WILLIAM
ARCHER
ON
IBSEN

MR. WILLIAM ARCHER

WILLIAM ARCHER ON IBSEN

The Major Essays, 1889 - 1919

Edited by

THOMAS POSTLEWAIT

Contributions in Drama and Theatre Studies, Number 13

Greenwood Press
Westport, Connecticut • London, England

Library of Congress Cataloging in Publication Data

Archer, William, 1856-1924.
  William Archer on Ibsen.

  (Contributions in drama and theatre studies, ISSN 0163-
3821 ; no. 13)
  Bibliography: p.
  Includes index.
  1. Ibsen, Henrik, 1828-1906—Criticism and interpre-
tation—Addresses, essays, lectures.   I. Postlewait,
Thomas.   II. Title.   III. Series.
PT8895.A73   1984   839.8'226   84-15744
ISBN 0-313-24499-5 (lib. bdg.)

Library of Congress Catalog Card Number: 84-15744
ISBN: 0-313-24499-5
ISSN: 0163-3821

First published in 1984

Greenwood Press
A division of Congressional Information Service, Inc.
88 Post Road West
Westport, Connecticut 06881

Printed in the United States of America

10 9 8 7 6 5 4 3 2 1

Bernard Shaw: "Indeed, none of us would reprint as well
               as Mr. Archer."

               Our Theatres in the Nineties, 5 June 1897

TABLE OF CONTENTS

Acknowledgements

I wish to thank those people and organizations that provided me with help in this project: Mrs. Elinor Finley, William Archer's niece, who gave me the initial approval for collecting and publishing these essays; Mrs. Enid M. Foster, librarian of the British Theatre Association, who allowed me full access to Archer's papers and generously helped me, as did the staff of the B.T.A., with all my many requests; Professor Joseph Donohue, who, as Series Editor for Greenwood Press's Contributions in Drama and Theatre Studies, has been a model literary adviser; Professor Bernard Dukore for his fine scholarly advice on matters of theatre history and biography; Professor Robert Scanlan for his most helpful suggestions and encouragement on how I present my advocacy for Archer; Professor August Staub, my chairman in the Department of Drama and Theatre, for providing me with summer research funds so I could finish this project; Mr. Nathan Dean, Vice-President, Office of Research, University of Georgia, for research support; and, Mrs. Kerry Nash, my resourceful typist, who conquered the idiosyncracies of a messy manuscript and the limitations of a word processor in order to produce camera-ready copy for my publisher. I also wish to thank Massachusetts Institute of Technology for two research grants that provided time and travel funds. Finally, my deepest thanks goes to my wife, Marilyn, for all of her support and understanding.

Thomas Postlewait
University of Georgia

Introduction

        William Archer (1856-1924) was one of England's great theatre
critics, possibly the most consequential because of his various
campaigns for the revival of drama on the London stage. Over a
period of almost five decades, beginning in 1877 at the age of
twenty-one, Archer fought for the new drama in several of its
manifestations, battling vigorously for "a literature in the
theatre," and against its reactionary censors. His mission,
which of course had its most notable success with the drama of
Ibsen, grew out of a commitment to an idea of the theatre that
placed the playwright at the center of production considerations,
not the actor-manager nor scenic spectacle. In other words, his
campaign for Ibsen and the other new dramatists was also a
campaign against certain aspects of the Victorian theatre.
        This advocacy is what primarily distinguishes Archer as a
critic. No doubt, when compared to some of the other major
theatre and drama critics in the history of the London stage (such
as Dr. Johnson, William Hazlitt, or Max Beerbohm), Archer lacks
certain qualities of style and analysis. We do not turn to him,
as we do to Shaw, for lively wit nor do we expect, as with
Coleridge, great leaps of imaginative synthesis. Instead, Archer
offers us, as T. S. Eliot acknowledged, "great lucidity and
consistency,"[1] a careful control of information and argument
presented in logical terms. Archer is the epitome of the critic
as rationalist, a writer skilled at analyzing how and why
something works (or fails to work) on the stage. He is masterful
at dissecting a play's strengths and weaknesses (see, for
instance, "Ibsen's Apprenticeship," "Ibsen's Craftmanship," "The
Pillars of Society," and "John Gabriel Borkman" in this
collection). Anyone who has read through the five volumes of
his The Theatrical World of 1893-1897, which contain his weekly
reviews, knows how well he defines the qualities, both positive
and negative, of works as various as Henry James's Guy Domville,
Lord Tennyson's Becket, Dumas fils' La Femme du Claude, and
Wilde's The Importance of Being Earnest. And in his reviews we
can fine some of the best analysis anywhere on melodrama, its
nature and its appeal. Also, although not usually granted,
Archer's skill in analyzing acting can be quite effective, as is

illustrated by his various reviews on the Ibsen actresses: Janet Achurch, Elizabeth Robins, Mrs. Patrick Campbell, Eleonora Duse, Alla Nazimova.

Of course, like all critics, Archer had his blind spots and prejudices. In his advocacy for dramatic realism, he often slighted earlier drama, including Restoration comedy and Jacobean tragedy. And even though he obviously enjoyed much about Shaw's drama, he continually failed to understand Shaw's strategies of plot design and characterization. As he wrote in 1907:

> Out of Mr. Shaw's fourteen or fifteen plays, I dislike three and a half; the remainder I hold in different degrees of esteem, but all of them I relish more or less, and some of them intensely. The merits of Mr. Shaw, the playwright, are not for a moment in question . . . .[But], as a matter of fact, I don't think technique is Mr. Shaw's strong point.[2]

The limitations that we find in Archer's criticism, primarily an over-emphasis upon realism and its techniques, cannot be dismissed, but they should not blind us to his strengths as a critic. In fact, his limitations derive from his very strengths: the lifetime commitment to Ibsen and the new drama. Archer was an advocate, a man with a mission. From his earliest essay on Ibsen, "Henrik Ibsen's New Drama" (1878), until his last book, The Old Drama and the New (1923), he fought for a radical change in the English stage and drama. If he seemed a bit old-fashioned at the end, this is because he was so successful in his mission. The battle was won. By the 1920's the new realism had become the established norm, especially on the English stage.

Today, somewhat surprisingly, we have lost sight of just how important Archer was in the Ibsen campaign. Quite often we focus on Shaw as the dominant person, in part because he is such a literary giant. Also, G. B. S. was a great self-propagandist, a marvelous creator of a public persona. Even a critic as astute as John Gassner has given Shaw the primary and Archer the secondary role in the Ibsen campaign.[3] Although we have usually misread The Quintessence of Ibsenism, as J. L. Wisenthal has demonstrated in Shaw and Ibsen (1980), we have still given it pride of place in the fight for Ibsen in the 1890's. It and Shaw's handful of theatre reviews on the Ibsen's productions are often seen as more important than Archer's contributions.

Beyond this, we tend to classify Shaw and Archer as twin voices in the fight for social drama, a fight that we accuse them of reducing to Ibsenism, which is supposedly a misreading of the plays in terms of socialist principles. Wisenthal has shown that this view of Shaw is incorrect. In the case of Archer, nothing could be further from the truth. Even a cursory reading of

Archer's essays on Ibsen should illustrate that he never supported the attempts to read a social philosophy out of Ibsen's drama nor argued that Ibsen's genius could be explained by such social theory. Instead, Archer argued repeatedly that the social issues in the plays had to be seen as but one of many elements in the overall dramatic design. For Archer, Ibsen is first and always, even in the "social dramas," a poetic genius. This argument informs his disagreements with Shaw (see "The Quintessence of Ibsenism: An Open Letter to George Bernard Shaw"). Archer admired and praised Shaw's Quintessence, but he also felt the strong need to emphasize Ibsen's poetic rather than his social qualities as a dramatist. To confuse ourselves about this basic argument in Archer's writing is nothing less than an admission that we have completely misunderstood the essential Archer. No doubt, our common problem is that we have gotten our Archer second-hand, through others, who for various reasons have misrepresented him.[4] In fact, a great disjunction now exists between how his contemporaries perceived him and how we have come to characterize him. The gap needs closing.

To his contemporaries, Archer was unquestionably the leader of the Ibsen campaign in England. Bernard Shaw, J. T. Grein, Harley Granville Barker, Max Beerbohm, Edmund Gosse, James Agate, Charles Charrington, Janet Achurch, and Elizabeth Robins all acknowledged his role as the paramount advocate for Ibsen. In the words of Harley Granville Barker: "from first to last Archer's own influence on the English theatre was considerable."[5] How considerable is of course the issue.

For Edmund Gosse, another of the important campaigners for Ibsen, there was no doubt about Archer's preeminence:

> Of Mr. Archer it is difficult for an English student of Ibsen to speak with moderation. . . .It was Mr. Archer and no other who was really the introducer of Ibsen to English readers. . . .For a quarter of a century he was the protagonist in the fight against misconstruction and stupidity; with wonderful courage, with no less wonderful good temper and persistency, he insisted on making the true Ibsen take the place of the false, and in securing for him the recognition due to his genius.[6]

Although Archer always discounted the idea that he showed courage in fighting for Ibsen, he did lead the battle in the 1880's and 1890's. Thus, J. T. Grein, who founded the Independent Theatre Society in 1891, which opened with a censored production of Ghosts, credits Archer far more than himself with "the revolution of our Drama in 1891." For Grein, Archer "was the man with the iron features and the golden heart; I was the dwarf with the pluck of Puck."[7]

Grein's comment points us toward something crucial that is no longer widely recognized, even among theatre historians of the age, but once was common knowledge. Namely, that Archer took part in all aspects of the Ibsen campaign: reviewing, essay writing, translating, producing, and even directing. Besides writing close to 200 reviews and essays on Ibsen, an amazing number, he translated most of the plays, revising many of them as new editions were published between 1889 and 1908. Without doubt, he was the premier Ibsen translator for his generation, both in quantity and quality. We may discover flaws in his phrasing, for he attempted to be as true as he could to the literal meaning of Ibsen's words (at the expense of colloquial language sometimes), but we should consider that his contemporaries, including other translators and theatre people, almost unamiously praised his work highly. During his lifetime, these translations sold in the hundreds of thousands, probably reaching millions of readers. And, just as importantly, if not so impressive numerically, his translations were used for almost all of the productions of Ibsen well into this century. For example, there were twenty-four productions of Ibsen in London between 1889, when A Doll's House was performed (with Janet Achurch as Nora), and 1897, when John Gabriel Borkman, A Doll's House, The Wild Duck, and Ghosts each had productions. Of these, twenty-two used Archer's translations.

The reviewing and translating, by themselves, surely place Archer as the leader of the Ibsen campaign, but he did even more than this. He also took part actively in many of the key productions of the plays. Archer helped supervise and direct daily rehearsals for the following first productions: A Doll's House, with Janet Achurch and Charles Charrington, Novelty Theatre, 1889; Rosmersholm, with Florence Farr, Vaudeville Theatre, 1891; Ghosts, with Mrs. Theodore Wright, Independent Theatre Co., Royalty Theatre, 1891; Hedda Gabler, with Elizabeth Robins and Marion Lea, Vaudeville Theatre, 1891; The Master Builder, with Elizabeth Robins and Herbert Waring, Trafalgar Square Theatre and Vaudeville Theatre, 1893; Little Eyolf, with Elizabeth Robins, Janet Achurch, Mrs. Patrick Campbell, and Courtenay Thorpe, Avenue Theatre, 1896; John Gabriel Borkman, with Elizabeth Robins, W. H. Vernon, and Genevieve Ward, Strand Theatre, 1897. These were most of the crucial productions in the campaign, the ones that caused intense interest and controversy. In each case, Archer worked closely with the actors on everything from changes in the phrasing (which he knew quite well were necessary for the stage) to delivery and blocking. The prompt books for several of these productions reveal part of what he did. And letters to actors during rehearsals provide even more evidence that Archer was fully involved in preparing the productions.[8]

In essence, then, Archer was everywhere in the Ibsen campaign. Here are a few examples. When Janet Achurch and Charles Charrington decided to venture a production of Ibsen, they came to Archer in 1889 and asked him not only to provide the translation of A Doll's House (after having read an essay of his a few weeks earlier advocating a production of this play), but also to help with the rehearsals. He agreed, in both cases. When Shaw decided to deliver a lecture at the Fabian society on Ibsen (the lecture which became the basis of the Quintessence), he came to Archer for an oral translation of Brand and Peer Gynt so he could talk about them. In fact, discussions with Archer initially got Shaw interested in Ibsen. And when Archer published his essay, "Ghosts and Gibberings," in 1891, Shaw proceeded to quote substantial parts of it in the Quintessence, which was published late that year.

When J. T. Grein decided to form the Independent Theatre Company, he did so on Archer's advice. And when Grein decided to open with Ghosts, he received Ibsen's permission only by promising that Archer would provide the translation and watch over the rehearsals.[9] Grein continued to depend upon Archer throughout the history of the Independent Theatre Society, especially with the productions of Ibsen between 1891 and 1897. When Elizabeth Robins decided to produce and star in Hedda Gabler she conspired with Archer in revising Edmund Gosse's inadequate translation, which for legal reasons she was obligated to use because Gosse's publisher, William Heinemann, controlled the rights (until, that is, Archer appealed to Ibsen, who sided with Archer). She also asked Archer to help with the rehearsals. This was the beginning of their close partnership that carried them through productions of The Master Builder, Rosmersholm, the fourth act of Brand (which Archer especially admired), Little Eyolf, and John Gabriel Borkman. The last was done under the banner of the New Century Theatre Company, which they founded.

During this crucial first decade of Ibsen productions and controversy, very little happened without Archer. He translated and published nineteen of Ibsen's plays, with some of them also being issued in revised editions. When a play was being produced, he almost always found some way to write about it, while yet maintaining a reputation of scrupulous honesty and rectitude (although Shaw teased him wonderfully in letters of 1891 about his attempts to maintain this critical persona). In 1889, when A Doll's House was produced, he wrote four articles about it. In 1891, when several plays were produced, he wrote nine reviews and essays on Ibsen. And in 1893, when Elizabeth Robins starred as Hilda Wangel in the first production of The Master Builder, Archer published no less than ten reviews and essays on this play and production alone. Hardly a year passed for forty years, 1880-1920, that Archer did not publish something on Ibsen. And in certain years he was an Ibsen factory. For example, in 1906, the year of Ibsen's death, besides commencing work on the collected edition of the plays (published in eleven volumes between 1906 and 1908, with separate introductions for each play),

Archer published eighteen articles on various aspects of Ibsen's works, life, and dramatic genius. And so the campaign went, year in and year out. Is it any wonder that the newspapers and journals of the time often referred to Archer as "the prophet of the new drama"?

Robins fell deeply in love with Archer, Shaw considered him one of his dearest friends, J. T. Grein, a Dutchman, came to London after having read some of Archer's writings on Ibsen and drama, Granville Barker took up both Shaw and Archer as mentors and closest colleagues, keeping a picture of Archer on his mantelpiece and dedicating the Prefaces to Shakespeare to Archer. Almost everyone respected him, in other words. And yet, today, for us he is "drab Archer," the man whom we now quite often slight or just ignore. Our lost perspective on Archer and the Ibsen campaign is therefore not merely a matter of reductive characterization (whereby Archer becomes for us only a caricature of himself), but, more seriously, a case of critical failure to understand one of the most important theatre critics and periods in the history of the London stage.

Our problem of misrepresentation and ignorance has been augmented, unfortunately, by the difficulties of ready access to the essays and reviews he wrote on Ibsen. Except for the five volumes of The Theatrical World of 1893-1897 (which the better libraries have on the shelves, usually gathering dust), the many theatre reviews that Archer wrote are buried in the newspapers and journals for which he regularly wrote: London Figaro, World, Tribune, Nation, Pall Mall Gazette, St. James's Magazine, Daily Chronicle, Morning Leader, and others. Not surprisingly, very few critics have gone to the trouble to read these reviews, which in some cases are only available in London (although this is no excuse for the inadequate histories and criticism on the Ibsen era and on Archer). And even Archer's major essays on Ibsen (here gathered for the first time in Part One of this collection) have been scattered in various journals, such as Fortnightly Review, New Review, Edda. These essays are basically unknown to most critics and scholars. The one exception is "Ghosts and Gibberings," which Shaw quotes extensively in the Quintessence and Michael Egan reprints in Ibsen: The Critical Heritage (1972). Somewhat more available, although seldom dug out, are Archer's separate introductions to each of the plays in the eleven volumes of the Collected Works, published in 1906-08. This edition, while available in most libraries, has long been out of print. Part Two of this collection brings most of these introductions together in one book for the first time.

So, here with this collection, we can begin to take the measure of Archer as an advocate for Ibsen. In these essays we are recovering one of the first major writers on Ibsen, who, along with Shaw, Gosse, Philip Wicksteed, and a few others (including Henry James who wrote four reviews and James Joyce who wrote one essay), fought critically for Ibsen in England—when fighting was necessary. Archer's essays reveal several aspects of his critical abilities: biographer, theatre historian, reviewer, literary critic. But before all else—and unifying these essays, from "Ibsen and English Criticism" (1889) to "The True Greatness of Ibsen" (1919)—there is Archer's continual advocacy for Ibsen the dramatic poet, as opposed to Ibsen the social philosopher or prophet. Archer's mission, so persistently and skillfully carried forward, was to place Ibsen's "true greatness" as a poetic genius before the English-speaking world. In this, Archer succeeded quite impressively.

These essays are gathered therefore in the spirit of both historical recovery and critical value. The reader should note that Archer wrote these essays for various occasions and publications, without any plan for collecting them, so there is bound to be some repetition of key points. This redundancy is slight, however, and preferable, I believe, to any editorial surgery. These twenty-seven essays, the most important of Archer's extended studies of Ibsen (as opposed to theatrical reviews), are printed without cuts, except for the removal of a discussion of the problems of translating Peer Gynt (from the essay on Peer Gynt in Part Two). I have added headnotes and some footnotes (identified as mine) throughout Part One because I felt that these essays would benefit, in presentation, from some pertinent background information. Otherwise, I have let Archer speak for himself. What he has to say, as the foremost advocate for Ibsen in England during the days of campaign, may be of surprising note and worth to readers today.

Footnotes

1. T. S. Eliot, "Four Elizabethan Dramatists," <u>Selected</u>
<u>Essays</u>, new ed. (New York: Harcourt, Brace, and World, 1964), p.
92.

2. William Archer, "Youth in the Judgment Seat," <u>Tribune</u>,
May 25, 1907.

3. John Gassner, "William Archer," and "Bernard Shaw and
the Making of the Modern Mind," in <u>Dramatic Soundings</u>, ed. Glenn
Loney (New York: Crown Publishing, 1968).

4. See, for example, Martin Esslin, "Ibsen and Modern
Drama," in <u>Ibsen and the Theatre</u>, ed. Errol Durbach (London:
Macmillan, 1980); George Rowell, <u>Theatre in the Age of aIrving</u>
(Oxford: Basil Blackwell, 1981); and William Quinn, "William
Archer," <u>Dictionary of Literary Biography: Modern British</u>
<u>Dramatists</u>, 1900-1945), 2 vols., ed. Stanley Weintraub (Detroit:
Gale Research, 1982).

5. Harley Granville Barker, "The Coming of Ibsen," in <u>The</u>
<u>Eighteen-Eighties</u>, ed. Walter de la Mare (Cambridge: Cambridge
University Press, 1930), p. 163.

6. Edmund Gosse, <u>Ibsen</u> (London: Heinemann, 1907), pp.
vii-viii & p. xi.

7. J. T. Grein, "William Archer," <u>The Illustrated London</u>
<u>News</u>, 10 Jan. 1925, p. 68.

8. I have discovered, recently, five prompt books, with
notes in Archer's hand, among the collection of his papers and
books at the British Theatre Association, London. See my
companion study, <u>Prophet of the New Drama: William Archer and</u>
<u>the Ibsen Campaign</u> (Greenwood), for the history of Archer's
unparalleled roll in this crucial period in the history of the
London stage.

9. Letter of Ibsen's to Grein, 20 Feb. 1891; quoted in
Michael Orme [Mrs. Grein], J.T. <u>Grein: The Story of a Pioneer</u>
(London: John Murray, 1936), p. 85.

WILLIAM
ARCHER
ON
IBSEN

PART ONE

ESSAYS FROM THE VARIOUS JOURNALS (1889-1919)

These twelve essays cover much of Archer's professional career. They represent, along with the introductions to the individual plays, his major writing on Ibsen. The early essays are occasional, written in the heat of battle, but they are not ephemeral. They were made to do service for a particular situation in the Ibsen campaign and now they define in great part that situation. That is, they are not only a record of the history but also a part of the history itself because they helped to shape events and attitudes. The later essays, starting with "The Real Ibsen" (1901), are Archer's contributions to the criticism, the literary history, and the biography of Ibsen. They present the assessment of Ibsen by the man who was most involved in introducing Ibsen's drama to the English-speaking world. They are, therefore, important essays in the history of Ibsen criticism. And, on their own merit, they are judicious assessments of Ibsen's greatness.

IBSEN AND ENGLISH CRITICISM

(Fortnightly Review, July 1889)

This essay was published immediately after
the successful production of A Doll's House
at the Novelty Theatre (June 7-28), starring
Janet Achurch as Nora. Archer was fully
involved as translator, co-director, and
critical advocate in the World, for which he
wrote weekly reviews. Although the critics
generously praised Achurch's performance,
they were in the main quite upset by the
play. And some of them, such as Clement
Scott, attacked the play, Nora, the
"unwomanly woman," Ibsen, and even Archer
himself for translating and advocating
Ibsen.

If we may measure fame by mileage of newspaper comment,
Henrik Ibsen has for the past month been the most famous man in
the English literary world. Since Robert Elsmere[1] left the
Church, no event in "coëval fictive art" (to quote a modern
stylist)[2] has exercised men's, and women's, minds so much as Nora
Helmer's departure from her Doll's House. Indeed the latter exit
may be said to have awakened even more vibrant echoes than the
former; for, while Robert made as little noise as possible, Nora
slammed the door behind her. Nothing could be more trenchant than
her action, unless it be her speech. Whatever its merits or
defects, A Doll's House has certainly the property of stimulating
discussion. We are at present bandying the very arguments which
hurtled around it in Scandinavia and in Germany nine years ago.
When the play was first produced in Copenhagen, some one wrote a
charming little satire upon it in the shape of a debate as to its
tendency between a party of little girls around a nursery

tea-table. It ended in the hostess, aged ten, gravely declaring that had the case been hers, she would have done exactly as Nora did. I do not know whether the fame of A Doll's House has reached the British nursery, but I have certainly read some comments on it which might very well have emanated from the abode of innocence.

Puerilities and irrelevances apart, the adult and intelligent criticism of Ibsen as represented in A Doll's House, seems to run on three main lines. It is said, in the first place, that he is not an artist but a preacher; secondly, that his doctrine is neither new nor true; thirdly, that in order to enforce it, he oversteps the limits of artistic propriety. I propose to look into these three allegations. First, however, I must disclaim all rights to be regarded as in any way a mouthpiece for the poet's own views. My personal intercourse with Henrik Ibsen, though to me very pleasant and memorable, has been but slight. I view his plays from the pit, not from the author's box. Very likely—nay, certainly—I often misread his meaning. My only right to take part in the discussion arises from a long and loving study of all his writings, and from the minute familiarity with A Doll's House in particular, acquired in the course of translating and staging it.

Is it true, then, that he is a dramatic preacher rather than a dramatic poet? or, in other words, that his art is vitiated by didacticism? Some writers have assumed that in calling him didactic they have said the last word, and dismissed him for ever from the ranks of the great artists. Of them I would fain enquire what really great art is not didactic? The true distinction is not between didactic art and "art for art's sake," but between primarily didactic and ultimately didactic art. Art for art's sake, properly so called, is mere decoration; and even it, in the last analysis, has its gospel to preach. By primarily didactic art I mean that in which the moral bearing is obvious, and was clearly present to the artist's mind. By ultimately didactic art I mean that which essays to teach as life itself teaches, exhibiting the fact and leaving the observer to trace and formulate the underlying law. It is the fashion of the day to regard this unconsciously didactic art, if I may call it so—its unconsciousness is sometimes a very transparent pose—as essentially higher than the art which is primarily and consciously didactic, dynamic. Well, it is useless to dispute about higher and lower. From our point of view the Australians seem to be walking head-downwards, like flies on the ceiling; from their point of view we are in the same predicament; it all depends on the point of view. Ibsen certainly belongs, at any rate in this modern prose plays, to the consciously didactic artists whom you may, if you choose, relegate to a lower plane. But how glorious the company that will have to step down along with him! What were the Greek tragic poets if not consciously

didactic? What is comedy, from time immemorial, but a deliberate
lesson in life? Down Plautus; down Terence; down Molière and
Holberg and Beaumarchais and Dumas! Calderon and Cervantes must
be kind enough to follow; so must Schiller and Goethe. If German
criticism is to be believed Shakespeare was the most hardened
sermonizer of all literature; but in this respect I think German
criticism is to be disbelieved. Shakespeare, then, may be left
in possession of the pinnacle of Parnassus; but who shall keep
him company? Flaubert, perhaps, and M. Guy de Maupassant?

The despisers of Ibsen, then, have not justified their
position when they have merely proved, what no one disputes, that
he is a didactic writer. They must further prove that his
teaching kills his art. For my part, looking at his dramatic
production all round, and excepting only the two great dramas in
verse, Brand and Peer Gynt, I am willing to admit that his
teaching does now and then, in perfectly trifling details, affect
his art for the worse. Not his direct teaching--that, as it seems
to me, he always inspires with the breath of life--but his
proclivity to what I may perhaps call symbolic side-issues. In
the aforesaid dramas in verse this symbolism is eminently in
place; not so, it seems to me, in the realistic plays. I once
asked him how he justified this tendency in his art; he replied
that life is one tissue of symbols. "Certainly," I might have
answered; "but when we have its symbolic side too persistently
obtruded upon us, we lose the sense of reality, which, according
to your own theory, the modern dramatist should above all things
aim at." There may be some excellent answer to this criticism; I
give it for what it is worth. Apart from these symbolic details,
it seems to me that Ibsen is singularly successful in vitalising
his work; in reproducing the forms, the phenomena of life, as well
as its deeper meanings. Let us take the example nearest at
hand -- A Doll's House. I venture to say--for this is a matter of
fact rather than of opinion--that in the minds of thousands in
Scandinavia and Germany, Nora Helmer lives with an intense and
palpitating life such as belongs to few fictitious characters.
Habitually and instinctively men pay Ibsen the compliment (so
often paid to Shakespeare) of discussing her as though she were
a real woman, living a life of her own, quite apart from the
poet's creative intelligence. The very critics who begin by
railing at her as a puppet end by denouncing her as a woman.
She irritates, troubles, fascinates them as no puppet ever
could. Moreover, the triumph of the actress is the dramatist's
best defence. Miss Achurch might have the genius of Rachel[3] and
Desclee[4] in one, yet she could not transmute into flesh and blood
the doctrinary doll, stuffed with sawdust and sophistry, whom
some people declare Nora to be. Men do not shudder at the agony
or weep over the woes of an intellectual abstraction. As for
Helmer, I am not aware that any one has accused him of
unreality. He is too real for most people--he is commonplace,

unpleasant, objectionable. The truth is, he touches us too nearly; he is the typical husband of what may be called chattel matrimony. If there are few Doll's-Houses in England, it is certainly for lack of Noras, not for lack of Helmers. I admit that in my opinion Ibsen has treated Helmer somewhat unfairly. He has not exactly disguised, but has omitted to emphasize, the fact that if Helmer helped to make Nora a doll, Nora helped to make Helmer a prig. By giving Nora all the logic in the last scene (and she is not a scrupulous dialectician) he has left the casual observer to conclude that he lays the whole responsibility on Helmer. This conclusion is not just, but is specious; and so far, and so far only, I grant that the play has somewhat the air of a piece of special pleading. I shall presently discuss the last scene in greater detail; but even admitting for the moment that the polemist here gets the better of the poet, can we call the poet, who has moved freeely through two acts and two-thirds, nothing but a doctrinary polemist?

Let me add that A Doll's House is, of all Ibsen's plays, the one in which a definite thesis is most tangibly posited--the one, therefore, which is most exposed to the reproach of being a mere sociological pamphlet. His other plays may be said to scintillate with manifold ethical meanings; here the light is focussed upon one point in the social system. I do not imply that A Doll's House is less thoroughly vitalized than Ghosts, or Rosmersholm, or The Lady from the Sea. What I mean is, that the play may in some eyes acquire a false air of being merely didactic from the fortuitous circumstance that its moral can be easily formulated.

The second line of criticism is that which attacks the substance of Ibsen's so-called doctrines, on the ground that they are neither new nor true. To the former objection one is inclined to answer curtly but pertinently, "Who said they were?" It is not the business of the creative artist to make the great generalisations which mark the stages of intellectual and social progress. Certainly Ibsen did not discover the theory of evolution or the doctrine of heredity, any more than he discovered gravitation. He was not the first to denounce the subjection of women; he was not the first to sneer at the "compact liberal majority"[5] of our pseudo-democracies. His function is to seize and throw into relief certain aspects of modern life. He shows us society as Kean was said to read Shakespeare--by flashes of lightning--luridly, but with intense vividness.[6] He selects subjects which seem to him to illustrate such and such political, ethical, or sociological ideas; but he does not profess to have invented the ideas. They are common property; they are in the air. A grave injustice has been done him of late by those of his English admirers who have set him up as a social prophet, and have sometimes omitted to mention that he is a bit of a poet as well. It is so much easier to import an idea than the flesh and blood, the imagination, the passion, the style in which it is clothed. People have heard so much of the "gospel according to Ibsen" that they have come to think of him as a mere hot-gospeller, the Boanerges[7] of some strange social propaganda. As a matter of fact Ibsen has no gospel whatever, in the sense of a systematic body of doctrine. He is not a Schopenhauer, and still less a Comte. There never was a less systematic thinker. Truth is not, in his eyes, one and indivisible; it is many-sided, many-visaged, almost Protean. It belongs to the irony of fate that the least dogmatic of thinkers--the man who has said of himself, "I only ask: my call is not to answer"--should figure in the imagination of so many English critics as a dour dogmatist, a vendor of social nostrums in pilule form. He is far more of a paradoxist than a dogmatist. A thinker he is most certainly, but not an inventor of brand new notions such as no one has ever before conceived. His originality lies in giving intense dramatic life to modern ideas, and often stamping them afresh, as regards mere verbal form, in the mint of his imaginative wit.

The second allegation, that his doctrines are not true, is half answered when we have insisted that they are not put forward (at any rate by Ibsen himself) as a body of inspired dogmas. No man rejects more consistently than he the idea of finality. He does not pretend to have said the last word on any subject. "You needn't believe me unless you like," says Dr. Stockmann in An Enemy of the People, "but truths are not the tough Methuselahs people take them to be. A normally constituted truth lives, let us say, some seventeen or eighteen years; at most twenty." The telling of absolute truths, to put it in another way, is scarcely Ibsen's aim. He is more concerned with destroying conventional lies, and exorcising the "ghosts" of dead truths; and most of all concerned to make people think and see for themselves. Here again we recognise the essential injustice of regarding a dramatic poet as a sort of prophet-professor, who means all his characters say and makes them say all he means. I have been asked, for example whether Ibsen intends us to understand by the last scene of A Doll's House that awakened wives ought to leave their husbands and children in order to cultivate their souls in solitude. Ibsen intends nothing of the sort. He draws a picture of a typical household; he creates a man and woman with certain characteristics; he places them in a series of situations which at once develop their characters and suggest large questions of conduct; and he makes the woman, in the end, adopt a course of action which he (rightly or wrongly) believes to be consistent with her individual nature and circumstances. It is true that this course of action is so devised as to throw the principles at stake into the strongest relief; but the object of that is to make people thoroughly realise the problem, not to force upon them the particular solution arrived at in this particular case. No two life-problems were ever precisely alike, and in stating and solving one, Ibsen does not pretend to supply a ready-made solution for all the rest. He illustrates, or, rather, illumines, a general principle by a conceivable case; that is all. To treat Nora's arguments in the last scene of A Doll's House as though they were the ordered propositions of an essay by John Stuart Mill is to give a striking example of the strange literalness of the English mind, its inability to distinguish between drama and dogma. To me that last scene is the most moving in the play, precisely because I hold it the most dramatic. It has been called a piece of pure logic--is it not rather logic conditioned by character and saturated with emotion? Some years ago I saw Et Dukkehjem acted in Christiania.[8] It was an off season; only the second-rate members of the company were engaged; and throughout two acts and a half I sat vainly striving to recapture the emotions I had so often felt in reading the play. But the moment Nora and Helmer were seated face to face, at the words, "No, that is just it; you do not understand me; and I have never understood you--till to-night"--at that moment, much to my own surprise, the thing suddenly gripped my heartstrings; to use an expressive Americanism, I "sat up"; and every phrase of Nora's threnody over her dead dreams, her lost illusions, thrilled me to the very marrow. Night after night I went to see that scene; night after night I have watched it in the English version; it has never lost its power over me. And why? Not because Nora's sayings are particularly wise or particularly true, but because, in her own words, they are so true for her, because she feels them so deeply and utters them so exquisitely. Certainly she is unfair, certainly she is one-sided, certainly she is illogical; if she were not, Ibsen would be the pamphleteer he is supposed to be, not the poet he is. "I have never been happy here--only merry. . . .You have never loved me--you have only found it amusing to be in love with me." Have we not in these speeches the very mingling of truth and falsehood, of justice and injustice, necessary to humanise the character and the situation? After Nora has declared her intention of leaving her home, Helmer remarks, "Then there is only one explanation possible--You no longer love me." "No," she replies, "that is just it." "Nora! can you say so?" cries Helmer, looking into her eyes. "Oh, I'm so sorry, Torvald," she answers, "for you've always been so kind to me." Is this pamphleteering? To me it seems like the subtlest human pathos. Again, when she says "At that moment it became clear to me that I had been living here for eight years with a strange man and had borne him three children--Oh, I can't bear to think of it! I could tear myself to pieces"--who can possibly take this for anything but a purely dramatic utterance? It is true and touching in Nora's mouth, but it is obviously founded on a vague sentiment, that may or may not bear analysis. Nora postulates a certain transcendental community of spirit as the foundation and justification of marriage. The idea is very womanly and may also be very practical; but Ibsen would probably be the first to admit that before it can claim the validity of a social principle we must ascertain whether it be possible for any two human beings to be other than what Nora would call strangers. This further analysis the hearer must carry out for him, or her, self. The poet has stimulated thought; he has not tried to lay down a hard-and-fast rule of conduct. Again, when Helmer says, "No man sacrifices his honour even for one he loves," and Nora retorts, "Millions of women have done that!" we applaud the consummate claptrap, not on account of its abstract justice, but rather of its characteristic injustice. Logically, it is naught; dramatically, one feels it to be a masterstroke. Here, it is the right speech in the right place; in a sociological monograph it should be absurd. My position, in short, is that in Ibsen's plays, as in those of any other dramatist who keeps within the bounds of his form, we must look, not for the axioms and demonstrations of a scientific system, but simply for "broken lights" of truth, refracted through character and circumstance.[9] The playwright who sends on a Chorus or a lecturer, unconnected with the dramatic action, to moralise the spectacle and put all the dots on all the i's, may fairly be taken to task for the substance of his "doctrines." But that playwright is Dumas, not Ibsen.

Lastly, we come to the assertion that Ibsen is a "coarse" writer, with a morbid love for using the theatre as a psychological lecture-room. Here again I can only cry out upon the chance which has led to so grotesque a misconception. He has written some twenty plays, of which all except two might be read aloud, with only the most trivial omissions, in any young ladies' boarding-school from Tobolsk to Tangiers. The two exceptions are A Doll's House and Ghosts--the very plays which happen to have come (more or less) within the ken of English critics. In A Doll's House he touches upon, in Ghosts he frankly faces, the problem of hereditary disease, which interests him, not in itself, but simply as the physical type and symbol of so many social and ethical phenomena. Ghosts I have not space to consider. If art is for ever debarred from entering upon certain domains of human experience, then Ghosts is an inartistic work. I can only say, after having read it, seen it on the stage, and translated it, that no other modern play seems to me to fulfil so entirely the Aristotelian ideal of purging the soul by means of terror and pity. In A Doll's House, again, there are two passages, one in the second and one in the third act, which Mr. Podsnap could not conveniently explain to the young lady in the dress-circle.[10] Whether the young lady in the dress-circle would be nay the worse for having them explained to her is a question I shall not discuss. As a matter of fact, far from being coarsely treated, they are so delicately touched that the young person suspects nothing and is in no way incommoded. It is Mr. Podsnap himself that cries

out--the virtuous Podsnap who, at the French theatre, writhes
in his stall with laughter at speeches and situations à faire
rougir des singes.[11] I have more than once been reproached, by
people who had seen A Doll's House at the Novelty, with having
cut the speeches which the first-night critics pronounced
objectionable. It has cost me some trouble to persuade them that
not a word had been cut, and that the text they found so innocent
contained every one of the enormities denounced by the critics.
Mr. Podsnap, I may add, has in this case shown his usual alacrity
in putting the worst possible interpretation upon things. Dr.
Rank's declaration to Nora that Helmer is not the only man who
would willingly lay down his life for her, has been represented
as a hideious attempt on the part of a dying debauchee to
seduce his friend's wife. Nothing is further from the mind of
poor Rank, who, by the way, is not a debauchee at all. He knows
himself to be at death's door; Nora, in her Doll's House, has
given light and warmth to his lonely, lingering existence; he
has silently adored her while standing with her, as with her
husband, on terms of frank comradeship; is he to leave her for
ever without saying, as he puts it, "Thanks for the light"?
Surely this is a piece either of inhuman austerity or of
prurient prudery; surely Mrs. Podsnap herself could not feel a
suspicion of insult in such a declaration. True, it comes
inaptly at that particular moment, rendering it impossible for
Nora to make the request she contemplates. But essentially,
and even from the most conventional point of view, I fail to see
anything inadmissible in Ranks conduct to Nora. Nora's conduct
to Rank, in the stocking scene, is another question; but that is
merely a side-light on the relation between Nora and Helmer,
preparatory, in a sense, to the scene before Rank's entrance in
the last act.

    In conclusion, what are the chances that Ibsen's modern
plays will ever take a permanent place on the English stage?
They are not great, it seems to me.[12] The success of A Doll's
House will naturally encourage Ibsen's admirers to further
experiments in the same direction--interesting and instructive
experiments I have no doubt. We shall see in course of time The
Young Men's League, The Pillars of Society, An Enemy of the
People, Rosmersholm, and A Lady from the Sea--I name them in
chronological order. But none of these plays presents the double
attraction that has made the success of A Doll's House--the
distinct plea for female emancipation which appeals to the
thinking public, and the overwhelming part for an actress of
genius which attracts the ordinary playgoer. The other plays, I
cannot but foresee, will be in a measure antiquated before the
great public is ripe for a thorough appreciation of them. I
should like to see an attempt made to produce one of the poet's
historical plays, but that would involve an outlay for costumes
and mounting not to be lightly faced. On the other hand I have

not the remotest doubt that Ibsen will bulk more and more largely
as years go on in the consciousness of all students of literature
in general, as opposed to the stage in particular. The creator
of <u>Brand</u> and <u>Peer Gynt</u> is one of the great poets of the world.

GHOSTS AND GIBBERINGS

(Pall Mall Gazette, 8 April 1891)

This essay, which delighted Henry James, Bernard Shaw, and many other supporters of Ibsen, was published at the height of the public controversy over the single performance of Ghosts on 13 March 1891 by the Independent Theatre Society. It illustrates, with satiric intent, the hysterical nature of the opposition to Ibsen. By bringing together these abusive statements from the press, Archer was able to reveal and ridicule the foolishness of the opposition. Also, and just as importantly, he kept the controversy going by rallying the supporters of Ibsen.

"Ibsen's positively abominable play entitled Ghosts. . . . This disgusting representation. . . .Reprobation due to such as aim at infecting the modern theatre with poison after desperately inoculating themselves and others. . . .An open drain: a loathsome sore unbandaged; a dirty act done publicly; a lazar-house with all its doors and windows open. . . .Candid foulness. . . .Kotzebue turned bestial and cynical.[1]. . .Offensive cyncism. . . .Ibsen's melancholy and malodorous world. . . . Absolutely loathsome and fetid. . . .Gross, almost putrid indecorum. . . .Literary carrion. . . .Crapulous stuff. . . .Novel and perilous nuisance."-- Daily Telegraph (leading article). "This mess of vulgarity, egotism, coarseness, and absurdity." -- Daily Telegraph (criticism). "Unutterably offensive. . . . Prosecution under Lord Campbell's Act.[2]. . .Abominable piece. . . .Scandalous."-- Standard. "Naked loathsomeness. . . .Most damned and repulsive production."-- Daily News. Revoltingly suggestive and blasphemous. . . .Characters either contradictory in themselves, uninteresting or abhorrent."-- Daily Chronicle. "A repulsive and degrading work."-- Queen. "Morbid, unhealthy, unwholesome and disgusting story. . . .A piece to bring the stage

into disrepute and dishonour with every right-thinking man and
woman."-- Lloyd's. "Merely dull dirt long drawn out."-- Hawk.
"Morbid horrors of the hideous tale. . . .Ponderous dullness of
the didactic talk. . . .If any repetition of this outrage be
attempted, the authorities will doubtless wake from their
lethargy."-- Sporting and Dramatic News. "Just a wicked
nightmare"-- The Gentlewoman. "Lugubrious diagnosis of sordid
impropriety. . . .Characters are prigs, pedants and profligates.
. . Morbid caricatures. . . .Maunderings of nookshotten Norwegians
. . . .It is no more of a play than an average Gaity burlesque."
--W. St. Leger in Black and White. "Most loathsome of all Ibsen's
plays. . .Garbage and offal."-- Truth. "Ibsen's putrid play
called Ghosts . . . So loathsome an enterprise."-- Academy. "As
foul and filthy a concoction as has ever been allowed to disgrace
the boards of an English theatre. . . .Dull and disgusting. . . .
Nastiness and malodorousness laid on thickly as with a trowel."
-- Era. "Noisome corruption."-- Stage.

Henrik Ibsen.--"An egotist and a bungler."-- Daily
Telegraph. "A crazy fanatic and determined Socialist. . . .A
crazycranking being. . . .Not only consistently dirty but
deplorably dull."-- Truth. "As a dramatist, I consider the poet
Calmour his superior."-- Hawk. "The Norwegian pessimist in
petto(!)."--W. St. Leger in Black and White. "Ugly, nasty,
discordant, and downright dull.. . .A gloomy sort of ghoul, bent
on groping for horrors by night, and blinking like a stupid old
owl when the warm sunlight of the best of life dances into his
wrinkled eyes."-- Gentlewoman. "A teacher of the aestheticism of
the Lock Hospital."-- Saturday Review.

Ibsenites (i.e., persons who omit to foam at the mouth when
the name of Ibsen is mentioned).--"Lovers of prurience and
dabblers in impropriety who are eager to gratify their illicit
tastes under the pretence of art."-- Evening Standard.
"Ninetyseven per cent. [Nothing like accuracy!] of the people who
go to see Ghosts are nasty-minded people who find the discussion
of nasty subjects to their taste, in exact proportion to their
nastiness."-- Sporting and Dramatic News. "The socialistic and
the sexless. . . .The unwomanly women, the unsexed females, the
whole army of unprepossessing cranks in petticoats. . . .Educated
and muck-ferretting dogs. . . .Effeminate men and male women. . .
.They all of them--men and women alike--know that they are
doing not only a nasty but an illegal thing. . . .The Lord
Chamberlain[3] left them alone to wallow in Ghosts. . . .Outside a
silly clique, there is not the slghtest interest in the Scandinavian humbug or all his works. . . .A wave of human folly."
-- Truth.

These are a few extracts from a little book I am compiling
--on the model of the Wagner Schimpf-Lexicon--to be entitled
"Ibsenoclasts: or, an Anthology of Abuse."[4] It will be an

entertaining little work, I promise you; but the time for
publication has not yet come. The materials, it is true, are
already abundant; but they keep on pouring in every day, and are
likely to do so for some time to come. I am anxious to make the
compilation a complete and classic handbook of obloquy--a Baedeker
to Billingsgate,[5] as it were; and such is the wealth of our
incomparable mothertongue that, despite the industry of a hundred
"frumious" critics during the past month or so, I cannot suppose
that the well of wormwood is as yet exhausted, or that such
virtuosos in vituperation will for the future be forced
ingloriously to repeat themselves. Besides, the full irony and
humour of the situation cannot be quite apparent to the general
reader, or to the critics themselves, until a certain time shall
have elapsed. As yet, the contributors to the above florilegium
can barely have recovered from the moral epilepsy into which
Ghosts--so far, and so far only, justifying their denunciations
--appears to have thrown them. By the time I publish my complete
Manual of Malediction, they will have come to themselves again,
and will be able to read with a smile--though perhaps a somewhat
sickly one--the babble of their delirium.

For the present I would fain "assist nature" and hasten
their recovery by confronting, in one particular, the Ghosts of
their heated imagination with the actual play as it was
represented and as he who runs may read it. That the average
man should profess himself bored by it, is only natural and
proper. If it were pleasant and acceptable to the average man,
it would entirely fail of its aim. The "ghosts" of the moral
world are not to be "laid" by a single exorcism. The first effect
of any disturbance of their repose is naturally to make them
"squeak and gibber in the Roman streets."[6] It is not even to be
expected that the average man, in his exasperation, should take
the slightest trouble to think out what the poet means, or to
represent truthfully what he says. Yet I own I am surprised at
the unanimity with which the critics have averred that the tragedy
is mainly, if not exclusively, concerned with what the
Anti-Jacobin calls the "loathsome details of disease born of
depravity." Scarcely a paper but says the same thing, in almost
the same words. The most precise of all, perhaps, is the St.
James Gazette: "No detail is omitted. We see the patient before
us. His symptoms are described with revolting minuteness; the
quivering of an eyelid or the drooping of a lip is duly noted:
the course of the disease, in its origin, development, and
culmination, traced with a precision worthy of a professor of
anatomy. The very theatre seems to be turned into a hospital."
Nothing can be more explicit than this statement; yet it is
absolutely without foundation. Oswald tells his mother that he
is suffering from softening of the brain--not a pleasant
announcement, certainly, but with nothing particularly "loathsome"
about it. The only "symptoms" mentioned are a severe headache and

bodily and mental lassitude, which cannot surely be called
"revolting" phenomena. There is not a single allusion to
"quivering eyelids" or "drooping lips"; the "origin, development,
and culmination" of Oswald's disease are not "traced with
precision," for they are not traced at all. Instead of no detail
being omitted, no detail is given. I do not for a moment suggest
that the writer deliberately stated what he knew to be false. He
wrote under the overpowering impression of what is undoubtedly a
very terrible scene or series of scenes. The intense reality of
the thing was vividly present to his mind, and he lacked time, and
perhaps energy, to consider very closely how that effect of
reality had been produced. In assuming that it must have been
produced by "revoltingly minute" descriptions, of which, as a
matter of fact, there is no trace, he bore unconscious testimony
to the subtle art of the poet. Of course it may be argued that
the horror of the scene, by whatever means produced, is beyond
human endurance, and consequently outside art. That is a rational
position, which may be rationally discussed when the critics have
quite recovered from their convulsions. But the fact remains that
in Ibsen's dialogue there are none of the "loathesome" medical
details which bulk so hugely before the "red and rolling eye" of
the critical imagination.

There is a scene in Truth--one of those fragrant and
wholesome plays beside which Ibsen, of course, seems unendurably
"fetid" and "malodorous"--in which a party of men who have been
lying egregiously to their womenfolk through two whole acts at
last determine that they must tell the truth.[7] After they have
expatiated for some time on the moral elevation begotten by this
resolve, one of them demurely suggests that they had better
settle what the truth is to be. I would make the same suggestion
to the Ibsenoclasts. Members of the same staff, at any rate,
might surely arrive at a working agreement as to what is to be the
truth about Ibsen. I print side by side two extracts from the
Daily Telegraph of March 14, the first from a dramatic criticism
on page 3, the second from a leading article on page 5:

> There was very little to offend the ear directly. On
> the Ibsen stage their nastiness is inferential, not
> actual. They call a spade a spade in a roundabout and
> circumlocutory fashion.
> It can no more be called Greek for its plainness
> of speech and candid foulness than could a dunghill at
> Delphi or a madhouse at Mitylene.

What is the bewildered man in the street to make of
such conflicting oracles? Is Ibsen "candidly foul" or only
"inferentially nasty"? Where doctors (of indecorum) differ, who

shall decide? Mr. Macdougall perhaps? But now we are met by a still more baffling discrepancy of judgment. When we find Mr. Clement Scott[8] and the critic of the Daily Telegraph flatly contradicting each other, chaos seems to have come again. Towards the close of last month Mr. Clement Scott was invited to take part in a debate on Ghosts at the Playgoer's Club. He was unable to attend, but sent a letter to represent him in the discussion. In this letter, as reported in the Detroit Free Press of February 28, there occurs the following sentence:--"None can doubt the cleverness, the genius, the analytical power of the 'Master'." After so emphatic a deliverance from so high an authority we began to take heart of grace, and to imagine that Ibsen might not be such a blockhead after all. But, alas! we reckoned without the critic of the Daily Telegraph. Ghosts, he assured us on March 14, not much more than a fortnight after the date of Mr. Scott's letter, "might have been a tragedy had it been treated by a man of genius. Handled by an egotist (!) and a bungler, it is only a deplorably dull play. There are ideas in Ghosts that would have inspired a tragic poet. They are vulgarized and debased by a suburban Ibsen. You want a Shakespeare, or a Byron (!), or a Browning to attack the subject-matter of Ghosts as it ought to be attacked. It might be a noble theme. Here it is a nasty and a vulgar one." Now, which are we to believe--Mr. Scott, or the literary oracle of the largest circulation, who reckons Byron among the great tragic poets? Is Ibsen a genius or merely an egotist and a bungler? I fear the weight of the evidence is in favour of the latter judgment; for I observe that a third eminent authority, the critic of Truth, sides with his colleague of the Telegraph against Mr. Scott. He writes of "the Ibsen dust-bin, and exclaims: "Literature forsooth! Where is a page of literature to be found in the whole category of Ibsen's plays? It is an insult to the word." This settles the matter! The man who can write of "the whole category" of Ibsen's plays must be an unimpeachable authority on literature. Mr. Scott and the rest of us must even yield to this categorical assurance, and own Ibsen no genius but a suburban egotist.

This article, I shall be told, is purely negative, and contains no rational discussion of the merits and demerits of Ghosts. True; but who can carry on a rational discussion with men whose first argument is a howl for the police?

THE QUINTESSENCE OF IBSENISM:

AN OPEN LETTER TO GEORGE BERNARD SHAW

(New Review, November 1891)

> Archer's "open letter" was his way of writing
> a book review of The Quintessence of Ibsenism,
> which had just been published (W. Scott). The
> two friends carried on an extended debate about
> Ibsen for years, while also working together in
> the general campaign for Ibsen's plays. Shaw's
> feisty response can be found in a long letter
> of 25 October 1891 and a short letter of 26
> Oct. In the case of Archer and Shaw, oppo-
> sition was indeed true kinship.

My Dear G. B. S.,

On that summer afternoon of last year when you read
your Fabian Essay on Ibsen (it was not yet quintessentiated) to
A. B. W.,[1] my wife, and myself, under the elm-trees by Walden
Pond,[2] I fear you found us the very worst audience you ever
addressed. A. B. W. confesses that after a brief but desperate
effort to adjust his mind to your novel terminology, he gave it
up in despair, and fell to considering the prospects of the
root-crops. For my part, I was seasoned beforehand to your
freakish irrationalism, your perverse Schopenhauerism[3]--may I say
your Shawpenhauerism? I was thus in a position, while recognising
the acuteness and ingenuity of your analyses of individual plays,
to scoff at the jargon in which you had chosen to expose the
ground-work of your theory--a darkening of counsel (so it seemed
to me) by sheer metaphysical verbalism. My criticisms, like the
remarks of Bret Harte's Californian controversialist, were so
"frequent and painful and free," that I have ever since regarded
your self-restraint in not pitching me into the alluringly
viscous horse-pond as a sufficient refutation of your doctrine of
human motives. You maintain that we do not "do things for
reasons, but simply "find reasons for what we want to do." Now
you will scarcely deny that you wanted to plunge me into the

duckweed--that your Will, with a big W, made for my immersion; and
no one who knows your powers of casuistry will doubt that you
could have found a score of excellent reasons for so doing. (I
will not insult so eminent a light-weight as the author of Cashel
Byron's Profession[4] by suggesting that any physical difficulty
could act as a deterrent.) The fact remains, however, that the
depths of that tarn (as Ibsen is our theme, let us be Ibsenesque)
are as yet unplumbed by me; whence it ensues that your action was
not governed by your Will with a big W, but was the resultant of
a plexus of perfectly comprehensible motives acting upon your
(lower-case) will; or in other words, that you behaved, in spite
of yourself, not like a high-and-mighty Realist (to adopt your
own terminology), but like a grovelling, logic-chopping, "canny"
Rationalist. And this although your opening chapters are devoted
to proclaiming that you "don't believe there's no sich person!"
    Indeed, I cannot but suspect you of having taken my
criticisms more rationally than I had ventured to hope. It seems
to me that there is less jargon in the completed book than there
was in the initial essay. You may point to this as a proof that I
am gradually becoming a convert to Shawpenhauerism, alleging that
the difference lies, not in your text, but in the eyes with which
I read it. Perhaps so; but a very little labour of the file may
do a great deal in the way of dejargonisation. Be this as it
may, the "Quintessence" as it now stands is in every way a great
improvement on the first draft. The analyses of the plays are
little masterpieces of dialectical and literary dexterity. Your
treatment of Brand and Peer Gynt fills me with envious awe. I
have read and re-read these poems until I know them as intimately
as Mr. Ruskin knows Giotto's Campanile; you, on the other hand,
have never read them at all, but have merely picked up a vague,
second-hand knowledge of their outlines;[5] yet you have penetrated
their mystery (I speak in all seriousness) much more thoroughly
than I have--more thoroughly even than Mr. P. H. Wicksteed,[6]
whose marvellous familiarity with their text far surpasses mine.
The reason is plain enough: Mr. Wicksteed and I (philosophical
bias apart) are bewildered by the multitudinous details,
fantastic, mystical, often, to all appearance, mutually
destructive, the touches of local and temporary satire, the
outbursts of tumultuous creative rapture, by which you remain
blissfully undisturbed. You study the great twin-towered
cathedral, so to speak, on paper, taking in at a glance the
ground-plan and elevations; we see it in all its amazing
lavishness of form and colour, light and shade, fretwork and
tracery, an elaborately-orchestrated piece of "frozen music."
I do not believe and you do not pretend, that the architect
himself, while rearing the pile, had the ground-plan and
elevations as clearly in his mind's eye as you have them in yours;
but they may be substantially correct for all that. In your
accounts of the later plays, and especially of Rosmersholm and

Hedda Gabler, there are several details of interpretation with which I cannot agree; and you have throughout reduced the poet's intentions and the motives of his characters to diagrammatic definiteness which will tend to strengthen the predisposition, already inveterate in some quarters, to regard Ibsen, not as a poet, but as the showman of a moral wax-work. That cannot be helped; it is a drawback inseparable from expository criticism. I do not for a moment doubt that, on the whole, your analyses will help the candid reader not only to understand Ibsen as a thinker, but to appreciate him as a poet; as for the uncandid reader, he must be left to time and his own conscience. Not that I accuse all those who "see nothing in Ibsen" of disingenousness. Most of them suffer from sheer obtuseness to the higher order of dramatic effects--a malady which may co-exist with more than average sensitiveness to other forms of literary excellence.

Granting, however, that you have succeeded in the main in following up the line of thought which runs through Ibsen's plays, from Brand onwards--granting, too, that your peculiar use of the terms "Idealist" and "Realist" is justified by convenience--I return to the consideration of what I still regard, even in its modified form, as your perverse Shawpenhauerism. Why give your doctrine a wantonly obscurantist air by vapouring about "the will to live," as though that were a substantive discovery of Schopenhauer's, and not merely a convenient and luminous name for a phenomenon or group of phenomena which had been more or less clearly recognised from time immemorial? That the name, and the philosophic synthesis it implies, marked a great advance towards lucidity of thought, I, for my part, most potently believe. I profess myself a convinced Schopenhauerist. I have not read Schopenhauer any more than you have; but I had thought my way to many of his conclusions (and Hamlet's) before I had so much as heard his name. This I say to show that my objection to your Shawpenhauerism arises from no mere sectarian prejudice, unless it be a prejudice to shrink from attributing Mesopotamian blessedness to any formula whatsoever. My point is that by juggling with the words "will" and "reason," you not only make a simple matter needlessly obscure, but give countenance to other word-jugglers who use their sleight-of-hand to reactionary ends. Because the eye is an imperfect organ--because it cannot see what is not in sight and is subject to illusion in what it does see--are we therefore to renounce its aid altogether and elect to walk blindfold? I assure you that is a perfectly natural--I will not infuriate you by saying "logical"--deduction from your babble about "the age of reason going its way after the age of faith."

The quintessence of Ibsen's doctrine, according to you, is simply that circumstances alter cases. "He protests," you say, "against the ordinary assumption that there are certain supreme ends which justify all means used to attain them; and insists that every end shall be challenged to show that it justifies the

means.   Our ideals, like the gods of old, are constantly
demanding human sacrifices.   Let none of them, says Ibsen, be
placed above the obligation to prove that they are worth the
sacrifices they demand." Well and good; but what is this but the
old utilitarian, rationalist morality?   I am firmly convinced that
you originally wrote "to prove that they are consistent with the
greatest good of the greatest number," and then suddenly
remembered that that phrase smacked of the Age of Reason, now
happily transcended.   But, having expunged it, you promptly
restated it in a vaguer form; small blame to you, say I, for your
beloved "will to live" is implicit in the Benthamite formula.[7] Of
course that formula, like all the rest, must be challenged and put
on trial--and that, mark you, in the Court of Reason.   As it
stands, the phrase is what you call an Ideal, what Ibsen calls a
"Genganger"--for who denies that rationalism as well as theology
has its "Ghosts"? Strictly considered, indeed, it is meaningless;
for there is nothing to show whether it implies "the greatest
number consistent with the highest good" or "the highest good
consistent with the greatest possible number."   But whatever its
verbal defects, it points in the right, because in the only
possible, direction, and you, my ingenuous sophist, in the very
act of scoffing at it, are throwing the search-light of reason
along the path it indicates.   Whither that path will lead us I do
not pretend to foresee.   You, with charming inconsistency, appear
to look forward to a time when there shall be no general rules of
conduct, but every act shall be regulated by a special judgment,
a deliberate ratiocination, as to its utility.   My faith in human
reason is not so robust.   I am rather inclined to speculate upon
a scientific morality, a set of formulas or ideals, if you choose
to put it so, based upon a thorough knowledge of what we are as
yet but groping after--the laws of physical and mental hygiene;
a morality to which the human will (psychological, not
metaphysical), tamed, and, as Ibsen would say, acclimatised, in
the course of generations, shall submit without a struggle and
with no conscious sacrifice of freedom.   You may object that this
implies an unthinkable state of stable equilibrium; but the
approach to perfect civilisation may be asymptotic, not absolute;
and furthermore, how do you know that the "constant growth of the
will," which you so confidently postulate, may not prove to be a
"Genganger"?   I admit that my stable moral world will not be at
all amusing; but perhaps by that time our sense of humour will
have been tamed, along with so many other inconvenient spiritual
promptings.
     Mr. Birrell[8] has remarked somewhere or other that if Macaulay
were to come to life again, a good many of us would be more
careful than we are how we write about him.   This saying came to
my mind, with Voltaire's name in place of Macaulay's, as I
read your curt dismissal of his immortal _Je n'en vois pas
la nécessité._[9]   What fun he would have made of your "universal

postulate," your solemn quibbling with the word "necessity," and
your ingenuous belief that you had proved Reason to be nowhere in
the race when you had only shown, what no one dreamed of denying,
that Instinct, or if you prefer it "will to live," has always had
a certain start of her! Why, man alive, where do you find any
necessity, natural, logical, or moral, for the individual life?
Nature, it is clear, "does not see the necessity" any more than
Voltaire or "the late lamented guillotine," as Ibsen calls it. By
a convenient metaphor, we call her "careful of the type," but she
is notororiously careless of the single life." You, I suppose,
will scarcely maintain the theological position that--

> We, like sentries, are obliged to stand
> In starless nights, and wait the appointed hour.[10]

There remains only the logical necessity, deduced from your
"universal postulate" of the will to live; and hourly experience
proves to us that it is not universal at all. We are all of us
answering the question "To be, or not to be?" every moment of our
lives, and our answer at any given moment is the resultant of a
complex set of forces of which instinct or habit is only one,
though doubtless in most cases the most potent. We can all
conceive circumstances which would turn the scale against the
primal instinct; every day of the year, every hour of the day,
some of us--a certain percentage--find ourselves placed in such
circumstances. And remember that the suicides who come within
the ken of the coroner are but a vanishing minority of those who
deliberately die because the will to live is not their strongest
motive. Is it not clear, indeed, that the man who first "did not
see the necessity" was the founder of civilisation? (By the way,
he was probably a woman.) We are what we are in virtue of the
impulse which causes some more or less human ancestor of ours to
tag an adverb to his will to live. The instinct is no longer
crude and absolute, even among the higher animals. Among men,
it has developed into the will to live nobly, or respectably, or
ostentatiously, or (in nine cases out of ten) comfortably. Our
dear Hedda Gabler was full of the will to live beautifully, and
when she found that she had mistaken the way, when she no longer
believed in vine-leaves in the hair, her will was to die
beautifully--and she fulfilled it. Poor little Hedvig, too--did
she "see the necessity"? No, it was her father who acknowledged
himself "face to face with the universal postulate."

> Hialmar, having seen her body
>   Borne before him on a shutter,
> True to Shawpenhauerism,
>   Went on eating bread-and-butter,[11]

and no doubt making phrases about the will to live.

I know, my dear G. B. S., that this is a wrangle about words; that we do not differ as to the facts; and that you will be prepared with an ingenious vindication of the set of terms you choose to employ. My point is that in using them you play into the hands of superstition and reaction. And you do yourself injustice; for let me end this diatribe by saying that the affection I have long felt for you—no pitiful false shame shall make me fall back on a more conventional word—is founded on the belief that less, perhaps, than any other man I have ever known, do you "see the necessity."

WILLIAM ARCHER.

THE MAUSOLEUM OF IBSEN

(Fortnightly Review, July 1893)

Part of Archer's aim in this essay, as in "Ghosts and Gibberings," was to counter the vituperative criticism of Ibsen's drama by the London theatre critics. His main target was Clement Scott, the most famous and widely-read of the anti-Ibsenite critics. Scott wrote for the Daily Telegraph, London's largest newspaper, and was past editor of Theatre magazine. Beyond this aim, Archer provided a history of the early performances and the publishing of Ibsen in London.

"The Master Builder bids fair to raise a mausoleum in which the Ibsen craze may be conveniently buried and consigned to oblivion."
        Illustrated Sporting and Dramatic News, 25 Feb. 1893

For the past four years, ever since June 7, 1889, when A Doll's House was produced by Mr. Charles Charrington and Miss Janet Achurch at the Novelty Theatre, the compact majority of English theatrical critics has been assiduously, energetically, one may almost say unintermittently, occupied in building the mausoleum of Ibsen. Mausoleum, perhaps, is scarcely the word; cairn or barrow would be nearer it. Each critic has simply brought his "chunk of old red sandstone"--his pebble of facetiousness, his 'arf-brick of abuse, his boulder of denunciation--and has added it at random to the rude pyramid under which the flattened remains of Henrik Ibsen were supposed to lie. When, at intervals, they have rested from their work, it has only been to look upon it and pronounce it very good. How often have we been informed, in tones of complacent assurance, that "we have heard the last of Ibsen," that "Ibsenism" (or, if the critic be a wit, "Ibsenity") "has died a natural death," that "the cult" or "the craze," is "played out," that "Ibsen has been tried in the balance and found wanting," that "the public won't have Ibsen at any price," and so forth, and so forth! There is probably not a conservative critic in London who has not announced to his readers some four or five times within the said four years that Ibsen is authentically dead at last, until even the great public, one fancies, must be beginning to regard the intelligence with suspicion. And when, after each of these announcements, it has manifestly appeared that Ibsen was not dead at all, but rather more alive than ever, the critics, with truly heroic pertinacity, have sought finally to crush him, by adding to the same old mausoleum or cairn--piling Pelion upon Ossa, Ossa upon Olympus, until the pyramid of execration has reached a magnitude almost unprecedented in literary history. Strange it should never occur to them that, since all this lapidation fails of its object, the reason can only be that Ibsen is not under that stone-heap at all, but only an effigy, a simulacrum, a "contrapshun" as Uncle Remus would call it, compounded of their own imaginings, and bearing but the faintest resemblance to the real Ibsen. In brief, the mausoleum is a cenotaph.

My purpose in this paper is not critical but purely historical. I desire to give a few, a very few, specimens of the treatment accorded to Ibsen by the immense majority of the critics, and then to show, by means of a few facts and figures, that, despite these incessant thunders of condemnation, the works of Ibsen have met with very remarkable acceptance on the stage, and have, in book form, attained an astounding and, so far as I know, unprecedented success.

Except in one quarter, to be hereafter noticed, A Doll's House, on its first production, was treated with comparative leniency. The acting was very highly and very justly praised. The critics, to their credit be it said, have all along admitted that Ibsen gives his actors incomparable opportunities--an odd characteristic in a dramatist so pitiably ignorant of the rudiments of his art. It is surprising--almost startling--to find that those who ventured to admire the play, apart from the acting, were already regarded as a sect of devotees. The term "Ibsenite" occurs in the first line of Mr. Clement Scott's first notice. Whether he invented it I do not know; but whoever may claim the credit of it, this policy of treating the poet as a hot-gospeller, and those who took pleasure in his creations as adepts of some esoteric doctrine, was exceedingly astute, and its prompt adoption at the very outset of the campaign showed the truest tactical genius. Already in the fifth line of the same article we hear of "the amiable fads of the gifted author." How many thousand times has the word "fad," with its derivatives, been repeated in the same connection! Then, in a second article (Daily Telegraph, June 18, 1889), we learn that "there are already signs of weakness in the over-vaunted Ibsen cause. The Ibsenites, failing to convince common-sense people of the justice of their case, are beginning, as a last resource, to "abuse the opposing counsel." Hard words and ill names are flying about." The ground thus cleared, the writer proceeds to analyse the character of "the socialistic Nora." At the beginning she is "all heart like a cabbage," at the end she is "a mass of aggregate conceit and self-sufficiency." And this "foolish, fitful, conceited, selfish, and unlovable Nora is to drive off the stage the loving and noble heroines who have adorned it, and filled all hearts with admiration from the time of Shakespeare to the time of Pinero. . . .The noble women of drama and fiction, the Andromaches and Penelopes, and the Iphigenias and Unas and Imogens and Constances and Jeanie Deans, are to be thrust aside for deformed and stunted and loveless creatures, whose unnatural selfishness the modern dramatist extols, and with whose puny natures the modern essayist professes to be in love!" Here already we have another feature of the opposition tactics fully exemplifies--the trick of assuming that to admire Ibsen is to loathe and despise all other dramatists from "Shakespeare to Pinero." It is an adroit and effective device, and has done good service in its day.

Other deliverances on A Doll's House must be given more briefly:--

> "By the new school of theorists the genre ennuyeux is assigned a place of distinction; for A Doll's House, with its almost total lack of dramatic action, is certainly not an enlivening spectacle."-- Times.

> "It would be a misfortune were such a morbid and unwholesome play to gain the favour of the public." -- Standard.

> "Such a starting-point has dramatic possibilities. A Sardou might conceivably turn to excellent account on the stage. . .It is simply as a mild picture of domestic life in Christiania that the piece has any interest at all. It is a little bit of genre painting, with here and there an effective touch."-- Daily News.

> "Of no use--as far as England's stage is concerned -- Referee.

> "Unnatural, immoral, and, in its concluding scene, essentially undramatic."-- People.

> "Ibsen. . .is too faddy and too obstinately unsympathetic to please English playgoers."-- Sunday Times.

> "Strained deductions, lack of wholesome human nature, pretentious inconclusiveness. . .Cannot be allowed to pass without a word of protest against the dreary and sterilizing principle which it seeks to embody"-- Observer.

> "The works of the Norwegian playwright are not

suitable for dramatic representation--at any rate on
the English stage."-- St. James's Gazette.

In these remarks, of course, there is nothing surprising,
nothing excessive. I quote them merely to show how, from the very
first, the public has been untiringly assured that it does not
want Ibsen, and that his plays are tedious. Two years passed,
during which only two Ibsen performances were given--one matinee
of The Pillars of Society and one of A Doll's House. All his
prose dramas, however, had meanwhile been translated and
published. Then, on February 23rd, 1891, Miss Florence Farr[1]
produced at the Vaudeville a hitherto unattempted play--
Rosmersholm--and this time the critics spoke out with no uncertain
note. Only one of them wavered, the critic of the Daily
Telegraph, who admitted that "Say what we will about Ibsen, he
unquestionably possesses a great power of fascination. Those who
most detest his theories, his doctrines, his very methods of art,
confess to a strange absorbing interest." These startling
admissions were very far from finding an echo in the Press in
general. If gall had been poured forth on A Doll's House,
Rosmersholm was douched with vitriol--

> "A handful of disagreeable and somewhat enigmatical
> personages. . . .Ibsen is a local or provincial drama-
> tist.-- Times.
> "Impossible people do wild things for no apparent
> reason. . .Those portions of the play which are compre-
> hensible are utterly preposterous. . .Ibsen is neither
> dramatist, poet, philosopher, moralist, teacher,
> reformer--nothing but a compiler of rather disagreeable
> eccentricities."-- Standard.
> "The brain-sick extravagancies of the Norwegian
> playwright."-- Daily News.
> "His play is morbid, in fact it is not a play but
> a tiresome exposition of a fantastic theory that no
> healthy mind can accept. . .Ibsenism, a craze happily
> confined to a few. . .Ibsen worship is a hysterical
> thing.-- Morning Advertiser.
> "A dreary and dismal function was that undergone at
> the Vaudeville on Monday afternoon."-- Sporting and
> Dramatic News.
> "A singularly gloomy and ineffectual function was
> that undergone at the Vaudeville on Monday afternoon."
> -- Observer.
> "Love, truth, religion, and self-respect have still
> some hold upon us, and it is hardly likely that Ibsen's
> gloomy ideas will be generally accepted."-- Morning
> Post.

"Mr. Ibsen's silly sayings."-- Evening News.
"The stuff that Ibsen strings together in the shape of plays must nauseate any properly-constituted person." -- Mirror.
"Ibsen's gruesome play. . .His repulsive drama. . . Greeted with the silence of contempt when the curtain finally fell."-- People.
"Studies in insanity best fitted for the lecture-room in Bedlam. . .At the fall of the curtain there was loud applause, and but the faintest attempt at hissing."-- Stage.
"The whole affair is provincial and quite con-temptible Saturday Review.
"Mr. Ibsen does not call Rosmersholm a farce; but that is because of his modesty. . .To judge it seriously either as literature or as drama is impossible."-- St. James's Gazette.
"The style and matter of most of his work is always tiresome, frequently childish, and the subject often morbid and unwholesome. . .method tedious to the last degree of boredom. . .Here and there he gives expression to pretty ideas reminding me of Tom Robertson."-- Punch.
"These Ibsen creatures are neither men nor women, they are ghouls, vile, unlovable, unnatural, morbid monsters, and it were well indeed for society if all such went and drowned themselves at once."-- Gentle-woman.
Rosmersholm is not very dramatic. It is hardly at all literary. . .It is without beauty, without poetry, without sense of vista. It is not even dexterously doctrinaire. . .The farce is almost played out."-- MR. F. WEDMORE in Academy.
"There are certain dishes composed of such things as frogs and snails, stews in which oil and garlic reek, and dreadful compounds which we taste out of sheer curiosity, and which, if we expressed our honest, candid opinion, we should pronounce to be nasty and unpleasant . . .Rosmersholm is beyond me."-- Topical Times.
"To descant upon such morbid, impracticable rubbish would be an insult to the understanding of every reader, except an Ibsenite. . .If Herr Ibsen were well smothered in mud with his two creations and with every copy of his plays, the world would be all the better for it." -- Licensed Victuallers' Gazette.

Alas, poor Ibsen! It is well that he does not read English, else who knows but the disesteem of the Licensed Victuallers' Gazette might drive him into his mausoleum in good earnest.

Less than a month later (March 13th, 1891) <u>Ghosts</u> was produced at the first performance of the Independent Theatre. The frenzy of execration with which it was greeted must be within the memory of all my readers. I compiled at the time a <u>Schimpflexikon</u>--a Dictionary of Abuse--which was published in the <u>Pall Mall Gazette</u> of April 8th under the title of "<u>Ghosts</u> and Gibberings."[2] I somewhat repent me of this title, which smacks of the controversial methods of the enemy; but the temptation was irresistible. The <u>Schimpflexikon</u> itself I shall not reproduce, but shall merely cull a few of its choicest epithets: Abominable, disgusting, bestial, fetid, loathsome, putrid, crapulous, offensive, scandalous, repulsive, revolting, blasphemous, abhorrent, degrading, unwholesome, sordid, foul, filthy, malodorous, noisome. Several of the critics shouted for the police. The critic of the <u>Daily Telegraph</u>, having repented his moment of backsliding over <u>Rosmersholm</u>, and recovered his moral tone, declared that "<u>Ghosts</u> might have been a tragedy had it been treated by a man of genius. Handled by an egotist and a bungler it is only a deplorably dull play. There are ideas in <u>Ghosts</u> that would have inspired a tragic poet. They are vulgarised and debased by a suburban Ibsen. You want a Shakespeare, or a Byron(!), or a Browning to attack the subject matter of <u>Ghosts</u> as it ought to be attacked. It might be a noble theme. Here it is a nasty and a vulgar one."

Nothing daunted by the tempest, Miss Elizabeth Robins and Miss Marion Lea produced <u>Hedda Gabler</u> only five weeks later (April 20th, 1891).[3] This time the "suburban Ibsen," the "egotist and bungler," was found by the <u>Daily Telegraph</u> to have produced a "ghastly picture beautifully painted." "It was like a visit to the Morgue. . . .There they all were, false men, wicked women, deceitful friends, sensualists, egotists, piled up in a heap behind the screen of glass, which we were thankful for. . . . There were the dead bodies, and no one could resist looking at them. Art was used for the most baleful purpose. It is true that the very spectacle of moral corruption was positively fascinating. . . .Would indeed that, after this Morgue inspection, after this ghasty spectacle of dead bodies and suicides, after this revolting picture of human frailty and depravity, there could be a break in the cloud. . . .But alas! there is no gleam to be seen in the dark raincloud of Ibsenite pessimism!. . .What a horrible story! What a hideous play!" Most of my readers are probably aware that there is only one dead body in <u>Hedda Gabler</u>, seen for something like a quarter of a minute just as the curtain falls. But what must the readers of the <u>Daily Telegraph</u> have gathered from the outburst I have just quoted? "I should like so much to see the piece you're in," a lady said to Mr. Scott Buist, the excellent Tesman of the cast, "but I don't think I could stand anything so horrible." "Horrible! How do you mean?" he enquired. "Why, you have the Morgue on the stage, haven't you?"

was the reply. And I have no doubt many thousands of people were under the same impression, on that 21st (not 1st) of April.[4] The other critics, if less imaginative, were no less denunciatory.

"Ibsen's plays regarded as masterpieces of genius by a small but noisy set of people, but. . .the tastes of English playgoers are sound and healthy, and the hollowness and shams of the Ibsen cult need only be known to be rejected."-- Standard.

"Dr. Ibsen's social dramas have yet to prove their power to interest cultivated audiences; for the limited number of worshippers who proclaim these productions as masterpieces of art and stagecraft. . .cannot be accepted as a fair sample even of the educated public." -- Daily News.

"Robust common-sense of ordinary English audiences will confirm the adverse judgment pronounced upon the morbid Norwegian dramatist by all save a clique of faddists anxious to advertise themselves by the aid of any eccentricity that comes first to hand. . . .Already, we fancy, the craze has had its day."-- Sporting and Dramatic News.

"One left the theatre filled with depression at the sorry spectacle that had been set before them (sic)." -- Reynolds' Newspaper.

"A few steps out of the hospital-ward and we arrive at the dissecting-room. Down a little lower and we come to the deadhouse. There, for the present, Ibsen has left us. . . .Miss Elizabeth Robins has done what no doubt she fully intended to do (!). She has made vice attractive by her art. She has almost ennobled crime. She has glorified an unwomanly woman," & c., & c. Mr. C. SCOTT in the Illustrated London News

"Hideous nightmare of pessimism. . .The play is simply a bad escape of moral sewage-gas. . . .Hedda's soul is acrawl with the foulest passions of humanity." -- Pictorial World.

"The piece is stuff and nonsense; poor stuff and "pernicious nonsense." It is as if the author had studied the weakest of the Robertsonian comedies, and had thought he could do something like it in a tragic vein."-- Punch.

"It is not, possibly, so utterly repulsive as others that have been seen, but, nevertheless, it is offensive."-- Lloyd's News.

"The more I see of Ibsen, the more disgusted I am with his alleged dramas."-- London.

"Utterly pessimistic in its tedious turmoil of knaves and fools. . . .Other plays from the same tainted source."-- The People.

"Full of loathesomeness."-- The Table.

"Things rank and gross in nature alone have place in the mean and sordid philosophy of Ibsen. . . .Can any human being feel happier or better from a contemplation of the two harlots at heart who do duty in Hedda Gabler? . . .Insidious nastiness of photographic studies of vice and morbidity. . . .It is free from the mess and nastiness of Ghosts, the crackbrained maunderings of Rosmersholm, the fantastic, shortsighted folly of A Doll's House. . . .The blusterous little band of Ibsen idolaters. . . ."-- Saturday Review.

"Strange provincial prigs and suburban chameleons. . . .The funereal clown who is amusing us. . . is given to jokes in very questionable taste. We are reminded again and again of Goethe's famous stage direction, "Mephistopheles macht eine unanständige Geberde," and it is a coarseness of this sort which, I fear, constitutes Ibsen's charm for some his disciples. . . .For sheer unadulterated stupidity, for inherent meanness and vulgarity, for pretentious triviality. . . no Bostonian novel or London penny novelette has sur-passed Hedda Gabler."

Mr. ROBERT BUCHANAN in the Illustrated London News.

And now, before passing on to examine the latest layer or story of the mausoleum--the onslaughts on The Master Builder--I wish to return for a little while upon the earlier layers, and look at some of the largest blocks or boulders, which I have hitherto purposely passed over. Speaking of the 1889 production of A Doll's House, I said that the critics, with one exception, treated it leniently. The exception was the critic of Truth. This gentleman, as we shall see, announced himself from the first as a very malleus hereticorum,[5] and kept up that character, with an ever-increasing fury of conviction, until--well, until about the time when Mr. Clement Scott departed on his journey round the world. It is commonly understood that Mr. Scott is the author of these articles. They bear the impress of his very characteristic style, and a public statement connecting him with them has elicited from him, not a disclaimer of their authorship, but an assertion of the sacred privileges of anonymity. Now, here I differ from Mr. Scott; I do not admit these sacred privileges. Whether a writer shall or shall not sign his articles is a question between him and his editor; but what he shall write, in unsigned no less than in signed articles, is a question between him and his conscience. I deny the right of any man to shirk responsibility for his words merely because he has not put his name to them. Anonymity should be rather an obligation than a privilege. If we must go forth to battle wearing the Cloak of

Darkness, we ought, at least, to be doubly careful not to hit below the belt. I offer no apology, then, for quoting the following utterances as Mr. Scott's, if indeed they are Mr. Scott's. But as I read them over I can scarcely believe it. If they are not his--if he, or, in his absence, the Editor of Truth, will state in so many words that he did not write them--I will make the most public apology for having for a moment connected him with them, though I shall in fact have done him a substantial service in giving him this opportunity for such a disclaimer. Whoever may be their author, they certainly deserve to be immortalized among the curiosities of criticism. I regret that my own name figures so prominently in the first article of the series; but the reader will readily acquit me of quoting it in a spirit of vain-glory. Further comment is unnecessary. I shall merely preface my extracts with a brief citation from an article signed by Mr. Clement Scott, in the Illustrated London News of February 28, 1891: "It seems to many of us a great pity that the discussion on Ibsen and all his works cannot be carried on with a little more exercise of temper and forbearance. It looks suspiciously like the knowledge of a weak cause when rude invective and coarse motive are flung at the head of any one."

"It was a great night on Friday for the Ibsenites. They were determined to worship at the shrine of their great apostle and saint. The erudite Archer had long ago been put forward, or had put himself forward, as the evangelistic herald to lighten our darkness, and to prepare the way of Henrik Ibsen in the dramatic wilderness. . . .Certain Philistine heretics some five years ago had the temerity to lay their sacrilegious hands on A Doll's House. . . .Breaking a Butterfly was the result, and naturally the Ibsenites put the failure down to "Ibsen ruined.". . .On this memorable occasion outspoke the erudite Archer. . .and made one unfortunate admission. He declared, ore rotundo, that "Ibsen on the English stage is impossible. He must be trivialized." And Archer proved his case up to the hilt on Friday at the Novelty Theatre, where a scant audience of unnatural-looking women, long-haired men, atheists, Socialists, egotists, and Positivists, assembled to see Ibsen when nothing was eliminated that was satirical or unpleasant, and to gloat over the Ibsen theory of woman's degradation and man's unnatural supremacy. . . . Ibsen is impossible on the English stage because he wants to preach nonsense and not to play sense. He is impossible because he is the idol of a clique of "faddists.". . .It is well that Ibsen should have been exploited and exposed. . . .By this time the Ibsen bubble must have burst, and a very good thing too."--

<u>Truth</u>, June 13th, 1889.
  "An obscure Scandinavian dramatist and poet, a
crazy fanatic, and determined Socialist, is to be
trumpeted into fame for the sake of the estimable
gentlemen who can translate his works, and the enterprising tradesmen who publish them. . .The unwomanly
women, the unsexed females, and the whole army of
unprepossessing cranks in petticoats. . .sit open-
mouthed and without a blush on their faces, whilst a
Socialist orator reads aloud <u>Ghosts</u>, the most loathesome
of all Ibsen's plays. . .If you have seen one play by
Ibsen you have seen them all. A disagreeable and nasty
woman: an egotistical and preachy man; a philosophical
sensualist; dull and undramatic dialogue. The few
independent people who have sat out a play by Ibsen. . .
have said to themselves, Put this stuff before the play-
going public, risk it at the evening theatre, remove
your claque, exhaust your attendance of the Socialistic
and the sexless, and then see where your Ibsen will be.
I have never known an audience yet that cared to pay to
be bored."-- <u>Truth</u>, March 19, 1891.
  "THE IBSEN FOLLY. Has it never struck the enthusiastic opposers of "free theatres" and "independent
managers," and self-advertising Dutchmen,[6] and Ibsenites generally, that they are giving quite unneccesary
notoriety to a wave of human folly. . .? Outside a
silly clique there is not the slightest interest in the
Scandinavian humbug and all his works. The public at
large knows nothing about him. If they ever take the
trouble to listen to him, they will hiss him contemp-
tuously off the stage. Those who read Ibsen, instigated
by this absurd "booming" of a very insignificant person,
find him not only consistently dirty but deplorably
dull. Now, if people like dirt let them have it. Let
them feed on it if they care for it. The decent house-
holder puts his garbage and offal outside the door,
to be taken away by the scavenger in the morning. But
some well-bred and educated dog is sure to rout over
the pile and to bury his nose in the nastiest morsel.
The better-bred and educated the dog, the more he
relishes the worst scrap of carrion. This is human
nature. But cannot we leave this muck-heap to the
educated and muck-ferreting dogs? If we hunt the hounds
away, they will always turn to the delightful pile
again. . . .The scene between the Rank Doctor and the
Squirrel Nora is too dirty for discussion by decent
people. Apart from that bit of dirt the play is dull.
There is a scene and countless suggestions in <u>Rosmer-
sholm</u>. . .that would be too gross for any respectable

man to start as a discussion at any dinner-table where
the sexes are mingled. Apart from that, the play is
dull to the pitch of desperation. . .And as to Ghosts. .
.if certain eccentric women choose to rout in these
muck-heaps, it does not much concern the general public.
. . .They all of them, men and women alike, Ibsenites
and Socialists, know that they are doing not only a
nasty but an illegal thing. . .The Lord Chamberlain
wisely left them all alone to wallow in Ghosts. . .What
would have been the good to hunt away these educated
individuals from the Ibsen dust-bin? They would all
have returned to it again. They know it is nasty, and
they pretend to conceal their love of nastiness with a
love of literature. Literature, forsooth! Where, may I
ask, is a page of literature to be found in the whole
category of Ibsen's plays? It is an insult to the word.
Ibsen, so far as I can see, is a crazy, cranky being
who has derived his knowledge of life from some half-
civilised Norwegian village. . . .He sees filth in
his Norway society, and imagines that all the world is
filthy as well. This is not philosophy, it is folly.
To my mind, three things have been triumphantly proved
by the recent performances: First, that Ibsen is no
philosopher at all; secondly, that his plays are not
literature; thirdly, and most important of all, that his
so-called plays are dull to the point of desperation. .
. .Men. . .and women. . .came to see something spicy. .
.They came to gloat, and they remained to yawn. . . .I
don't think the fifty-shilling subscriptions will roll
in very fast to the exchequer of the enterprising Dutchman, who has a soul for art, but also a very keen eye
to the main chance!"-- Truth, March 26, 1891.

"There was only one thing to be done with Ibsen so
as to popularise him with a set of boobies, and that was
to treat him with religious fervour. This hoary-headed
old atheist is the craze to-day in the same way that
Oscar Wilde's aestheticism was the craze a few years ago
. . . .At the command of the hack translators of Ibsen,
they fall down at the feet of the cynical old preacher
of Schopenhauerism, Voltarism, and pessimism!. . .Listen
to this old grey Norwegian wolf as he chuckles in his
den. . . .This is the art of Ibsen, to make us love the
hideous, the ugly, and the depraved. Read the character
of Hedda Gabler. . . .She is a fiend in human form. She
is a revolting, abominable, heartless woman. See her
acted by Miss Elizabeth Robins! Do we hate her, do we
despise her, do we condemn her? No; we admire her for
her very wickedness. . . .When art is the propagandist
of faithlessness and lawlessness, it becomes a serious

question whether Faith has not a right to look after
its own creed, Morality its own mission, and the Law its
own dignity."-- Truth, April 30th, 1891.

"Mr. J. M. Barrie's parody, Ibsen's Ghost,[7] came
rather too late in the day, for poor old Ibsen is as
dead as a door-nail. . . .Nobody cared twopence for the
Scandinavian playwright or all his wild romance, and no
one would have heard of him had not the critics and
crotchetmongers fought over his corpse. The coup-
de-grace, if it were wanted, will be given by chaff"
-- Truth, June 4th, 1891.

"Old Ibsen is as dead as a door-nail. He was a
"bogey" at the best--a turnip at the top of a long pole.
. . .But let not the satirists and burlesque-writers lay
the flattering unction to their souls that it was they
who killed this perky old Cock Robin. . . ."-- Truth,
June 11th, 1891.

These extracts are all from articles in Truth treating
directly of Ibsen's works, or of parodies upon them. They might
be indefinitely extended if one included side-flings of similar
"epieikeia, or sweet-reasonableness," from articles professing to
deal with other topics.

We come now to the uppermost course (for the present) in the
pyramid of invective. On the 20th of last February, Mr. Herbert
Waring[8] and Miss Robins produced The Master Builder at the
Trafalgar Square Theatre, and this is how it was greeted by the
Press:--

"Dense mist enshrouds characters, words, actions,
and motives. . . .A certain kind of interest in the
Norwegian writer's strange dramas. . . .One may compare
it, to put an extreme case, to the sensations of a man
who witnesses a play written, rehearsed, and acted by
lunatics."-- Daily Telegraph.

"Assuredly no one may fathom the mysteries. . .of
the play, so far as it can be called a play. . . .If it
did not please, it most unquestionably puzzled. . . .It
is not a moment to be understood that we personally
recommend any one to go and see it."-- Standard.

"Here we contemplate the actions of a set of lunatics each more hopeless than the other. . . .Platitudes
and inanities. . . .The play is hopeless and indefensible."-- Globe.

"People sit and make themselves think that it is
great because they know it is by Ibsen. . . .The same
work with an unknown name they would most assuredly
ridicule and hiss."-- Echo.

"A feast of dull dialogue and acute dementia. . . .

The most dreary and purposeless drivel we have ever heard in an English theatre. . . .A pointless, incoherent, and absolutely silly piece."-- Evening News.

"Rigmarole of an oracle Delphic in obscurity and Gamp-like in garrulity. . . .Pulseless and purposeless play, which has idiocy written on every lineament. . . . Three acts of gibberish."-- Stage.

"A distracting jumble of incoherent elements. There is no story; the characters are impossible, and the motives a nightmare of perverted fingerposts." -- Saturday Review.

"Sensuality. . .irreverence. . .unwholesome. . . simply blasphemous."-- Morning Post.

"Dull, mysterious, unchaste."-- Daily Graphic.

"A play to which even the Young Person may be taken with no more fear of harm than a severe headache. . . . Ibsen is a master of the chaotic and meaningless epigram . . . .Thrilling moments in last act marred by bathos. The rest idle babble."-- Figaro.

"Presents human life in a distorted form, and is entirely without intelligible purpose." -- Mr. MOY THOMAS in the Graphic.

"Same old dulness prevails as was the feature of his previous prosy pratings."-- England.

"The blunder has been made. Master-Builder Solness has been played. . . .Hilde Wangel is perhaps the most detestable character in the drama's range. . .victim of nymphomania(!). . .deliberate murderess. . .mean, cheap, hateful, stands out in dishonourable distinctness."-- Pall Mall Gazette.

"Ibsen has written some very vile and vulgar plays. . . . The Master Builder bids fair to raise a mausoleum in which the Ibsen craze may be conveniently buried and consigned to oblivion.-- Sporting and Dramatic News.

So much for the critical mausoleum. Was ever artist in this world denounced with greater fury, with more unwearying persistency? It must be remembered that I have only selected a few bricks from the pyramid. It would be easy to multiply such extracts twentyfold. "This is all very well," the reader may say, "but how about the other side of the case?" There has, of course, been a good deal of sane and competent Ibsen criticism during these four years, and some, no doubt, extravagantly enthusiastic. But both in bulk and influence the favourable, or even the temperate, criticism, has been as nothing beside the angrily or scornfully hostile. All the great morning papers, the leading illustrated weeklies, the critical weeklies, with one exception, and the theatrical trade papers, have been bitterly denunciatory. If, now and then, I have quoted from obscure prints for the sake of preserving some delicious absurdity of criticism, the great mass of my extracts have been taken from papers of influence and position. The upshot of the whole is that the "Scandinavian humbug," the "hoary-headed old Atheist," the "determined Socialist,"[9] the "suburban Ibsen," is dull, dreary, dirty, dismal, and dead; that no one ever did take any sort of interest in his works; and that if the English public could possibly be got to pay the smallest attention to such an incurable "egotist and bungler," its healthy common-sense would rise up in revolt, and it would "hiss him off the stage." If hard words (and foul words) could kill, in short, how very dead Ibsen would be!

Let us see, now, how dead he is--first in the book market, then on the stage.

About four years ago The Pillars of Society, Ghosts, and An Enemy of the People were published in a shilling volume, one of the Camelot Classic series. Of that volume, up to the end of 1892, Mr. Walter Scott had sold 14,367 copies. In 1890 and 1891 the same publisher issued an authorised uniform edition of Ibsen's prose drama in five volumes, at three and sixpence each. Of these volumes, up to the end of 1892, 16,834 copies had been sold. Thus, Mr. Walter Scott alone has issued (in round numbers) thirtyone thousand volumes of the works of the man for whom nobody "outside a silly clique" cares a brass farthing. But these figures in reality understate the case. The "volume" is an artificial unit; the natural, the real unit, is the play; and each volume contains three plays. Thus we find that one publisher alone has placed in circulation ninety-three thousand[10] plays by Ibsen. Other publishers have issued single-volume editions of A Doll's House, Ghosts, Rosmersholm, The Lady from the Sea, Hedda Gabler, and The Master Builder, some of which (and especially Mr. Heinemann's copyright editions of the last two plays) must have had a very considerable sale. Thus, I think, we are well within the mark in estimating that one hundred thousand prose dramas by Ibsen have been bought by the English-speaking public in the course of the past four years. Is there a parallel in the history of publishing for such a result in the case of translated plays? Putting Shakespeare in Germany out of the question (and he has been selling, not for four years, but for a century), I doubt whether any translated dramas have ever sold in such quantities. Ibsen himself must have had a very large sale in Germany; but there his plays are to be had for threepence each, while here, on an average, they cost at least three times that sum. In English publishing, at any rate, such sales are absolutely unprecedented. The publishers to whom I proposed a collected edition of the Prose Dramas before Mr. Scott undertook it, dismissed the idea as visionary, roundly declaring that no modern plays could ever "sell" in England; and, except in the one case of Ibsen, experience justified this assertion. It will be said that the works of the French dramatists, Dumas, Augier, &c., are not translated, because people read them in the original. But do there exist in England at the present moment one hundred thousand plays by all the modern French dramatists put together—Dumas, Augier, Sardou, Meilhac, Labiche, Gondinet, and all the rest? I very much doubt it. Of course, it would be folly to deny that the very frenzies of hostility above exemplified have defeated their own ends and helped more than anything else perhaps to arouse and sustain public interest in Ibsen. But when did deserved denunciation ever secure popularity for a writer? If a book is dull, and the critics say so, people will not find it interesting out of sheer perversity. Not until criticism, in declaring a writer tedious, prosy, "dull to the point of desperation," contradicts itself on its very face by the eager emphasis of its invective, does the public begin to wonder whether the dulness which so potently excites the critics may not have in it some stimulus, some suggestion, in a word some interest, for the general reader as well. It is quite true, as the publishers assured me, that for fifty years or more the English public had lost the habit of reading plays, and that to many people the unaccustomed dramatic form is in itself an annoyance. Yet in spite of this drawback, in spite of the foreignness of Ibsen's subjects, his atmosphere and his point of view—in spite, too of the loss in sheer beauty of style which he necessarily suffers in translation—the fact remains that 100,000 of his plays are at this moment in the hands of the reading public. Whether the interest in his works will wax or wane no one can predict. For the present it shows no symptom of flagging. But even if it were to fall dead to-morrow, I think it will be admitted that these 40,000 volumes,[11] these 100,000 plays, form a tolerably handsome "mausoleum."

Now as to the stage—but before stating the facts of the case let me suggest a few preliminary considerations. Except in omnivorous Germany, have translated plays ever been known to take very deep root on a foreign stage? In adaptations there has been for centuries a brisk international trade—the French have borrowed from the Spaniards, we and all the world from the French, and so forth—but translations have been few and far between. In England least of all have we shown any appetite for them. Even of Molière we have made, for the stage, only crude and now almost forgotten adaptations. Since, then, Ibsen—translated, not adapted—has met with some acceptance in the English theatre, that fact is in itself practically unique. If he had indeed been "impossible" on the English stage, he would have had as companions in impossibility Corneille, Racine, Molière, Marivaux, Hugo, Musset, Lessing, Goethe, Schiller, Lope, and Calderon;[12] no such despicable confraternity. As a matter of fact, and in the face of the unexampled tempest of oboloquy in the Press, seven of his plays—not adapted, but faithfully translated—have been placed on the English stage. If our theatrical history presents any para-

llel to this, I shall be glad to hear of it; I can certainly
think of none. "This is all very fine," cry the adversaries,
"but we do not deny that there is a 'silly, noisy, &c., &c.,
clique of faddists' who applaud these productions. What we
maintain is that the great public, the paying public, will not
have Ibsen at any price." It is undoubtedly true that the compact
majority of the critics has done all that lay in its power to
frighten the paying public away from any theatre where Ibsen is
being played; and their invectives, though they doubtless cut both
ways, have on the whole tended to diminish the chances of
pecuniary success. Especially effective has been the persistent
accusation of "indecorum"--an accusation which cannot but be
injurious in a country where the theatre is so largely a family
institution. The cry is beginning to lose its effect, for
open-minded playgoers, who have braved the warnings of the Press,
have discovered for themselves that of all writers for the stage
Ibsen is the farthest remote from any taint of lubricity. It is
certain, as the critic of Truth puts it, that any one who has gone
to the theatre with the view of "gloating over" his improprieties,
must have been grievously disappointed. But a superstition so
adroitly implanted and sedulously fostered takes time to die, and
thousands of people are doubtless kept away from Ibsen
performances by the notion that they are not entertainments "to
which a daughter can safely take her mother." Yet in spite of
denunciation and misrepresentation, Ibsen's plays have by no means
made the pecuniary fiasco industriously predicted and insinuated
by the hostile critics. It is true that (apart from The Master
Builder [13] which, as I write, is still being performed, so that its
balance-sheet cannot be finally made up) I know of only one
instance in which any very considerable profit has been made out
of an Ibsen production; but taking the others all round, he may
fairly be said to have paid his way and a little more. Of the
production of The Lady from the Sea at Terry's Theatre,[14] I know
nothing, and do not include it in my calculations. Ghosts, again,
has never been licensed, so that no money has been taken for its
two performances. As to the five remaining plays I am enabled to
state with tolerable accuracy the total amount paid by the London
public in order to see them on the stage, between June 7, 1889,
and March 18, 1893. The public, says the critic of Truth, will
not "pay to be bored," but somehow or other they have paid £4,876
to be bored (and of course bewildered, nauseated and all the rest
of it) by Ibsen. Of these five plays The Pillars of Society was
played only once and Rosmersholm twice to receipts amounting in
all to £276. Thus it appears that for the privilege of being
bored by the "prosy prating" of A Doll's House, the "Morgue
inspection" of Hedda Gabler, and the unchaste drivel and
gibberish" of The Master Builder, the London public (who "will
not have Ibsen at any price," has paid, up to March 18, the pretty
handsome price of £4,600.[15]

Let me not be understood to put this forward as, in itself, a very imposing result. I know that successful production at a fashionable West-End theatre will draw as much money as this in a single month. But consider the circumstances of the case! Here are a set of foreign plays, representing society in a small and little-known country; not adapted, but translated; not produced at leading theatres with the prestige and popularity of the actor-managers to support them, but acted under all sorts of disadvantages at second-rate theatres,[16] by actors (in many cases) comparatively unknown to the great public; bitterly denounced and ridiculed by the vast majority of the Press, and yet, in the face of all these difficulties, making so much financial success as fairly to pay their own way, and leave a margin over! In the case of Hedda Gabler the margin was a very large one. The net profit on the ten matinees, after all expenses paid, amounted to £281, or an average of £28 on each performance--a rate of profit which the most prosperous actor-manager would scarcely despise; and, when the play was put in the evening bill, it drew houses which, under ordinary circumstances, would have been fairly remunerative, though, as the manager had to pay two sets of salaries (to the Hedda Gabler company, and to the regular company of the theatre, who were meanwhile unemployed), he could not run it beyond a month. What becomes, then, of the assertion that "the public will not have Ibsen at any price"? Does it not rather seem that there is a public, and not a very small one, which will have Ibsen at any price, despite such a chorus of critical anathema as was never heard before in the history of the English stage?

I am far from predicting that Ibsen will ever be really popular on the English stage, though such a prediction would seem less extravagant to-day than the prediction of the success he has actually achieved would have seemed ten years ago. It is possible, as a French critic, M. Doumic, has recently been arguing, that "a certain mediocrity" is essential to great popular success on the stage. I have very little doubt that criticism will soon come to take a saner view of his works, and that they have a certain future before them even in the theatre. It is scarcely to be expected, however--it would contradict all experience, here and elsewhere--that they should take deep and permanent hold upon the English stage. Scarcely to be expected, and scarcely to be desired; for no theatre can for long live healthily on imported material. Each nation should produce, in its own theatre, its own criticism of its own life. Criticism of life from a foreign standpoint and illustrated by foreign examples, may be very interesting and fascinating, but cannot, in the long run, satisfy our souls. I look forward to a time when Ibsen, having completed the work which many even of his enemies admit that he has well begun, of lifting the theatre on to a higher intellectual plane, shall himself be heard no more, or heard but rarely, upon the English stage. By that time, in a

certain sense, this great Master Builder will have built his own
mausoleum; but not a mausoleum of oblivion. It will have tower
aloft, like Hilda's castle, "with the vane pointing upwards at a
dizzy height"; and, looking up at it, we shall seem to hear harper
i luften--"harps in the air."

    P.S. This article was in type before the recent series of
Ibsen performances at the Opera Comique[17] was so much as thought
of, and while Mr. Beerbohm Tree's production of An Enemy of the
People at the Haymarket was still in the vague future. The Opera
Comique performances resulted in a clear profit, and I believe Mr.
Tree has, up to the present, had every reason to be satisfied with
the financial result of his experiment.

THE REAL IBSEN

(International Monthly, Feb. 1901)

> This was the first of a series of essays written
> between 1901 and 1919 in which Archer presented
> his assessment of Ibsen's greatness.   One of
> the consistent aims in these essays is Archer's
> determination to   correct   misinformation   and
> misperceptions—to separate, that is, the "real
> Ibsen" from the "distorted simulacrum" of him
> that many people chose to see.   In this essay
> Archer   analyzed   five   "popular   errors"   about
> Ibsen: that   he   lacks   style,   that   he   is   an
> inefficient craftsman, that he is a pessimist,
> that he has no humor, and that he is a "provin-
> cial" or "suburban" playwright.

Over all artists, past or present, Henrik Ibsen may claim one
undesirable preeminence: he has been, if not more deeply, at any
rate more widely, misunderstood.   If his fame endures for another
fifty years, someone will doubtless write a "History of Ibsen
Criticism in the Nineteenth Century" to the no small entertainment
of our grandsons.   Never, certainly, was there any man about whom
more nonsense was talked in so brief a space of time.   It is at
the outside twelve years since Ibsen became known to the world at
large.   Down to 1888 or thereabouts, very few people beyond the
limits of Scandinavia and Germany had even heard his name.   In the
five years between 1888 and 1893 his fame spread through England,
America, France, Italy.   Since 1893, he has had only two rivals in
respect of world-wide renown—Tolstoy and Zola.   This quaint
trimvirate has unquestionably held the centre of the literary
stage during the past decade; and Ibsen has been, not certainly
the best known, but the most furiously canvassed, and the most
hopelessly misunderstood, of the three.   I propose to point out
some of these and to show how they have arisen.
Let us note at the outset one fact so obvious that it is
often disregarded.   In respect of language, Ibsen stands at a

unique disadvantage. Never before has a poet of world-wide fame
appealed to his world-wide audience so exclusively in
translations. To the Greek poets, the world of culture was the
Hellenic world. Their works were not translated into the
barbarian tongues, for such barbarians as were capable of culture
made a knowledge of Greek their first step towards attaining it.
The Roman poets conquered the world in an idiom which was already
imperial. It was not in translations that Dante and Petrarch won
the homage of Europe. So long as English remained a merely
insular tongue, Shakespeare was practically unknown abroad, and
grotesquely misunderstood by the few that had heard of him. All
the critics who made his European fame read him in the original.
Cervantes became world-famous because he wrote in prose. Lope and
Calderon are mere names to the world at large because their
language is little read, and because, being poets, they lose
fatally in translation. The language of the French poets has
been, since the Renaissance, the universal tongue of culture, just
as Latin was during the middle ages. When Goethe and Schiller
began to write, German was already much more widely known than
Norwegian to-day; yet I am sure a little research could bring
together a bouquet of early Goethe-criticisms almost as absurd,
though not one thousandth part as numerous, as the "anti-Ibsenite"
criticisms of the past ten years. The great Russians, again,
Turgueneff and Tolstoy, write a language almost as little known as
Ibsen's in Western Europe and American. But they, like Cervantes,
write in narrative prose. Their works can be translated without
too much loss or distortion of "values."

   "But Ibsen," you say, "is also a prose-writer." That is just
where the mistake comes in. Ibsen is a dramatic poet; and Brand
and Peer Gynt, the works which, more than any others, establish
the scale of his intellectual stature, are written in brilliant,
richly-rhymed lyrical verse, which is the despair of the
translator. If you do not know Brand and Peer Gynt, you know
Ibsen only as a fragment, a torso; if you know them in
translations, you may guess at his true greatness, but you cannot
realize it. Having myself translated Peer Gynt, I am in a
position to say with some confidence that these poems are
untranslatable. If they are ever to be adequately rendered in
English, it must be by a poet with all Mr. Swinburne's mastery of
metres. It may safely be said that ten people know Ibsen's prose
plays for one who has read Brand or Peer Gynt even in translation.
Who can wonder, then, that a poet so imperfectly known should be
so largely misunderstood?

   But it is not merely his great dramas in verse that suffer in
translation. The dramatic prose of his modern plays also suffers,
not so much as verse indeed, but far more than any narrative
prose. As I do not know Russian, I cannot tell how much the
beauty of Tolstoy's style is obscured in the French or English
renderings which most of us read; but we have no reason to suppose

that the substantial value of his work is impaired. Ibsen's
dialogue, on the other hand, is incredibly difficult to render
with any justice. Its beauty,--its real and often remarkable
beauty,--is almost as elusive as the charm of verse. Its
simplicity is apt to come out as commonness, its high-lights of
imagination are too often transmuted into mere flashes of
eccentricity. Working in the intensely compressed dramatic form,
Ibsen has far fewer words than Tolstoy at his command; and in
precisely the same ration is each individual word more important
to the full expression of his meaning. A slovenly or cumbrous
phrase, a loose approximation, the missing of a fine shade of
meaning or emphasis, does far more harm to Ibsen than it would to
Tolstoy, or any other narrative writer. His prose has not,
indeed, the deliberate, rhetorical beauty of Maeterlinck's or
D'Annunzio's; but the unobtrusive beauty peculiar to it is all the
more difficult to reproduce.

Ibsen, in short, is by far the most widely renowned poet
produced, in modern times, by so small a nation as Norway. His
Danish-Norwegian language is spoken by some four and a half
million people in all, and the number of foreigners who learn it
is infinitesimal. The sheer force of his genius has broken this
barrier of language, but the fragments of it, so to speak,
inevitably cumber his path. It is his fate to come before, not
only the general reader, but the scholar and critic, in a more or
less halting form. George Brandes is the only critic of European
reputation who reads him in his own language; and even Brandes'
criticism has but recently been translated into English.[1]

Again, the mere fact that he writes nothing but dramas is a
serious bar to anything like ready comprehension of his meaning on
the part of the English-speaking peoples. For reasons which it
would take too long to analyze, we have lost, and are but slowly
regaining, the habit of reading prose plays. To many people it
is a positive labor to read dialogue, while very few possess the
alertness of imagination necessary to conjure up the
stage-picture on which the dramatist's effect depends. Thus Ibsen
is not only presented to the public in imperfect form, but even
such form as the translator has succeeded in giving his work is
imperfectly discerned by the great majority of readers.

In another way, too, the fact of his being a dramatist
operates to his disadvantage. It brings his works, whether on the
stage or in book form, primarily within the jurisdiction of the
theatrical critics. It is the theatrical, not the literary,
critic who has the first word about him, and gives opinion its
initial trend. In France this is no special disadvantage, for
there theatrical criticism stands fairly on a level with literary
criticism. But can we say the same of England and America?
Certainly not of England. Ibsen was first brought to the
knowledge of the British public through a chorus of unexampled
ineptitudes of anonymous newspaper criticism; and although not

even the writers of these articles would now repeat or defend their colossal absurdities, the bias once given to the popular mind has not by any means exhausted itself. In a word, Ibsen had to run the gauntlet of Anglo-Saxon stupidity before he could gain the ear of Anglo-Saxon intelligence. Every nameless scribbler of theatrical paragraphs had had his little say about him before the voices of such men as Mr. W. D. Howells, Mr. Henry James, Professor Brander Matthews, Professor Gilbert Murray, or Mr. W. L. Courtney could make themselves heard.

Nor must I omit to mention among sources of misunderstanding the facile hero-worship of those who saw in A Doll's House a sort of Woman's-Rights manifesto, and hailed Ibsen as the preacher of a social, one might almost say a social-democratic, gospel. I am the last to deny that Ibsen has in some measure suffered from ignorant enthusiasm, as well as from ignorant obloquy.

Having thus indicated how impossible it was at the outset, --how difficult it must still be,--for the English-speaking world to see anything like the true Ibsen, I proceed to examine some aspects of the distorted simulacrum who has for ten years represented him in the popular view, and is only now beginning to give place to a juster image. The popular errors which I propose to scrutinize are these:

(1) That Ibsen is lacking in style, in literary form; (2) That he is an inefficient theatrical craftsman; (3) That he is a pessimist; (4) That he has no humor; (5) That he is "provincial" or "suburban."

I have already dealt incidentally with the first error. It is mainly due to the imperfections, some corrigible, others inevitable, of the translations in which alone Ibsen is known to the vast majority of readers. No one who can read Norwegian doubts for a moment that the author of Brand and Peer Gynt (to say nothing of Love's Comedy and the small but priceless volume of lyrics), is a consummate master of language, and one of the great poets of the century. In point of mere style, diction, poetic force, and color, one must go far to find parallels to the fourth act of Brand or Aase's death-scene in Peer Gynt, to name only two out of twenty equally magnificent passages. As for the prose plays, the illusion of lack of style arises not merely from deficiencies of translation, but in some degree from a narrow ideal of dramatic style in the mind of the critic. From the time of the Restoration even to our own day, wit, epigram, a highly artificial surface-polish, has been traditionally regarded as necessary to any dramatic prose that aspired to the dignity of literature. Etherege set the fashion, Congreve perfected it. Sheridan popularized it, and recent years the "epigrammatic" imbecilities of the cup-and-saucer school[2] have caricatured it. Without for a moment depreciating Congreve and Sheridan, one cannot but point out that the exclusive predominance of their "sparkling" ideal of dialogue has had a baneful effect upon

English drama, so that even now the first idea of the amateur who sits down to write a play is to make his characters talk as unnaturally as possible. Critics no less than playwrights have unthinkingly given their undivided homage to this conception of style in prose drama; and, finding Ibsen's characters talk naturally, instead of in antitheses, word-plays, and conceits, they concluded that he had no style at all, and expressed himself with mere haphazard commonness. But the universally relevant ideal of style is simply "the right word in the right place"; and Ibsen puts the right word in the right place just as unerringly as Congreve, only that, aiming at a different order of effect, he necessarily judges "rightness" by a different criterion. His style is terse, tense, full of color and character. Where there is room for eloquence, it is eloquent; where there is room for beauty, it is beautiful. And as an inventor of biting phrases and haunting cadences he is without a rival in modern drama.

The criticism which saw in Ibsen an inefficient craftsman, --a "bungler" was the consecrated term in the early nineties,--is already so obsolete that I need scarcely waste time in discussing it. Every critic who knows the meaning of the word technique now sees in Ibsen a master technician. This is admitted even by people who dislike the uses to which he puts his mastery, and prefer a simpler, less retrospective and introspective method. If I were asked to name the most consummate instance of technical genius in modern drama, I think I should point to Rosmersholm. But here, and in others of his later plays, Ibsen has gone so far beyond the currently accepted French technique that it is not surprising that newspaper critics, fed upon a few misunderstood maxims of Dumas and Sarcey,[3] should fail to appreciate his craftsmanship. The odd thing is that the critics who called him a "bungler" founded that opinion, not upon his late plays, but mainly upon Pillars of Society and A Doll's House: plays which are absolutely French in their methods and (except in the final scene of A Doll's House) masterly examples of the very technique which the critics professed to appreciate and expound. If they had criticized these two plays as somewhat conventionally and artificially "well-made," they would have had a strong case. As a matter of fact, they saw a man cutting a number of exceptionally intricate figures upon the ice, and thought it a good opportunity to aver that he did not know the rudiments of skating.

Let me not be understood to imply that Ibsen's technique is invariably flawless. In his latest plays, from Little Eyolf onwards, he shows a certain lack of staying-power, seeming to lay great bases for a comparatively inadequate superstructure. Even in some of his earlier works, such as The Lady from the Sea, his grip slackens a little towards the end. But occasional flaws of execution leave unaffected the fact that, far from being ignorant or inexpert in the technique of theatrical art, he has practically re-created it and enormously enhanced its efficiency.

No critical dogma has more universal currency than that which declares Ibsen to be a pessimist; yet nothing can be more clearly demonstrated than that, in the philosophic sense of the term, he is not a pessimist at all. Pessimism is the doctrine which holds life to be fundamentally and irremediably evil, pleasure a fleeting dream, pain an enduring reality, and all efforts at the amelioration of human conditions a mere fostering of that illusion which nature has implanted in us to further her own inscrutably sinister ends. Leopardi,[4] one of the greatest and most consistent of pessimists, has summed up the creed in the following sentence: "Men are miserable by necessity, and resolute in believing themselves to be miserable by accident." But no one is more resolute than Ibsen in the latter belief. He does not say with Leopardi, "Life is bad at the best"; he says "Life is bad because so many men happen to be knaves and fools; let us correct human knavery and folly, and life will be eminently worth living." Perhaps this is an overstatement of his position. It would be difficult to bind him down to a positive assertion of the ultimate value of life. But at least he is sufficiently hopeful to have no doubt of its being worth while to correct such evils as are plainly corrigible. Dr. Brandes has long ago defined very exactly Ibsen's attitude toward life, in calling him an "indignation-pessimist." Indignant he is at the prevailing paltriness of the human character. He is always and essentially a satirist. But pessimism, in the true sense of the word, leaves no room for satire and indignation. If life is evil to the core, why tinker at the incidental evils on the surface? Every seeming improvement in human conditions merely creates an opening for new life,—new sentience, new misery,—to rush in. This is the logical position of philosophic pessimism; it is almost entirely foreign to Ibsen.

"But," it may be said "'indignation-pessimism' is only another word for misanthropy. Ibsen may not be a philosophic pessimist, but you cannot deny that he is a misanthrope." I do deny it, most strenuously. While he has satirized human baseness and proved egoism to its most elusive recesses, he has also celebrated human goodness and nobility with all the force of his genius. I should think it unfair to go back to his romantic plays in order to prove this, were it not that one figure dating from his romantic period—Peer Gynt—is often alleged as the final evidence of his misanthropy. Let us look, then, through the whole roll of his works. His early plays abound in figures of ideal nobility: Eline Gyldenlöve in Lady Inger, Ornulf, Gunner, Sigurd, Dagny, in The Vikings, Margrete and Sigrid in The Pretenders, Svanhild in Love's Comedy. Even the erring and tragic figures, Lady Inger, Hjördis, King Skule, (and to this class we may also assign Julian the Apostate) are drawn with profound sympathy. There is not a trace of misanthropy about them. If there is a figure of ideal beauty in all literature it is surely Agnes in

Brand--the perfect embodiment of wifely and motherly love,
courage, fortitude, and self-devotion. Brand himself, too, though
an erring, not an ideal, figure, errs on the side of nobleness.
Was Molière a misanthrope because he drew Alceste? Surely not;
yet Molière opposed to Alceste, not an Agnes, but a Célimène.
In Peer Gynt, again, Ibsen incarnated all the baser attributes of
the Norwegian character as he saw it in a moment of bitter
indignation. Yet even Peer Gynt he drew with a certain sympathy.
He did not put the venom into his portraiture that Molière infused
into his presentment of Tartuffe. Rather he treated him with
something of the kindliness which Shakespeare bestowed upon
Falstaff. And as a set-off against Peer Gynt, have we not the
exquisite figure of Solveig? For that matter, it seems to me that
Peer's mother, Aase, the ignorant, sharp-tongued, warm-hearted,
devoted old woman, drawn with such irresistible humor and pathos,
should be a sufficient answer to those who read misanthropy into
Peer Gynt.

I pass over, among the modern plays, the somewhat
conventional League of Youth and Pillars of Society. They are
transition products. The poet was feeling his way towards a new
form, and was not expressing himself quite adequately. It would
be unfair to take such sentimentally flawless heroines as Lona
Hessel and Martha Bernick as representing Ibsen's definite view
even of feminine human nature, or to dwell upon such optimistic
"tags" as "The spirits of Freedom and Truth,--these are the
Pillars of Society." It is worth noting, however, that, here as
elsewhere in Ibsen's work, satire falls chiefly upon the male sex,
while women are portrayed with a gentler and often with an
idealizing touch. I am not here concerned with the justice or
injustice of this partiality, which is probably no more than a
survival from the romanticism of the poet's youth. What I wish
to point out is that the natural tendency of the pessimist is to
cog the dice on the other side, and to regard women as an
essentially inferior race, the symbols and instruments of that
primal curse "the will to live." Ibsen has been regarded, not
without a certain reason, one of the pioneers of the "feminist"
movement. But optimism and pessimism are not more
mutually-exclusive than "feminism" and pessimism.

There remain to be considered the prose dramas from A Doll's
House onwards, --what proofs of misanthropy do we find in them?
Is Nora Helmer, is Mrs. Alving, the creation of a misanthrope?
Until her world of illusions comes tumbling about her ears, Nora
is the "womanly woman" of the philistine ideal; absolutely
devoted to her husband and children, bright, unselfish,
courageous, "domesticated" in the highest degree. You may or may
not like her, but you cannot doubt that Ibsen treats her with
abundant sympathy. Mrs. Alving, again, is a model of fortitude
and self-devotion,--a heroine in the fullest sense. If there is
one character in all his plays that admittedly typifies Ibsen

himself, it is Dr. Stockman in <u>An Enemy of the People</u>,--a character of irrepressible, almost Dickensish amiability, a model of rectitude, public spirit, and all the domestic virtues, a lover of his kind, if ever there was one. Yet the man who created him, and in some respects made him his mouthpiece, is a hater of his kind! The next play, <u>A Wild Duck</u>, is gloomy, beyond a doubt; but is it not irradiated by the exquisitely beautiful and lovable figure of little Hedvig? In <u>Rosmersholm</u>, again, the atmosphere is tragic; but Rosmer himself, though weak, is a character of great nobility and charm. The personages of <u>The Lady from the Sea</u> are almost all amiable, and the play, as a whole, may almost be called optimistic in tone. In the later plays, again, we have such characters as Aunt Julia in <u>Hedda Gabler</u>, Asta and Borgheim in <u>Little Eyolf</u>, Ella Rentheim in <u>John Gabriel Borkman</u>,--all drawn with perfect sympathy, all showing a rooted faith in the nobler possibilities of human nature. Yet even a favorably disposed critic like Mr. A. W. Pinero can attribute to Ibsen that pessimism which "despairs not only of human happiness, but of human virtue"! This from the creator of <u>The Gay Lord Quex</u>[5] to the creator of Agnes, of Mrs. Alving, of Stockmann, of Hedvig, of Rosmer! Truly 'tis a mad world, my masters.

Of all the illusions which beset the popular mind with regard to Ibsen, none is more persistent than that which makes him out a gross and unseemly writer. I have made elsewhere a collection of some of the terms of abuse which were launched at him by English critics at the time when he first became known in England. We will, if you please, "take them as read." They are neither agreeable nor edifying; for, if Ibsen is not gross himself, he has undeniably been the occasion of much grossness in his critics. Let one very mild specimen suffice. It appears from the New York <u>Critic</u> that when Mrs. Erving Winslow, in 1890, proposed to give a reading of <u>An Enemy of the People</u> in the drawing-room of a leader of Washington society, the lady in question rejected the idea, on the ground that she could lend no countenance to "that foulmouthed Ibsen, who recognizes no law, human or divine." Now, how has the rumor got abroad that Ibsen is "foul-mouthed"? Mainly, I think, through the accident that the plays which first introduced him to the English speaking public were <u>A Doll's House</u> and <u>Ghosts</u>. It happens that in the first of these he incidentally touched upon the very terrible subject of the heritage of physical evil entailed upon children by the vices of their fathers; while in the second he made it the basis of his action. The subject is one of wide relevance, of immense importance; and it cannot for a moment be pretended that Ibsen's allusions to it are in themselves gross or indelicate. It was the bare fact of his alluding to such a topic at all that startled the prudery of critics who will applaud without stint the most cynical immorality, the most unblushing glorifications of debauchery, if only they are French in origin and frivolous in tone. Moreover, there was a single passage in A Doll's House--the famous silk stocking passage--the psychological significance of which was not at once apparent, and which, therefore, lent itself to misunderstanding. The very fact that there was not a trace of sensual appeal in Ibsen's treatment of these "unpleasant" topics--that he neither glorified passion nor sentimentalized frailty--made the critics resent still more fiercely the shock to their accepted standards of propriety. Knowing Ibsen solely in these two works for as yet his other plays were untranslated) they were unable to see him in anything like his true proportions, or to realize how absolutely episodic in the history of his genius was his touching upon the theme of congenital disease. Yielding to that hysterical impulse of exaggeration which always overcomes Mr. and Mrs. Grundy[6] on such occasions, they imagined him persistently and ghoulishly gloating over these physical horrors. The word went forth that he was a "foul-mouthed" and foul-minded person; and henceforward, in each new play that came within their ken, people set themselves with ludicrous assiduity to discover recondite and unnameable improprieties in passages of absolute innocence. Once set the critical imagination questing on the track of filth, and it will scent asafetida in a bank of violets.

Even this superstition is gradually dying out, and people are beginning to realize that while Ibsen deals firmly, frankly, and boldly with the moral questions arising out of sex-relationships, no writer is more thoroughly exempt than he from any suspicion of complacently dallying with inflammatory topics, stimulating the sensual imagination, or in any way pandering to vulgar pruriency. It is true that he writes for men and women, not for babes and sucklings. It is true that he sometimes (in Little Eyolf, for example) casts an uncomfortably fierce light upon the conventional moralities of marriage. But that he has any morbid predilection for the ignoble, the malodorous, or the indecent, is of all critical slanders the most flagrantly untrue.

We come now to the allegation that Ibsen has "no sense of humor." This illusion may be called the last infirmity of noble minds. Many critics who recognize Ibsen's greatness in almost every other respect, are still to be found laying it down as an axiom that humor has been denied him. As a matter of fact, it was precisely Ibsen's humor that first attracted me to the study of his works. In 1872, when my acquaintance with him began, only one of his social plays, The League of Youth, was in existence. This is a brilliant comedy, verging now and then upon farce. The man who can read or see it and declare that the author has no sense of humor, would be capable of making the same deduction from The School for Scandal, or She Stoops to Conquer. Then, again, I was fascinated by the glittering wit of Love's Comedy (it loses fatally in translation) and by the delightfully amusing character of the Sheriff in Brand. As for Peer Gynt, what is it if not a

carnival of humor, of whimsical mirth, of fantastic drollery? It
is a great deal more than that, of course, but it is that or
nothing. If the creator of Aase has no humor, we may certainly
say the same of the creator of Mrs. Hardcastle or of Mrs.
Micawber.[7] If there is no humor in the Troll-King's Court, in
Peer Gynt's Adventures in Africa, and in his colloquies with the
Strange Passenger and with the Button Moulder, why then there is
no humor in Rabelais, in Swift, or in Heine. These things, as I
say, were what first attracted me to Ibsen, before his modern
plays were written. Conceive, then, the amazement with which I
heard it proclaimed by English critics that my favorite
poet-humorist was a smileless fanatic, without a gleam of humor
in his composition!

Looking back, however, at this distance of time, I can see
how the opinion arose. Here, again, we must remember that it was
not Peer Gynt or The League of Youth that first brought Ibsen
prominently into notice, but A Doll's House and Ghosts. These
plays (with Pillars of Society) were not only the first plays the
critics knew, but, for some time, the only ones they could
possibly know, except by vague report. Now these plays are
certainly not devoid of humor,--witness the characters of Lona
Hessel and Hilmar Tönnesen, of Engstrand, nay, of Helmer himself,
--but it is a somewhat grim, unlaughable humor, which critics,
impressed by the general atmosphere of intense seriousness, might
not inexcusably overlook. Then A Doll's House was seized upon by
the fanatics of female emancipation as a manifesto in their favor,
and criticism, necessarily ill-formed, was only too ready to
accept the "Ibsenite" view of Ibsen as himself a fanatic. The
least dogmatic of thinkers,--the poet who has said of himself
"My calling is to question, not to answer"--was written down
a fervid dogmatist, a solemn stump-orator. And such a
pre-conception is much more easily implanted than eradicated. It
is true that the very next play which followed on Ghosts was a
piece of genial, hearty, liberal humor, containing in Thomas
Stockmann the most entirely lovable character that Ibsen ever
drew. It is true that the next, again, though gloomy enough in
all conscience, introduced us to Hjalmar Ekdal, a figure of humor
all compact, a monumental creation, worthy to rank with Daudet's
Numa Roumestan or Mr. Meredith's Sir Willoughby Patterne.[8] In the
theatre and out of it people laughed till they were tired over
An Enemy of the People and The Wild Duck. But what of that? The
critics who had staked their reputation on Ibsen's total lack of
humor simply took refuge in the assertion that they were laughing
at him, not with him, and that he did not himself see or intend
the ludicrous effects he produced. Some simple-minded persons
actually believed this, and had a sense of triumphing over Ibsen
when they shook with laughter at Hjalmar Ekdal. But it is here
more than anywhere else that the bad faith of "anti-Ibsenite"
criticism manifested itself. It became with some writers a delib-

erate trick, an artifice of war, to pretend that an absorbed and smileless solemnity was the only proper attitude of an Ibsen audience, and that every smile that ran around the theatre was a smile at the poet's expense. This assumption, due at first to sheer ignorance, was persisted in by some writers when in their hearts they know a great deal better.

The critics who, after seeing An Enemy of the People, can still accuse Ibsen of possessing no humor, recall to me an anecdote of the great Norwegian comedian, Johannes Brun, who created several of Ibsen's most amusing characters. As a very young man, he joined the newly established Norwegian Theatre in Bergen, much against the wishes of his relatives. One old uncle in particular was not to be reconciled to his nephew's calling, and resolutely declined to go near the theatre. At last, rumors of the young man's success somewhat softened him, and one evening he accepted a ticket for the play. Johannes acted one of his most brilliant parts to the delight of the audience, and then took his uncle home with him to supper. For a long time the old man said not a word about the performance, obviously avoiding the subject. Finally, Johannes took the bull by the horns, and asked him point blank how he had liked the play. "Well Johannes" said the old gentleman seriously "you mustn't be hurt by what I am going to say. I am an old man, and I see things that you don't see. You didn't know it, but all those people were laughing at you! I could scarcely keep from laughing myself. You have no talent for acting, my dear lad." It is by an exactly similar process of reasoning that critics who have listened to the laughter evoked by Thomas Stockmann and Hjalmar Ekdal, or by the colloquy between John Gabriel Borkman and Foldal, conclude that the man who created these characters has no humor.

Even when driven to admit that Ibsen has plenty of positive or creative humor, some critics take refuge in the assertion that he lacks the negative humor which should prevent him from introducing grotesque or trivial touches out of season, and calling forth untimely laughter. This is really a part, a sub-section, of that accusation of provincialism, which is the last fallacy I propose to examine. Even an intelligent and sympathetic critic like Mr. W. L. Courtney[9] thinks it worth while to complain that the tragic drama that you find in Ibsen is "singularly mean, commonplace, parochial,--as if Apollo, who once entered the house of Admetus, was now told to take up his habitation in a back parlor in South Hampstead." "There may be tragedies in South Hampstead," Mr. Courtney continues, "although experience does not consistently testify to the fact; but at all events from the historic and traditional standpoint, tragedy is more likely to concern itself with Glamys Castle, Melrose Abbey, Carisbrooke or even with Carlton House Terrace."

It is not to be denied that Norway is a comparatively poor country, and that Ibsen's modern plays (he has given us his Glamys and Carisbrooke tragedies in Lady Inger, The Vikings, and

The Pretenders) deal with distinctly middle-class or bourgeois society. There is no hereditary aristocracy in Norway; there is not even very much of a plutocracy. Ibsen's characters are government officials, bankers, merchants, doctors, engineers, journalists. He actually descends to a photographer and a rat-chaser. Now to people who habitually adorn the gilded saloons of the nobility, whose acquaintances are mostly Dukes and Marquises, and who, as Mr. W. S. Gilbert puts it, never nod to any one under the rank of a stockbroker, it is naturally painful to be invited to consort, even in imagination, with such a plebeian crew. Our English playwrights treat us much better. Moving, as we all know, in the most exclusive circles, they seek their tragic motives either in the mansions of Mayfair, or in the baronial halls of the aristocracy, their friends. I have just occupied an hour in going through the chief plays of our leading dramatists, and making a small peerage and baronetage from among their characters. I find that they introduce us to two Princesses, four Dukes, three Duchesses, five Marquises, one Marchioness, eleven Earls, seven Countesses, five Viscounts, and sundries, (such as Baronets, Ladies of undefined rank, and Honorables) to the number of about ninety-five. There is nothing "provincial," nothing "suburban" about this, is there? What could be more metropolitan or "smarter" than such a catalogue? How odd it is, then, that the "parochial" Ibsen should be world-famous, while Mr. Pinero and Mr. Henry Arthur Jones are barely struggling into notice outside the English-speaking countries!

This illusion of centrality is one of the most insidious, and certainly not the least ludicrous, to which human nature is subject. We do not often find it so crudely stated as in Mr. Courtney's antithesis between "South Hampstead" and "Carlton House Terrace";[10] but no one is ever wholly exempt from it. We cannot disabuse our minds of the idea that our own particular parish is the hub of the universe, and that habits which are not our own, manners which differ from ours, even names with which we are not familiar, are essentially inferior, contemptible, ludicrous. A quaint instance of this may be found in Mr. F. Anstey's very clever parodies entitled, Mr. Punch's Pocket Ibsen.[11] The humor of these burlesques is irresistible, the satire, in the main, quite legitimate. The odd thing is that a man of education, like Mr. Anstey, should apparently conceive that there is something inherently absurd in the Norwegian language, as it appears in the titles of Ibsen's plays. He thinks it funny to represent these titles by gibberish phrases, as though it were a ridiculous foible on Ibsen's part to designate his plays by combinations of letters which happen to mean nothing to Mr. Anstey. This is precisely the attitude of the traditional British sailor to the confounded lingo of the parley-voos, which, being incomprehensible to him, is necessarily despicable. We laugh at the sailor; I am at a loss to know why we should laugh with Mr. Anstey.

The whole idea of Ibsen's "provincialism" and lack of preventive humor, so to speak, proceeds from the same illusion, in somewhat subtler forms. There are a good many things in his plays,--traits of Norwegian manners and so forth,--which quite naturally raise a smile in England or America, just as French manners in America, and American manners in England. This sense of the ludicrous is unavoidable, and is harmless so long as it is unaccompanied by a sense of superiority,--so long as we remember, in smiling, that our neighbors have an equal right to smile at us. But this is just what English critics do not remember. They postulate some sort of supernal validity for the conventions to which they happen to be accustomed, and hold it inherently ridiculous on Ibsen's part to portray a society in which these conventions do not obtain. With French conventions they are more or less familiar; some of them they think ridiculous, others they regard as highly distinguished and "chic"; but at any rate they do not accuse French authors of being provincial and lacking humor because they depict French manners. Germany, a little more remote than France, is a good deal more provincial. If translations of German plays were as widely read and closely canvassed as the translations of Ibsen, I fear they would be found decidely suburban. But Germany, after all, is a great country, which may reasonably claim to have manners of its own. Norway, on the other hand, is a very small nation and still more remote than Germany from Carlton House Terrace, which is, by hypothesis, the centre of civilization. It follows, then, that the manners and customs of the Norwegians must be inherently ridiculous; and the artist who can dream of gravely depicting them is obviously devoid of a sense of humor.

But there lurks behind the complaint of Ibsen's "parochialism" a good deal more than the mere illusion of centrality. It springs in many cases (though, not, I am sure, in that of Mr. Courtney) from sheer artless snobbery. In dealing with modern life, the Anglo-American stage has of recent years devoted itself almost exclusively to pictures of rank and wealth. We are accustomed in the theatre to the society of marquises and millionaires; or, if we admit middle-class life at all, it is always of that order which apes, in its external appointments, the habits of the class above it. Now the Norwegian society depicted by Ibsen is frankly bourgeois. For instance, I do not remember a single liveried servant in all his plays. Hedda Gabler dreams of setting up a flunkey; but her husband exclaims at the bare idea of such extravagance. It does not appear that any of his personages are "carriage people." No doubt the Chamberlain in The League of Youth, Werle in The Wild Duck, Rita of "the gold and the green forests" in Little Eyolf, and one or two others would keep carriages; but I cannot remember that the fact is ever mentioned. It is true that Mrs. Wilton, in John Gabriel Borkman, possesses a covered sleigh, with silver bells; but she is a foreigner and an altogether exceptional person. For the most part, Ibsen's characters do their locomotion on foot, and when ladies go home from evening parties it is the custom for gallant cavaliers to escort them. Such suburban practices are very shocking to many worthy people. Again, Ibsen's habitual employment of champagne as a sort of symbol of rollicking festivity, if not of unbridled luxury, is vastly ridiculous to your clubman, your metropolitan man-about-town, who prides himself on an exact knowledge of the etiquette of the wine-list. In these and a hundred other trifling matters Ibsen betrays the fact that he is dealing with a community in which two thousand five hundred dollars a year means wealth and five thousand dollars a year opulence. That is the melancholy truth; there is no disguising it; and if people of narrow means were necessarily people of narrow emotions, criticism would have every right to deplore this unfortunate limitation of his art. But it has yet to be proved that the capacity of human beings for sin and suffering, for exultation and agony, varies in direct proportion to their yearly income; and until this is proved, the insistence on Ibsen's "provincialism" or "suburbanism" is, what I have ventured to call it, a piece of irrelevant snobbery. One may, of course, prefer the drama of dukes, drawing-rooms, smart frocks, and powdered menials; but such a preference is not criticism. There are thousands of people who prefer the drama of dancing girls to the drama of dukes,-- The Belle of New York to The Second Mrs. Tanqueray --but they do not, therefore, go about to call Mr. Pinero "parochial." [12]

I am far from denying that there are touches of mannerism in Ibsen which sometimes provoke an unintended smile. To people in whose eyes these surface oddities bulk so large that they cannot see the master-poet behind them, I can only apologize for having bored them with this discussion. The operation for the removal of their mental cataract is far beyond my surgery.

A master-poet--that term sums up the real Ibsen. He is a great creator of men and women, a great explorer of the human heart, a great teller of stories, a great inventor and manipulator of those "situations," those conjunctures and crises in which human nature throws off its conventional integuments and expresses itself at its highest potency. He is more of a seer than a thinker. He has flashes of intense insight into the foundations of things; but it is none of his business to build up an ordered, symmetrical, closely-mortised edifice of thought. Truth is to him many-sided; and he looks at it from this side to-day, from the opposite side to-morrow. The people who seek to construct a "gospel," a consistent body of doctrine, from his works, are spinning ropes of sand. He is "everything by turns and nothing long." [13] He is neither an individualist nor a socialist, neither an aristocrat nor a democrat, neither an optimist nor a pessimist. He is simply a dramatist, looking with piercing eyes

at the world of men and women, and translating into poetry this
episode and that from the inexhaustible pageant. Poetry,--poetry:
that is the first word and the last of any true appreciation of
Ibsen. It is largely because he has applied to purposes of poetry
a vehicle hitherto used only for prosaic ends that he has been so
strangely misunderstood. But the period of misunderstanding is
passing away, and the real Ibsen is emerging from the mists in
which prejudice and imperfect knowledge have enveloped him, to
take his predestined place among the great poets of the nineteenth
century.

IBSEN'S APPRENTICESHIP

(<u>Fortnightly</u> <u>Review</u>, Jan. 1904)

This essay, which might have been titled "Ibsen and the Well-Made Play," is a study of Ibsen's early days as a stage manager and beginning playwright. Archer charts the development of the Norwegian theatre and Ibsen's central role in it. He argues here for the influence of Eugene Scribe's drama on the early plays, but also for the importance of the last act of <u>A Doll's House</u> because this scene between Nora and Torvald is, for Archer, the flowering of Ibsen's true genius as a social dramatist.

French critics are very fond of trying to make out that Henrik Ibsen borrowed all his ideas from French writers of the first half of the nineteenth century, and especially from George Sand. A sharp little skirmish on this subject took place some time ago between Dr. George Brandes and M. Emile Faguet, the Frenchman attacking, and the Dane defending, Ibsen's originality. Dr. Brandes had certainly the right end of the stick. It is impossible to prove, of course, that some of George Sand's ideas, floating in the air, may not have found their way into Ibsen's mind. But he does not read French; he has certainly never studied George Sand, or consciously undergone her influence; and to say that he reproduces or echoes her is a manifest error. It is not he, but the world he depicts, that has been to some extent influenced by George Sand.

If the French are determined to claim some share in the making of Ibsen, they must shift their ground a little. He did not get his ideas from George Sand, but he got a good deal of his stagecraft from Eugene Scribe, and the playwrights of his school.[1] Ideas he could not possibly get from Scribe, for the best of all reasons; but he can be proved to have been familiar, at the outset of his career, with the works of that great inventor and manipulator of situations, from whom there can be little doubt that he acquired the rudiments of dramatic construction. He ultimately outgrew his teacher, even in technical skill, and his later plays, from Ghosts onward, show the influence of Scribe mainly in the careful avoidance of his methods. Nevertheless it was in the Scribe gymnasium, so to speak, that he trained himself for his subsequent feats as a technician.

Down to the year 1850, there was not only no Norwegian drama, but no Norwegian theatre. There was a playhouse in Christiania,[2] but the actors were all Danes; and the scant theatrical entertainments of the smaller towns were supplied by companies of Danish strollers. The Danes were in every sense of the word foreigners. It is true that the language spoken by the Norwegian townspeople was, in vocabulary, practically identical with Danish; but the Danish pronunciation differed from the Norwegian far more than (for instance) the most marked American pronunciation differs from English. The separation of Norway from Denmark in 1814 had been followed by a notable development of Norwegian nationalism in poetry, in painting, and in music; but it was commonly regarded as hopeless for Norway to think of possessing a drama of her own. People had come to regard Danish as the natural language of the stage, very much as French is regarded as the natural language of diplomacy.

Fortunately this was not the view of Ole Bull, the great Norwegian violinist. In 1849 he returned to his birthplace, Bergen, from a triumphal foreign tour, bringing back a forest of laurels and a pocketful of money. He found in Bergen a poor, bare little theatre, built in 1800, which had been used partly by Danish strollers but mainly by the amateur actors of the lively little town. Even amateur acting had, however, for years fallen into desuetude; so that when Bull conceived the idea of establishing a Norwegian theatre, he found absolutely no material ready to his hand. There existed no such person as a Norwegian actor or actress, no such thing as a Norwegian play of the slightest merit. Even Henrik Ibsen's Catiline (published in the following year) was as yet only a roll of manuscript in the desk of a druggist's apprentice at Grimstad.

Ole Bull, however, found a warm welcome for his idea among some of the leading citizens of Bergen. Was not Ludvig Holberg,[3] the immortal founder of the Danish theatre and drama, a "Bergenser" by birth? And did not Bergen pride itself upon its gaiety of temper and its quick artistic sympathies? There was a strong conservative party, indeed, which shrank from the notion of hearing "raw" Norwegian spoken on the stage; but in the main Bull met with encouragement, rather than ridicule, when he inserted the following "announcement" in the local papers:--

NORWEGIAN THEATRE IN BERGEN.
Ladies and Gentlemen who wish to make a profession
of Singing, Instrumental Music, Acting, or National

Dancing, are offered engagements. Original dramatic and musical compositions will be accepted and paid for according to circumstances. Applications should be sent in writing, as early as possible, to "The Norwegian Theatre in Bergen."

OLE BULL.

Bergen, 23 July, 1849.

Quaint stories are related, it need scarcely be said, of the applicants who presented themselves in answer to this advertisement; but among the very first, by an extraordinary stroke of luck, was a boy of seventeen, named Johannes Brun, who proved to possess a comic genius of the rarest order. I was unfortunate enough never to see Brun (who died some years ago), and cannot therefore speak of him from personal knowledge; but the unanimous testimony of the best judges declares him to have been the greatest actor Norway has as yet produced, incomparable in purely comic parts, and in characters of mingled humour and pathos. An excellent actress, Louise Gulbrandsen, who afterwards became Brun's wife, was also among the earliest applicants; and, altogether, Bull succeeded in getting together a company of eight men and five women, most of whom proved to have some real talent. A private experimental performance was given on November 30th, 1849, when the programme consisted of a comedy of Holberg's, Mozart's Jupiter Symphony, and a monologue in the local dialect, spoken by Johannes Brun. This was the nearest approach they could achieve to Norwegian drama! The actual opening of the theatre took place on January 2nd, 1850. Again a comedy of Holberg's was given, with the overture to Egmont, the Jupiter Symphony, and Bull's Visit to the Soeter, performed by the master himself.

Incredibly, pathetically small, according to our ideas, were the material resources of this gallant enterprise. The town of Bergen had only 25,000 inhabitants; performances were given only twice, or at the outside, three times, a week; and the highest price of admission was only two shillings. What can have been attempted in the way of scenery and costumes it is hard to imagine. Of a three-act play, produced in 1852, we read that "the mounting, which cost £22 10s., left nothing to be desired." Some idea of the financial conditions of the enterprise may be gathered from the fact that when, in 1851, Bull applied to the Norwegian Parliament for an annual subvention, the sum he demanded (in vain) was only £450--less than a single Saturday's receipts at a popular London theatre.

But what do material limitations matter to the man who is in league with destiny! Bull felt that the time was ripe for a Norwegian drama, and though he had no trained actors, a poor and scanty public, and very little money, he determined to have the theatre swept and garnished, and ready for the drama when it should arrive. At the very outset, as we have seen, he laid his hand on a genius in the person of Johannes Brun. In his second season a Bergen schoolgirl, Lucie Johannesen (afterwards Fru Wolf), joined his company, and rapidly developed into an actress of the first order. And in his third season, looking about for some one to replace the local and temporary state-managers whom he had previously employed, he pitched upon a black-bearded student at the University of Christiania, who happened to be none other than Henrik Ibsen. When Ibsen, five years later, returned to Christiania, another student, somewhat younger than he, was ready to take his place--Björnstjerne Björnson,[4] to wit. If Bull had had the power to create men for his purpose, instead of merely selecting them, he could scarcely have done better than this.

A few anecdotes will serve to illustrate the primitive conditions of the theatre in which Ibsen was to serve his apprenticeship. One or two idylls of peasant life--pieces with little or no action, but full of songs and dances--were the only semblance of national drama that Bull found ready to his hand; and, being himself a musician, he naturally hoped to cultivate this artform. He even aimed at the development of a national school of dancing, founded upon the violent "hallings" and "spring dances" of the upland peasantry. To this end, he engaged a number of peasant performers, with disastrous results. In the first place, the rake of the stage put the dancers out, so that they tumbled about like ninepins; in the second place, their wild caprioles, which were characteristic and fitting in the house-place at home, seemed merely barbarous in the framework of the theatre. The attempt to introduce the "real pig" into the realm of make-believe was no more successful in this case than in the fabulous instance cited, fifteen years afterwards, by Peer Gynt. On the other hand, a peasant violinist, the Miller Boy, whom Bull brought to Bergen from distant Haukelid, seems to have made some success. The story of this engagement, as related in Blanc's history[5] of the Bergen theatre, has a touch of the old saga-time in it. One of Bull's peasant dancers, Jacob by name, was deputed to summon the Miller Boy to Bergen.

Proud of his embassage, Jacob set off on snow-shoes over the mountains, and did not fail to announce his errand in every village he passed. When he arrived at Haukelid, Thorgeir was not at home; but his wife at once prepared his bundle, since there couldn't be the smallest question as to his accepting the call. As soon as Thorgeir returned, he lay down to sleep, in order to make an early start the next day, and before sunrise he and Jacob were on the road. They were awaited in all the villages and hailed with great satisfaction. But at one place a rich peasant had invited a party to hear Thorgeir play, confidently anticipating his assent. When Thorgeir declared that he could not delay his journey, since Ole Bull was awaiting him in Bergen, the peasant went the length of offering him ten dollars (£2 5s.), to alter his resolution. "No, I cannot," replied Thorgeir, "Ole is expecting me, and I am to play in Norway's Theatre." Then the peasant turned purple in the face, and it was evident that he was prepared to use force. Seeing this, Jacob took Thorgeir aside and said, "Pretend to consent, but say you are tired and must have sleep. They will show you to a room; then wait until you hear me whistling, take your fiddle, and jump out of the window." So said, so done; and, Jacob having meanwhile secured a pair of horses, they mounted and rode away. But the guests had now assembled, and the defection of the Miller Boy was soon discovered. Enraged at the insult, the men of the party rushed to the stable, and were soon on the track of the fugitives. They overtook them at the next village, in a very ugly frame of mind; and, as they came up, Jacob drew his knife. But now the Miller Boy, usually so taciturn, became eloquent. He said that any one who barred their way was a traitor to his country. He was summoned by Ole Bull to play in Norway's Theatre, and woe betide the man who hindered him. On his way back he would play for them three days and nights on end, if they demanded it; but now they must leave him to fulfil his mission in peace. This speech had the desired effect, the knives were sheathed, and the travellers went on unmolested.

This story is surely significant. It shows how instinctive and how widespread was the longing for, and faith in, the appearance of a national art, which was to have its seed-plot in "Norway's Theatre."

Meanwhile, the police authorities of Bergen were not minded to let any art, national or otherwise, spring up without their sanction and supervision. They claimed, as of right, three places at every performance. Bull objected, rather on principle, it would seem, than because of any difficulty in sparing the seats; and when the police pressed their claim, he assigned them the three worst seats in the house, attaching to the wall above them a placard measuring five feet by twenty inches, inscribed with the legend:--"Places for three policemen." This the authorities took as an insult, and prosecuted Bull for, I suppose, an offense equivalent to lèse-majesté. The case was gravely tried, and is gravely reported. Bull's advocate argued that it could scarcely be construed as high treason if the words "Royal Box" were inscribed over the box allotted to the Royal Family. It is not very clear which side actually won the case, but the police carried their point, and were thereafter suffered to see the play unpilloried.

A story told by Professor Dietrichson,[6] who was a boy in
Bergen when the theatre was established, illustrates (perhaps with
a touch of burlesque) the severe economy which the management was
compelled to practise. A relation of Dietrichson's, a lady of a
certain age, in whom no one before (or afterwards) divined the
existence of any dramatic talent, was among the first to rally to
Bull's appeal for actors and actresses. For some unexplained
reason, she was engaged as "second old woman." But her
elocutionary powers were impaired by the fact that she had lost
one of her front teeth. It was no easy matter in those days, and
in Bergen, to have the loss made good; but the management came
nobly to the rescue, and bore the expense of the necessary
dentistry. After two seasons, the improvised actress retired; and
it was related that when she did so she had to leave her tooth
behind her, that work of art being the property of the theatre.
"Certain it is," says Dietrichson, "that she whistled in her
speech as much after as before her theatrical experiences."

Another anecdote of Dietrichson's relates to one of those
misadventures which may occur in the best regulated theatre, but
shows, too, how the untrained actor is apt to lose his head--in
this case, in a double sense. Dietrichson says:--

> A certain Herr Lunde, who played the Emperor in
> Deinhardstein's Hans Sachs, had in one scene to cast
> aside a cloak which disguised him, and reveal to the
> astonished bystanders the jewels glittering on his
> breast, and especially the insignia of the Golden
> Fleece. Unfortunately, when the moment came, he found
> it impossible to unfasten the hooks of the cloak. After
> struggling with them for some time in vain, he chose a
> heroic method of saving the situation. Seizing the
> cloak by the lower hem, he lifted it like an upturned
> smock-frock over his head, which he thus totally con-
> cealed, at the same time duly revealing the Golden
> Fleece and other Imperial splendours on his bosom.
> Then out of the depths of the enveloping drapery, came
> a muffled voice inquiring, "Say, know ye now the Roman
> Empire's lord?"

The last of these Bergen anecdotes has Johannes Brun for its
hero. Something very similar has, I fancy, been related of other
comedians; but even if it be not literally true in the present
case, it doubtless illustrates, aptly enough, the attitude of some
of the worthy burghers of Bergen towards the theatre. One of
these old gentlemen, an uncle of Brun's, was intensely disgusted
at his nephew's choice of a profession, and resolutely declined to
go near the theatre.

> At last rumours of the young man's success somewhat
> softened him, and one evening he accepted a ticket for

the play. Johanes acted one of his most brilliant
parts, to the delight of the audience, and then took his
uncle home with him to supper. For a long time the old
man said not a word about the performance, obviously
avoiding the subject. Finally Johannes took the bull by
the horns, and asked him how he had liked the play.
"Well, Johannes," said the old gentleman seriously, "you
mustn't be hurt by what I am going to say. I am an old
man, and I see things that you don't see. You didn't
know it, but all those people were laughing at you! I
could scarcely keep from laughing myself. You have no
talent for acting, my dear lad!"

The legend may perhaps be adapted to the circumstances; but
the circumstances--the simplicity and inexperience of a great part
of the public--were certainly such as to render it plausible.

Ibsen's connection with the Bergen Theatre lasted from
November 6th, 1851, until the summer of 1857--that is to say, from
his twenty-fourth to his thirtieth year. He was engaged, in the
first instance, "to assist the theatre as dramatic author"; but in
the following year he received a "travelling stipend" of £45 from
the management, to enable him to study the art of theatrical
production in Denmark and Germany, with the stipulation that on
his return he should undertake the duties of "scene-instruktör"
(nearly, though not exactly, equivalent to our "stage-manager")
at a yearly salary of £67. It is not easy to discover who was the
actual manager during these years. Ole Bull, always flighty and
erratic, did not even pretend to direct the fortunes of the
theatre he had founded. Indeed, he was absent from Bergen the
greater part of the time. At the beginning of the second season,
while still exercising a general right of supervision, he deputed
his authority to a committee of ten citizens of Bergen, mostly
merchants and professional men. But no theatre was ever actually
managed by a committee of ten, and it does not appear in whose
hands the effective authority rested. It is probable that the
choice of plays lay mainly with Ibsen; but, on the other hand,
there seems to have been very little choice in the matter. For
the most part, the Bergen Theatre simply reproduced the repertory
of the Copenhagen Royal Theatre and People's Theatre; and the
Danish stage, like that of Europe in general, was in those days
flooded with the works of Scribe and his school.

None of Ibsen's biographers has as yet undertaken an exact
analysis of the plays with which he must have been familiar (since
they were rehearsed under his supervision), during his stay in
Bergen. Yet one could scarcely make a more important
contribution towards the history of his artistic development. For
my own part, I cannot pretend to supply this want with any
completeness. The task would demand more space and time than I
can devote to it. But with the aid of Blanc's excellent book,

above cited, I can give a brief catalogue of the principal plays that passed through his hands.

It appears that 145 plays in all were produced during Ibsen's tenure of office. Of these more than half (75) were French, 21 being by Scribe himself, while at least half of the remainder were by adepts of his school--Bayard, Dumanoir, Mélesville, &c. During the two months of 1851 that followed Ibsen's accession to office, four French plays were produced, La Somnambule, by Scribe, two by Mélesville, and one by Ancelot. In the following year (1852) eighteen French plays were produced, among them D'Ennery's Don César de Bazan, Scribe's Bataille de Dames, L'Ambitieux, and La Tutrice, with several minor pieces by the same author, two plays by Bayard, La Jeunesse de Henri V., by Alexandre Duval (a writer of the very beginning of the century), and Ponsard's Charlotte Corday. During this year Ibsen must have been writing his play, St. John's Night, which was produced on January 2nd, 1853, the third anniversary of the foundation of the theatre. This is the only play of Ibsen's that has never been published; but from the full account of it given by Blanc, it is evident that there was very little French influence traceable in it. It seems to have been a crude and confused production, full of lyrical sentiment of the Danish school. Yet even here the budding satirist--the creator of Peer Gynt--manifests himself. We are told that one of the characters was a gloomily romantic and patriotic poet of the long-haired type, who for a long time cherished an imaginative devotion to the "Huldra," a mountain sprite or pixie of the national mythology; but learning one day that she had a tail, "he was forced to give her up."

In the year 1853, fourteen French plays were added to the repertory of the Bergen theatre, the most important being Sandeau's Mademoiselle de la Seiglière, Dumas's Cathérine Howard, Mélesville's Chevalier de St. Georges, Le Mariage au Tambour, by Leuven and Brunswick, and Si Dieu le veut by Bayard and Biéville. Foundation Day (January 2nd), 1854, was celebrated by the production of Ibsen's one-act play, The Warrior's Barrow, which however, had been written four years earlier, and produced in Christiania in 1850. The French productions of 1854, again fourteen in number, included Scribe's two great dramas of intrigue, Adrienne Lecouvreur, and Les Contes de la Reine de Navarre, along with the same author's comedy, Les Indépendants; Dumas's La Fille du Régent; Bayard's Un Fils de Famille (known in England as The Queen's Shilling); and Arago and Vermond's Mémoires du Diable. Now in these years (1853 and 1854, Ibsen must have been busied upon his first great historic drama, Lady Inger of Oestraatt, which was produced January 2nd, 1855. Although the romantic environment of the play and the tragic intensity of Lady Inger's character tend to disguise the relationship, there can be no doubt that this play is, in essence, simply a French drama of intrigue, constructed after the method of Scribe, as exemplified

in Adrienne Lecouvreur, Les Contes de la Reine de Navarre, and a
dozen other French plays, with the staging of which the poet was
then occupied. It might seem that the figure of Elina, brooding
over the thought of her dead sister coffined in the vault below
the banqueting hall, belonged rather to German romanticism; but
there are plenty of traces of German romanticism even in the
French plays with which the good people of Bergen were regaled.
For the suggestion of grave-vaults and coffined heroines, for
example, Ibsen need have gone no further then Dumas's Cathérine
Howard, which he produced in March, 1853. I do not, however,
pretend that his romantic colouring came to him through the
French. It came to him, doubtless, from Germany, by way of
Denmark. The point I would emphasise is that the conduct of the
intrigue in Lady Inger shows the most unmistakable marks of his
study of Scribe and the great French plot-manipulators. Its
dexterity and its artificiality alike are neither German nor
Danish, but French. Ibsen had learnt the great secret of
Scribe--the secret of dramatic movement. The play is full of
those ingenious complications, mistakes of identity, and rapid
turns of fortune, by which Scribe enchained the interest of his
audiences. Its central theme--a mother plunging into intrigue
and crime for the advancement of her son, only to find that her
son himself has been her victim--is as old as Greek tragedy. The
secondary story, too, that of Elina's wild infatuation for Nils
Lykke--who proves to have been the betrayer and practically the
murderer of her sister--could probably be paralleled in the ballad
literature of Scotland, Germany, or Denmark, and might, indeed,
have been told, in verse or prose, by Sir Walter Scott. But these
very un-Parisian elements are handled in a fundamentally Parisian
fashion, and Ibsen is clearly fascinated, for the time, at any
rate, by the ideal of what was afterwards to be known as the
"well-made play."

The year 1855 witnessed the production of twelve French
plays, two of them (La Part au Diable and Mon Etoile), by Scribe,
and almost all by imitators or collaborators of his. During this
year Ibsen was writing The Feast at Solhaug, produced with great
success on January 2nd, 1856. In this piece he is accused of
having imitated Svend Dyring's House, a very popular Danish play
by Henrik Herz. He has himself warmly rebutted the suggestion,
and the truth is, no doubt, that he and Herz both based their
style upon the same model--that of the Danish Kjoempeviser, or
romantic ballads. But, despite the strong lyrical element in the
dialogue, The Feast at Solhaug still has that crispness of
dramatic action which marks the French plays of the period. It
may indeed be called Scribe's Bataille de Dames writ tragic.
Here, as in the Bataille de Dames (one of the earliest plays
produced under Ibsen's supervision), we have the rivalry of an
older and a younger woman for the love of a man who is proscribed,
on an unjust accusation, and pursued by the emissaries of the

royal power. One might even, though this would be forcing the point, find an analogy in the fact that the elder women (in both plays a strong and determined character) has in Scribe's comedy a cowardly suitor, while in Ibsen's tragedy, or melodrama, she has a cowardly husband. In every other respect the plays are as dissimilar as possible; yet it seems to me far from unlikely that an unconscious reminiscence of the Bataille de Dames may have contributed to the shaping of the Feast at Solhaug in Ibsen's mind. But more significant than any resemblance of theme, is the similarity of Ibsen's whole method to that of the French school --the way, for instance, in which misunderstandings are kept up through a careful avoidance of the use of proper names, and the way in which a cup of poison, prepared for one person, comes into the hands of another person, and is, as a matter of fact, drunk by no one, but occasions the acutest agony to the would-be poisoner, who is led to imagine that she has murdered the two people who are dearest to her in the world. All this ingenious dovetailing of incidents and working up of misunderstandings, Ibsen unquestionably learned from the French. The French language, indeed, is the only one which has a word-- quiproquo --to indicate the class of misunderstanding which, from Lady Inger down to The League of Youth, Ibsen employed so freely.

The only French play of note added to the Bergen repertory in 1856 was Scribe's highly characteristic production. Le Verre d'Eau, in which he formulates his theory that the great effects of history result from the most trifling causes and coincidences. On January 2nd, 1857, was produced Ibsen's three-act romantic drama, Olaf Liliekrans. It is, with the exception of Catiline, and possibly St. John's Night, the most immature of his writings, with very little technical character of any sort. One could pretty confidently guess that it dated from a period before he came under French influence; and as a matter of fact it was conceived, and partly written, as early as 1850. A painfully elaborate and artificial scene of quiproquo in the second act may, however, have been added during the revision which the play doubtless underwent in 1856, before it was put in rehearsal. Olaf Liliekrans was the last of Ibsen's plays produced in Bergen. In the summer of 1857 he removed to Christiania, to fill the post of artistic director at the Norwegian Theatre, recently established in that city. Le Gendre de M. Poirier was the only French play of much importance mounted in Bergen during the last months of his stay there.[7] After a short interregnum, he was succeeded in his Bergen "instructorship" by Björnstjerne Björnson.

So far as my investigation has gone, I have found no proof--for the suggested relationship between Bataille de Dames and The Feast at Solhaug is the merest vague possibility--no proof of any direct borrowing on Ibsen's part from his French models. Should further inquiry confirm this result, it will show him to have possessed from the outset a very rare originality.

Young playwrights, as a rule, find it almost impossible to avoid, consciously or unconsciously, adapting to their own purposes the inventions of their predecessors. Shakespeare, Molière, Corneille, were cases in point. It will sometimes happen that a beginner will construct a whole plot, as he thinks, entirely out of his own head, and then discover that what he believed to be invention was merely the revival of half-effaced memories of other plays. It need not have surprised us to find even conscious borrowings, in Ibsen's early works, of particular situations and devices from the great French storehouse. As Scott adapted in Kenilworth the scene between Egmont and Clärchen, in Goethe's tragedy, so Ibsen might without reproach have woven into the texture of this play or that some episode evidently suggested by Scribe or Dumas. I have discovered no instance of the kind, and am inclined to doubt whether further research will bring any to light. If students with more leisure than I have, are minded to pursue the inquiry, I would direct their attention to the situation in Lady Inger, where that wily woman expresses her confidence in the good faith of Olaf Skaktavl, and Nils Lykke, who are intriguing against each other for her political support. She fills two goblets with wine, and hands them to her guests; then, when they have drunk, she looks from one to the other and says, "Now I must tell you--the one goblet contained a welcome for my friend; the other--death for my enemy!" Whereupon the two cry out simultaneously, "Ah! I am poisoned!" and "Death and hell, you have murdered me!" This is a situation so entirely in the spirit of Dumas that one would almost be surprised to find that he did not invent it. If it occurs nowhere in his works, nor in those of his disciples, I think the search for definite borrowings on Ibsen's part may be abandoned.

None the less it is certain that he borrowed from the French playwrights of the second quarter of the nineteenth century the structural technique which he employed in his writings for the stage, from Lady Inger down to The League of Youth. The whole action of The League of Youth turns on a series of quiproquos, and several of its individual incidents could be paralleled in a score of French plays. For example, the whole intrigue of the letters which makes such capital sport in the fourth and fifth acts, is like a highly elaborated version of the letter incident in Scribe's Mon Etoile, produced in Bergen in 1855. But though The League of Youth marks the culmination of the French influence, I think it can still be traced in the three play which come next in order. It is visible in some of the most important episodes of Emperor and Galilean; it pervades Pillars of Society; and it is strong in the first two acts of A Doll's House. In the tarantella scene at the end of the second act, Ibsen may be said to have worked the Gallic virus out of his system. It is a last spasmodic effort in the art of keeping up the dramatic tension by means of external devices. In the last act of A Doll's House, Ibsen has once for all disengaged his true individuality. Thenceforward his technique is absolutely his own. It has become so subtle in its simplicity that the conventional critic, accustomed to the obvious artifices of the French school, is apt to declare that Ibsen has no technique at all. The truth is that having mastered all that Scribe and his followers had to teach him, he outgrew and renounced their doctrine. But to me it seems scarcely doubtful that had he not served his apprenticeship in that workshop, he would never have been the master-craftsman he ultimately became.

HENRIK IBSEN: PHILOSOPHER OR POET?

(Cosmopolitan, Feb. 1905)

> At the turn of the century probably no writer
> was put forward more insistently than Ibsen as
> an advocate for women's rights. In this essay
> Archer takes up this issue and argues strongly
> and perceptively that to read a philosophy of
> feminism out of Ibsen's plays is to misread not
> only Ibsen's intentions but also the way plays
> such as Ibsen's develop characterization and
> meaning.

Never a year and scarcely a month now passes without the
publication of some elaborate study of the philosophy of Henrik
Ibsen. In my own little library, I have a whole shelf devoted to
books about Ibsen; yet my collection is very far from complete.
And almost all these books, be they English, French, German,
Danish, Swedish, or what not, are concerned with Ibsen the
thinker, not with Ibsen the poet. Mr. Bernard Shaw's brilliant
little study, The Quintessence of Ibsenism, may be taken as the
type of this method of criticism. One critic after another passes
Ibsen through his own particular alembic, and each produces a
different quintessence. A great deal of ingenuity is often
expended on the confectioning of these chemical extracts; but
unfortunately the real Ibsen is nowhere to be found in them.
This poet whom, of all others, men are most intent on boiling
down, bottling up and labeling, happens to be, of all others,
the most illusive, the most impersonal, one might almost say the
most irresponsible. I do not mean that there is no value in the
lucubrations of the expositors. Many of them preach very
interesting sermons on texts supplied them by Ibsen—sermons in
which Ibsen himself would probably find a great deal to approve.
Their error lies in imagining that Ibsen is primarily a thinker,
and only in the second place a poet; so that, if only they search
long enough, they are bound to find a consistent body of doctrine
in his works. That is the one thing they will not find, for the
good reason that it is not there.

Ibsen is a great poet, a great creator of men and women, a great inventor and manipulator of those critical conjunctures in life which are the material of drama. He is also, no doubt, a moralist. He has a high ideal of human character, and he scourges unsparingly both the individual and the social turpitudes which prevent the realization of that ideal. But he has no definite, consistent, clearly thought-out moral or social system to inculcate. His primary concern is the projection of character, and its development by aid of an interesting, moving, absorbing action. As no serious action in life is devoid of moral significance, so there is no play of Ibsen's that does not raise a number of moral issues. It may even be for the sake of one or more of these moral issues that he chooses one action rather than another. But his characters always live a life of their own, independent of any ethical intention in the play. Only where the poet falls distinctly beneath himself do we feel that their speech or action is conditioned by his moral design; and, on the other hand, they often, as it were, take the bit between their teeth, and leave the moral design away in the dim distance. Moreover, the ethical intentions discernible in one play are often inconsistent, superficially at any rate, with those of the next. Being, as I say, a poet, and not a systematic thinker, Ibsen sees one side of a case intensely at one moment, and the other side at another moment, with no less intensity. In this multiplicity of his points of view we have the reason why so many different people are able to "quintessentiate" their own doctrines out of Ibsen's work. The doctrines are there beyond dispute; but the process of quintessentiation consists in ignoring the contradictory doctrines which are there no less.

Take, for instance, the work of M. Ossip-Lourié, a Franco-Russian writer of some repute, on La Philosophie Sociale dans le Théâtre d'Ibsen. Here is the second sentence on the first page of M. Lourié's book: "The plays of Ibsen are not so much dramatic productions as philosophic essays touching the vital questions of humanity. Their action is of secondary importance; their incidents are forced, unexpected, brusk; their main interest resides in the conflict of ideas." And on the next page: "Some of his pieces may be considered as "absolutely foreign to dramatic art." Now it is of course for M. Lourié to say where, for him, the main interest of Ibsen's plays resides; but if he finds it in the conflict of ideas, as distinct from the characters and their doings and sufferings, then it is evident that he does not read Ibsen as Ibsen desires to be read--nay, as one ought in common reason to read him. If his plays are "not so much dramatic productions as philosophic essays," it is a great pity that he should have couched them in the cumbrous and baffling dramatic form. If "some of his pieces are absolutely foreign to dramatic art," he must be indeed a sad bungler; for it is abundantly clear, both from internal and from external evidence, that he tried his

best to make them dramas, and not philosophic essays. If M.
Lourié had said "foreign to theatrical art," one could have
understood his meaning, though it would still have been
unfortunately expressed. The two great dramas in verse, Brand and
Peer Gynt, are too long for the actual stage, and contain many
passages which are difficult of scenic realization. Still more
obviously do the vast proportions of the "world-historic drama,"
Emperor and Galilean, unfit it for the narrow boards of a modern
playhouse. These pieces, when they are acted, must be freely
curtailed, like Goethe's Faust Schiller's Wallenstein trilogy,
and, for that matter, Shakespeare's Hamlet. But I presume M.
Lourié would scarcely call Faust and Hamlet foreign to theatrical
--and still less to dramatic--art. As a matter of fact, both
Brand and Peer Gynt have been frequently and successfully acted.
If the fourth act of Brand and Aase's death-scene in Peer Gynt be
not among the highest achievements of modern drama, their "social
philosophy" will certainly not justify their existence. In the
former there is only a slight incidental trace of "social
philosophy" to be discovered, in the latter there is none at
all--it is pure unadulterated dramatic poetry. Of course, there
is ethical import in both scenes: there is ethical import in
every true and vivid portrayal of human character. But the value
of the scenes lies not in their ethical import, but in the
splendor of their imagination, the poignancy of their drama. For
these things M. Ossip-Lourié, like so many Ibsen commentators, has
apparently no eyes.

It is not in the least doubtful how Ibsen himself desires to
be regarded. He has asserted again and again, in opposition to
his expositors, that he is not primarily a thinker, but a
dramatist. He did his best to impress this even on M. Lourié, who
quotes from a private letter of his (dated 19th February, 1899)
the following words: "I would beg you to remember that the
thoughts thrown out in my plays proceed from my dramatic
personages who utter them, and are neither in matter nor in form
to be attributed to me personally." Still more explicit is one
of the poet's declarations to Count Prozor, his French translator:
"If," he says, "in transporting to the stage certain men and women
whom I have seen and known, certain facts which I have witnessed
or which have been related to me--and if, in throwing an
atmosphere of poetry over the whole--I succeed in stimulating the
minds of my audiences, different ideas will germinate in different
brains, and will no doubt have had my play for their point of
departure. And of course I don't deny that, as I wrote, such and
such ideas may have traversed my own mind too. But this is
entirely a secondary matter. The main thing in a theatrical
creation is, and must be, action, life." It is abundantly
manifest, then, that if M. Lourié and the other quintessentiators
are right in regarding Ibsen's plays as primarily philosophic
essays, in which the action is a more or less negligible quantity,

Ibsen's life-work must be, from his own point of view, a gigantic failure. But they are not right: they are utterly and hopelessly wrong. In another paper I have tried to suggest certain reasons and excuses for their error. Here let me confine myself to showing, very briefly, in one typical instance, how impossible it is to extract from Ibsen's works a consistent body of social doctrine--impossible, that is to say, without arbitrarily ignoring whatever does not happen to tally with the case you want to make out.

As Ibsen's most famous play is <u>A Doll's House</u>, in which Nora Helmer somewhat vehemently asserts her right to a soul of her own, it is commonly assumed that Ibsen is above everything a champion of "women's rights"--of "female emancipation," in the sense which political agitators assign to the term. Mr. Lourié has not the slightest doubt on this point. "Ibsen," he says, "has consecrated the puissance of his pen to the defense of Woman"; and he goes off into a demonstration that "the modern woman has already proved that she possesses the same intellectual capacities as man, and that there is no branch of human activity in which she cannot replace, and often even surpass him." Apparent exceptions to this rule are explained on the ground of inadequate education, insufficient opportunity, ingrained prejudice, and so forth. In short, M. Lourié gives us a treatise of several pages on the ordinary topics of latter-day feminism.

But there is not a word of all this in Ibsen. He nowhere seeks to show that woman "possesses the same intellectual capacities" as man; he nowhere claims for her a right to take part with man in every "branch of human activity." He allows her a soul to be saved, and he makes one of his heroines seek her own salvation in breaking out of the cage of marriage. Beyond this, I defy any one to discover in Ibsen the smallest championship of "woman's rights" in the sectarian sense of the word. Would he give women the suffrage? He does not say. Does he consider them fitted for the learned professions, for commerce, for engineering, for soldiering, for sailoring? If he does, he has kept the secret. He has drawn many noble women, true; but also many vulgar, base, and abominable women. If every poet who drew beautiful female characters were a champion of "woman's rights," it would be the most gloriously championed cause in all history.

Were I arguing for the sake of argument, I should adopt M. Lourié's own method and totally disregard the chronological sequence of Ibsen's works. M. Lourié seems to conceive that Ibsen began his poetic career with a ready-made social philosophy complete at every point--that there has been no change or development in his views--and that therefore every phrase in his writings, whatever its dates and whatever its context, may be cited in evidence of his personal and permanent opinion on whatever point it refers to. In short, M. Lourié chops up all Ibsen's dramas into shreds and snippets, shuffles them together,

and whenever his eye happens to fall upon a scrap that apparently
harmonizes with his own opinions, pops it into his text. Were I
thus to ignore chronology and build upon Ibsen's earlier plays,
the plays of his romantic period, from Cataline right down to Peer
Gynt, it would be the easiest thing in the world to prove that his
views were the very opposite of those M. Lourié assigns to him.
He was inclined during this period to a romantic idealization of
woman; but his ideal woman was precisely the antithesis of M.
Lourié's ideal. She never dreamed of claiming equality with man
or independence of man. She was submissive, long-suffering, self
sacrificing, domestic in the most old-fashioned sense of the word.
When a woman, of this period, asserts any will, any individuality
of her own (as in the case of Furia, Lady Inger, Hjordis), it is
invariably to plunge into crime. The sympathetic heroines one and
all accept with scarcely a murmur the most infamous usage at the
hands of their men-folk. Ingeborg in The Pretenders has an
interview with King Skule--the man who has loved and deserted
her--in which she gives up to him the one joy left her in life,
their son. For a moment King Skule is touched by her devotion,
and thus, (in the first edition) their dialogue ran:

> King Skule: Every fair memory from those days I have
>   wasted and let slip.
> Ingeborg: It is man's right to forget.
> King Skule: And meantime you, Ingeborg, loving faith-
>   ful woman, have sat here in the North, guarding and
>   treasuring your memories in ice-cold loneliness.
> Ingeborg: It is a woman's happiness to remember.

And then, as she leaves the hall, realizing that her son and
his father, absorbed in each other, have already no thought for
her, she says to herself, "To love, to sacrifice all, and be
forgotten, that is woman's saga." So the speeches stood in the
first edition. On the remonstrance of George Brandes, the poet
slightly modified them, and Ingeborg now says: "It was your
right," "It was my happiness," and "To love, to sacrifice all,
and be forgotten, that is my saga." Thus she no longer enunciates
general principles, but simply expresses personal feelings. It
is impossible to doubt, however, that at the time when The
Pretenders was written, and even for years afterward, Ibsen was
not at all disinclined to accept the view as she at first worded
it. I do not mean that he deliberately held the doctrine that to
love, to sacrifice all and be forgotten, is woman's highest duty
and destiny. My whole argument is that he does not deliberately
hold to doctrines, but creates characters. Still, this
reactionary, this medieval-romantic view of "the woman question"
was so far from being abhorrent to him, that he made the two
latest and loveliest heroines of his romantic period act up to it

literally, and showed no suspicion that in so doing they were
betraying the cause of their sex. Ingeborg's formula tells the
whole story of that exquisite creation Solveig in Peer Gynt: she
loves, she sacrifices everything, and is forgotten. As for Agnes
in Brand--an ideal character if ever there was one--she utterly
sinks her individuality in that of her fanatic husband, and
sacrifices to his superhuman, his inhuman, "categorical
imperative," not only her own life, but that of her child as
well.   M. Lourié is full of admiration for Agnes; but he
conveniently closes his eyes to the fact that she is the absolute
negation of the modern woman who holds the assertion of her
own rights and the development of her own individuality to
be her first and her holiest duty.   Imagine Agnes at the
polling-booth![1]
     But I admit, nay, assert, that these plays of Ibsen's
romantic period cannot reasonably be cited as evidence on either
side of this case.   It is only because M. Lourié himself cites
them that I have thought it worth while to show what their
evidence really amounts to.   There is no doubt that during the
years when Ibsen was making his first experiments in prose drama
of modern life, he began to be interested in a more self-assertive
and independent type of female character. Selma, in The League
of Youth, is his first study in this direction.   In Pillars of
Society, Lona Hessel is an accomplished type of the "strong-minded
woman" (there is no difficulty in conceiving her at the
polling-booth), while Dina Dorf is a transitional figure, filling
up the gap between Selma and Nora. Finally, in Nora, we have
undoubtedly a prophetess of individuality and emancipation; and
the last scene of A Doll's House, admirably dramatic though it be,
seems to me one of the very few passages in Ibsen where the desire
to give utterance to a general point of view is suffered to
interfere with absolute dramatic propriety.   I think the poet was
seduced into letting Nora develop the principles of her revolt
more rapidly and more articulately than is quite consistent with
the particular fable in which he has placed her. No doubt he felt
a very strong sympathy with Nora. He has drawn her from first to
last with a loving care which places this beyond question; and
when we find in his next play such a character as Mrs. Alving, we
see clearly that at this period Ibsen thought the assertion of
feminine individuality one of the most dramatic motives in modern
life.   Of its social importance, nay, inevitability, he was no
doubt equally convinced; for Ibsen is always an "outpost thinker";
conservatism--the attitude of "the little narrow-chested,
short-winded crew that lie in our wake"--has no meaning for him.
But it is one thing to realize that a movement is in the main just
and inevitable, another thing to accept and proclaim the dogmas of
its partisans. This Ibsen never does. He sees around and beyond
all parties.   It is not his business to commit himself to any
credo or any program. Beyond the simple admission that society

has done itself an injury by ignoring, thwarting and deforming much of what is best in feminine human nature, there is no judgment on "the woman question" to be found in Ibsen. Mr. Lourié's dogma of the equality, nay, identity, of talent in the sexes is, I repeat, foreign to him. As for M. Lourié's assertion that "the women of Ibsen are superior beings," with the implication that he has them so of set purpose, out of sheer sex-partizanship, nothing could be farther from the obvious facts of the case.

In his romantic period--yes. Then he was apt to make his women "superior beings"; but their superiority, as I have shown, lay precisely in their renunciation of all that modern feminism claims for their sex. But as soon as we emerge from the romantic period, we leave behind us the region of "superior beings." Nora is superior to Helmer, no doubt, and Mrs. Alving to her deceased husband; but that is because Helmer is a prig and an ass, while Chamberlain Alving was am imbecile debauchee. Nora's complaint is precisely that the influence of her father and her husband has left her in so many respects an inferior being that she is unequal even to the task of bringing up her own children. As for Mrs. Alving, she is no doubt a fine and strong character; but Ibsen has himself protested against the notion that she is to be taken as an ideal. "It has been said," he writes, "that the play preaches nihilism. Nothing of the sort. It is none of my business to preach anything whatever. It only points to the nihilism fermenting under the surface, at home as elsewhere. And how can it be otherwise? A Pastor Manders will always act as a goad to one or other Mrs. Alving. And just because she is a woman, she will, when once started, go to the uttermost extreme."[2] Does such an utterance as this savor of sectarian woman-worship? And even if he had verged in the direction of idealization in Mrs. Alving, has he not redressed the balance by placing at her side that abject creature of corruption, Regina? With Ghosts, moreover, his interest in the assertion of female individuality ceases. Petra in An Enemy of the People is a piece of portraiture, no more--a bright, self-reliant modern girl, her father's daughter, but neither the symbol nor the mouthpiece of any particular doctrine. And from this point onward the poet deals one hard stroke after another at feminine human nature. Hedvig in The Wild Duck is a beautiful child, but she is no more than a child; and though her mother, Gina, has elements of good in her, she is scarcely a "superior being." In Rosmersholm there are two women--one living and one dead. The dead woman, Beata, was a morbid weakling, only half sane; the living woman, Rebecca, is a strong character, indeed, but she happens to be a cold-blooded murderess. Ellida in The Lady from the Sea is a neurotic personage, smacking of Charcot and La Salpetrière.[3] Her claim for "freedom" is wholly psychological, not in the least social. Bolette in the same play is a charming type of the old-fashioned, dutiful, domestic girl, while Hilda, is an irrepressible little minx. Hedda Gabler, a superb masterpiece of characterization, is a degenerate type hovering on the verge of criminality, while Thea Elvsted is an inarticulate, clinging, "womanly woman" in the most retrograde sense of the word. This catalogue, however, is becoming tedious. Look at Hilda and Mrs.Solness in The Master Builder, at Rita and Asta in Little Eyolf, at Gunhild Ella Rentheim and Mrs. Wilton in John Gabriel Borkman, at Irene and Maia in When We Dead Awaken --where do you find in any of them either the "superior being" of the feminist ideal, or the propagandist, direct or indirect, of a theory which would make woman interchangeable with man in regard to all the activities of life? Only two of the characters enumerated can even be called sympathetic--Asta and Ella Rentheim --and neither of these displays the smallest ambition to transcend the limits laid down for her sex by the most conventional of social theories.

M. Lourié is so determined to make Ibsen not only a creator of women but a champion of woman, that he actually lavishes admiration even on Rebecca West and Hedda Gabler. Now I am far from saying that there is not a great fascination in both these characters. In Rebecca there is even an element of nobility; while Hedda, though essentially malign and mischievous, has some traits which reproduce themselves in so many of us, that I, for one, am by no means inclined to join in simply stoning her. But to represent such characters as "superior beings," proving that Ibsen (to adapt Malvolio's phrase) thinks nobly of the feminine soul and in no way approves the opinion of Schopenhauer, is to misrepresent him grotesquely. Nay, not only grotesquely, but injuriously; for it is to make him out a flagrantly immoral writer. To put forward such characters as ideals would be no less immoral than absurd; and Ibsen certainly never dreamed of doing so. It would be rational, though very far-fetched, to argue that in these later plays Ibsen championed the emancipation of woman by showing what distortions and vices of character her servitude has begotten in her. But to represent him as idealizing woman in order to emphasize her claim to freedom and equality, is to fly in the face of the plainest facts.

The truth is that from the date of Ghosts--or at latest of An Enemy of the People--anything like an active interest in the social emancipation of woman seems to have faded from the poet's mind. I do not mean that he ceased to sympathize with it, but merely that he had no longer any use for it as a dramatic motive. From The Wild Duck onward, we find him more and more absorbed in psychology, with little or no bearing on sociology, and more and more addicted, withal, to pure poetry. His interest in building "houses for human beings," as Solness puts it, has waned. He now builds towers from the summit of which we can hear, more and more clearly, the music of "harps in the air." M. Lourié does not seem to have heard of a characteristic incident that happened in

Christiania some years ago. I unfortunately cannot lay my hand on the exact reference,[4] but the gist of the episode is clear in my mind. A number of ladies actively interested in the "Kvindesag"--the Woman's Cause--organized a little festival in honor of their chosen champion, Henrik Ibsen. The poet submitted with the best grace he could assume; but when the time came for him to acknowledge the homage of his hostesses, he made one of his brief, pregnant speeches, beginning with the remark that he did not know what the "Kvindesag" was! He then went on to say that, in his estimation, motherhood, with the training of the new generations, was the first of woman's rights and the greatest of woman's privileges--a very ancient and respectable doctrine, but not at all what the leaders of the Woman's Cause had expected to hear from him. A typical instance, this, of the misadventures which are certain to befall whomsoever seeks to force upon Henrik Ibsen the apostolate of any sect or party.

Let me give one more example of the way in which M. Lourié presses the most unlikely passages from play after play into the service of his own particular views. Among the quotations by aid of which he thinks to show that the innate superiority of woman is one of Ibsen's dogmas, we find the following from John Gabriel Borkman:

> Borkman (indignantly): Oh, these women! They wreck and ruin life for us! Play the devil with our whole destiny--our triumphal progress.
> Foldal: Not all of them!
> Borkman: Indeed? Can you tell me of a single one that is good for anything?
> Foldal: No, that's the trouble. The few that I know are good for nothing.
> Borkman (with a snort of scorn): Well, then, what's the good of it? What's the good of such women existing --if you never know them?
> Foldal: Yes, John Gabriel, there is good in it, I assure you. It is such a blessed, beneficent thought that here and there in the world, some- where, far away--the true woman exists after all.
> Borkman: Oh, do spare me that poetical nonsense!

It is immediately on the heels of this passage, and as a more or less formal deduction from it, that M. Lourié lays it down that "the women of Ibsen are superior beings"! By what possible right can he decide that the poet is uttering his own thoughts through the mouth of Foldal? If we must conceive him to be speaking his own thoughts at all, why may not Borkman be his mouthpiece? It is manifest to any one who reads the whole scene (one of the greatest he ever wrote) that Ibsen is treating both Borkman and Foldal with the grimmest of irony. He is laughing at both,

unquestionably; but Foldal is throughout the scene, as he
certainly is in this particular passage, the more ridiculous of
the two.   It may be said that Foldal is, without knowing it,
expounding the secret of Borkman's tragedy--that had Borkman
possessed the insight to recognize the "true woman" in Ella
Rentheim, his misfortunes would never have happened. But that is
simply to say that if Borkman had been another man his fate would
have been different. It needs no champion of feminism to tell us
that a man who, for the sake of worldly ambitions, throws over a
more or less amiable woman, and marries an unamiable woman in her
stead, makes a dire mistake.   It is a perfectly gratuitous
proceeding to translate this plain and simple moral into a
glorification of the Foldal-Lourié ideal of "the true woman."
But I beg M. Lourié's pardon--I am wrong in hyphening the
"Foldal-Lourié ideal."   Even if Ella Rentheim represented the
Foldal idea, and even if some remnant of this ideal (a survival
of his romantic period) lurked in the poet's own soul, it would
remain absolutely certain that this ideal differs in almost every
respect from the feminist ideal of M. Lourié.   It is only by
wilful deafness to Ella Rentheim's most passionate and fervent
utterances that any one can mistake her for a prophetess of
equality and emancipation.

Is it not evident that the passage quoted is purely dramatic,
the natural utterance of the two characters concerned, the poet
having no thought of committing himself to the views of either?
I take it to be one of many passages in his works which he wrote
with a mischievous twinkle in his eye, well knowing that he was
spreading a snare for the quintessentiators.   In the autumn of
1887, I spent a day with Ibsen at Saeby in Jutland. When I asked
whether he had then any work in hand, he answered, with the
aforesaid twinkle in his eye, "Oh, yes, I'm compounding some
tomfoolery for next year."   The "tomfoolery" in question turned
out to be The Lady from the Sea.   The speech seems to me to throw
a flood of light upon the mood in which the poet regards his work.
I do not mean that he does not take it seriously, or that he is
guilty of deliberate mystification; but I am sure that he is
sometimes conscious of a malign glee in giving rein to his purely
dramatic imagination--even spurring it, perhaps, with the thought
of the bewilderment of commentators.

It may perhaps be thought that I am, personally, an opponent
of female emancipation, and am simply trying, like M. Lourié, to
read my own views into Ibsen. This is not so. Though I do not
quite believe with M. Lourié that woman can do everything that
man can do, as well and probably better, I am in favor of removing
all legal restrictions on her activities.   I would always vote,
for instance, in favor of female suffrage, though I am not quite
inconsolable at the tardiness of its coming. This topic of female
emancipation is only one out of many that I might equally well
have chosen to illustrate my point--namely, that the poet whom the

commentators are always striving to enlist in this or that party or sect, in reality stands entirely outside sects and parties, and simply uses them for his dramatic purposes. If you want a deliberate and consistent body of doctrine, you must go, not to Ibsen, but to Tolstoy. In his own person, in one of his lyric poems, Ibsen has said, "My calling is to question, not to answer." One of the very few characters--two or three at most--in which we are justified in recognizing some trace, some aspect, of the poet's own personality, says of himself, "I am glad that it is my mission to be the thirteenth at table."[5] At all our banquets of sectarian self-gratulation Ibsen plays the part of this disquieting guest, as he did at that feminist festival in Christiania.

IBSEN IN HIS LETTERS

(Fortnightly Review, Mar. 1905)

Ibsen's letters were published in Danish and German editions in 1904. The English edition, translated by J. N. Laurvik and Mary Morison, came out in 1905. The publication of these letters, rather remarkable since Ibsen was still alive, attests to the importance he had attained throughout Europe. He had established, in James Joyce's words, an empire over the modern mind. In this essay Archer traces the history of Ibsen's development from national obscurity to international eminence, as this can be seen in his letters, especially in those to Björnstjerne Björnson, the Norwegian dramatist, and Georg Brandes, the Danish literary critic.

Henrik Ibsen's letters, collected in two solid volumes under the careful editorship of Herr Halvdan Koht and Dr. Julius Elias, form the best possible substitute for that autobiography which he again and again thought of writing, but always put aside till it was too late. In a certain sense, the letters are more convincing evidence of his frames of mind than any reminiscences could have been; especially as the poet's declared intention was to make his life and his writings mutually explanatory, and weave them into a consistent whole. His work would have been in some sort an apologia, and open to the suspicion with which we regard all special pleading. Without doubting his sincerity, we should have doubted, now and then, whether his memory did not show him rather the man he wished he had been than the man he was. But letters —such manifestly unaffected letters as these—afford the best possible record of the mood of the moment. The insight they give us is fragmentary, no doubt; but at least it is not warped by the intervention of any refracting medium.

Ibsen was not a born letter-writer. The form was never congenial to him. His pen did not fly over the paper, but travelled over it slowly, laboriously, conscientiously. He did not shine in direct utterance of any sort, but was a dramatist to the marrow. Even his lyrics--the best of them, at all events--are either fables or dramas. In this repect he offers a curious contrast to Byron, whom in some other respects he resembles --notably in his voluntary exile, his passionate estrangement, from his native land. In direct self-expression Byron was always most at his ease--Ibsen, least. Byron tried to write drama and could not; Ibsen could scarcely write anything else. The bulk of these volumes would be considerably reduced if all Ibsen's apologies for his dilatoriness as a correspondent were cut out, along with all his expression of distaste for letter-writing and inability to discuss this subject or that except by word of mouth. To his less intimate correspondents, too, his formalities of compliment are oppressive. He is too often the polite letter-writer, and little else.

Nevertheless, the book is extraordinarily interesting, and even fascinating. It throws a flood of new light on the poet's outward and inward life. Like many men who hate letter-writing, he could, when he worked himself up to it, or when a sudden impulse overcame his chronic distaste, express himself with remarkable freedom and vivacity. All his letters to Björnson[1] and to George Brandes[2] are documents of the utmost value; and the same may be said of many occasional epistles to other correspondents. As he grows older, his habit of reticence gains upon him; yet even in the ceremonious letters of his later life there are many memorable phrases, and character-traits that one would not willingly let die.

The new knowledge conveyed in these volumes may be roughly marshalled in four divisions. It concerns (1) the outward conditions of the poet's life, (2) his artistic development, (3) his political and social ideas, (4) his personal character. I propose to glance at a few salient points under each of these headings.

I.

There is ample evidence in the early letters of the harassing poverty in which some of the best years of his life were passed. Not until he was nearly forty could it be said that his "bread-sorrows" were over. At Bergen his salary as theatre-poet and artistic instructor was under £70 a year. At the Norwegian Theatre in Christiania his nominal salary was £130, but when the theatre went bankrupt it was considerably in arrears. At the Christiania Theatre his nominal salary was about £6 a month, but it was never paid in full. From The Vikings, the most successful play he had written up to 1863, he made in five years just about £50. When it was produced at the Christiania Theatre, he was

offered an "honorarium" of 6 15s., and told that if he was not
content with that he should have nothing at all. What wonder
that, with incomings such as these, and with a wife and child to
support, he ran into debt! But even his debts bear witness to the
narrow circumstances in which he lived, for in 1863 they did not
amount to much over £100. It is pitiful to read his repeated
applications to the Government for one of the miserable "stipends"
which the Storthing sometimes doled out to poets and artists. At
last, in 1864, he is allotted a "travelling stipend" of £90, and
with that he sets off to Rome. But he leaves debts behind him,
and has to borrow here and there from wealthy acquaintances in
order to eke out his travelling pittance. What these continual
money-troubles must have meant to a man of Ibsen's proud and
sensitive spirit, it is only too easy to imagine. His letters
(which, however, are scanty during this period) show him less
galled and humiliated than might have been expected. Even his
first years in Italy were passed in direful straits. His original
"stipend" was only a single dole, not a yearly allowance. In 1866
he applies to King Carl for an annual "poet-pension." "It is
not," he says, "for a secure income that I am here contending, but
for the life-task which I immovably believe that God has imposed
upon me--the task which of all others seems to me the most
important and most necessary--that of awakening the people of
Norway and inducing them to think greatly." His petition is
granted, and he writes to the Minister who informs him of the
fact: "My future is now assured, and I can pursue my vocation
undisturbed." His future is assured by an allowance of £90 a
year!

In the history of the pecuniary arrangements which enabled
him to go to Rome and to support himself there, the most
interesting feature is the enthusiastic and unwearied help
afforded him by Björnson. It was not until 1859 that they formed
any close intimacy, but for seven or eight years after that they
were the warmest friends. Björnson, though more prosperous as an
author than Ibsen, had little enough money to lend; but he gave a
more convincing proof of friendship in persuading other people to
come to the aid of his brother-poet. Nor was Ibsen chary in his
expressions of gratitude. For instance, in September, 1865, he
writes from Ariccia:

The great thing--absolutely the greatest thing for
me and my fortunes that has ever happened--is that I
have met and really found you; and I can never requite
you except by an affection which neither my friends nor
your enemies shall ever impair.

I shall speak later of the vicissitudes this friendship
underwent; they belong to the history of Ibsen's character rather
than to that of his outward circumstances. The most enduring

benefit Björnson conferred upon him was an introduction to
the great publishing house of Gyldendal in Copenhagen. The
publication of Brand by that firm preceded by about two months the
allotment of the annual pension. The poem was a great success,
and the pinch of need was over. A few days before Brand appeared,
Ibsen added a postscript to a letter to Björnson: "For this once
I avail myself of your suggestion that I should not prepay my
letters. I do so by necessity, not choice." In other words, "My
poverty, but not my will, consents."[3]

But in spite of all troubles and anxieties, Ibsen's first
years in Italy were probably the happiest of his life. His
enjoyment of nature and art--of nature especially--was very keen,
and his sense of liberation, in his escape from Norway, was ever
present to him. He rejoiced in Rome itself. "Everything here,"
he writes, "is stupendous, but there is an indescribable peace
over it all. No politics, no commercial spirit, no militarism,
leaves its one-sided imprint on the population." It was a very
different Rome on which he turned his back twenty years later. In
1865 he wrote to Björnson: "I often lie for half a day among
the tombs on the Via Latina or the Via Appia Antica, and I do not
think this idling can be called waste of time. The Baths of
Caracalla have also a peculiar attraction for me." Did he know,
I wonder, that they had been one of Shelley's favorite haunts?
For some time after his arrival in Italy he wrestled in vain with
the idea of the play which afterwards became Emperor and Galilean.
But at last, one day in the summer of 1865, business brought him
from Ariccia into Rome. He strayed into St. Peter's, and there
the idea of Brand flashed into his mind. "I suddenly saw in
strong and clear outline what I had to say. I have now thrown
overboard the thing I had been torturing myself with for more than
a year, and in the middle of July I began something new which went
as nothing has ever gone with me." He is now hard at work on it
(at Ariccia), seeing no one, and reading nothing but the Bible
--"which is strong and bracing." "I have a suspicion," he
continues, "that my new poem will not ingratiate me with our
legislators [on whom his pension depended]; but God confound me if
I either can or will strike out a single line of it, to suit the
taste of these waistcoat-pocket souls." In another letter (also
to Björnson) he describes the state of exaltation in which, amid
all his anxieties and distresses, he wrote Brand. "I felt," he
says, "a crusader's rapture."

After Brand and Peer Gynt (which followed close upon it) had
made him famous and assured his economic position, the course of
his life ran very smoothly. Its main features were his many
migrations, the gradual extension of his fame beyond the limits of
Scandinavia, and the controversies aroused by his later works.
These external facts have long been public property, and on them
his letters throw little new light. I pass, therefore, to the
glimpses of his artistic development which the letters afford.

II.

In the first place, it is interesting to note the literary influences to which he was subjected in the impressionable years of his early manhood. We know from one or two of his immature works that the sentimental romanticism of Oehlenschlaeger[4] must have attracted him for a time; but there is no trace of this influence in his letters. In 1852, when he was sent by the management of the Bergen Theatre to study the Danish stage in Copenhagen, he writes to his employers: "In respect to the repertory we have been very fortunate, having seen Hamlet and several other plays of Shakespeare, and also several of Holberg's." The other plays of Shakespeare which he probably saw at this time were King Lear, Romeo and Juliet, and As You Like It. Of these, Lear and As You Like It must greatly have impressed him, for he cites them years afterwards; but it does not appear that his acquaintance with Shakespeare was ever wide or deep. On the other hand, Holberg, the great Danish-Norwegian comedy-writer of the eighteenth century, was throughout life his favorite author. His letters abound in Holberg quotations; he declares him to be the one writer he never tires of reading; and on the only occasion when I, personally, ever saw Ibsen greatly excited, a phrase from Holberg rose to his lips.

In a former article in this REVIEW, I have shown that his constant employment for several years in mounting the plays of Scribe and his school must have had a determining influence on his technique; but he clearly recognised, at an early period, that it was an influence to be outgrown. When some French critics tried, most absurdly, to class him as an imitator of Dumas fils, Ibsen wrote to Brandes: "I owe absolutely nothing to Dumas in respect to dramatic form--except that I have learnt from him to avoid certain glaring errors and clumsinesses of which he is not infrequently guilty." He could never rest satisfied with semi-realism of form; for that his sense of logic was too imperious. Before the appearance of The League of Youth, his first prose play of modern life, he wrote to Brandes: "I have been very scrupulous as to form, and have, among other things, achieved the feat of working out my theme without the aid of a single soliloquy, or even aside." This self-denying ordinance he somewhat relaxed on returning to historical drama in Emperor and Galilean; but when Mr. Gosse[5] suggested that it had better have been written in verse, he energetically dissented. "The illusion," he said, "which I wanted to produce was that of reality; I wanted to give the reader the impression that what he was reading had actually happened. . . .My new play is not a tragedy in the old sense of the word; I have tried to represent human beings, and therefore I have not allowed them to speak 'the language of the gods'." Ten years later, when a Norwegian actress, Fru Wolf, asked him for a prologue to be spoken at her benefit, he replied to the effect that a self-respecting dramatic artist ought to be chary of reciting even a single verse upon the stage, so much harm had metre done to the art of acting. This was no doubt the utterance of a momentary fanaticism; but it harmonises with the austere repression of every lyric impulse which reached its height, just about the date of this letter, in An Enemy of the People. In his later plays, as we know, poetry regained the upper hand, and more and more encroached upon realism, in spirit, if not in outward form.

The making of a play meant, for Ibsen, an extraordinary effort of mental concentration. He put everything else aside, read no books, attended to no business that was not absolutely imperative, and lived for weeks and months with his characters alone. He writes in June 1884: "I have in these days completed a play in five acts. That is to say, I have roughed it out: now comes the more delicate manipulation of it, the more energetic individualisation of the characters and their mode of expression." This play was The Wild Duck. A month or two later he writes: "The people in my new play, in spite of their manifold frailties, have through long and daily familiarity endeared themselves to me. . . .I believe that The Wild Duck will perhaps lure some of our younger dramatists into new paths, and that I hold to be desirable." In 1890, when he has finished Hedda Gabler, he writes to Count Prozor:[6] "It gives me a strange feeling of emptiness to part from a piece of work which has now, for several months, exclusively occupied my time and my thoughts. Yet it is well that it has come to an end. The incessant association with these imaginary people was beginning to make me not a little nervous."

Of aesthetic theory, other than that which he himself constructed for his own use and behoof, Ibsen was very impatient. One of his first remarks on coming in contact with the art of antiquity and of the renaissance is that "as yet, at any rate, I can often see only conventions where others profess to find laws." Antique sculpture he cannot at first "bring into relation to our time." He misses "the personal and individual expression, both in the artist and in his work." "Michael Angelo, Bernini, and his school I understand better; those fellows had the courage to play a mad prank now and then." He afterwards saw deeper into the nature of antique art; but in 1869, after he had been five years in Italy, he wrote: "Raphael's art has never really warmed me; his creations belong to the world before the Fall." Yet of anything like pre-Raphaelitism, in the English sense of the term, he was entirely innocent. Florentine art, so far as we can see, had nothing to say to him. On his return to Rome in 1879, he bought a number of "old masters," partly from taste, partly as an investment; but he does not mention the name of a single painter. My impression is that the paintings he used to have around him would be but slightly esteemed by English connoisseurs; but, when I have visited him, I have had little attention to spare for his

picture gallery. It is noteworthy, by the way, that at the Vienna
Exhibition of 1873 he found the English art-section to consist
"almost exclusively of masterpieces."[7] In his youth, it will be
remembered, he had himself given a good deal of time to painting.

This, however, is a digression: I return to his views on
aesthetic theory in general. When he has been a year in Italy,
he writes to Björnson that the most important result of his
travels has been the elimination from his mind of the aesthetic
system, "isolated and claiming inherent validity," which formerly
had power over him. "Aesthetics in this sense now appear to me as
great a curse to poetry as theology is to religion. You," he
continues, "have never been troubled with this sort of
aestheticism, you have never gone about looking at things through
your hollow hand." Some years later, when a Danish critic,
Clemens Petersen, has tried Peer Gynt by his aesthetic standard,
and pronounced it "not really poetry," Ibsen retorts (in a letter
to Björnson) with a splendid arrogance that Dante or Milton might
have envied: "The book is poetry; or if it is not, it shall
become poetry. The concept 'poetry' in our country, in Norway,
shall refashion itself in accordance with the book." In the same
letter he continues: "If it is to be war, so be it! If I am no
poet, I have nothing to lose. I shall set up as a photographer.
My contemporaries up in the north I will deal with individually,
man by man. . . .Nothing shall escape me--no thought or feeling
lurking behind the words in any soul that deserves the honour of
being noticed." This was written in a moment of hot indignation;
but it can scarcely be said that when the indignation cooled the
purpose had evaporated.

Of criticism in general Ibsen writes: "The majority of
critical strictures reduce themselves, in the last analysis, to
reproaches addressed to an author because he is himself, and
thinks, feels, sees, and creates like himself, instead of seeing
and creating as the critic would have done--had he had the power."

Ibsen is never tired of insisting that all his writings--even
his romantic plays--stand in intimate relation to his own life.
"I have never," he declares, "written anything merely because, as
the saying goes, I had 'hit on a good subject'." He repeats again
and again, to different correspondents, a distinction of which the
full force escapes me. Everything he has produced, he says, has
its origin in something he has not merely experienced (oplevet)
but lived through (gennemlevet). Perhaps he is here repeating in
another form the definition of poetry as "emotion recollected in
tranquillity";[8] but this seems scarcely consistent with an idea
he more than once repeats, that poetic production purges the
system of fermenting elements which would become poisonous if not
expelled. A few examples may perhaps make his meaning clearer.
Catiline was written in the little philistine town of Grimstad,
where (as he seems to imply) he stood in very much the same
relation to respectable, conservative society in which Catiline

stood to the ruling oligarchy of Rome. "Lady Inger of Ostratt is founded on a love-affair, hastily entered and violently broken off . . . .The Vikings I wrote when I was engaged to be married. For Hjördis I employed the same model who afterwards served for Svanhild in Love's Comedy. . . .The fact that everyone was against me, that there was no one in the outer world who could be said to believe in me, could not but give rise to the strain of feeling which found utterance in The Pretenders. . . .Brand is myself in my best moments—just as, by self-dissection, I have brought to light many of the character-traits both of Peer Gynt and of Stensgaard." In the latter character (the hero of The League of Youth) he was commonly accused of having drawn Björnson. Replying in advance to this accusation, he wrote: "People in Norway will perhaps say that I have depicted real persons and circumstances. This is not the case. I have, however, used models, which are as indispensable to the writer of comedy as to the painter or sculptor." Here again, I must own that the distinction baffles me. I can only imagine the meaning to be that he takes "composite photographs," not individual likenesses. As a matter of fact, Stensgaard was doubtless intended rather as a warning to Björnson than as a portrait of him.

The confession that parts of Peer Gynt and Stensgaard are the result of self-dissection may be compared with Mr. Meredith's similar admission (to Stevenson) with regard to Sir Willoughby Patterne.[9] Ibsen not infrequently insists on the sternness of his self-criticism. To a lady correspondent he writes: "You must not think that I am so unkindly disposed towards my countrymen as many people accuse me of being. At any rate, I can assure you I am no more indulgent to myself than to others." And, again, to Björnson: "You may be sure that in my leisure moments I probe, and sound, and anatomise pretty searchingly in my own inward parts; and that at the points where it bites the sorest."

III.

On his political and social utterances I need not dwell long, for the most important of them, occurring in letters to George Brandes, have long ago been quoted by that critic, in his Ibsen and Björnson. It was to Brandes, for example, that he expressed his lack of interest in "special revolutions, revolutions in externals, in the political sphere," adding, "What is really wanted is a revolution of the spirit of man." Familiar, too, is his remark that "he who possesses liberty otherwise than as an aspiration possesses it soulless, dead"; and, again, "I confess that the only thing about liberty that I love is the fight for it; I care nothing about the possession of it." These, and all his most noteworthy political deliverances, will be found in Brandes's invaluable essay.

A systematic political thinker Ibsen never was or could be.
His views were full of incompatibilities, which he did not dream
of harmonising. The only thing he consistently detested
throughout life was opportunism. He was, if one may coin a word,
an impossibilist.[10] That a course of action was useless and
hopeless was, in his eyes, the best reason for pursuing it. His
bitter contempt for the inaction of Norway and Sweden when Denmark
was crushed by Prussia was one of the forces that drove him into
exile and kept him in estrangement from his country. It did not
occur to him to inquire whether there would have been any use in
their rushing into the quarrel. The humiliation which he then
felt was, as appears from one of his letters, a main reason for
his abandoning the field of national history and legend. He no
longer took any pleasure in evoking the great past of his country,
seeing that the men of to-day stood to the men of the sagas in the
relation of a modern Levantine pirate to a hero of Homer. His
impulse now was to hurl scorn at his degenerate countrymen
through the mouth of Brand, and to embody in Peer Gynt their
pusillanimity, their egoism, their "halfness." And of this
feeling we find a curious echo in the very last letter included
in these volumes. It is written in December, 1900, to a Dutch
journalist who had upbraided him for some mildly pro-British
utterance with regard to the South African War. Ibsen does
not attempt to discuss the merits of the case, but answers: "You
say that the Dutch are the Boers' natural defenders in Europe:
why have not your countrymen chosen a point of more strategic
importance for their defensive operations? I mean South Africa.
And then, this method of defending kinsmen with books, and
pamphlets, and open letters! May I ask, Mr. Editor, if you could
not have found more effective weapons?" "Mr. Editor" probably
thought the sneer very unreasonable; but it was precisely the
reproach which in Brand, and in his lyrics at the time of the
Danish war, the poet had flung in the teeth of his own countrymen.

One of the contradictions of Ibsen's political thinking lay
(it seems to me) in the fact that he accepted the idea of definite
national units, while he would fain have denied them all
organisation. His hatred of "the State" appears over and over
again in these letters. He does not shrink from utterances of
sheer anarchism; but he does shrink from--or rather he never
attains to--the idea of internationalism or cosmopolitanism,
without which anarchism is surely unthinkable. Ibsen is always a
tribeman, though as life goes on his conception of the tribe
widens. In early life, he was an ardent "Scandinavian"--a
champion, that is to say, of the political union of the three
northern kingdoms. "I began," he wrote to George Brandes in 1888,
"by feeling as a Norwegian, I developed into a Scandinavian, and
have now come to rest in all-embracing Germanism. . . .I believe
that national consciousness is dying out, and that it will be
replaced by race-consciousness." This course of thought is not

unlike that which Mr. George Wyndham[11] set forth in his recent
Rectorial Address at Glasgow. Much earlier (1872) Ibsen had told
Mr. Gosse that the introduction of his works into England was one
of his "dearest literary dreams" because "the English people
stands so near to us Scandinavians." Without criticising the
race-idea, from the point of view either of science or of
expediency, one cannot but inquire how a race, any more than a
nation, can maintain and assert itself in anarchic incoherence?
The race-unit, no less than the nation-unit, must surely be an
organism. Anarchism implies the negation of the unit, the
absorption of all units in a homogeneous mass. How little Ibsen
cared for consistency appears when we find him, in the 'nineties,
acknowledging the benefits conferred on Germany by the
drill-sergeant, and placing "discipline" in the forefront of the
ethical requirements of his countrymen.

Inconsistency of thought need not surprise us in a poet who
had so strongly emphasised the relativity and consequent
impermanence of truth. "A normally constituted truth," says Dr.
Stockmann, "lives--let us say--seventeen or eighteen years; at the
outside twenty." But this estimate is only a flourish of the
worthy Doctor's. Ibsen himself would probably have been the first
to admit that, on the plane of expediency at any rate, five
minutes may perfectly suffice to turn a truth into a falsehood.
His mind was intensive rather than extensive. He did not profess
or attempt to apprehend a thing in all its relations. He saw one
aspect of it vividly and stated it forcibly, without denying that
there might be other aspects of equal or greater validity. He
evidently believed that ideas, like organisms, must be sifted
through the struggle for existence, in order that the fittest may
survive. Consequently he never hesitated to throw out the thought
that for a moment dominated him, and let it take its chance among
the rest; well knowing, at the same time, that it might one day be
swallowed up by a larger and stronger thought, perhaps emanating
from his own brain.

This intensiveness is a symptom or consequence of a
slow-moving, brooding habit of mind which is manifest throughout
his correspondence. He is not prolific of ideas; he ruminates on
one or two at a time, until they embody themselves in dramatic
form, and he "gets them off his heart." A letter to George
Brandes, dated April 1872, contains the germs of two plays,
published, respectively, ten and fourteen years later. "I hear,"
he says, "that you have founded an association. . . . .How far
your position is thereby strengthened, I cannot judge: it seems
to me that he is strongest who stands alone." And again, with
reference to some controversy in which Brandes was engaged, he
thus apostrophises him: "Be dignified! Dignity [or, better,
distinction] is the only weapon in such conflicts." In these
two utterances we have the root-ideas of An Enemy of the People
and Rosmersholm; and similar germs of other plays may be discerned

every here and there in his letters, at dates which indicate that
he brooded over them for years. That he could, on occasion,
warm into conversational brilliancy is proved by two witnesses:
Professor Dietrichson,[12] who was with him in Rome in the 'sixties,
and the painter Grönvold,[13] who saw a good deal of him in Munich
in '77. But Dietrichson admits that these occasions were rare.
Thoughts did not, as a rule, flash upon him as he talked;
he was more apt to draw, with great deliberation, on the
previously-formed ideas which were slowly revolving in his brain.
I happened to be with him frequently at the time when the
publication of Ghosts had raised a storm in Scandinavia; and I
find his letters of these weeks studded with the very phrases
which he used to me in conversation.

IV.

There can be little doubt that his slowness of mind and
unreadiness of self-expression was a determining feature of his
character. In his very first letter to Björnson, on the subject
of some trivial misconception that had arisen between them, he
says:--

> I do not deny that I can understand your suspicion;
> and I lay the blame for it, not so much on you, as on
> myself. I know that it is a defect of mine to be power-
> less to draw near in intimacy to the people to whom I
> ought to be able to reveal myself wholly and entirely.
> . . .I feel that in personal relations I have at my
> disposal only a false expression for what is in my
> inmost soul--for my real self. Therefore I prefer to
> shut it away; and that is why we have sometimes stood,
> as it were, observing each other from a distance. But
> this, or something like it, you must certainly have
> seen; otherwise your friendship for me could not have
> remained so rich and warm.

He detested untruth, and he found it impossible to express
the whole truth as to his inner self, except in poetic form;
wherefore he shut himself up in an aloofness which to some people
seemed morose and savage. "Do you know"--he writes to Björnson,
in vindicating the "earnestness" which has shaped his course
through life--"do you know that I have cut myself off for good
from my own parents, from my whole kindred, because I could not
be at rest in a relation of half-understanding?" As we read this
we think, not without a shiver, of Brand's refusal to bring
comfort to his mother on her death-bed, and ask ourselves whether,
after all, Peer Gynt was not wiser as well as kinder when he drove
the dying Aase to Soria-Moria Castle, to the castle east of the

sun and west of the moon? It is pretty clear that Ibsen sometimes put the same question to himself. To two members of his family he did write occasionally--to his favourite sister, Hedvig (the model for Hedvig in The Wild Duck), and to a half-brother of his father's. It is evident from these letters that he retained a warm feeling for his home and for the parents who had sent him out into the world at the age of fourteen. But his nature was, once for all, that of the uncompromising Brand, not of the pliant Peer Gynt; and there was probably not a little of the same unyielding mettle in the parents who had bred such a son. It is not for us to judge him, then, in this relation. He was very likely right in feeling that a half-understanding--an attempt to rub along together on the surface of things--would only have meant misery to all concerned.

It is in his relation to Björnson that his character can be best studied and will be most canvassed. Up to the end of 1867, their friendship is still warm, despite sundry interventions of "the devil in person" to make mischief between them. For instance, Ibsen seems to have thought Björnson remiss in not having averted Clemens Petersen's attack on Peer Gynt,[14] alluded to in a former quotation; but Björnson explains his conduct, and all irritation vanishes. Ibsen writes:--

> The thought of that cargo of rubbish which I un-
> loaded in my last epistle has left me, in the interim,
> not a single hour of peace or self-contentment. The
> worst thing a man can do to himself is to do injustice
> to others. . . .I read your letter again and again every
> day, and read myself free from the torturing thought
> that I have wounded you.

But even in this letter a new cloud, no bigger than a man's hand, appears on the horizon; for we find Ibsen vindicating his own principles and conduct in the matter of accepting ribbons and crosses, which are anathema to the dogmatic republican, Björnson. The cloud soon gathers volume and covers the whole sky. Only a year later, Ibsen refuses to contribute to a magazine with which Björnson's name is connected; and six months later again he writes to Brandes:--

> What you tell me of Björnson does not surprise me.
> For him only two classes of people exist: those of whom
> he can make use, and those who may stand in his way.
> For the rest, though Björnson is an excellent psycholo-
> gist in respect to his own creations, he calculates very
> badly where real people are concerned.[15]

Though Stensgaard,in The League of Youth, was not intended for Björnson, the play undoubtedly satirised Björnson's party, and

he did not hesitate to denounce it as an act of assassination
(literally, "sneak-murder"). In 1870, Ibsen thought of making a
conciliatory move by dedicating to his brother-poet a new edition
of The Pretenders; but some news (or gossip) from Christiania
caused him to abandon the design. In 1872, Björnson's political
action had become so distasteful to Ibsen that he wrote of the
Norwegian Ministry: "People who can let Jaabaek and Björnson go
at large are only fit to be locked up themselves." At that time
Björnson was still an evangelical Christian, and religious as well
as political considerations severed the former friends. Before
the appearanace of Emperor and Galilean, Ibsen believed (rightly
or wrongly) that Björnson went about denouncing it in advance as
"sheer atheism," though he had not read a line of it.

But towards the end of the 'seventies the orbits of the two
stars gradually drew together again. On the one hand, Björnson
abandoned his religious standpoint; and on the other, after the
appearance of A Doll's House, the conservatives could no longer
pretend to make party capital out of Ibsen. When the controversy
over Ghosts broke out, Ibsen wrote (January 24th, 1882): "The
only person who in Norway has openly, freely, and boldly taken up
arms for me is Björnson. That is like him. He has indeed a great
king-like mind, and I shall never forget his action." In August
of the same year, on the twenty-fifth anniversary of Björnson's
first appearance in literature, Ibsen wrote to him:--

> Your works stand in the first rank in literary
> history, and will always stand there. But if I had to
> determine what should one day be inscribed on your
> monument, I would choose these words: "His life was
> his greatest poem."

Two years later, the two poets met at Schwaz, in the Tyrol,
and their friendship was fully renewed. It would probably be too
much to say that it has since been entirely untroubled, but
malicious gossip has vastly exaggerated any little friction that
may have arisen between them. In a novel published in 1889,
Björnson paid an exquisite, though indirect, tribute to Ibsen's
genius; and when he went to congratulate Ibsen on his
seventy-fifth birthday, it is recorded that Ibsen said, with tears
in his eyes, "Thou art, after all, the man I have most loved."
(Du er dog den jeg har holdt allermest af.)

Which was to blame in the years of estrangement? Both, no
doubt, in some degree. Björnson was impulsive and reckless; Ibsen
was suspicious and apt to brood, in his loneliness, over fancied,
or exaggerated, wrongs. Björnson had too many friends, Ibsen too
few. The fundamental trouble was that Björnson, an ardent, almost
fanatical, partisan, could not understand or forgive Ibsen's
systematic refusal to cast in his lot with any party. Between two
such men it was inevitable that misunderstandings should arise;

yet one cannot but feel that, considering the manifold benefits Björnson had conferred on him, a little more patience and tolerance on Ibsen's part would not have been amiss.

One thing is clear--namely, that it was no petty literary jealousy that sundered the two poets. The people who love to read their own littleness into the minds of great men have represented that each of these two grudged the other his genius and the homage it brought him. There is not the slightest evidence of any such feeling on either side. The fact that Ibsen's fame over-shadowed Björnson's in the world at large was resented by some of Björnson's Norwegian adherents; but there is nothing to show that the poet himself shared their resentment. Their rivalry in the literary field was never other than noble.

Throughout his letters we find Ibsen notably free from the characteristic foibles of the literary man. Clemens Petersen's attack on Peer Gynt is the one criticism that stings him into what may be called personal wrath. For the rest, though he is often indignant, it is with the indignation of the exasperated satirist, not of the fretful author. George Brandes criticised Peer Gynt on its appearance almost as unsympathetically as did Petersen; of Hedda Gabler, too, he wrote in the most disparaging terms; but neither criticism made any difference in Ibsen's friendship for him. No one could ever guess from these letters that their writer had been, for ten years or so, the most furiously assailed and reprobated of European authors. He resolutely acted up to his own advice to Brandes: "Be dignified!" It was, indeed, one of the contradictions of his nature, that while intellectually an ultraradical he was temperamentally an aristocrat. This was the source of many of the seeming inconsistencies in his doctrine --inconsistencies which he would probably have said that it must be the task of the future to harmonise. His ideal was a democracy of aristocrats; and his moods of pessimism were those in which he feared that this must for ever remain a contradiction in terms.

In 1874, he wrote to Mr. Gosse that the delicacy of his (Mr. Gosse's) lyrics ought to be specially appreciated by "the English nation, whose practical efficiency is in such a wonderful way combined with a pure and noble habit of feeling, which makes it, as a whole, a nation of aristocrats, in the best sense of the word." Could he have foreseen even a few of the epithets habitually attached to his name by the English Press of the early 'nineties, he might have found something to modify in this panegyric.

IBSEN AS I KNEW HIM

(The Monthly Review, June 1906)

This is one of Archer's minatures in the art of biography (like "Ibsen in His Letters"). Published a few weeks after Ibsen's death, it was one of several essays in 1906 that Archer wrote in tribute and remembrance to the man who had most dominated his intellectual life.

I

It was in December 1881 that I first met Henrik Ibsen. He was then fifty-three years of age. His romantic plays and his dramas in verse, Brand and Peer Gynt, already lay far behind him. During the seventies he had written the vast "world-historic drama," Emperor and Galilean, and the second and third of his prose plays of modern life, Pillars of Society and A Doll's House. His name was as yet little known outside the three Scandinavian kingdoms, though A Doll's House was beginning to make its way on the German stage. He stood, in fact, on the threshold of his world-wide renown, though neither he nor any one else clearly foresaw it.

He was living in Rome, where I, too, had settled down for the winter. The desire to know the creator of Peer Gynt was not the least among the motives that had taken me thither. Though I might have procured introductions from Norway, I had somehow not thought of doing so. I trusted to meeting him at the Scandinavian Club, but found that, as a British subject, I was not eligible. The Committee, however, overcame the difficulty by making me an honorary member; and it was, in fact, in the rooms of the Club, in a sombre palazzo on the Via de' Pontefici, hard by the Mausoleum of Augustus, that I first encountered the poet.

The occasion was one of the Saturday evening social gatherings which brought together all the Scandinavians in Rome. I had been about a quarter of an hour in the room, and was

standing close to the door, when it opened, and in glided an
undersized man with very broad shoulders and a large leonine head,
wearing a long black frock coat with very broad lapels, on one of
which a knot of red ribbon was conspicuous. I knew him at once,
but was a little taken aback by his low stature. In spite of all
the famous instances to the contrary, one instinctively associates
greatness with size. His natural height was even somewhat
diminished by a habit of bending forward slightly from the waist,
begotten, no doubt, of short-sightedness and the need to peer into
things. He moved very slowly and noiselessly, with his hands
behind his back--an unobtrusive personality, which would even have
been insignificant, had the head been strictly proportionate to
the rest of the frame. But there was nothing insignificant about
the high and massive forehead, crowned with a mane of (then)
iron-grey hair, the small and pale but piercing eyes behind the
gold-rimmed spectacles, or the thin-lipped mouth, depressed at the
corners into a curve indicative of iron will, and set between
bushy whiskers of the same dark grey as the hair. The most
cursory observer could not but recognise power and character in
the head; yet one would scarcely have guessed it to be the power
of a poet, the character of a prophet. Misled, perhaps, by the
ribbon at the buttonhole, and by an expression of reserve, almost
of secretiveness, in the lines of the tight-shut mouth, one would
rather have supposed oneself face to face with an eminent
statesman or diplomatist.

He moved from group to group, exchanging a few words with
this or that acquaintance, but never engaging in any long or
animated talk. Not without trepidation, for I had heard legends
of his unapproachableness and occasional harshness, I asked the
President of the Club to introduce me. It was clear that my name
conveyed nothing to him, and this relieved me not a little; for I
had been guilty of an unauthorised adaptation of Pillars of
Society, produced (for one performance) in London some months
before; and he might, not unjustly, have resented my action in the
matter. He had, as a matter of fact, heard of the performance,
and he took my rather lame explanations in perfectly good part.
Of bearishness there was no trace in his manner; on the contrary,
it was marked by a ceremonious, old-world courtesy. He invited
me to call upon him, and my audience was over. As we parted, I
asked him when we might expect his new play. He believed it was
that very day to be published in Copenhagen.

The new play was Gengangere -- Ghosts. At that moment he was
as far as I was from foreseeing the storm of obloquy it was to
bring down upon his head, and the controversy that was to rage
around it all the world over.

I determined not to call upon him until I had read the new
play. Day after day, I worried the shopmen at Loescher's
bookstore in the Corso for the copy I had ordered; but it was
close upon Christmas before it arrived. However, I had devoured,

if not digested, it before the Christmas-Eve festival at the Club,
when my second meeting with the poet took place. Here I will
quote from a letter written the following day, merely translating
into English the phrases I had reported in Norwegian.[1]

The first thing that met my eyes when I entered the
room was the great Henrik, resplendent with all his
orders, and looking really leonine. I must say I
share a little of Björnson's objection to the orders;
but, after all, it is customary to wear them, and too
great respect for the powers that be is not, as a rule,
his weak point. I sat quite close to him at dinner,
but, unfortunately, back to back. At dessert, up got a
prosy old Dane and proposed Ibsen's "skoal," which was
drunk with enormous enthusiasm. (N.B.--I think my copy
of Gengangere is the only one which has penetrated to
Rome, except his own.) Like all the other people round,
I had the honour of clinking glasses with him, and then
he made a very short reply. He said that it was a
great pleasure to him, &c., that Christmas was usually
regarded as a season of peace, but that for him it was
often very much the reverse, since his books generally
appeared a little before Christmas. But he did 'not
believe that peace was the most desirable condition; on
the contrary, he held warfare to be more wholesome for
human nature. At the same time, it was always very
pleasant to him to find that people, however much their
points of view might differ from his, did not let that
interfere with their kindliness of feeling towards him.
That was the substance of his speech, and it did not
consist of many more words.
After dinner, as the tables were being cleared
away, I stood in the lobby talking to Fröken (Miss)
R----, who had been Ibsen's table-companion. She declares that she has the distinction of being the only
lady he ever danced with--in Bergen, many years ago.
I suggested that perhaps the honour was greater than
the pleasure, and she admitted that there was a good
deal in that. Just then Ibsen came up and shook hands
with me. The conservation turned on smoking, as he
was smoking a cigar, and offered Fröken R---- one. He
said he couldn't work without smoking--not cigars, but
a short pipe, so that you didn't know you were smoking
until it was done and you had to refill it. Then he
said people talked as if some special things were poi-
sons, and some not; but in fact there is no such thing
as poison. Certain substances, under certain conditions
and in certain quantities, do more or less harm, and

that you could say of everything. For instance, cold
water, if you come plump into it from a height, will
kill you. I thought of Peer Gynt, and his plunge from
the Gendin Edge.

Afterwards I talked a good deal with Fröken R----
about him. She said that people were very unjust to his
character, and that he himself had more than once said
to her: "You mustn't think that I am entirely heartless
and unfeeling." She said, too, that he hated to talk
about his books; that he carried his reluctance to the
point of mania. Consequently, I was rather surprised
when, further on in the evening, Ibsen came up to me,
and, after we had discussed the Ring Theatre fire, said:
"You would scarcely believe what a sensation my new play
is making in the North." He asked if I had read it, and
told me that he was getting heaps of letters every
day about it. I told him a villain in the Berlingske
Tidende had anticipated the very thing I was looking
forward to saying about it some day or other, namely,
that he had made good his promise of placing "a torpedo
under the Ark." He then said he doubted whether it
would be acted just yet, on account of its tendency. It
was always the same; when he wrote Love's Comedy there
was a great outcry, another when he wrote Peer Gynt,
another over Pillars of Society; but little by little
people got accustomed to the pieces. Just then I was
called away, and as we parted Ibsen apologised for not
having been to see me. I told him I did not for moment
expect it, but hoped he would let me call upon him. He
said I should be heartily welcome, we shook hands, und
damit basta.

My remark about the torpedo referred to a poem, "To my Friend
the Revolutionary Orator," in which Ibsen said that the only
thorough-going revolution recorded in history was the Flood. But
even that remained incomplete, for Noah seized the dictatorship.
"Let us do it again, radicals!" he concluded. "But both men and
orators will be needed for that. If you bring about a Deluge on
the face of the earth, I'll gladly place a torpedo under the Ark."
I remember to this day the look of surprise with which he received
the allusion. In that look lay the germ of his next play, An
Enemy of the People-- it was Dr. Stockmann's surprise on finding
that his demonstration of the rottenness of society was regarded
by society as something less than a cause for unmixed gratitude.
Strange as it may seem, Ibsen had not been prepared for the
tempest which Ghosts was arousing. In a few days more the
club-room was littered with papers in which critics scoffed at him
as a "pale Ghost of his former self," and poets bewailed him as
"A Fallen Star." George Brandes, I remember, was almost the only
Scandinavian critic who preserved his sanity and his courage.

A week later, on New Year's Eve, there was again a "festa" at the Scandinavian Club.   A tall, lanky, and very bald Dane, speaking in a shrill voice with a strong Copenhagen accent (unpleasing to the Norwegian ear) made himself very prominent throughout the evening, acting as a sort of self-appointed Master of the Ceremonies.   Towards midnight, after the ladies had left, the President and Secretary of the club, Ibsen, one or two other men and I sat round a table in one of the smaller rooms chatting, when this Dane came in, and began talking and laughing very loudly.   Ibsen visibly fumed for several minutes, until the Dane addressed to the President some question which I did not catch. Then Ibsen turned upon him, his eyes blazing, and thundered, "What have you to do with that?   That is a matter for the Committee." I merely asked the question," the Dane replied, and went on talking at a great rate.   Ibsen rose, muttered something very audibly about an "intolerable person!"   and left the room.   The party immediately broke up; and as we were putting on our coats in the hall, I heard Ibsen, in saying good-night to the Secretary, quote some derogatory epithet from Holberg, and apply it to "den skallede, vaemmelige genganger!"--"that bald, loathsome ghost!" This was the only occasion on which I, personally, saw his temper ruffled, though rumour tells of many others.   At the time, I thought the Dane's punishment excessive; but the Secretary told me afterwards that in "downing" him, as Johnson would have said, Ibsen had merely expressed the general sense of the Club.

II.

In those days, at the corner of the Corso and the Via della Mercede, there stood a very bright and well-managed café, known as the "Nazionale."   The Corso has since been widened at this point, and the comparatively small "Nazionale" has expanded into "Aragno's," the rendezvous of all Rome.   Entering this café on the afternoon of January 2, 1882, I observed in the inmost corner a huge, broad-brimmed wide-awake hat, and gleaming through the shadow it cast, the gold spectacles of Henrik Ibsen.   In earlier days, when he was writing Brand, at Ariccia, he was known to the peasants of the Alban Hills as "Il Cappellone," the man with the big hat; and his friends, in allusion to the lining of the said headpiece, used to call it "The Blue Grotto."   It was doubtless a successor to the original "Blue Grotto" that he was wearing, as he sipped his glass of vermouth and looked at the Illustrirte Zeitung.   I took a seat, with a friend, near the door.   Presently Ibsen rose to leave, and as he passed out he stared at me shortsightedly, without recognition.   But apparently he recalled my face on reaching the street, for in a minute or two he reopened the glass-door,   came up to my table, and entered into con-versation.   I again quote from a letter written at the time:

. . .He says he can read English with difficulty, but
his son can read it quite well; and he spoke of Gosse's
translations of some extracts from Peer Gynt.[2]   In the
course of the talk, I elicited the melancholy fact that
he has quite given up verse, so far as the drama is concerned, at any rate.   I suppose another Peer Gynt was
scarcely to be expected; but I must say I'm sorry to
hear he is entirely devoting himself to prose.[3]   Then of
course we got on Gengangere. He said "The people in
the North are terrible.   I write a play with five
characters and they insist on putting in a sixth--namely
Ibsen.   There never was a play with less utterance of
personal opinion in it."   Then he went on to say that
his idea had been to show, in Fru Alving, how a badly
educated, badly trained woman was certain to be driven,
by men of Pastor Manders' way of thought and feeling,
into opposite extremes. . . .Then I asked him right out:
"How do you figure to yourself what occurs after the
curtain falls? Does she give her son the poison or
not?"   He laughed, and said in his sort of unctuous,
deliberate drawl: "That I don't know. Every one must
work that out for himself. I should never dream of
deciding such a difficult question. Now, what do you
think?" I said that if she did not "come to the rescue"
it was no doubt the result of a genganger, a ghost,
still "walking" in her--always assuming, I added, that
the disease was ascertained to be absolutely incurable.
He said he thought the solution perhaps lay there: that
the mother would always put off and put off "coming to
the rescue," on the plea that while there is life there
is hope. . . .Then we chuckled over Ploug's remark that
it was questionable whether Oswald could inherit disease
through merely smoking his father's pipe.[4]   But here I
noticed a little thing which seems to show that the
criticisms rather gall him; for he accused Ploug of
purposely misrepresenting him, so as to gain a temporary
advantage over him, in the eyes of people who hadn't
read the play. I suggested that it was probably a mere
piece of carelessness, and he admitted it might be, but
said, what was quite true, that a critic had no business
be careless in that way.

During the next two months I saw Ibsen frequently, at his
house, at the Club, and at the Caffè Nazionale. He had a flat in
the Via Capo le Case, close to the corner of the Via Sistina. It
was, if I may use the expression, a comfortable, yet comfortless
flat--well furnished, but with no air of home about it. All his
pictures, I fancy, were packed up and lying at Munich, and he had
not even many books about, for he was never a great reader. His

writing-room was very bare and painfully orderly. It has been
reported that he kept on his writing-table various nicknacks and
little figures, which he regarded as fetishes, and without which
he could not work. I never saw anything of the kind, either in
Rome, Munich or Christiania; and photographs of his study in
Christiania confirm my scepticism.[5]

Almost every afternoon he sallied forth from his flat and
walked slowly by the Via Capo le Case and the Via della Mercede,
to the Caffè Nazionale, where he would spend an hour or so,
sometimes in looking over the German and Italian papers, more
often gazing into vacancy, and lost in thought. The dim blue
eyes, at such times, saw nothing of the cosmopolitan crowd in the
glittering cafe, but were fixed, or I am much mistaken, upon
far-off Norway and its grey "provincial" life--saw the mob
breaking Stockmann's windows, or little Hedvig slipping, pistol
in hand, into the garret where the Wild Duck lived. Six years
earlier, in an address to the Norwegian students, he had said:
"A poet is by nature long-sighted. I have never seen my homeland
and its life so clearly, so closely, or in such relief as when I
have been farthest sundered from it in space."

My friends and I used to frequent the Caffè Nazionale almost
as regularly as did Ibsen; but, of course, I did not often intrude
upon his cogitations. I find only one other note of a talk with
him in Rome, from which the following passage may be quoted:

I spoke to him about Kierkegaard,[6] and he declares
it is all nonsense to say that Brand has anything to do
with Kierkegaard. He says he always draws from models
to some degree, and that a man who formed a sort of
model for Brand was a certain Pastor Lammers. This man
went out of the State Church, taking any number of
people with him; then saw he was on the wrong track, but
neither could nor would take his followers back into
the fold, and so left them in the wilderness and came
abroad. Ibsen knew him in Dresden. However, he can't
have been by any means an exact prototype of Brand, for
Ibsen says he was full of the joy of life, went to the
theatre, and was something of a painter and musician.
Brand played the organ, but that was his only accom-
plishment, that I ever heard of. We spoke of
Turgeuneff, whom Ibsen praised highly; and as I happened
to have Une Page d'Armour with me, we discussed Zola.
Ibsen hasn't read anything of his, he says, and is inclined to undervalue him, from what he has read about
him. I was rather interested to hear this, for, of
course, the Morgenblad[7] is profoundly convinced that
Gengangere is directly inspired by the study of Zola.

To my other meetings with him in Rome I find only general references in the papers before me, but they entirely bear out my recollection of his invariable courtesy and cordiality. And here let me ask how many great writers would have given so much time and patience to a wholly irrelevant youth who had no sort of claim upon them--not even that of a formal introduction: In after years Ibsen might--indeed, he did--consider himself under some sort of obligation to me; but in those far-off Roman days he knew nothing of me except that I could more or less imperfectly express myself in his language, and had made an unauthorised and partly garbled version of one of his plays. That he could be morose and even repellent on occasion is plain from well-authenticated anecdotes; but I think his treatment of me during these first months of our acquaintance ought absolutely to acquit him of any charge of systematic or habitual churlishness. He was never a man of many words; he always spoke slowly and (as George Eliot is said to have done) under a manifest sense of responsibility; but within the limits of his phlegmatic temperament I always found him not only courteous, but genial and even communicative.

Here, too, I cannot help touching upon a more delicate subject; for to avoid it would be to lend colour to idle and malicious reports. The often-repeated stories of his over-indulgence in stimulants were, to the best of my belief, such gross exaggerations as to be practically falsehoods. My personal observation on this point is confirmed by the report of one of his oldest and most intimate friends who, some years ago, discussed his character quite frankly with me, told me many anecdotes illustrative of his peculiarities, but wholly repudiated this slander. On convivial evenings at the Scandinavian Club I have seen him drink one or two small tumblers of thin Italian wine, but no more. At the Caffè Nazionale he would slowly sip a glass or two of vermouth--the most temperate of potations. This I have observed day after day and week after week; for the amiable gossip that was current in Norway would not but make me keep my eyes open. In Germany, in Denmark, in Norway I have been with him repeatedly, have seen him evidently pursuing his daily habit in the matter of spirituous liquors, and have always noted the moderation of that habit. On one public occasion, when it was afterwards spread abroad that he had conspicuously exceeded, I both walked and talked with him, and can positively assert that there was no truth whatever in the scandal. He was certainly no teetotaler, and it is even possible that he relied on the stimulus of stimulants more than strict hygienists may consider wise; but that he was in any serious sense of the word intemperate I utterly disbelieve.

It may be said, once for all, in this connection, that, like most small communities, Norway is a hot-bed of tittle-tattle. Everybody knows everybody, and everybody knows a great deal more about everybody else than they know themselves. One has only to read Ibsen's plays to realise the prevalence and power of personal gossip. Ibsen was at one time violently unpopular in his own country; and though in his old age his fame was looked upon as a national possession, the habit of malicious and mendacious chatter about his concerns still held its ground. My brother was one day going to call upon him in Christiania, and remarked to a friend resident in the town, that if Ibsen was not at home, he hoped he might see Fru (Mrs.) Ibsen. "Oh no," said his friend, "you won't see her; she hasn't been able to live with him for years." My brother paid his call, and the first person he saw on crossing the threshold was Fru Ibsen. The incident was typical.

III.

After leaving Rome, I did not again meet Ibsen for five years. In the summer of 1887 I spent some weeks in the south of Norway, and determined to return to England by an untried route --crossing to Frederikshavn in Jutland, and then proceeding by rail to Hamburg and Flushing. On the day before I started, I saw a paragraph in a Norwegian paper to the effect that Henrik Ibsen was spending the summer at the little town of Saeby, a few miles from Frederikshavn. I telegraphed for permission to call upon him, and received a cordial answer. My impressions of that visit are noted in a letter from which I make the following extracts:

Frederikshavn is a very bright-coloured, cheerful, clean little place, and the country about it is delicious--a perfectly level sea-shore, and then, about a quarter of a mile inland, a low table-land, broken by deep watercourse, very wide for the driblets of water in the bottom of them. You see a magnificent sweep of coast, with, about seven miles southward, a projecting point on which stands a large church. This is Saeby. I found at the hotel in Frederikshavn a Norwegian business-man, a very decent old fellow, who was going to drive to Saeby. I proposed to share the conveyance, the more so as I had a Huntley and Palmer biscuit tin full of roses from A---- J---- for Fru Ibsen. The old boy consented with alacrity, and away we drove at the rate of about five miles an hour, in the queerest old trap you ever saw. It was a delightful drive--a perfect summer day, the corn ripe all round, the wild flowers brilliant, and the Cattegat dancing in the sunlight. All the way we could see Saeby Church straight ahead; and at last we rattled over a bridge, past a lovely old water-mill and into the quaint main street of Saeby--one storey houses with great high gables, all brightly painted.

The moment we were over the bridge I saw a short, broad figure ahead, in an inordinately long black frock-coat, and a tall hat made of black silk, looking far too small for the immense head. It was Ibsen, evidently on the look out for me. I stopped the trap, we greeted each other with effusion, and then he insisted that I should drive to the Hotel Harmonien, where he was staying, he following on foot. This scene proceeded to the speechless amazement of my fellow traveller, whom I had found to be a fine old stock-conservative, and had therefore not informed of my purpose in visiting Saeby. Ibsen, with his white necktie, appeared for all the world like a most respectable parson; but I am sure my friend looked at his boots to see if they were normal, and would not have been surprised if he had produced a torpedo from his coat-tail pocket, and proceeded to place it under the ark in which we were travelling. We drove into the courtyard of Harmonien, and, by the time I had settled with my companion, Ibsen arrived.

He took me up into an enormous, barely-furnished, room on the first floor, with four (if not five) windows, and two bedrooms opening off it at the back. This formed his apartment; and here we sat and talked for about an hour, until Fru Ibsen came in from a walk in Saeby Forest. I presented the flowers, which she promptly rescued from the biscuit-box, and received with enthusiasm. Indeed, they made a slendid show, and she was immensely touched by their being a "greeting from Norway." After another hour we had dinner, coffee, and cigars. Then I thought the "Old Man" would want to take his siesta, so I proposed to go for a walk in the forest and return in an hour or two. So said, so done. . . . But on my way back I lost myself in the forest, and did not reach Saeby till six o'clock. Then we had tea, or supper, and at eight I set off to walk back to Frederikshavn.

Now for a few Ibseniana. I must say, in the first place, that the "Old Man" was really charming throughout --perfectly frank and friendly, without the least assumption, or affectation, or stiffness of any sort. . . . Unfortunately, I have a morbid shrinking from talking to people about their own works, so that our conversation was, on the whole, far too much devoted to mere small-talk and (strange to say) politics, Norwegian, Danish, and Irish. However, I shall jot down a few of the things that turned up in the course of the talk.

He said that Fru Ibsen and he had first come to Frederikshavn, which he himself liked very much--he could knock about all day among the shipping, talking to the sailors and so forth. Besides, he found the neighborhood of the sea favourable to contemplation and constructive thought. Here, at Saeby, the sea was not so easily accessible. But Fru Ibsen didn't like Frederikshavn because of the absence of pleasant walks about it; so Saeby was a sort of compromise between him and her. Fru Ibsen afterwards added that the Norwegian steamers at Frederikshavn were a source of perpetual temptation to her.

For the present Ibsen is not writing anything, and hasn't been all last winter, because his time has been greatly taken up with business connected with the production of his plays in Germany. He told me, what I had already read in the Norwegian papers, that there had been a regular Ibsen controversy in Berlin--that a certain set of critics had taken to exalting him to the skies and flinging him at the head of their own poets. They won't hear even of Spielhagen[8] and Paul Heyse,[9] being (Ibsen says) very unjust to the latter--which is particularly unpleasant for him (Ibsen), as he now lives near Heyse in Munich, and they are very good friends. Ibsen's account of Heyse is that he values himself on his plays, which are weak, while he despises his stories, many of which Ibsen holds to be masterpieces. It is this increase of business in connection with his plays that now forces him to live north of the Alps --besides the fact that the S.P.Q.R.[10] have pulled down his house in the Via Capo le Case.[11] There has been a whole literature of pamphlets in the Ibsen controversy, of which he gave me one and promised to send me others.

Little did I foresee at that time how, two years later, the "Ibsen controversy" was destined to spread to England and America, and to rage for the next ten years with a virulence worthy rather of the Byzantium he had depicted in Emperor and Galilean than of the western world and the nineteenth century. He went on to tell me of the reception his plays had met with in Germany and of the repeated suppression of Gengangere by the police; but as all this is now matter of history, I omit the details. Meanwhile, he said, he was revolving plans, and hoped to have "noget galskab faerdigt til naeste aar"--"some tomfoolery ready for next year." The "tomfoolery" in question proved to be The Lady from the Sea. It was evident from all his talk that he was himself at this time fascinated by that wonder and glory of the sea which was to be the motive of his next creation. I remember straining, and overstraining, the resources of my Norwegian in an attempt to convey to him some conception of the greatness of Mr. Swinburne as a poet of the sea, and, in so far, a kindred spirit.

I tried [the letter continues] to get at the genesis of a piece in his head, but the fear of seeming to cross-examine him prevented me from obtaining any very explicit answer. It seems that the idea of a piece generally presents itself before the characters and incidents, though, when I put this to him flatly, he denied it. It seems to follow, however, from his saying that there is a certain stage in the incubation of a play when it might as easily turn into an essay as into a drama. He has to incarnate the ideas as it were, in character and incident, before the actual work of creation can be said to have fairly begun. Different plans and ideas, he admits, often flow together, and the play he ultimately produces is sometimes very unlike the intention with which he set out. He writes and re-writes, scribbles and destroys, an enormous amount, before he makes the exquisite fair copy he sends to Copenhagen.

As for symbolism, he says that life is full of it, and that, consequently, his plays are full of it, though critics insist on discovering all sorts of esoteric meanings in his work of which he is entirely innocent. He was particularly amused by a sapient person in Aften-posten[12] who had discovered that Manders in Ghosts was a symbol for mankind in general or the average man, and therefore, called Manders. He also spoke of some critic who had found the keynote of Emperor and Galilean in Makrina, a character of no importance whatever, introduced simply because it happened that Basilios had, as a matter of fact, a sister of that name.

In politics [the letter continues] he came out very strong against the "compact majority."

Here, unfortunately, I ceased to report, and branched off into discussions foreign to the present purpose.[13] One remark, however, I may be pardoned for quoting. Speaking of Ibsen as a thinker, not as a poet, I said: "He is essentially a kindred spirit with Shaw." At this time Mr. Bernard Shaw had barely heard of Ibsen's name, and The Quintessence of Ibsenism—nay, the very word, "Ibsenism"—was as yet undreamt of. Have subsequent events, then, justified my observation? Only, I think, in a very limited sense. But this earliest juxtaposition of the two names seemed worth putting on record.

IV.

Three years passed before I again saw Ibsen. In the meantime A Doll's House had been produced by Mr. and Mrs. Charrington[14] at

the Novelty Theatre, London (June 1889), English translations of
this and other plays were pouring from the press, and the
"Ibsenite" and "Anti-Ibsenite" factions were fulminating against
each other in the English and, to some extent, in the American
press.   In August 1890 I passed through Munich on my way to
Oberammergau, and spent a day with Ibsen and his wife and son. I
again quote from a letter written a few days later.

My first business in Munich, after making sure of
my seat for the Passion Play, was to call upon Ibsen. .
. .His fame in England and America is, as he says, "a
fairy-tale" to him. . . .He is obviously older, but
looks very well, and is quite alert and cheerful. He
trotted me round a vast exhibition of modern pictures,
where there is a portrait of himself by a Norwegian
named Smith--a vivid enough, but far from flattering
one. He won't go into the room where it hangs, but
waited round the corner. Just as I discovered it, an
Englishman and his wife were standing before it. The
man looked up his catalogue, and said, "Oh, that's
Ibsen, the Norwegian poet"; whereupon the lady replied
with the greatest interest, "Oh, is it? Well, now,
that's just what I should have expected him to look
like." I was tempted to tell them they need only step
into the next room to see the original; but, instead, I
reported their conversation to the "Old Man," who was
amused. Sigurd Ibsen[15] joined us at lunch, and we had a
long talk about all sorts of things--mainly about
translations and performances in England, America, &c.
You would see from Shaw's letter which I sent you
that Ibsen was supposed to be infuriated at having been
classed as a Socialist by G.B.S.[16] He explained to me,
however, that his rage existed only in the imagination
of the Daily Chronicle interviewer. What he really said
was that he never had belonged, and probably never would
belong, to any party whatsoever; but he expressed
himself as pleasantly surprised to find that English
Socialists, working on scientific lines, had arrived at
conclusions similar to his. This the Chronicle interviewer (a Berlin Jew) twisted into an expression of
unpleasant surprise that any one should have the auda-
city to make use of his name in Socialist propaganda.
The Old Man was quite put out about this, for the
thing had got into the German and Danish papers too.
While I was with him he received a letter from Vollmar,
one of the Socialist leaders in the Reichstag, and a
friend of his, asking him what the devil he meant by
this seemingly contemptuous disclaimer, not only of
Socialism, but of all sympathy with Socialism. Ibsen

had already written a letter to Braekstad,[17] intended
for the English papers; and he forthwith sat down to
write a German translation of this letter for Vollmar.
    Fru Ibsen and he had an amusing little scene
apropos of this incident. She said, "I warned you when
that man came from Berlin that you would put your foot
in it. You should have let me see him; women are much
more cautious than men in what they say." Whereupon the
Old Man smiled grimly, and said that wasn't generally
supposed to be the strong point of the sex; adding that
since the interviewer was going to lie about what he
said, it didn't much matter whether he was cautious or
not. Then Fru Ibsen suggested that he ought not to have
seen him at all, and I closed the discussion by assuring
her that in that case he would have made up the
interview entirely from his inner consciousness.

    Again, on my return from Oberammergau, I had a long chat with
Ibsen at his favourite table in the "Cafe Max," opposite the
Hoftheater, but have kept no notes of what passed. His rooms in
Munich, further down the Maximilianstrasse, were lofty and
handsome, but still, to my thinking, unattractive. He never
seemed really "at home" until I saw him in his flat in
Christiania. Of his home life I can only say that at all times I
received a most pleasing impression of it. Of the loyal devotion
of his wife and son, and their enthusiasm for his ideas, there
could not be a moment's doubt.

                              V.

    In 1891 Ibsen returned to Norway, after an absence (save for
brief visits) of more than a quarter of a century. He made
Christiania his abiding-place, and seldom left it, settling in the
new quarter on the Palace hill, first in Viktoria Terrasse, but
ultimately in Arbins Gade. It was there that, in 1898 and 1899, I
saw him again and saw him frequently.
    He had now become a European celebrity, and thousands of
tourists have seen him, and hundreds described or depicted him,
taking his daily walk down Karl Johans Gade, or sitting at his
own particular window in the cafe of the Grand Hotel. He was also
the favourite victim of the inventive newsmonger. Either in
Christiania or in Copenhagen--probably in the latter--there was a
regular manufactory of Ibsen legends. Whenever other "news" was
slack, a telegram about Ibsen's health, or about his friendships
and enmities, or about his next play, or about his "autobiography"
would be fabricated and disseminated: to be tardily followed, and
never overtaken, by an official contradiction. I would especially
warn all Ibsen-biographers against a most circumstantial story of

his illness, his "Apologia," and his relations with Björnson, purporting to be written by Dr. George Brandes, which was circulated in the autumn of 1901, and was pure invention from first to last.

In the spring of 1898 he celebrated his seventieth birthday, and a number of his English admirers, headed by Mr. Edmund Gosse, presented him with a large silver goblet, technically known as a ciborium. This gift, as he told me both by letter and by word of mouth, gave him peculiar pleasure. It occupied a place of honour in his drawing-room when I visited him in August of the same year. In his study, a bright corner-room looking out upon the palace park, I was somewhat surprised to notice, holding a very prominent position, a huge gilt-edged and brass-clasped family Bible. "You keep this close at hand," I said, pointing to it. "Oh, yes," he replied, "I often read in it--for the sake of the language." Among some fine old pictures in his study, was a large and striking modern portrait. "Who is that?" I asked. "That is Strindberg," he replied. "Oh, do you know him?" I asked, a good deal interested. "No, I don't know him at all," was the reply, "but I rejoice in that portrait. I think he looks so delightfully mad."

Of my conversations with Ibsen in these years I have only fragmentary notes. In 1898, my brother, to whom the letters above quoted from were addressed, was with me in Christiania, and shared in our talks. In 1899, it was the festivities connected with the opening of the National Theatre that took me to Norway; and though I saw Ibsen several times during those crowded days, there was little opportunity for quiet conversation.

In one of his poems, written in 1870, and entitled, "A Balloon-Letter," he had said,

> Yes, the age for Beauty hungers--
> That's what Bismarck little guesses.

He had now came to doubt whether he was right in that. Perhaps it was rather truth that the age was hungering for. But the two ideas tended, by psychological necessity, to flow together; and he could not but hope that the religious idea might one day follow suit, and blend with the idea of the true and the beautiful, into something different from any of those ideas as they at present exist. This course of thought--though he did not seem to realise it at the moment--runs exactly parallel with his transition from romanticism to realism, and from that again to a poetic elevation bordering on mysticism.

He spoke of the mission which the Government had assigned him in his youth, to travel through the country and collect folksongs. As a matter-of-fact, he picked up no folk-songs at all, but brought back a store of folk-tales--all told him by one man, however. On the other hand, he gathered many impressions,

which afterwards used in Brand. He came to one valley where the
parsonage had just been destroyed by an avalanche. The pastor and
his wife were living in one room of a peasant's house. The wife,
who had just given birth to a child, occupied a screened-off
corner, while the husband transacted all the business of the
parish in the remainder of the room. The scenery of Brand was
mainly suggested to him by a side valley off the Geiranger Fjord
--the Sunnelvsfjord, I think he said. He also spoke of coming
down from the Jotunfjeld at a place where he looked straight down
upon a steeple in the valley hundreds of feet below, and could
see no possible way of descent. It appeared, however, that there
was a path cut in the face of the precipice, and by this he made
his way down, in company with a Catholic priest and a sick woman
tied on to a horse.

He wrote Brand and Peer Gynt (which appeared with only a
year's interval between them) at very high pressure, amounting to
nervous overstrain. He would go on writing verses all the time,
even when asleep or half awake. He thought them capital for the
moment; but they were the veriest nonsense. Once or twice he was
so impressed with their merit that he rose in his night-shirt to
write them down; but they were never of the slightest use. At
Ariccia he used to get up at four or five in the morning and go
for a long walk; then, when he came back, he was in good trim for
writing.

He began Peer Gynt at Ischia and finished it at Sorrento. He
set to work upon it with no definite plan, foreseeing the end,
indeed, but not the intermediate details. For instance, he did
not know that Peer was to go to Africa. "It is much easier," he
said, "to write a piece like Brand or Peer Gynt, in which you can
bring in a little of everything, than to carry through a severely
logical (konsekvent) scheme, like that of John Gabriel Borkman,
for example."

I had often heard him confess to a great distaste for seeing
his own plays on the stage. This time he went more at large into
his reasons. "I have quite definite conceptions," he said, "of my
own characters, and the actors come between me and those
conceptions, in some cases permanently distorting or obscuring
them." It was one of the drawbacks to the various festivals that
had been held from time to time in his honour--in Berlin,
Meiningen, Copenhagen, Stockholm, &c.--that he was always expected
to sit out one or more of his plays. I was reminded of Dr.
Schlenther's account of the first production of Ghosts in Germany,
at the Augsberg Stadttheater.[18] Ibsen was present, whether at the
dress-rehearsal or at the performance I do not remember. He sat
with a friend in the stalls, and throughout the performance kept
on pinching his companion and ejaculating, "Oh! oh!" in apparent
agony, varying the exclamation at some points--as when Regina made
her entrance in peasant costume--with an emphatic "Oh, nein!"
English and American stage-managers please note!

It was true, he said, that he had for a time entertained some idea of writing a sort of literary autobiography--an account of the external circumstances, and the conditions of thought and feeling, that had generated each of his works. The upshot would have been--so he believed, at any rate--a demonstration of the continuity and consistency of his process of development. But he had put the idea aside, and was now (1898) maturing the scheme of a new drama. "I have turned the characters out to grass," he said. "I hope they will fatten." In 1899 he told me that the play was nearly finished, and that he thought of calling it A Dramatic Epilogue--a sort of summing-up, I understood him to imply, of the work of his later life. That play was--alas!-- When We Dead Awaken.

On September 1, 1899, Ibsen and Björnson sat side by side in the place of honour at the opening of the Norwegian National Theatre. That night crowned the life-work of the two men. They had created a national drama which had gone forth over all the world; and here at last it had found a fitting home in their own country which they had so loved--and chastened. A few days later, I parted from Ibsen for the last time, at his house in Arbins Gade. Punctilious as ever in his courtesy, he accompanied me to the outer door and we shook hands on the threshold. Nearly twenty years had passed since I first saw him in the dim old Roman salon; and in all that time, whether in speech or writing (though we had had business relations not quite without complexity) I had met with nothing but kindness, consideration, and cordiality at his hands. What I said I do not remember, but doubtless it was not the right thing. The right thing to have said was very plain. Thinking of all that I owed to the poet and the man, I should have used the simplest and most comprehensive of the formulas of gratitude in which Norwegian abounds, and said to him, "Tak for alt," or "Thanks for all."

IBSEN'S CRAFTSMANSHIP

(Fortnightly Review, July 1906)

> This essay picks up at the point where "Ibsen's
> Apprenticeship" left off: Scribe's influence
> on Ibsen. It carries the analysis of Ibsen's
> craftsmanship through the well-made play to
> Ibsen's own mastery of his retrospective
> technique. For Archer, who sees a progressive
> movement in the prose drama toward the "new
> method" of Ghosts and subsequent plays, the
> turning point is A Doll's House. In the last
> act Ibsen finally breaks with the well-made
> play, "almost at a definite line on which one
> can lay one's finger."

In a former article in this Review[1] I examined the repertory
of the Bergen Theatre during the six years of Henrik Ibsen's
connection with it, and showed that, in the exercise of his
functions, he must have closely studied some seventy-five French
plays, most of them belonging to the then dominant school of
Eugène Scribe. I suggested, very briefly, that the influence of
these studies was apparent in all his plays (except the three
dramas in verse), from Lady Inger right down to A Doll's House.
In that play, as it seemed to me, he finally outgrew and cast off
the domination of the French school; but he would never have been
the master-technician he ultimately became had he not first
learnt, and then deliberately unlearnt, the formal dexterities of
Scribe and his disciples. I now propose to illustrate a little
more fully this reading of the history of his technical
development.

It is no longer necessary to insist on the fact that Ibsen
was a consummate craftsman. In the days when the great Ibsen
controversy raged throughout Europe, the hostile critics declared his work to be childishly simple, regarding it, apparently,
as a sort of eccentric improvisation. No one now doubts that
its seeming simplicity is only the mask of a complexity beyond all
precedent. Ibsen's dialogue is a marvellously-adjusted mosaic,

in which every tiniest tessera has its definite and carefully-studied function. But this art of adjustment is not so much an invention as a development. We can trace its growth through play on play. And it distinctly grew out of that delicacy in the adjustment of external incidents which Ibsen acquired in the school of Scribe.

Perhaps it may not be altogether misleading if we put the matter thus: Scribe's contribution to theatrical technique was the art of constant movement.[2] Every scene and almost every speech of his plays shook the kaleidoscope and brought about a more or less marked and interesting change in the fortunes or relations of his characters. He led the spectator through a continuous series of small "peripeties," and thus kept his attention, his interest in the process of events, constantly on the alert. He never allowed three minutes to elapse without some marked alteration, more or less surprising, or exciting, or moving, or entertaining, in the posture of affairs. This art of external movement Ibsen acquired and practised in his earlier plays. In The League of Youth he exercises it very much as Scribe himself would have done. But, as play follows play, he gradually applies it more and more deliberately to different ends, until at last, instead of external movement, it is psychological movement on which he is intent. With him, too, the pattern, the posture of affairs, is never stationary; but the changes take place in the souls of the actors, and are often scarcely discernible in their external fortunes and relations until the final catastrophe is reached. Movement, in fine, is the secret of Ibsen's theatre, as it is of Scribe's; but the movement is spiritual instead of material.

Of the plays of his Bergen period I have spoken in the article referred to above. Let me only say here that the most remarkable of them, Lady Inger, though it contains all the germs of his future greatness, is so clearly prentice-work that it might almost be taken for a caricature both of German romanticism, with its grave-vaults and coffins, and of French intrigue, with its mistakes of identity brought about through the careful abstinence of all concerned from reasonable clearness of expression.

In The Vikings at Helgeland (1858)--the first play he wrote after leaving Bergen--Ibsen had made an extraordinary technical advance. He aimed at, and he achieved, something of the stern simplicity of the sagas from which he took his material. The tragedy grows, indeed, out of an incredible mistake of iden-tity--a mistake which, in the earliest, mythical form of the legend, is brought about by supernatural means. Ibsen, eschew-ing supernatural agency, places the thing on the plane of romance. Sigurd's personation of Gunnar in the killing of the bear and carrying-off of Hjördis is an incident to be conven-tionally accepted, just as we conventionally accept the dis-guises and substitutions of one person for another which abound in

Elizabethan drama. But in The Vikings this mythical or ultra-romantic motive is placed outside the frame of the play. It has occurred years before the action opens, and thus taxes our credulity far less than if it were "subjected to our faithful eyes." It is one of those initial postulates which, according to Sarcey's famous maxim (a corollary to the Horatian principle), we are always ready to accept without cavil.[3] Apart from this postulate, the action of The Vikings is entirely logical, and is carried forward without trickery of any sort. The supremely pathetic situation of the second act arises, no doubt, from a misunderstanding of Örnulf's purpose in setting forth in pursuit of Kaare; but the misunderstanding is natural and even inevitable; it was not in Örnulf's character to be explicit as to his intentions. The soliloquy, too, is almost suppressed, for Hjördis's mutterings in the third act are little more than the ejaculations which in fact are often wrung from us by strong emotion. There are, indeed, two extremely inartistic "asides" in the final scene--Dagny's "So bitterly did she hate him!" and Gunnar's "Then after all she loved me!" But these are worse than merely technical flaws; they are symptoms of the romantic-sentimental psychology which is still dominant in the play. Taking it as a whole, one may almost say that the technique of The Vikings is in advance of its substance. The French principle of change, of movement, is realised with little or no resort to French artifice. It seems as though Ibsen had already assimilated what is good, and rejected what is bad, in the technique of Scribe.

But this is a fallacious appearance. Ibsen eschews artifice, not because he theoretically rejects it, but because he feels it to be out of keeping with the heroic simplicity of the characters and manners he is delineating. When we pass to The Pretenders, in itself an immeasurably greater work, we find him falling back without a qualm upon all the methods of French intrigue-spinning.

To realise what Scribe and his school had done towards the subtilising of the dramatic mechanism, we need only compare The Pretenders with one of Shakespeare's, or even of Schiller's or Oehlenschlager's, historical plays. Here is a theme of which all the elements are present in Shakespeare's histories--rival pretenders to the throne, turbulent nobles of either faction, a crafty churchman undermining the temporal power in the interest of his order. How, then, would Shakespeare have treated it? He would have been content to take from Snorri Sturlasson, as he did from Holinshed, a few episodes suitable for rhetorical expansion, and to string them loosely together, perhaps with a comic underplot still more loosely attached to them. However dramatic in its individual scenes, his plays would have been essentially epical in its general form. Now a certain amount of the epical element is doubtless discernible in Ibsen's play. It has not the absolute unity and concentration of, say, the Oedipus Rex, or of

Rosmersholm, or even of The Vikings. But its complex interweaving of motive and event is totally foreign to the technique of historical drama as it was understood before the days of Scribe and Dumas. Everywhere we have a sense of nice measurement and forethought, the winding up of springs, the fitting of wheel into wheel, the careful adjustment of balance and counterpoise. It is, in brief, a very elaborate mechanism with which we have to deal, involving, on the designer's part, a totally different order of effort from that which went to the making of an Elizabethan chronicle-play, or any modern play on the same model, such as Tennyson's Becket or Queen Mary. I am not asserting superiority on either side. I am only registering a difference, and a difference which would not have existed, at any rate in the same degree, had not Ibsen studied in the school of the French mechanicians.

It is especially in this play, indeed, that Ibsen proves himself a master of intrigue, by drawing a master of intriguers. Bishop Nicholas is a cunning dramaturge, a sort of ecclesiastical Scribe, who pulls the strings of the action to further his own sinister purposes. Partly out of pure malevolence, and partly in the interests of the Church, he is determined that no king shall sit secure on the throne of Norway, and to that end he plays, by a hundred artifices, upon the characters of the rival pretenders, King Haakon and Duke Skule. His death scene, in which he devotes the last energies of his being to the construction of what he calls a perpetuum mobile to keep the King and the Duke irreconcilably at strife, is an extraordinary instance of the intimate blending of intrigue with character-study. It is a marvel no less of psychological than of constructive subtlety; and the soliloquy in which the Bishop first conceives the idea of his perpetuum mobile is notable as a perfect definition of the very art which the poet himself was exercising throughout the play.

It may be said that we have a counterpart to the fusion of the play of character with the play of intrigue, not in Shakespeare's Histories, but in Othello. This is true, in a sense; but beside Bishop Nicholas, Iago is a veritable bungler in villainy. We forget the clumsiness of his wiles in the masterly dialogue of that incomparable third act; but every unprejudiced critic has recognised that his happy-go-lucky machinations do not in the least deserve to succeed, and are, in fact, predestined to the discovery which overtakes them. Bishop Nicholas's subtleties are ten times subtler, and he dies triumphing in the completion of his perpetuum mobile. His character, as a whole, is much more complex and more profoundly studied than Iago's, but that is nothing to my present purpose. What I wish to point out is that the mere intrigue of The Pretenders is handled with a dexterity to which, even in Othello, his masterpiece in this kind, Shakespeare makes no pretension. Bishop Nicholas outmanoeuvres Iago, because he has learnt his tactics in the school of Scribe.

It is to be noted that Ibsen found in history only the barest hints for the Bishop's character. The whole invention and elaboration is his own. He elaborated it in that form, because he found in himself the requisite virtuosity for the piecing together of a complex mechanism; and at the same time he made this virtuosity subserve, in Haakon and Skule no less than in the Bishop himself, a power of character-projection and analysis far beyond the range of his French models. The worser side—the artificiality—of the French technique is felt chiefly in the miraculous exactitude with which incidents, probable enough in themselves, are made to occur at the very moment when dramatic effect requires them. Just when Haakon feels the need of Vegard Vaeradal's support, the news of Vegard's death is brought to him. Just when Bishop Nicholas is chuckling over the non-appearance of the document which proves or disproves Haakon's legitimacy the document arrives. Just as Haakon is wondering what has brought the wrath of heaven upon him, his mother appears to remind him of his harshness to her. Just as Skule is yearning for the love and trust of a son and successor, the son, of whose existence he had not dreamed, comes knocking at his door. This method of, so to speak, giving the cue for each turn of fortune, is an artificiality which it took Ibsen long to outgrow.

In The Pretenders the soliloquy is freely employed. If it occurred merely in the Bishop's death-scene it might be defended as a touch of realism, for the old man's feverish exaltation would very probably find vent in spoken words. But both Skule and Haakon soliloquise at points where no such defence can be urged. These are the last instances in Ibsen's prose plays of the purely conventional soliloquy. Oddly, enough, he does not employ it in Emperor and Galilean, in which his technique is, for the rest, sufficiently melodramatic. He deals largely in spectacular surprises and contrasts, and even presents us with the well-worn operatic effect of two choruses chanting alternately a pagan paean and a Christian dirge. But the architecture of this giant drama would demand a study all to itself.[4] I must hasten on to an examination of the plays of modern life, which began in 1869 with The League of Youth.

If Francisque Sarcey could have seen The League of Youth before he was prejudiced against Ibsen by his later works, he would certainly have found it a piece after his own heart—a little languid perhaps in the first and third acts, but in the second, fourth, and fifth a model of the "well-made play." Every detail confirms this classification. Half the action hinges upon misunderstandings and mistakes of identity, or, in the jargon of French criticism, on "quiproquos." The misconception on which the splendid comedy of the second act is based, and several of the minor misunderstandings, are brought about by that vagueness of expression, that sedulous care not to mention names, which is one of the stock devices of French comedy. A forged document is made to pass through almost as many adventures as the "scrap of paper" in Les Pates de Mouche.[5] Stensgaard and Bastian Monsen, both wishing to propose to Madam Rundholmen, both do so in writing (for no particular reason), and each (for no particular reason) gives his letter to Aslaksen to deliver. Then, when Stensgaard changes his mind, and determines to deliver his letter himself, Aslaksen mixes the two up and hands him Bastian's letter instead of his own. All this is so deftly managed that, in the rush of the action, we are scarcely conscious of its artificiality; but a moment's reflection shows us that it comes, not from life, but from mid-century French comedy. Who is not familiar with the scene in which Stensgaard, making a proposal to Madam Rundholmen on behalf of Bastian Monsen, does it in such ambiguous terms that she thinks he is wooing her on his own account? There is no more favourite device in the whole repertory of farce-effects. It was not in its first youth when Dickens employed it in Pickwick. Every detail in the structure of the play tells the same tale --Ibsen is simply using in masterly fashion the tools provided for him, as for Europe at large, by the French playwrights of the school of Scribe.

It is evident, too, that he still conceives comedy as a sort of game which neither author nor audience must be expected to take too seriously. This appears particularly in the way in which the end is patched up. As soon as Stensgaard has run the gauntlet of rejection by all three ladies to whom he has made his mercenary advances--as soon as he has been dismissed with contumely, in a scene which resembles a symmetrical dance-figure rather than any conceivable episode in real life--the rest of the characters beam with smiles, and proceed to fall into one another's arms. The Chamberlain forgives his son, who has forged his name, and, reversing the whole policy of his life, goes into partnership with him. His rebellious daughter-in-law, Selma, is reconciled to her husband; Daniel Heire abandons his law-suits; even Aslaksen is invited to sit at the Chamberlain's table; and the moral of the comedy is formulated in what may almost be called a set "tag." The whole thing has been a storm in a teacup. It has blown over; everyone (except Stensgaard) is the wiser and the better for it; and they are all going to live happily for ever afterwards. We are even provided with the statutory "love interest," though it takes a subordinate place. Dr. Fieldbo, the entirely reasonable and sympathetic personage (the first and last in Ibsen's modern plays), after wandering through the action in sententious superiority, is rewarded with the hand of Thora Bratsberg. All this complacent conventionality acts as a sort of oil to the cogs and cranks of the mechanism, and comes from the same emporium.

If I were asked to name the perfect model of the well-built play of the French school, I should not go either to Augier or Sardou for an example, but to Ibsen's Pillars of Society. In

symmetrical solidity of construction, complexity combined with
clearness of mechanism, it seems to me incomparable. Yet at the
same time I should call it by far the least interesting of all
the works of his maturity.

In one respect it shows him very distinctly feeling forward
towards his later method. In The League of Youth the whole of the
action passed, so to speak, within the frame of the picture.
Nothing depended on the bygone history of the characters. What
little we learn of Stensgaard's, Heire's, Selma's antecedents
comes in quite incidentally, and is not in the least necessary to
our comprehension of the story. In Pillars of Society, on the
other hand, what is presented on the stage is only the second half
of a drama, the first half of which was enacted fifteen years
before the rise of the curtain. The action, in fact, consists
almost entirely in the gradual revelation of the truth concerning
a series of begone events. More and more, as time goes on, does
this become Ibsen's formula. His characters are occupied in
raising curtain after curtain from the past, in probing deeper
and deeper towards some hidden truth; and as soon as this is
reached and realised, they are on the brink of the catastrophe.
It has been said, not without justice, that Ibsen's later plays
are all retrospect and catastrophe; and it has, with equal
justice, been pointed out that, in so far as his method is identical
with that of Sophocles in the Oedipus Tyrannus.

In Pillars of Society, as I have said, he is only feeling his
way towards the "retrospect and catastrophe" formula. A good deal
of action within the frame of the picture, or, in other words, of
intrigue, is created by the fact that the principal character,
Karsten Bernick, energetically, and even by criminal devices,
struggles against the elucidation of the past, thereby
approaching in some measure to the villian of ordinary melodrama.
When the formula is more fully developed (as in the typical
instance of Rosmersholm) the process of elucidation, once begun,
proceeds by such inevitable degrees that no one dreams of
struggling against it. Veil after veil is torn from the face of
truth as though by some invisible, ineluctable destiny. There is
a sense of fatality in the air which accentuates the kinship
between Ibsen and the tragic poets of antiquity.

All the complex threads of the action in Pillars of Society
are interwoven with astonishing clearness. In the nice adjustment
of motive and incident, the play may hold its own with such
masterpieces of intrigue as Scribe's Adrienne Lecouvreur and
Sardou's Fedora. In its structure it belongs entirely to this
school; it is in matters unconnected with structure--for instance,
in the masterly scene of casuisty between Bernick and Rorlund in
the fourth act--that Ibsen's true originality manifests itself.
In some respects, moreover, he is still under the influence, not
only of Scribe, but of the French Romanticists. He is still
intent on what may be called the external irony of picturesque

antithesis. For instance, it is while the streets are illuminated in his honour, and while a torchlight procession of his fellow-citizens is approaching to do him homage, that Karsten Bernick learns of the flight of his son in the coffin-ship which he himself is sending to sea. This is the sort of effect which Victor Hugo loved and would have applauded. Its somewhat cheap emphasis is very foreign to Ibsen's later manner.

It need scarcely be pointed out, too, that in _Pillars of Society_ Ibsen has not outgrown the convention of the happy ending. In _The League of Youth_, essentially a light comedy, the perfunctoriness of the close does not trouble us. But when, in _Pillars of Society_, Olaf is brought safe home, and Bernick, converted in the crisis of emotion, makes a clean breast of his misdeeds and proclaims himself a reformed character, we feel that Ibsen is not yet taking his art quite seriously. He still holds with Scribe that the business of the dramatist is not to obey psychological necessity, but to invent plausible means of evading it, in the interests of popular optimism.

It is in _A Doll's House_ that he finally breaks with French tradition, and breaks with it, one may say, almost at a definite line on which one can lay one's finger. The first two acts, and the first half of the third act, are thoroughly French in method. First we have the confidante, Mrs. Linden. She has a certain character of her own, for Ibsen could not, if he would, draw a mere lay figure. But she and her character do not belong to the spiritual essence of the play. Her function is mechanical. She has to listen to Nora's confidences, in order that we may overhear them; and she has to influence the upshot of the action by soften the heart of Krogstad. She is external, if I may so phrase it, to the psychological chemistry of the action. She serves, now as a rod to stir the mixture, now as a ladle to skim it; but she has no part in the chemical process itself. In Ibsen's later plays, you will scarcely find another charcter of the slightest prominence to whom this description applies.

The long scene between Nora and Mrs. Linden constitutes a formal exposition of that part of the action—a good half—which lies outside the frame of the picture. It ends with Nora's cry, "Oh, what a wonderful thing it is to live and to be happy!"—and instantly there comes a ring at the bell, and Krogstad's shadow falls across Nora's glee. Here we have an instance of the old traditional irony; a case of Nemesis in miniature; an exclamation of happiness giving the cue for the entrance of disaster. Again, a little further on, we have the same antithesis in a heightened form. Nora, romping with her children, is so absorbed in the game, that when Krogstad comes to strike the fatal blow at her happiness, he actually stands amongst them before she is aware of his presence. An admirable stage-effect this is, no doubt, and introduced most skilfully and naturally. But in the light of Ibsen's later method, one sees that it is of the stage, stagey.

Such so-called "dramatic" conjunctures do, no doubt, occur in life; but as the dramatist sees deeper into the inexhaustible wealth of essential drama in the human soul, he is less and less tempted to concern himself with surface accidents such as this.

Krogstad reveals to Nora the true import of her action in signing her father's name, and leaves her a prey to terror which she strives in vain to shake off. And here mark the ingenuity with which Krogstad's own delinquency is made to throw a lurid light upon Nora's. In a scene which forms a sort of counterpart to that between Bernick and Rörlund before alluded to, Nora tries to find comfort in getting Helmer to say that Korgstad's offence was not unpardonable; but he, little dreaming what is at stake, merely hammers the nail deeper into her soul. This scene (the last scene of the first act) is manipulated with the utmost skill, but produces an unmistakable effect of artificiality. Note, for instance, Helmer's remark, "Nearly all cases of early corruption may be traced to lying mothers." We cannot but echo Nora's question" "Why--mothers?" We feel that Ibsen here gives the conversation a slight twist, a little kink as it were, which is not absolutely unnatural, indeed, but is too clearly designed to dot the i of the situation. Again, Nora's withdrawal of her hand when Helmer says, "It gives me a positive sense of physical discomfort to come in contact with such people," is merely an old stage trick turned outside in. Sardou, too, had he written the scene, would infallibly have made Nora say, "How warm it is here!" That is the established remark for a character who wishes to dissemble great mental perturbation.

The second act, as we all know, culminates in the famous tarantella-scene--a crowning and final instance of that striving after picturesque antithesis which is as old in drama as Euripides at least, but is specially affected by the French romantic playwrights and their Spanish progenitors. There is no more favourite antithesis than that of revelry and horror--witness the marble guest appearing at Don Juan's orgie, or the Miserere in Lucrèce Borgia extinguishing the mirth of the doomed roysterers. The analogy between these scenes and that of Nora's tarantella may not at first be apparent; but a little examination will show that Ibsen simply screws up the effect a peg or two by making the contrast between gaiety and horror no longer lie in the mere inert juxtaposition of the two elements, but in Nora's active assumption of feverish merriment in order to mask her resolve of suicide. Reduce the scene to its bare formula--a woman dancing on the brink of the grave--and you see how ultra-romantic, how Spanish, how Hugoesque it is. But it is not merely in the actual tarantella-scene that Ibsen strives for this effect of antithesis. That scene is only the culmination of an antithesis running through the whole play. He has deliberately selected the season of Christmas festivity to form a radiant background to the horror of Rank's doom and Nora's agony. While Nora is learning from

Helmer the true import of her innocent felony, she is mechanically
decking a Christmas-tree with candles and tinsel. While Rank is
telling her that the clutch of death is at his heart, she is
preparing her masquerade dress. In the last act, as the sense of
impending disaster deepens, we hear the gay rhythms of the
tarantella from the ball-room above. Nora enters with the dread
of death in her eyes, and decked out in the parti-coloured dress
of an Italina contadina. Throughout there runs this strain of
insistent antithesis—the familiar medieval antithesis of the
rose-wreathed skeleton, the Dance of Death. There is something
theatrical about it, almost operatic, which even the exquisite
skill of the manipulation, and the wealth of character and meaning
compressed into the conventional framework, cannot quite disguise.
It is admirable in its kind, but the kind is not the highest.
    The following sentences from an American criticism of A
Doll's House, written when the play was first produced in New
York, are exactly typical of a hundred English criticisms
published about the same time. "The piece under consideration,"
says the critic, "is almost totally devoid of dramatic action.
There is only one really dramatic incident, and that occurs when
Nora dances a tarantella. All the rest is words. It is seldom
that such a cataract of vapid talk has been let loose in a
theatre." With unerring instinct, this gentleman lays his finger
on the most strained, unnatural, in a word theatrical, effect in
the play, and calls it the only dramatic incident. But now mark
a curious point.   This tarantella scene, with all its
theatricality, is hardly ever effective on the stage. I have seen
many Nora's, first and last, and four of them very remarkable
actresses: Fru Hennings, who originally created the character in
Copenhagen; the incomparable Eleonora Duse; Madame Réjane; and our
own Miss Achurch. But I have never seen any actress attain an
effect in the tarantella-scene at all proportionate to the effort.
People applaud, of course—they will always applaud a dance—but
it is the dance they are thinking of, not the situation. The
scene is disappointing, just as so many scenes of great external
picturesqueness are disappointing on the stage—the idea dwarfs
the reality. It is so obviously, so aggressively, theatrical,
that we expect from it a greater thrill than it can ever give us.
    Well now, is it not curious—is it not significant—that
immediately after this passage of violent theatricality, not to
say staginess-immediately after he has wrung the last dregs of
effect out of his apparatus of Christmas-tree, masquerade, tinsel,
and tarantella—Ibsen should suddenly, at a given moment, throw
it all aside, never to be taken up again, and end this very play
in the strain of pure drama, sober and searching, devoid of all
mechanical accessories and antithetic fripperies, to which he ever
afterwards adhered? There is a point where Nora, after Helmer has
"forgiven" her, goes off the stage into her own adjoining room,
and when Helmer asks her what she is going to do, replies, "To

take off my masquerade dress." At that point, as it seems to me, it was Ibsen himself who, consciously or unconsciously, threw off all masquerade. He put away from him whatever was external and mechanical in the French technique. He had mastered and done with it. In Pillars of Society, and now in the first two acts of A Doll's House, he had developed the method of Scribe, on a line parallel to that of Sardou, and had reached a point about even with that at which Sardou has remained stationary. He had—to employ a somewhat grotesque image—danced his tarantella, and was henceforth to apply to soberer and more artistic purposes the skill, the suppleness, in a word the virtuosity he had thus acquired. When Nora, in her every-day clothes, confronts the astonished Helmer and says, "It's not so late yet. Sit down, Torvald; you and I have much to say to each other," it is the true Ibsen, of his latest and greatest period, that for the first time appears on the scene.

When I first saw A Doll's House acted, in Christiania, the Nora was a neophyte of no great talent, and the effect of the play, up to the middle of the third act, came far short of my expectations. The tarantella especially fell very flat; but indeed the action, as a whole, did not at all "grip" me as it had in reading—until the point was reached where Nora and Helmer sat down, one on each side of the table, with the lamp between them, to make up the accounts of their matrimonial bankruptcy. Then the drama seized and held me as in a vice, and every phrase of Nora's threnody over her dead dreams, her lost illusions, thrilled me with an emotion such as I had never before experienced in the theatre. I was then a quarter of a century younger than I am now, and was not in the least biassed by any technical theories. I was perfectly content with the Scribe-Sardou formula, and went to the theatre predisposed to condemn this final scene, inasmuch as it set that formula at defiance. It was no theoretical, pumped-up rapture that seized me—indeed, it took me utterly by surprise. Nor do I now mean to say that the scene is unassailably excellent. I think it is an extreme example of psychological compression. Nora has attained, in a crisis of twenty minutes, an intellectual clearness with regard to her position, which, as a matter of fact, she would scarcely have acquired in months of reflection. But though the scene is open to criticism in many respects, I take it to be the first clear example of that power in which lies the peculiar greatness of Ibsen's later plays—the power of impregnating thought with emotion, and making psychological analysis palpitate with dramatic interest. Other dramatists give us patches of analysis, interludes of thought, scattered throughout an action which exists independently of them, and which, from the strictly technical point of view, they merely cumber and delay. In Ibsen, at his best, the psychology and the action are inextricably interfused; the psychology is the action; and he has the art of unfolding the soul-history of his personages with such cunning gradations, such vivid surprises, such lightning-like flashes of clairvoyance, that his analysis has all the thrill of adventure, all the fascination of romance.

When we contrast the stern, severe simplicity of Ghosts, with the shimmering artificiality of A Doll's House (up to the final scene) we cannot but feel that between the two plays a revolution occurred. My own conjecture is that the revolution actually occurred during the composition of A Doll's House. I cannot help thinking that Ibsen originally designed the play to have a "happy ending," like that of The League of Youth or Pillars of Society, and that Mrs. Linden's influence over Krogstad was invented and adapted to that end. Then, I take it, as his work advanced, the poet himself began to realise the higher possibilities of his art, renounced the trickery of the "happy ending," and, in the final scene, made the first essay of the new powers which he felt to have developed within him. Ghosts, the first play written entirely under the new method, showed him not yet quite at his ease with it. Majestic, impressive though it be, it is a little too simple, a little heavy in its handling. Then the poet relaxed the tension in an admirable comedy, An Enemy of the People. If we compare it with its predecessor in a similar key, The League of Youth, we cannot but recognise an enormous artistic advance. Then comes that terrible tragi-comedy, The Wild Duck, a work almost as far ahead of A Doll's House in creative potency as A Doll's House itself is ahead of, say, Still Waters Run Deep. But if I am asked what I take to be Ibsen's technical masterpiece, I reply with very little hesitation, Rosmersholm. That marvellous play seems to me flawless in structure. It has all the closeness of texture of the earlier, and all the poetry of the later, plays. Ibsen's very greatest period, I take it, extended from The Wild Duck to The Master Builder, inclusive, though the middle play of this group, The Lady from the Sea, falls somewhat below his highest level. After The Master Builder, we can trace a little relaxation of mental fibre, in the fact that he lays foundations which seem somewhat out of proportion to the superstructure he raises upon them. He did nothing--absolutely nothing--more masterly from a purely dramatic point of view than the first act of Little Eyolf or the second act of John Gabriel Borkman; but in the conclusion of both these plays the lyric poet gets somewhat the better of the dramatist. And yet--after all--I am inclined to think that this is merely the inevitable consummation of the process of evolution I have tried to suggest. In breaking away from the French formula, which is, with all its merits, essentially prosaic, Ibsen was merely setting free the poetical element in his genius. When the poet of Brand and Peer Gynt produced The League of Youth and Pillars of Society, it was indeed a case of Apollo serving in the house of Admetus. Having learned all that that bondage could teach him, he finally cast it off in the last scene of A Doll's House, and in each of his later plays gave freer scope to the divinity within him.   It is reported that when someone asked him how he wrote his plays, he answered, "I take an incident from life within my own experience or knowledge; I throw in a little poetry; and that's how it's done!"   A very simple recipe, if only you happen to be Henrik Ibsen.

IBSEN'S IMPERIALISM

(The Nineteenth Century, Feb. 1907)

In this analysis of Emperor and Galilean,
the play that Ibsen worked on longest and
considered his masterpiece, Archer explains why
this "world-history drama," as Ibsen called
it, reveals a dramatist undone by metaphysics.
Archer's argument, although basically in accord
with those recent critics who have found an
Hegelian philosophy at work in Ibsen's drama,
does not support the view that this play bene-
fitted by its historical philosophy.   For
Archer, the imperialism of the idea of a "World
Spirit" hindered rather than helped Ibsen.

It is said that Henrik Ibsen, even towards the end of his
life, regarded Emperor and Galilean, a World-historic Drama, as
his masterpiece; and, whether this be so or no, there is ample
evidence in his letters that at the date of its completion (1873)
he held that opinion.   I doubt whether any critic of repute has
ever been found to agree with him.   It has been recognised from
the outset that, while the First Part of the great double drama is
full of vigour, colour, and movement, the Second Part is languid,
fragmentary, and more like a rather long-drawn historical romance
than a drama properly so called.   Even in the Second Part there
are magnificent patches of imaginative work; but the general
effect is one of effort, and effort of a rather cheap kind.   We
feel that, while the play is not very dramatic, it is distinctly
and insistently melodramatic.
    An examination of its development in the poet's mind, and of
its relation to its historic sources, reveals a curious reason for
this difference in style and effect between the two parts.   In the
following pages I shall attempt to show that, just as he was about
midway in its composition, Ibsen was seized and mastered by a
"world-historic" idea which impelled him, in the Second Part, if
not to alter his view of the character of his hero, at any rate to

belittle him by treating him as the pitifully purblind instrument
of an overruling destiny. This idea, as I understand it, was a
sort of imperialism--a belief in the efficacy of large political
or racial aggregates in promoting that "revolution of the spirit
of man" to which he looked for the salvation of the world.
That this idea was very clearly thought out, or that it was
successfully brought into harmony with his other ideas, I do not
contend. But we have the plainest evidence for the fact that it
took hold on him, and dominated his thought, during the years when
he was giving its final form to Emperor and Galilean.

The play was conceived during the first months of Ibsen's
first residence in Italy, in 1864; but it was put aside for six
years, while he wrote Brand, Peer Gynt, and The League of Youth.
In the autumn of 1870, while living in Dresden, he seriously
attacked the theme, and on the 18th of January, 1871, he wrote to
his publisher, Hegel,[1] that the First Part was finished. But this
"First Part" was not the five-act play we now possess, under the
title of Caesar's Apostasy. At that time he thought of making a
trilogy of the work; and the First Part referred to in this
letter to Hegel was a three-act play entitled Julian and the
Philosophers. No doubt it substantially corresponded with the
first three acts of Caesar's Apostasy, and ended with Julian's
elevation to the rank of Caesar. At that time (January 1871)
the poet hoped to have the whole play ready for the printers by
June. As a matter of fact, he took more than two years over what
he expected to complete in six months. In July 1871 he wrote to
Hegel, asking for more historical documents as to the career of
Julian--"It is facts that I require." At the same time he said:
"This book will be my chief work. . . .That positive view of the
world which the critics have so long been demanding of me they
will find here." Up to August of the following year (1872) he
still wrote of the play as being divided into three parts: Julian
and the Philosophers, three acts; Julian's Apostasy, three acts;
and Julian on the Imperial Throne, five acts. It is not clear at
what date he determined to fuse the six acts of the first two
plays into the five acts of the play we actually possess. The
announcement of this alteration first occurs in a letter to Hegel,
of February 1873, informing him of the completion of the whole
work.

It was in 1872 that Ibsen made, by correspondence, the
acquaintance of Mr. Edmund Gosse;[2] and to him he wrote in October
of that year:

> I am working daily at Julianus Apostata, and. . .am
> putting into this book a great part of my own spiritual
> life. What I depict I have, under other forms, myself
> gone through; and the historic theme I have chosen has
> also a much closer relation to the movements of our own
> time than one might at first suppose.

In a somewhat later letter to Mr. Gosse, he says: "I have
kept strictly to history. . .and yet I have put much self-anatomy
into this book." In the same key he wrote to his friend Ludvig
Daae immediately after the completion of the play: "There is in
the character of Julian. . . more of my own spiritual experience
than I care to acknowledge to the public."

Now let us note the exact day on which Ibsen told Hegel that
Julian and the Philosophers was completed, that he was hard at
work on the Second Part, and that he hoped to have all three parts
finished in six months. The day was the 18th of January, 1871
--the very day on which, at Versailles, King William of Prussia
was proclaimed German Emperor. That this event, and all that it
stood for, made a deep impression on Ibsen, we know on his own
authority. In 1888 he wrote to the Danish-German scholar Julius
Hoffory:

> Emperor and Galilean is not the first work I wrote
> in Germany, but doubtless the first that I wrote under
> the influence of German spiritual life. . . .During my
> four years' stay in Rome I had merely made various his-
> torical studies and taken sundry notes for Emperor and
> Galilean. I had not sketched out any definite plan, and
> much less written any of it. My view of life was still,
> at that time, national Scandinavian, wherefore I could
> not master the foreign material. Then, in Germany, I
> lived through the great time, the year of the war and
> the development which followed it. This brought with it
> for me, at many points, an impulse of transformation.
> My conception of world history and of human life had
> hitherto been a national one. It now widened into a
> racial conception, and then I could write Emperor and
> Galilean.

This puts it beyond doubt that a marked change of mental attitude
must have occurred during the actual composition of the play. We
know that before the day on which the imperialisation of Germany
became an accomplished fact--and therefore long before it was
possible for the poet to realise and take home to himself the
historic lessons of that event--the three acts of Julian and the
Philosophers were already written, and good progress made with
Julian's Apostasy. But when we next hear of the play, six months
later, we find that, far from being finished, it has apparently
made little or no advance. What has he been doing in the
interval? He has been, I suggest, readjusting his mental attitude
in the light of the "world-historic" events of which he is an
absorbed spectator.

In a letter to Hegel he speaks explicitly of "the growth of
the idea during the process of composition." At the end of the
six months of apparent inactivity we find him calling out (rather

late in the day, one would think) for facts. The inference is
that hitherto he has been poetising more or less freely on a
comparatively slight historic basis, but that his new idea
involves a closer sifting of the documents. And this inference is
fully borne out by a study of the play in its relation to history.
To put it broadly, but not, I think, unfairly: the First Part (as
it now stands) is true to the spirit of history, but not to the
letter, while the Second Part is true to the letter, but not to
the spirit. For the actual events, the individual scenes, of the
First Part, there is no historic foundation, except in the case of
the military insurrection which forced Julian to assume the
purple. Apart from some unimportant rearrangements to chronology,
the other events are such as may quite well have occurred, but
there is no evidence that they did actually occur. When we pass
to the Second Part, on the other hand, we find it a mere mosiac of
incidents and expressions taken bodily from the documents. Here
there is practically nothing fictitious save the fictions of the
ecclesiastical historians. Yet the general impression conveyed by
the Second Part is as false to history and unjust to Julian as the
general impression conveyed by the First Part is just and true.

In saying this, however, I am somewhat anticipating my
argument. All I have hitherto proved is that between January and
June 1871--that is to say, between the practical completion of our
present First Part and the commencement of the Second Part--a
momentous change of spirit and of method did as a matter of fact
take place. The First Part, no doubt, would afterwards be in some
degree modified in the light of later conceptions; but the changes
were certainly not sufficient to obscure the spirit in which it
was originally conceived, or to render it homogeneous with the
Second.

It is to be noted that not until after the six months' gap
between January and July 1871 does Ibsen announce to Hegel that
the play will contain "that positive view of the world which the
critics have so long been demanding." What, then, was that
"positive view"? It can have been nothing else than the theory
of the "third empire" which is to absorb both paganism and
Christianity, and is to mark, as it were, the maturity of the
race, in contrast to its pagan childhood and its Christian
adolescence. The theory is most clearly formulated in the scene
betwen Julian and Maximus at the end of the third act of the
Second Part, of which this is the essential portion:

    JULIAN. Who shall conquer? The Emperor or the Gali-
       lean?
    MAXIMUS. Both the Emperor and the Galilean shall suc-
       cumb.
    JULIAN. Succumb----? Both----?. . .
    MAXIMUS. Hear me, brother and friend of truth! I say
       you shall both succumb--but not that you shall

perish.

Does not the child succumb in the youth, and the youth in the man? Yet neither child nor youth perishes.

Oh, my best-loved pupil--have you forgotten our colloquies in Ephesus about the three empires?

JULIAN. Ah, Maximus, years have passed since then. Speak!

MAXIMUS. You know I have never approved your policy as Emperor. You have tried to make the youth a child again. The empire of the flesh is swallowed up in the empire of the spirit. But the empire of the spirit is not final, any more than the youth is. You have tried to hinder the growth of the youth, to hinder him from becoming a man. Oh, fool, who have drawn your sword against that which is to be--against the third empire, in which the twin-natured shall reign!

That this conception was no passing one, but was fundamental with Ibsen, is proved in many ways, but chiefly, perhaps, in a speech he delivered in Stockholm in 1887, fourteen years after the completion of Emperor and Galilean, in which he said:

I have sometimes been called a pessimist; and, indeed, I am one, inasmuch as I do not believe in the eternity of human ideals. But I am also an optimist, inasmuch as I fully and confidently believe in the ideals' power of propagation and of development. Especially and definitely do I believe that the ideals of our time, as they pass away, are tending toward that which, in my drama of Emperor and Galilean, I have designated as "the third empire." Let me therefore drain my glass to the growing, the coming time.

The analogy between this theory and the Nietzschean conception of the "Overman" need not here be emphasised.[3] It is sufficient to note that Ibsen had come to conceive world-history as moving under the guidance of a Will which works through blinded, erring and sacrificed human instruments, toward a "third empire" in which the jarring elements of flesh and spirit shall be reconciled.

It may seem like a play on the word "empire" to connect this concept with the establishment in January 1871 of a political confederation of petty States, compared with which even Julian's "orbis terrarum" was a world-empire indeed. But there can be no doubt that in Ibsen's mind political unification, the formation of large aggregates inspired by a common idea, figured as a preliminary to the coming of the "third empire." Of this there are many evidences. In no other sense can we read the letter to

Hoffory above quoted, or the letter to George Brandes in which he says:

> Only entire nations can join in great intellectual movements. A change of front in our conception of life and of the world is no parochial matter, and we Scandinavians have not yet got beyond the parish-council standpoint. Nowhere do you find a parish council anticipating and furthering the third empire.

In a later letter to Brandes (Munich, 30th of October, 1888) he says: "I began by feeling myself a Norwegian. I then developed into a Scandinavian, and now I have come to rest in collective Germanism." To the same purpose runs one of his commonplace-book reflections, recently brought to light; it is undated, but was evidently written before 1871: "We laugh at the four-and-thirty fatherlands of Germany; but the four-and-thirty fatherlands of Europe are equally ridiculous. North America is content with one, or--for the present--with two." Perhaps it may not be quite fanciful to find an evidence of the persistence of this habit of thought in the fact that the poet's last public utterances should have taken the form of protests against one-sided sympathy with the Boers in the South African war.

"But Julian," it may be said, "represented precisely this ideal of political cohesion which was revived in the unification of Germany; why, then, should Ibsen, in writing the second play, have (so to speak) turned against his hero?" Incidentally and by inheritance, Julian did indeed stand for Empire; but that was not the idea which animated his life. What he aimed at was, in effect, the maintenance of unnumbered local cults, in opposition to the spiritual unity which was the ideal, fiercely and intolerantly pursued, of the Christian Church. It was this very claim to universal validity that Julian could least endure in the doctrine of the Galileans. True, he was himself a monotheist in the Neo-Platonic sense. The gods were to him only emanations or symbols--departmental representatives, as it were--of God. This highly compressed statement does great injustice to the subtlety of this metaphysic, but is sufficiently accurate for the present purpose. It is not quite clear to us, and it was very likely not quite clear to Julian himself, whether he believed in the objective existence of the divinities he worshipped. Probably he did not; yet M. Gaston Boissier, a high authority on such a point, writes: "Je n'oserais pas dire avec autant d'assurance que M. Naville que l'anthropomorphisme lui est tout à fait étranger."[4] Be this as it may, he regarded the finite deities of polytheism as indispensable forms through which alone the human mind could contemplate or commune with the infinite; and he was quite willing that every nation or tribe should approach God through the gods to whom their fathers had paid homage. His own "Hellenism" he regarded as a very superior form of religion, but not as exclusively valid. He may have hoped that--with the improvements he sought to introduce into it, most of them borrowed from Christianity--it would ultimately spread even to the barbarians. But his tolerance of barbarian cults (such as the Jewish worship of Jehovah) was not only sincere--it was a fundamental element in his thought. Had Christianity been content to be a religion he would have seen no objection to it; what he would not suffer was its intransigent claim to be the religion. But Ibsen had come to think of this spiritual imperialism as precisely the most necessary step towards the realisation of the "third empire." A loose political unity could be of little avail without the spiritual fusion implied in a world-religion. It was Julian's tragic error to oppose this fusion; or rather, he was chosen as the "third great freedman under necessity" to give the final demonstration of the impotence of religious nationalism. Christianity, as it existed in the fourth century, possessed a metaphysic very similar to that of Neo-Platonic polytheism, and certainly in no way inferior; it possessed a greatly superior ethic; it opposed to the anarchy of paganism a highly-developed organisation and power of ecclesiastical discipline (both of which Julian attempted to imitate); and, above all, it possessed the inestimable advantage of offering for worship no mere symbols or figures of speech, but a historic divinity whose human character, as distinct from his theological functions, was eminently capable of exciting devotion and enthusiasm. That Julian should have set himself up against a religion thus equipped for world-conquest was, in Ibsen's eyes, a crime against the light, but a crime predestined to make the light shine forth the more irresistibly.

Since Julian's failure, however, was the most conspicuous and unalterable fact in the historical data, it may seem that Ibsen must from the outset have intended some such conclusion to his work as that which he actually gave it, and that the events of 1871 can at most have lent greater precision to ideas which must all along have been in his mind. But is this so certain? Ibsen could not make Julian succeed; but was it necessary to make him fail so pitiably and almost ignobly? Or, to bring the matter to a more definite point, is the Julian of the Second Part really the same man as the Julian of the First Part?

There may, indeed, be no irreconcilable contradiction between the two phases of Julian's character; yet one cannot but feel, I think, that in the Second Part the poet's attitude towards him has entirely changed. In the First Part he is in the main heroic, with moments of weakness; in the Second Part, he is in the main contemptible, with moments of heroism. The ultimate secret of this change is probably to be sought in Ibsen's repeated assertion, to Mr. Gosse and other correspondents, that he has "put into the book a part of his own spiritual life," and that "there is in the character of Julian more of his own spiritual experience than he cares to acknowledge to the public."

In what sense can he mean this? Every dramatist, of course, draws upon the potentialities of his own soul for many of the traits which he gives to his characters. Mr. Meredith declared to Robert Louis Stevenson that he found his Sir Willoughby Patterne mainly in his own breast;[5] and similarly Ibsen said that Brand represented the higher side, and Peer Gynt the lower side, of his own nature. That, in this sense, something of Julian came from within, is doubtless true; but as all the leading traits of his character came from without--from history, anecdote, invective, and above all from his own writings--he certainly could not be called a mere self-projection of the poet, as an entirely fictitious personage might be. In this sense, then, Ibsen can scarcely have meant his reiterated remark. Its truth, in this sense, would have been limited and not worth emphasising. What he meant, I suggest, was that he had himself gone through the same rebellion against Christianity--against book-worship, death-worship, other-worldliness, hypocrisy, intolerance--which he has portrayed in Julian. He had seen (in Rome) the ruins of the ancient world of light and glory sicklied o'er with the pale cast of mediaevalism; and he had sympathised to the full with Julian's passionate resentment against the creed which had defamed and defaced the old beauty in the name of a truth that was so radically corrupted as to be no longer true. Julian, then, as he first conceived the play, was to be the poet's own mouthpiece (within the limits imposed by his dramatic instinct), and to proclaim unequivocally what Carlyle would have called his "Exodus from Houndsditch."[6] He was to fail, indeed; but his failure was to be represented as a world-catastrophe. In the light of this conception, the First Part was planned and in great measure written. But then intervened the new idea, the spiritual imperialism, if I may so express it, arising out of the events of 1870-71. Further study of detail showed that the secret of Julian's failure lay in the hopeless inferiority of the religion he championed to the religion he attacked. That religion, with all its corruptions, came to seem a necessary stage in the evolution of humanity; and the poet asked himself, perhaps, whether he, any more than Julian, had even now a more practical substitute to offer in its place. In the concept of the "third empire" he found the keystone to his arch of thought, to which everything else must be brought into due relation. He re-wrote (it seems probable) the scene of the symposium at Ephesus (Part I., ACT III.) in order to emphasise this idea; and it entirely dominated and conditioned the whole of the second play.

But what was the effect of this concept? It was to make Julian a plaything in the hands of some power, some implicitly postulated World-Will, working slowly, deviously, but relentlessly towards a far-off, dimly-divined consummation. Christianity, no doubt, was also an instrument of this power; but it was an instrument predestined (for the moment) to honourable uses, while its opponent was fated to dishonour. Thus the process of the Second Part is a gradual sapping of Julian's intelligence and power of moral discrimination; while the World-Will, acting always on the side of Christianity, becomes indistinguishable from the mechanical providence of the vulgar melodramatist.

Whatever we may think of the historical or philosophical value of the theory of the "third empire," there can be little doubt that its effect upon the play has been artistically disastrous. It has led Ibsen to cog the dice against Julian in a way from which even a Father of the Church might have shrunk. He has not only accepted uncritically all the invectives of Gregory and the other Christian assailants of "Antichrist," but he has given to many historic events a fictitious twist, and always to Julian's disadvantage.

It would need a volume to apply to each incident of the Second Part the test of critical examination. I must be content with a rough outline of the distorting effect of the poet's preoccupation with his "world-historic" idea.

In the first place, he makes Julian much more of a persecutor than even his enemies allege him to have been. Nothing is more certain than that Julian was sincerely convinced of the inefficacy of violence as a means of conversion, and keenly alive to the impolicy of conferring upon his opponents the distinction of martyrdom. Tried by the standards of his age, he was a marvellously humane man. Compared with his uncle Constantine, his cousin Constantius, and his brother Gallus--to go no further back among wearers of the purple--he seems like a being of another race. It is quite true, as his enemies allege, that his clemency was politic as well as humane; but, whatever its motives, it was real and consistent. Gregory, while trying to make him out a monster, explicitly and repeatedly complains that he denied to Christians the crown of martyrdom. Saint Jerome speaks of his blanda persecutio, persecution by methods of mildness. The worst that can be alleged against him is a lack of diligence in punishing popular outrages upon the Christians (generally of the nature of reprisals) which occurred here and there under his rule. That he incited to such riots is nowhere alleged, and it is difficult to judge whether his failure to repress them was due to malicious inertia or to actual lack of power. The policing of the empire cannot have been an easy matter, and Julian was occupied during the whole of his brief reign in concentrating his forces for the Persian expedition. It cannot be pretended that his tolerance rose to the pitch of impartiality. He favoured pagans, and he more or less oppressed Christians; though a considerable part of his alleged oppression lay in the withdrawal of extravagant privileges conferred on them by his predecessors. In his attempt to undo some of the injustices that Christians had committed during their forty years of predominance--such as the seizure of temple glebes and so forth--he was doubtless guilty, on his own account, of more than one injustice. Wrong breeds wrong, and in a time of religious dissolution and reconstruction equity is always at the mercy of passion, resentment, and greed. There was even, in some of Julian's proceedings, a sort of perfidy and insolence that must have been peculiarly galling to the Christians. It would not be altogether unjust to accuse him of having instituted against the new religion a campaign of chicanery; but that is something wholly different from a campaign of blood. The alleged "martyrdoms" of his reign are few in number,[7] are, for the most part, recounted by late and prejudiced authorities, are accompanied by all the manifestly fabulous details characteristic of such stories, and are none of them, with the smallest show of credibility, laid to the account of Julian himself.

But what is the impression we receive from Ibsen? We are given to understand that Julian drifted into a campaign of sanquinary atrocity, full of horrors as great as those recorded or imagined of the persecutions under Decius and Diocletian. It is made to seem, moreover, that he was personally concerned in some of the worst of these horrors. We are asked to conceive his life as being passed with the mingled shrieks and psalms of his victims ringing in his ears. He is made to gloat in imagination over their physical agonies. ("Where are the Galileans now? Some under the executioner's hands, others flying through the narrow streets, ashy pale with terror, their eyes starting from their heads," &c.) He is haunted in his last hours by ghastly visions of whole troops of martyrs. Moreover, his persecutions are made particularly hateful by the fact that they either fall upon or threaten his personal friends. The companion of his childhood, Agathon (a fictitious personage), is goaded by remorseless cruelty to that madness which eventually makes him the assassin of Anti-christ. Gregory of Nazianzus is first made (what he never was) Julian's most cherished comrade, and is then shown as doing what he never did--playing a noble and heroic part in personally defying the tyrant. Mad and monstrous designs are attributed to Julian, such as that of searching out (with the aid of tortures) and destroying all the writings of the Christians. This trait appears to be suggested by a letter from Julian to the Prefect of Egypt, enjoining him to collect and preserve all the books which had belonged to George, Bishop of Alexandria:

> He had many of them concerning philosophy and rhetoric, and many that contained the doctrines of the impious Galileans. I would willingly see the last-named all destroyed, if I did not fear that some good and useful books might, at the same time, by mistake be destroyed. Make, therefore, the most minute search concerning them. In this search the secretary of George

may be of great help to you. . . .But if he try to
deceive you in this affair, submit him to the torture.

It is needless to remark upon the difference between a
rhetorical wish that all the Christian books in a particular
library might be destroyed, and an actual attempt to annihilate
all the Christian writings in the world. Thus not only are
clearest evidences of Julian's abstention from violence
disregarded, but all sorts of minor incidents are misrepresented
to his disadvantage.

A particularly grave injustice to his character meets us
almost on the threshold of the Second Part. The execution of the
treasurer, Ursulus, by the military tribunal which Julian
appointed on coming to the throne is condemned by all historians
and was regretted by Julian himself. No doubt he was culpably
remiss in not preventing it; but Ibsen, without the slightest
warrant, gives his conduct a peculiarly odious character in making
it appear that he deliberately sacrificed the old man to his
resentment of a blow administered to his vanity in the matter of
the Eastern ambassadors. There is nothing whatever to connect
Ursulus with this incident.

The failure of Julian's effort to rebuild the Temple of
Jerusalem is a matter of unquestioned history. It is impossible
now to determine, though it is easy to conjecture, what natural
accidents were magnified by superstition into supernatural
intervention. But what does Ibsen do? He is not even content
with the comparatively rational account of the matter given by
Gregory within a few months of its occurrence. He adopts Ammian's
later and much-exaggerated account; he makes Jovian (who had
nothing to do with the affair) avouch it with the authority of an
eye-witness; and, to give the miracle a still more purposeful
significance, he represents it as the instrument of the conversion
of Jovian, who was to be Julian's successor, and the undoer of his
work. Under ordinary circumstances, this would be a quite
admissable rearrangement of history, designed to save the
introduction of another character. But the very fact that the
poet is throughout the play so obviously sacrificing dramatic
economy and concentration to historic accuracy renders this
heightening of the alleged miracle something very like a
falsification of evidence. It arises, of course, from no desire
to be unjust to Julian, for whom Ibsen's sympathy remains
unmistakable, but from a determination to make him the tragic
victim of a World-Will pitilessly using him as an instrument to
its far-off ends.

But this conception of a vague external power interfering at
all sorts of critical moments to baffle designs which, for one
reason or another, it disapproves, belongs to the very essence of
melodrama. Therefore the incident of the Temple of Jerusalem
brings with it painful associations of The Sign of the Cross;[8] and

still more suggestive of that masterpiece is the downfall of the temple of Apollo at Daphne, which brings the second act of the Second Part to a close. Here the poet deliberately departs from history for the sake of a theatrical effect. The temple of Apollo was not destroyed by an earthquake, or in any way that even suggested a miracle. It was simply burnt to the ground; and though there was no evidence to show how the conflagration arose, the suspicion that it was the work of Christians cannot be regarded as wholly unreasonable.

An incident of which Ibsen quite uncritically accepts the accounts of Julian's enemies is his edict imposing what we should now call a test on the teachers in public (municipal) schools. This was probably an impolitic act; but an act of frantic tyranny it certainly was not. Homer and Hesiod were in Julian's eyes sacred books. They were the scriptures of his religion; and he decreed that they should not be expounded to children, at the public expense, by "atheists" who (unless they were hypocrites as well) were bound to cast ridicule and contempt on them as religious documents. It is not as though Christians of that age could possibly have been expected to treat the Olympian divinities with the decent reverence with which even an agnostic teacher of to-day will speak of the gospel story. Such tolerance was foreign to the whole spirit of fourth-century Christianity. It was nothing if not intolerant; and the teacher would have been no good Christian who did not make his lessons the vehicle of proselytism. There is something a little paradoxical in the idea that tolerance should go to the length of endowing the propagation of intolerance; and it is sheer absurdity to represent Julian's measure as an attempt to deprive Christians of all instruction, and hurl them back into illiterate barbarism. He explicitly states that Christian children are as welcome as ever to attend the schools.

As the drama draws to a close, Ibsen shows his hero at every step more pitifully hoodwinked and led astray by the remorseless World-Will. He regains, towards the end, a certain tragic dignity, but it is at the expense of his sanity. "Quos deus vult perdere prius dementat."[9] Now there is no real evidence for the frenzied megalomania, the Casarenwahn,[10] which the poet attributes to Julian. It is not even certain that his conduct of the Persian expedition was so rash and desperate as it is represented to have been. Gibbon (no partisan of Julian's) has shown that there is a case to be made even for the burning of the fleet. The mistake, perhaps, lay not so much in burning it as in having it there at all. Even as events fell out, the result of the expedition was by no means the greatest disaster that ever befell the Roman arms. The commonplace, self-indulgent Jovian brought the army off, ignominiously indeed, but in tolerable preservation. Had Julian lived, who knows but that the burning of the ships might now have ranked as one of the most brilliant inspirations recorded in military history?

It would be too much, perhaps, to expect any poet to resist the introduction of the wholly unhistorical "I am hammering the Emperor's coffin," and "Thou has conquered, Galilean." They certainly fell in too aptly with Ibsen's scheme for him to think of weighing their evidences. But one significant instance may be noted of the way in which he twists things to the detriment either of Julian's character or of his sanity. In the second scene of the fifth act, he makes Julian contemplate suicide by drowning, in the hope that, if his body disappeared, the belief would spread abroad that he had been miraculously snatched up into the communion of the gods. Now Gregory, it is true, mentions the design of suicide; but he mentions it as an incident of Julian's delirium <u>after</u> his wound. Gregory's virulence of hatred makes him at best a suspected witness; but even he did not hold Julian capable of so mad a fantasy before his intellect had been overthrown by physical suffering and fever.

Thus from step to step, throughout the Second Part, does Ibsen disparage and degrade his hero. It is not for me to discuss the value of the conception of the "third empire" to which poor Julian was sacrificed. But one thing we may say with confidence --namely, that the postulated World-Will does not work by such extremely melodramatic methods as those which Ibsen attributes to it. So far as its incidents are concerned, the Second Part might have been designed by a superstitious hagiologist, or a melodramatist desirous of currying favour with the clergy. Nay, it might almost seem as though the spirit of Gregory of Nazianzus--himself a dramatist after a fashion--had entered into Ibsen during the composition of the play. Certainly, if the World-Will decreed that Julian should be sacrificed in the cause of the larger imperialism, it made of Ibsen, too, its instrument for completing the immolation.

THE TRUE GREATNESS OF IBSEN

Lecture Delivered By

William Archer at University College, London

(Edda, 1919)

This was Archer's last attempt to provide a
perspective on Ibsen's greatness. By 1919
Ibsen was of course recognized as one of the
great writers of the modern age, but the view
of him as a social prophet persisted, and this
Archer tried, once again, to prove wrong.
Ibsen's ideas, he argues here, were in many
ways commonplace. The greatness comes from
Ibsen's understanding and representation of
human character, his ability to portray
character in dramatic action. So, more than
anything else, this essay is an argument
against Ibsenism, an argument that began
twenty-eight years earlier when Archer re-
sponded to Shaw's The Quintessence of Ibsenism.

Not long ago I came upon an article in the Times Literary
Supplement which began thus:

At all times is going on a struggle between certain
opposing principles. Among the confused sounds issuing
from the melee, one catches certain names, the rallying-
cries of the combatants, and among such of late
Nietzsche's, just, as some time ago, Darwin's, Ibsen's
or Tolstoy's.

Now most of you, I dare say, see nothing at all surprising in
these words; nor do I pretend that they actually surprised me.
But had I read them thirty years ago instead of the other day, I
should certainly have said to myself, "Ibsen! What on earth is

Ibsen doing in this company! Is Ibsen also among the prophets?"
I know as a matter of fact--indeed few people know better--that
Ibsen actually figures in men's minds as one of the tub-thumpers
of the world--a vendor of ideas, of doctrines, of social and
spiritual patent-medicines. But what I want to suggest to you
to-day is that this is precisely the great mistake people have
made about Ibsen. He has in no way deserved to be glorified--or
crucified--between Tolstoy and Nietzsche. Tolstoy, a very great
man,--in fecundity of creative genius greater, no doubt, than
Ibsen--was at the same time a preacher, a vendor of views. He
was actually the promulgator of a religion. Nietzsche, a very
great madman--probably the greatest that ever lived,--was nothing
if not a propounder of notions. But Ibsen was something quite
different. What religion can you get out of Ibsen? A vague sense
of the mystery of existence--nothing more. He makes his
characters talk about God because men do talk about God--they
think in terms of God--and to portray men while omitting this
characteristic would be like painting them without noses. But if
anyone can extract from all Ibsen's works his personal belief
about God or about man's relation to the unseen, all I can say is
that he or she can see further through a millstone than I can. As
for ideas, there are no doubt some general ideas in Ibsen's works.
There is the idea, for instance, that opinions, prejudices,
superstitions cling to us and hamper our conduct long after they
are really dead; that all truth and wisdom do not necessarily
reside with the compact majority; that if a man wants to ennoble
the world, he had better begin by ennobling himself. But did it
need any great genius to enunciate these ideas? Are they not
rather truisms, to which we can all yield assent the moment they
are uttered? Could any man attract the world's attention, or
arouse vehement hostility and partizanship, on the strength of
such discoveries as these? Assuredly not! Have they anything in
common with, for instance, Tolstoy's idea of the duty of
non-resistance or Nietzsche's distinction between master-morality
and slave-morality? I don't think you will tell me that they
have. Why, then, has Ibsen come to be reckoned among the
hot-gospellers? I suggest that it is by a curious critical
blunder. It is not an incomprehensible blunder--on the contrary,
it is easily accounted for--but I think it is time that any
serious student of Norwegian literature should try to divest his
mind of it.

     What was Ibsen, then, if not a great and original thinker?
He was a great poet, and, more specifically, a great dramatist.
That is what people either do not realise or insist on forgetting.
He is not the only poet to suffer in the same way. How many
hundreds of volumes have been written on Shakespeare's ideas and
opinions--his religion and his philosophy--from not one of which
would you ever learn that he had touched the summits of man's
achievement both in pure poetry and in that peculiar form of

imaginative creation which we call drama. What does it matter
what a man's ideas and opinions are, if he can write A Midsummer
Night's Dream and the third act of Othello, can create Hamlet and
Falstaff, and can make Cleopatra say:

> Show me, my women, like a queen; go fetch
> My best attires: I am again for Cydnus
> To meet Mark Antony. Sirrah Iras, go.
> Now, noble Charmian, we'll dispatch indeed;
> And when thou hast done this chore I'll give
>   thee leave
> To play till doomsday.

There you have character in a moment of crisis, uttering
itself, under a noble convention, coeval with the dawn of mimetic
art, in the choicest words a great imagination can supply. You
have, in short, drama in its most consummate expression; and when
a man can produce that, the profundity of his personal ideas, the
merits of what we call his "message", are matters, if not all
together indifferent, at all event of quite subordinate
importance.

To return, then, to Ibsen: It was not in the least a great
discovery that opinions, prejudices and superstitions cling to us
like burrs long after all real vitality has gone out of them: but
it was a great achievement to bring home to us the tragic
consequences of that familiar fact in one of those highly
condensed presentations of a crisis in human experience which give
us the peculiar and poignant emotion inseparably characteristic of
great drama. In Mrs. Alving Ibsen created a living, breathing
woman, revealed to us her life-history and the development of her
character (always under the stringent conditions of his most
exacting art form), and made her, out of the depth of her
experience, conjure up, and give consummate expression to, the
immortal image of Ghosts. In other words, he gave to a
sufficiently commonplace idea poetic life and form; and in that
poetic life and form lies the essential quality, the true
greatness, of his work.

So, too, the fact that the edicts of the ballot-box do not
sum up all virtue and wisdom, was the very reverse of an
epoch-making revelation. It was very well known in Athens and in
Rome; it was the first assumption of at least half of the
political philosophy of the world; even in the most democratic
countries, there were always devil's advocates, like our own
Carlyle, who took a mischievous delight in showing up the seamy
side of democracy. What Ibsen did with this old idea was to
embody it in a delightful comedy, full of the raciest human
nature; while at the same time he showed a mental grasp far
superior to Carlyle's in making Stockmann no reactionary, no
believer in the political virtues of either autocracy or oligar-

chy, but rather the prophet of a larger enlightenment, a democracy which should love, honor and obey its spiritual pioneers, instead of stoning and casting them out.

Not quite such a commonplace was the idea that the reformer of the world or of his nation ought to begin with reforming himself; yet it was far from being a novelty. I remember, for instance, an essay by that half-forgotten poet, James Thomson (B. V.),[1] the author of The City of Dreadful Night, which expounds, in a paradoxical vein, a new and simple recipe for producing a perfect world--namely that each of us should forthwith proceed to make him- or herself perfect. What Ibsen did with the idea, in Rosmersholm, was to give it poetic form of extraordinary nobility and beauty, in one of the tensest, most closeknit, most intricately elaborated dramas ever produced on this planet.

Here then lies the true greatness of Ibsen which I would urge you to study, to realise and appreciate. He is a great creator of character, and a great deviser of those conjunctures of circumstance in which character most vividly reveals itself under the conditions of stage representation. It may one day, perhaps, be recognised that his ideas, far from being the strength of his work, are its chief weakness. It cannot be denied that he seldom created quite freely. His studies of life are not wholly objective and dispassionate. There can be no doubt, for instance, that--to take a very clear case-- An Enemy of the People was inspired by the tempest of execration with which Ghosts was received. Stockmann is a dramatic adumbration of Ibsen himself, hooted and boycotted for telling inconvenient and unpalatable truths. Thus the play is in some measure a fable, one might almost say an allegory. The idea which disengages itself is not a mere by-product, but rather the germ of the whole construction. In so far as this is generally true of Ibsen's plays, it probably implies--or, shall we say, it implies according to the critical orthodoxy of the moment--a point of inferiority to such absolutely free creation as we find in Shakespeare. No Shakespearian critic will deny that, whatever general ideas may be discovered in Hamlet or Othello, in The Merchant of Venice or Henry IV, they are only by-products, and in no case the nucleus round which the drama has crystallised. Shakespeare did not say to himself, "Go to, I will illustrate such-and-such a moral or political thesis," and to that end devise the fable of Macbeth or Lear. In so far as general ideas did precede and condition the invention and development of Ibsen's plays, we may perhaps say, "the less Shakespeare he." But we do him the very gravest injustice if we fail to recognise that his creative genius almost always threw off the trammels of generalisation and moralisation, and produced, no mere illustrative apologue, but a living, pulsing work of art. The fable is generally there, but only in his weaker moments does it obtrude itself. And no one will ever extract from Ibsen the true, the intense, enjoyment he is capable of giving, who cannot disregard the element of fable, and centre his attention upon the pure drama--the presentment of character in action, always powerful and arresting, and elaborated, in some of his finest creations, with a technical virtuosity which I do not hesitate to call unique.

May I illustrate my point by going back--a very long way back--to the time of my first introduction to Ibsen? He swam into my ken when he was just about the middle of his career. It must have been in 1871 or 1872[2] that I first heard of him, and, having heard of him, bought and read Love's Comedy. The League of Youth was then his last published work, and he was struggling with the vast theme of Emperor and Galilean. By the time that "world-historic drama" appeared, I was fairly familiar with all his earlier plays. At that time, then, no one had discovered, or could discover, in his work those ideas with Tolstoy and Nietzsche. The whole series of his social dramas was yet to come--for that half-French farcial comedy The League of Youth can scarcely be said to belong to them. The very idea of "Ibsenism" --surely the strangest "ism" on record--slept in the womb of time. I became from the outset his most fervent admirer, but the thought of becoming, or being supposed to become, his disciple, never crossed my mind. What was it, then, that attracted me? Simply the great--one might already almost have said the colossal --dramatist. Of course I recognised in him--in the poet of Brand and Peer Gynt--a satirist as well; but it was the dramatist pure and simple that chiefly appealed to me--the man who knew how to extract from that wonderful instrument, the theatre, the intensest and most thrilling emotional effects. There you have the distinction in a simple word: it was emotion that I first sought and found in Ibsen, and that every one must seek and find who would understand him aright. Intellectual interest--the interest of social, or moral, or metaphysical theory--may underlie great drama, as the harmonies of the accompaniment underlie the melody of a song. But it is the melody that matters, the direct emotional appeal; and if that be lacking all the rest is naught. The true greatness of Ibsen lay in the invention and elaboration of dramatic melodies; and if you have no ear for these melodies --if you go to his plays in search of ethical, or political, or sociological doctrines--you would be much better employed in reading the works of Mr. Herbert Spencer.

Think, for example, of the first play in which he reached anything like maturity-- The Vikings at Helgeland. It is not one of his great works. He has taken the theme from the Volsung Saga, reduced it almost to the dimensions of domestic drama, and rather tediously sentimentalised it. He has treated it somewhat as Tennyson treated the Arthurian legend in the Idylls of the King. But in the second act he proved himself a very great dramatist, by inventing a situation of extraordinary intensity, in which the malignant ingenuity of Hjördis compasses its evil ends very much

as Iago does in the third act of <u>Othello</u>. There is this
difference, however, that Iago plays upon one very simple
instrument, whereas Hjördis has to produce discord by the skilful
manipulation of a whole orchestra of instruments, in themselves
predisposed to harmony. Very early in the banquet scene she says
to Sigurd: "Tell me, can thy ship sail with any wind?" He
replies: "Ay, when 'tis cunningly steered." "Good!" says she,
"I too will steer my ship cunningly, and make my way whither I
will." And that is what she does: we watch her tacking and
twisting throughout the scene, craftily availing herself of every
undercurrent of character and gust of circumstance, until she has
worked her wicked will, and has thereby brought upon herself the
revelation which humiliates her to the dust. Now that is the
specific privilege and glory of drama--it can show us human
character working, so to speak, at its highest pressure, in those
crises in which every moment is big with fate, and triumph and
disaster tread close upon each other's heels. In this scene, too,
we have the incomparable pathos of old Ornulf's return from
rescuing Gunnar's child, only to find that his own son, Thorolf,
the last of his stock, has meanwhile been done to death by Gunnar
himself. It is, in short, one of the greatest pieces of pure
drama ever invented: it gives us an aesthetic sensation which
may be high or low in quality, but is certainly unique in kind.

It is the fashion nowadays to scoff at situation, and I grant
that mere situation, divorced from character, is a poor enough
thing. But the situation which grows out of the interplay of
character and circumstance carries drama to its highest poignancy,
and may almost be called the peculiar glory of the theatre. The
other constituents in drama it shares with other forms of
art--with the lyrical eclogue, with the novel, even with the
Platonic dialogue. In the peaceful and leisurely development of
character the novel has a great advantage, and for the exposition
of ideas the dialogue is obviously the better form. But in the
situation we have what may be called character read by flashes of
lightning; and the apparatus for producing this effect the theatre
alone supplies--not necessarily the actual material playhouse, but
the theatre of the imagination, which if we cannot conjure up, we
may as well give up reading drama. Look, for instance, at the
play scene in <u>Hamlet</u>; look at the screen scene in <u>The School for
Scandal</u>; what are these but superb situations? And where is the
pedant or the prig who will pretend that they are examples of a
low form of art? The second act of <u>The Vikings at Helgeland</u> is a
great situation in the same sense, and as clearly proclaims its
author a great dramatist.

But certainly not to this play would I apply the epithet
which I ventured to use a few minutes ago--colossal. Nor was I
thinking of <u>Brand</u> and <u>Peer Gynt</u> when I used the word. They are,
indeed, colossal imaginative efforts, but they are not pure drama.
They contain long passages in which the satirist gets the better

of the dramatist, and the lyric poet, sometimes, takes the upper hand of both. If we define drama (and I think we may) as character exhibited in action, and in such dimensions as are suited to theatrical performance, I think we must admit that Brand and Peer Gynt are a great deal more than drama, and at the same time something less. No--the drama of Ibsen's early life to which I think the term colossal may fairly be applied is The Pretenders. It is colossal as Julius Caesar or Antony and Cleopatra is colossal; and outside of Shakespeare I know of nothing that can be compared to it. Faust, of course is not in the same class. Like Brand and Peer Gynt, it is a philosophical poem in dramatic form. It has wonderful passages of drama, but it overflows the dramatic mould on every side. Schiller's noble genius, of which I would be the last to speak with disrespect, was romantic and rhetorical rather than specifically dramatic. Where shall we find in his works such an intensely vital creation as Bishop Nicholas? How verbose, how abstract and sententious is his style, compared with the nervous directness of Ibsen's, in which every sentence reveals a new facet of character, or gives a new turn to the action! Is there anything in modern drama to compare with the death-scene of Bishop Nicholas, that "crowded hour of glorious life," in which the old reprobate, even with the fear of hell before his eyes, works with all the cunning of his wicked old brain to wreak upon his country the malignity begotten of his thwarted ambitions? It is a scene so wonderfully close-knit that to extract passages from it is to obscure its greatest merit; yet I am tempted to read you a passage which seems to me to touch the summit of pure drama:

[Here Archer read an extract from Act III of The Pretenders.³]

Where is the "Ibsenism" in that? Where is the doctrine, the thesis, the gospel? Do we talk of the Shakespearean in Iago, in Shylock, in Falstaff? Is one a Shakespearite because one thinks Macbeth and Lear great dramatic creations? I venture to say that the people who can with any justice be called "Ibsenites" think very little of The Pretenders, and that those who can appreciate The Pretenders will never be Ibsenites.

How magnificent, again, is the character of Earl Skule, that tortured soul, with too much ambition to rest content with any but the first place in the state, yet with too much conscience to be a successful usurper! What an admirable dramatic invention is the contrast between the dark, self-torturing Skule, and the radiant, happily-inspired, yet rather shallow Haakon! It is Haakon, you remember, who vindicates his right to the throne by conceiving what even his rival recognises as a true "king's thought"--the thought of making Norway not merely an assemblage of tribes, but a spiritually united nation. "Tis impossible!" cries Skule, when Haakon reveals to him his thought--"Norway's saga tells of no such thing." "For you 'tis impossible," says Haakon, "for you can but work out the old saga afresh; for me 'tis as easy as for the falcon to cleave the clouds." Then Skule is tempted to steal Haakon's thought and make it his own. He says to himself:

[Act IV,Skule's monologue and the scene with
Jatgeir the Icelandic skald.]

There speaks the great dramatist, the man of intense imagination, of deep insight into human soul, but, above all, endowed with the specific faculty of casting his ideas in the intensely concentrated and therefore intensely moving dramatic form. I think it may safely be said that if Ibsen had written nothing but The Pretenders he would have been secure of a place in the very first rank of dramatists.

What, now, of Brand and Peer Gynt? Where lies their true greatness? Is it in the satirical or philosophical ideas underlying them? I should be sorry to think so, for if so I fear their lease of life would be short. The satire--the criticism of the Norwegian national character which runs through them--is manifestly of local and temporary interest. It is often trenchant, generally amusing, sometimes rather cheap. At all events, it has none of the stuff of immortality in it. The philosophy, which forms, so to speak, the hilt of the satiric blade, is scarcely of permanent worth. There is a great deal of what may be called "fine confused thinking" in both works, and, as it is generally expressed with a great deal of wit and vivacity, it pleases us, apart from all question of its substantive value. But if we attempt to extract from either poem any new metaphysical insight, or even any consistent and helpful ethical doctrine, we shall find ourselves lost in a labyrinth of contradictions. Brand, indeed, is a curious instance of satire which turns and rends itself. Ibsen set out to use Brand as a scourge for what he thought the pusillanimity and half-heartedness of his countrymen, their spirit of compromise, their desire to serve both God and Mammon; but as he went on he could not help seeing, and practically confessing, that Brand's blind, self-righteous devotion to an ideal, conceived out of all relation to human nature and to reasonable human ends, was a greater calamity than the weaknesses he denounced and scarified. Ibsen afterwards declared that it was by mere chance that he had made Brand a priest--that he could have worked out the theme quite well with (for example) a sculptor for his hero. If he really thought so, he was deceiving himself. Brand clearly marks a stage in his own religious development. He had shed, or was shedding, the Christian element in Christianity; but the Jewish element—the conception of a jealous God, demanding utter devotion on the part of his creatures, and setting up "all or nothing" as his moral standard—still kept a strong hold upon him. In the process of writing Brand he probably made what Carlyle would have called his "exodus from Houndsditch",[4] or, less figuratively, his adieu to mythology; but the result is that the poem remains baffling and unclarified, a fierce vindication of a confessedly untenable ideal. Brand is a theological Gregers Werle—the apostle of an ethic based, not on science, but on sentiment.

In Peer Gynt we have a continuation of the assault made in Brand upon the Norwegian national character as Ibsen conceived it. Peer Gynt incarnates in his own person the foibles and vices which Brand denounced. We also find an emphatic enunciation of the general principle that "to be yourself is to slay yourself," and more than a hint of the romantic superstition as to the saving efficacy of a woman's love: the real Peer Gynt, the Peer Gynt of God's intention, being found to exist unsullied and unimpaired in Solveig's heart, or, more accurately, in her imagination. Now in all this, as it seems to me, there is nothing worthy of the name of philosophy. It is simply not true that to be yourself you must slay yourself. Exaggerations of altruism are just as hurtful, if not quite so common, as exaggerations of egoism. The conception of a world in which every one is concerned, not at all for his own welfare, but solely and entirely for that of other people, is just as ridiculous as the conception of a town whose inhabitants live by taking in each other's washing. As for the notion of a magical virtue, not, remember, in a woman's influence—for Solveig has exercised practically no influence upon Peer Gynt—but simply in a woman's "faith, hope and love," what is it but a romantic variant of the notion of transferred or imputed righteousness so prevalent in folk-lore and theology? As a scapegoat, whether human or animal, could bear in its own person the punishment due to a whole people or a whole race, so a saintly personage could accumulate so much merit as to have plenty over for the salvation of some sinner to whom he, or she, happened to be devoted. The plain truth is that

> No man can save his brother's soul
> Or pay his brother's debt,

and there is no reason to suppose that a woman's illusion is more efficacious in this respect than a man's. Indeed Ibsen, characteristically, scoffs at his own romanticism by making the voice of the Button-Moulder break in upon Solveig's lullaby with the reminder

> At the last crossroad we will meet again, Peer;
> And then we'll see whether—I say no more.

If, then, the satire of these poems is, like almost all satire, of transient interest, and if their philosophy will not bear rational criticism, what remains to constitute their greatness? Why, everything remains--everything that matters--for the poetry remains, the drama remains. As works of reflection they may be mediocre, but as works of imagination they are superb. Brand is much less vital than Peer Gynt, for in it reflection is apt to get the upper hand of imagination, and we have long passages in which the satirist and the moralist take the stage, while the dramatist scarcely gets a word in edgewise. Yet even in Brand the great dramatist reveals himself, not only in the magnificent fourth act with its almost intolerable pathos, a piece of absolutely unrivalled lyric drama, but also in scores of minor scenes and traits in which we see the touch of the man who by nature thinks and conceives dramatically. Note, for instance, the end of the first scene. You remember how Brand meets Einar and Agnes dancing over the mountain plateau, stops them on the verge of a precipice, and then has a long discussion with Einar in which he opposes his dark and stern theology to the young painter's hedonism. Agnes, meanwhile, listens intently and says never a word. When at last Brand goes his way, she awakes as from a reverie and says:

Is the sun set already?

Einar.

Nay, a shadowing cloud; and now 'tis past.

He wants her to resume their gay, light-hearted progress, their butterfly dance over the surface of life. He points to the shining fjord that lies below them, where the steamer that is to bear them away to the south has rounded a headland. "See," he says,

It is the steamer-thine and mine!
And now it speeds into the fjord
Then out into the foaming brine.
Tonight with thee and me aboard!
The mists have veil'd the mountain brow
Saw'st thou how vividly, but now,
Heaven's image in the water woke!

Agnes.

Oh, yes. But tell me--sawest thou--?

                    Einar.

   What?

                    Agnes.

   How he tower'd as he spoke?[5]

   There is the touch of the born dramatist. He can make
silence eloquent, and in barely a dozen words reveal what he
himself has called a revolution of the soul.
   As for Peer Gynt, is it not from first to last a piece of
sheer untrammelled, almost wantonly capricious imagination? I do
not say that satirical and philosophic intensions are not there
--we know, in fact, that they are--but they are so fused in the
fabric of pure fantasy that it is the easiest thing in the world
to ignore them, and the most difficult thing in the world to seize
and disengage them in consistent, hard-and-fast form. We are
reminded of "black vesper's pageants" as Antony describes them:

            Sometime we see a cloud that's dragonish:
            A vapour sometime like a bear or lion,
            A tower'd citadel, a pendent rock,
            A forked mountain, a blue promontory
            With trees upon't. . . .
                Then even with a thought
            The rack dislimns, and makes it indistinct
            As water is in water.

   No doubt there are passages, especially in the fourth and
fifth acts, where the satirist takes the bit between his teeth and
goes off for an independent canter. But in the main we have
simply a brilliant, many-coloured romance, like that of Ulysses,
or Aladdin, or Don Quixote, set forth in a series of episodes each
of which is a little drama in itself. The great scene, of course
--perhaps the summit of Ibsen's poetical achievement and in my
judgment one of the summits of nineteenth century literature--is
Aase's death scene, and the drive to Soria-Moria Castle. But
there are other pasages almost as inspired; for instance, the
marvellous parting of Peer Gynt and Ingrid at the beginning of the
second act; the saeter-girl scene; the coming of Solveig to Peer's
hut in the forest; and the eerie shipwreck scene which opens the
fifth act. The man who cannot read Peer Gynt for sheer delight,
as he would read Pickwick, or The Three Musketeers or Huckleberry
Finn, does not begin to understand the true greatness of Ibsen.
From this point of view, its intellectual weaknesses are trans-

muted into emotional strength. For my part, I do not hesitate to call Solveig one of the most exquisite figures in literature, and her rescue of Peer at the end a very beautiful and touching invention, on the folk-lore or fairy-tale level to which the whole poem belongs. It is only when we are asked to accept this piece of primitive romanticism as a serious contribution to ethical thought that reason rebels. It rebels, first and foremost, against the injustice done to Ibsen's genius by those who insist on regarding him primarily as a preacher. There have been many better preachers, but few greater poets.

I have now passed in review, you see, the principal works of the Ibsen whom I first knew in 1872 and 1873--the Ibsen who layed his spell on my youthful imagination. However high we may rank his later productions, no one can possibly deny that The Pretenders, Brand and Peer Gynt are among the greatest things he ever did; and assuredly it was not their philosophy, their doctrine, their message,--but, on the contrary, their poetry, their imagination, their drama--that captivated the boy of 17 or 18 who read and re-read them with ever-growing admiration. Well, ladies and gentlemen, I have remained, in regard to Ibsen, that boy of 17; and I counsel you to recapture some such youthful frame of mind if you want really to appreciate him. I did not, at that age, thoroughly understand him. In the intentions and sub-intentions of Brand and Peer Gynt there was a good deal to which I lacked the key. But if I did not wholly understand I wholly enjoyed, and that, I suggest, is what a poet primarily demands of his readers. To this day there are many people who understand Ibsen better than I do--and sometimes, I suspect, better than Henrik Ibsen did--but there is no one in England or anywhere who enjoys him more than I do. It has been my privilege to translate a good many of his works and to revise and re-revise translations made by other people. Consequently I have pored over him as a priest pores over his breviary. But all this familiarity has not dulled the edge of my enjoyment. His great scenes are as fresh and poignant to me as ever. I still marvel at the patient, exquisite art with which he builds up his complex mosaics of character and circumstance--just as I did when the little paper-covered books reached me fresh from the press in Copenhagen, or sometimes act by act in batches of proof-sheets. A very notable Danish critic, Henning Kehler, has recently subjected Ibsen's works to an extraordinarily searching analysis, in the pages of that greatest of literary quarterlies, Edda--a publication of which Norway may well be proud. The analysis, or perhaps one may rather say the dissection, has, on the whole a depreciative effect. It throws into relief mannerisms, superficialities, intellectual and technical foibles. It shows that some "ghosts" walked in Ibsen's mind as well as in Mrs. Alving's. But in order to shake off its somewhat chilling influence, one has only to take up one of the great plays and read

an act or two. The foibles may be there--some of them were fairly
apparent to most of us without the aid of Herr Kehler's scalpel.
But what is still more evident is the genius, the incomparable
creative imagination. That is why I conceive, rightly or wrongly,
that Ibsen is likely to last, to wear, as few dramatists have
lasted. There is a good deal of impermanent matter in his
work--matter that belongs to his age and generation--and it is
with this matter that the sect of Ibsenites (if it still exists)
is mainly concerned. But it is not of the essence of his genius.
His true greatness lay in his unique and incomparable gift of
compressing a crisis in human destiny into the narrow limits of
the dramatic form, and it will be long, I think, before people
whose nerves are tuned to the peculiar vibration which great drama
alone can impart, will cease to seek for it and to find it in the
works of Ibsen.

Of course there are striking inequalities in Ibsen. Just
about the time when I first came to know him, he was at a sort of
pause in his career--he was drifting about in a region of cross
currents and baffling breezes. The years he devoted to Emperor
and Galilean--in spite of the imaginative splendor of that
work--may almost be reckoned lost years in his development. Then
he set to work to teach himself, or rather to create for himself,
a new art. Pillars of Society--the first of his plays that came
to me hot from the press--was by far the poorest of his mature
works. It had not even the careless verve and humour of The
League of Youth. It was no better than a good many contemporary
French plays. In A Doll's House he revealed a new and striking
originality, mingled with a good deal of artifice and convention.
Ghosts, as Georg Brandes said, was a great and daring deed, and it
marked a long stride forward in the development of his peculiar
technique; but it was a little stiff, heavy, monotonous. It
lacked the extraordinary suppleness--the intricacy and yet
perspecuity of movement--that he was presently to attain. The
fact is that Ibsen was in those days deliberately aiming at a form
of art which did not give his genius free play. He was trying to
be a prosaic realist; he had, for the moment, clipped the wings
of his imagination. But they were soon to grow again. Not in An
Enemy of the People--that is still strictly prosaic: a
wonderfully vital comedy, but making its appeal to the intellect
rather than to the imagination. It was in The Wild Duck that
Ibsen attained to what may be called the full maturity of his
second period. Putting Brand and Peer Gynt aside, as dramatic
poems rather than pure dramas, we may call The Wild Duck
incomparably the greatest thing he had done since The Pretenders.
Indeed if anyone chose to call it the greatest thing he ever did,
it would be hard to say him nay. Thenceforward, with only one
slight declension in The Lady from the Sea, he produced
masterpiece on masterpiece, until his genius began to flag a
little in the third act of John Gabriel Borkman. Rosmersholm,

which followed The Wild Duck, is the most consummate and perfect example of his peculiar technic--that technic which gives his work its wonderful richness of effect, by presenting, as it were, two dramas in one, a drama of the past blending with, sustaining, conditioning the drama of the present. The Lady from the Sea, in spite of many beauties, is distinctly looser in fibre than any other of his works of this period. I well remember wondering whether it denoted a permanent decline in power, and the relief I felt on finding him, in Hedda Gabler, once more at the very summit of his mastery. Here is a play which surely gives a conclusive answer to the view of Ibsen as a hot-gospeller, a tub-thumper. What is the gospel, what the message, of Hedda Gabler? The play is simply the portrait of a lady--not a very pleasant lady, but one of whom many modern women (and men too) may say like John Newton, "There, but for the grace of God, go I".[6] As for Masterbuilder Solness, it always reminds me of a phrase I have more than once heard Ibsen apply, with a twinkling smile, to his own process of creation. If you asked him whether he had a play on the stocks, he would say, "Ja, jeg laver paa noget galskap til naeste aar"--"Yes I am concocting some tomfoolery for next year". Can we not imagine the old man chuckling over this magical piece of tomfoolery--literally a unique achievement, for it is like nothing else in the world. The realistic will o' the wisp has lost the last shred of its influence over his mind, and he is once more as pure a poet as he was in The Pretenders or Peer Gynt. And so he is in Little Eyolf--in that superb first act. Working up to its heart-breaking climax in the cry of "Krykken flyder" ("The crutch is floating")--in that cruel, almost ferocious, second act--and the third act, full of elevation, reconciliation, serene humanity. In John Gabriel Borkman, as I have said, his grip is somewhat slackening; but the scene between Borkman and Foldal in the second act is certainly one of the richest and most original things he ever did, while in John Gabriel's death scene he is at the height of his nobility.

And what is the common characteristic of all these plays we have been rapidly reviewing? It it not that each of them is an independent creation, a thing with a peculiar, inherent life of its own, not the aesthetic toy of a moment, but, as it were, a permanent enlargement of our spiritual experience? Whatever message, whatever doctrine there may be in them does not constitute their greatness, but, if anything, detracts from it. They are great simply and solely as pieces of creative imagination. Those of us who, in my judgement, truly appreciate them can as easily imagine the world without Hamlet or Faust, without Robinson Crusoe or David Copperfield, as without Peer Gynt or The Wild Duck or Masterbuilder Solness.

May I end, as perhaps I ought to have begun, by expressing the peculiar pleasure it gives me to take however humble a part in promoting the study of the Norwegian language and literature

within the walls of this great institution? My own very imperfect
knowledge of that language has been a source of quite incalculable
delight and inspiration to me.   To any one who is specially
interested in drama, Norwegian may fairly be called indispensable;
for it is not only the language of Ibsen, but the language of
Björnson, whose Sigurd Slembe is a thing of Shakespearian
greatness; and more especially, it is the language of one of the
greatest and most delightful dramatists who ever lived--namely
Ludvig Holberg. And Holberg is a writer who must be read in the
original, for he is absolutely untranslatable. Ibsen loses much
in translation, Bjornson loses more, but Holberg loses everything
--his greatest charm is his style, which is bereft of all its
aroma in another idiom.   But of course it is not to drama alone
that Norwegian furnishes the key--it opens to us treasures of
lyric poetry and of fiction, and not a little excellent criticism
and sociological writing. Let me add, since Ibsen is our special
theme, that I particularly welcome this movement for the study of
Norwegian since it relieves me and my coadjutors in Ibsen
translation of a great responsibility. In the days when a furious
battle raged round the name of Ibsen, I could not but feel partly
responsible for the delirious nonsense that was talked about him.
Small as is my sympathy with the Ibsenite,he is of course sane in
comparison with the anti-Ibsenite of those days, whose voice is
still occasionally heard in the land. I could not but feel that,
for those, wild misunderstandings, defects, inevitable defects, of
translation were partly to blame. "If they could but read The
Pretenders, Peer Gynt and The Wild Duck in the original," I said,
"it would be impossible for them to talk so idiotically." Now at
last Ibsen is being enabled (thanks to Mr. Grondahl)[7] to speak
in his own virile and noble tongue to an ever-increasing circle
of English readers; and in that fact, your Excellency, I rejoice
to see a guarantee, not only for fuller and truer appreciation of
your great poet, but for a more intimate sympathy and friendship
between the new England of the coming years, and the historic,
the beautiful, the illustrious country which you represent.

PART TWO

ESSAYS ON THE SEPARATE PLAYS

The following essays on The Pretenders, Peer Gynt, The League of Youth, and the twelve major prose plays, from Pillars of Society to When We Dead Awaken, were written by Archer for his eleven-volume edition of The Works of Henrik Ibsen (1906-08). In these "introductions" Archer usually provides the following: (1) the biographical background for the play, (2) a record of its conception and development through the notes and drafts (as they exist), (3) the publishing history, (4) the performance history, (5) the initial response, when significant, (6) Ibsen's comments and explanations, (7) an analysis of the play's craftsmanship, (8) a review of the basic themes, (9) some assessment of the characterization, and (10) a judgment on the play's place comparatively in Ibsen's overall achievement. This measured commentary on the plays, somewhat less argumentative than the approach followed in the other essays, offers a detailed, step by step history of a "world-poet" who changed both drama and the world. Across one whole generation, and well into the second, these essays provided, in the English-speaking world, the most reliable and extensive introduction to Ibsen's genius and greatness. Even today, we might note, they can still serve this function, while also offering their historical function as documents in the Ibsen campaign.

There is no essay on Brand because C. H. Herford provided this "introduction" for the Works. I have not included the essay on Emperor and Galilean because it is similar to "Ibsen's Imperialism" in Part One. Nor have I included the essays on the early plays written before The Pretenders. Otherwise, except for a section on translation which I have cut from the essay on Peer Gynt, these essays are unaltered and complete. Unless noted, the footnotes are all by Archer.

THE PRETENDERS

Six years elapsed between the composition of The Vikings and that of The Pretenders.[1] In the interval Ibsen wrote Love's Comedy, and brought all the world of Norwegian philistinism, and (as we should now say) suburbanism, about his ears. Whereas hitherto his countrymen had ignored, they now execrated him. In his autobiographic letter of 1870, to Peter Hansen, he wrote: "The only person who at that time approved of the book was my wife. . . .My countrymen excommunicated me. All were against me. The fact that all were against me--that there was no longer any one outside my family circle of whom I could say 'He believes in me'--must, as you can easily see, have aroused a mood which found its outlet in The Pretenders." It is to be noted that this was written during a period of estrangement from Björnson. I do not know what was Björnson's attitude towards Love's Comedy in particular; but there can be no doubt that, in general, he believed in and encouraged his brother poet, and employed his own growing influence in efforts to his advantage. In representing himself as standing quite alone, Ibsen probably forgets, for the moment, his relation to his great contemporary.

Yet the relation to Björnson lay at the root of the character-contrast on which The Pretenders is founded. Ibsen always insisted that each of his plays gave poetic form to some motive gathered from his own experience or observation; and this is very clearly true of the present play. Ever since Synnove Solbakken had appeared in 1857, Björnson, the expansive, eloquent, lyrical Björnson, had been the darling child of fortune. He had gone from success to success unwearied. He was recognised throughout Scandinavia (in Denmark no less than in Norway) as the leader of the rising generation in almost every branch of imaginative literature. He was full, not only in inspiration and energy, but of serene self-confidence. Meanwhile Ibsen, nearly five years older than he, had been pursuing his slow and painful course of development, in comparative obscurity, in humiliating poverty, and amid almost complete lack of appreciation. "Mr. Ibsen is a great cipher" (or "nullity"), wrote a critic in 1858; another, in 1863, laid it down that "Ibsen has a certain technical

and artistic talent, but nothing of what can be called 'Genius'."
The scoffs of the critics, however, were not the sorest trials
that he had to bear. What was hardest to contend against was the
doubt as to his own poetic calling and election that constantly
beset him. This doubt could not but be generated by the very
tardiness of his mental growth. We see him again and again (in
the case of Olaf Liliekrans, of The Vikings, of Love's Comedy, and
of The Pretenders itself), conceiving a plan and then abandoning
it for years--no doubt because he found himself, in one respect or
another, unripe for its execution. Every such experience must
have involved for him days and weeks of fruitless effort and
discouragement. To these moods of scepticism as to his own powers
he gave expression in a series of poems (for the most part
sonnets) published in 1859 under the title of In the Picture
Gallery. In it he represents the "black elf" of doubt, whispering
to him: "Your soul is like the dry bed of a mountain stream, in
which the singing waters of poetry have ceased to flow. If a
faint sound comes rustling down the empty channel, do not imagine
that it portends the return of the waters--it is only the dry
leaves eddying before the autumn wind, and pattering among the
barren stones." In those years of struggle and stress, of
depressing criticism, and enervating self-criticism, he must often
have compared his own lot and his own character with Björnson's,
and perhaps, too, wondered whether there were no means by which
he could appropriate to himself some of his younger and more
facile brother-poet's kingly self-confidence. For this relation
between two talents he partly found and partly invented a historic
parallel in the relation between two rival pretenders to the
Norwegian throne, Haakon Haakonsson and Skule Baardsson.

Dr. Brandes, who has admirably expounded the personal element
in the genesis of this play, compares Haakon-Björnson and
Skule-Ibsen with the Aladdin and Nureddin of Oehlenschläger's
beautiful dramatic poem. Aladdin is the born genius, serene,
light-hearted, a trifle shallow, who grasps the magic lamp with an
unswerving confidence in his right to it. ("It is that which the
Romans called ingenium," says Bishop Nicholas, "truly I am not
strong in Latin; but 'twas called ingenium.") Nureddin, on the
other hand, is the far profounder, more penetrating, but sceptical
and self-torturing spirit. When at last he seizes Aladdin's lamp,
as Skule annexes Haakon's king's thought, his knees tremble, and
it drops from his grasp, just as the Genie is ready to obey him.

It is needless to cite the passages from the scenes between
Skule and Bishop Nicholas in the second act, Skule and Haakon in
the third, Skule and Jatgeir in the fourth, in which this element
of personal symbolism is present. The reader will easily
recognise them, while recognising at the same time that their
dramatic appropriateness, their relevance to the historic
situation as the poet viewed it, is never for a moment impaired.
The underlying meaning is never allowed to distort or denaturalise

the surface aspect of the picture.[2]   The play may be read, understood, and fully appreciated, by a person for whom this underlying meaning has no existence. One does not point it out as an essential element in the work of art, or even as adding to its merit, but simply as affording a particularly clear instance of Ibsen's method of interweaving "Wahrheit" with "Dichtung."

So early as 1858, soon after the completion of The Vikings, Ibsen had been struck by the dramatic material in Haakon Haakonsson's Saga, as related by Snorri Sturlasson's nephew, Sturla Thordsson, and had sketched a play on the subject. At that time, however, he put the draft aside. It was only as the years went on, as he found himself "excommunicated" after Love's Comedy, and as the contrast between Björnson's fortune and his own became ever more marked, that the figures of Skule and Haakon took more and more hold upon his imagination. In June, 1863, he attended a "Festival of Song" at Bergen, and there met Björnson, who had been living abroad since 1860. Probably under the stimulus of this meeting, he set to work upon The Pretenders immediately on his return to Christiania, and wrote it with almost incredible rapidity. The manuscript went to the printers in September; the book was published in October, 1863 (though dated 1864), and the play was produced at the Christiania Theatre, under the author's own supervision, on January 17, 1864. The production was notably successful; yet no one seems fully to have realised what it meant for Norwegian literature. Outside of Norway, at any rate, it awoke no echo. George Brandes declares that scarcely a score of copies of the play found their way to Denmark. Not until Ibsen had left Norway (April, 1864) and had taken the Danish reading public by storm with Brand and Peer Gynt, did people turn back to The Pretenders and discover what an extraordinary achievement it was. In January, 1871, it was produced at the Royal Theatre, Copenhagen, where Emil Poulsen found in Bishop Nicholas one of the great triumphs of his career. It was produced by the Meiningen Company and at the Munich Hoftheater in 1875, in Stockholm in 1879, at the Königliches Schauspielhaus, Berlin, and at the Vienna Burgtheatre in 1891; and it has from time to time been acted at many other Scandinavian and German theatres.[3] The character of Nicholas has fascinated many great actors: what a pity that it did not come in the way of Sir Henry Irving when he was at the height of his power! But of course no English actor-manager would dream of undertaking a character which dies in the middle of the third act.

Ibsen's treatment of history in this play may be proposed as a model to other historic dramatists. Although he has invented a great deal, his inventions supplement rather than contradict the records. Chronology, indeed, he treats with considerable freedom, and at the same time with ingenious vagueness. The general impression one receives in reading the play is that the action covers a space of four or five years; as a matter of fact it covers twenty-two years, between the folkmote in Bergen, 1218, and Skule's death, 1240. All the leading characters are historical; and although much is read into them which history does not warrant, there is little that history absolutely forbids us to conceive. The general features of the struggle between the two factions--Haakon's Birkebeiner, or Birchlegs, and Skule's Vargbaelgs--are correctly enough reproduced. In his treatment of this period, the Norwegian historian, J. E. Sars, writing thirteen years after the appearance of The Pretenders, uses terms which might almost have been suggested by Ibsen's play. "On the one side," he says, "we find strength and certainty, on the other lameness and lack of confidence. The old Birchlegs[4] go to work openly and straightforwardly, like men who are immovably convinced of the justice of their cause, and unwaveringly assured of its ultimate victory. Skule's adherents, on the other hand, are ever seeking by intrigues and chicanery to place stumbling-blocks in the way of their opponents' enthusiasm." Haakon represented Sverre's ideal of a democratic kingship, independent of the oligarchy of bishops and barons. "He was," says Sars, "reared in the firm conviction of his right to the Throne; he grew up among the veterans of his grandfather's time, men imbued with Sverre's principles, from whom he accepted them as a ready-made system, the realisation of which could only be a question of time. He stood from the first in a clear and straightforward position to which his whole personality corresponded. . . .He owed his chief strength to the repose and equilibrium of mind which distinguished him, and had its root in his unwavering sense of having right and the people's will upon his side." His great "king's-thought," however, seems to be an invention of the poet's. Skule, on the other hand, represented the old nobility in its struggle against the new monarchy. "He was the centre of a hierarchic aristocratic party; but after its repeated defeats this party must have been lacking alike in number and in confidence. . . .It was clear from the first that his attempt to reawaken the old wars of the succession in Norway was undertaken in the spirit of the desperate gambler, who does not count the chances, but throws at random, in the blind hope that luck may befriend him. . . .Skule's enterprise had thus no support in opinion or in any prevailing interest, and one defeat was sufficient to crush him."

In the character of Bishop Nicholas, too, Ibsen has widened and deepened his historical material, rather than poetised with a free hand. "Bishop Nicholas," says Sars, "represented rather the aristocracy. . .than the cloth to which he belonged. He had begun his career as a worldly chieftain, and, as such, taken part in Magnus Erlingsson's struggles with Sverre; and although he must have had some tincture of letters, since he could contrive to be elected a bishop. . .there is no lack of indications that his spiritual lore was not of the deepest. During his long participation in the civil broils, both under Sverre and later, we see in him a man to whose character any sort of religious or ecclesiastical enthusiasm must have been foreign, his leading motives being personal ambition and vengefulness rather than any care for general interest—a cold and calculating nature, shrewd, but petty and without any impetus, of whom Haakon Haakonsson, in delivering his funeral speech. . .could find nothing better to say than that he had not his equal in wordly wisdom (veraldar vit)." I cannot find that the Bishop played any such prominent part in the struggle between the King and the Earl as Ibsen assigns to him; and the only foundation for the great death-bed scene seems to be the following passage from Haakon Haakonsson's Saga, Cap. 138: "As Bishop Nicholas at that time lay very sick, he sent a messenger to the King praying him to come to him. The King had on this expedition seized certain letters, from which he gathered that the Bishop had not been true to him. With this he upbraided him, and the Bishop, confessing it, prayed the King to forgive him. The King replied that he did so willingly, for God's sake; and as he could discern that the Bishop lay near to death, he abode with him until God called him from the world."

In the introduction to The Vikings at Helgeland, I have suggested that in that play Ibsen had reached imaginative and technical maturity, but was as yet intellectually immature. The six years that elapsed between The Vikings and The Pretenders placed him at the height of his intellectual power. We have only to compare Skule, Haakon, and Bishop Nicholas with Gunnar, Sigurd, and Ornulf to feel that we have passed from nobly-designed and more or less animated waxworks to complex and profoundly-studied human beings. There is no Hjordis in The Pretenders, and the female character-drawing is still controlled by purely romantic ideals;[5] but how exquisitely human is Margrete in comparison with the almost entirely conventional Dagny! The criticism of life, too, which in The Vikings is purely sentimental, here becomes intense and searching. The only point of superiority in The Vikings—if it be a point of superiority—is purely technical. The action of the earlier play is concentrated and rounded. It has all the "unity," or "unities," that a rational criticism can possibly demand. In a word, it is, in form as well as essence, an ideal tragedy. The Pretenders, on the other hand, is a chronicle-play, far more close-knit than Shakespeare's or Schiller's works in that kind, but, nevertheless, what Aristotle would call "episodic" in its construction. The weaving of the plot, however, is quite masterly, betokening an effort of invention and adjustment incomparably greater than that which went to the making of The Vikings. It was doubtless his training in the school of French intrigue that enabled Ibsen to depict with such astonishing vigour that master wire-puller, Bishop Nicholas. This form of technical dexterity he was afterwards to outgrow and bring into disrepute. But from The Vikings to Pillars of Society he practised, whenever he was writing primarily for the stage, the methods of the "well-made play"; and in everything but concentration, which the very nature of the subject excluded, The Pretenders is thoroughly "well-made."

With this play, though the Scandinavian criticism of 1864 seems to have been far from suspecting the fact, Ibsen took his place among the great dramatists of the world. In wealth of characterisation, complexity and nobility of emotion, and depth of spiritual insight, it stands high among the masterpieces of romantic drama. It would be hard to name a more vigourous character-projection than that of Bishop Nicholas, or any one dramatic invention more superbly inspired than the old man's death scene, with the triumphant completion of his perpetuum mobile. But even if the Bishop were entirely omitted, the play would not be Hamlet without the Prince of Denmark. The characters of Haakon and Skule, and the struggle between them, would still make one of the greatest historic dramas in literature.

It has not been generally noticed, I think, that Ibsen found in Björnson's King Sverre, published in 1861, a study of Bishop Nicholas in his younger days. The play, as a whole, is a poor one, and does not appear in the collected edition of Björnson's works; but there is distinct merit in the drawing of the Bishop's character. Furthermore, it ought to be remembered that The Pretenders was not the first work, or even the first great work, of its class in Norwegian literature. In 1862, Björnson had published his splendid trilogy of Sigurd Slembe, which, though more fluid and uneven than The Pretenders, contains several passages of almost Shakespearean power. It was certainly greater than anything Ibsen had done up to that date. Ibsen reviewed it on its appearance in terms of unmixed praise, yet, as one cannot but feel, rather over-cautiously.

If anything could excuse the coolness of Norwegian criticism towards The Pretenders, it was the great and flagrant artistic blemish of the Ghost Scene in the last act. This outburst of prophetico-topical satire is a sheer excrescence on the play, indefensible, but, at the same time, fortunately negligible. It is, however, of interest as a symptom of Ibsen's mood in the last months before he left Norway, and also as one of the links in that chain which binds all his works together. Just as Skule's attempt to plagiarise Haakon's king's-thought points backwards to Gunnar's moral lapse in taking advantage of the fraud on Hjördis, so the ironic rhymes of the Bagler-Bishop's ghost point forward to the lyric indignation and irony of Brand and Peer Gynt.

PEER GYNT

The publication of Brand, in March, 1866, brought Ibsen fame (in Scandinavia) and relieved him from the immediate pressure of poverty. Two months later the Storthing voted him a yearly "poet-pension" of £90; and with this sum, as he wrote to the Minister who had been mainly instrumental in furthering his claim, he felt "his future assured," so that he could henceforth "devote himself without hindrance to his calling." This first glimpse of worldly prosperity, no doubt, brought with it the lighter mood which distinguishes Peer Gynt from its predecessor. To call it the gayest of Ibsen's works is not, perhaps, to say very much. Its satire, indeed, is bitter enough; but it is not the work of an unhappy man. The character of Peer Gynt, and many of his adventures, are conceived with unmistakable gusto. Some passages even bear witness to an exuberance of animal spirits which reminds one of Ben Jonson's saying with regard to Shakespeare--"aliquando sufflaminandus erat."

The summer of 1866 Ibsen spent at Frascati, in the Palazzo Gratiosi, where he lived "most comfortably and cheaply." He found Frascati and Tusculum "indescribably delightful." From the windows of his study he could see Soracte, "rising isolated and beautiful from the level of the immense plain. . .the battlefield where the chief engagement in the world's history took place." So he writes in a letter to Paul Botten-Hansen, and immediately afterwards proceeds: "I shall soon be setting to work in good earnest. I am still wrestling with my subject, but I know that I shall get the upper hand of the brute before long, and then everything will go smoothly." But was the play here referred to Peer Gynt? Probably not; for, three months later, we find him still projecting a historical play, of the period of Christian IV. of Denmark, which was to have had for its hero a Norwegian freebooter named Magnus Heinesson, who came to a tragic end in the year 1589. It is in a letter to Hegel, dated from Rome, January 5, 1867, that we find the first unmistakable reference to Peer Gynt: "Now I must tell you that my new work is well under way, and will, if nothing untoward happens, be finished early in the summer. It is to be a long dramatic poem, having as its chief figure one of the Norwegian peasantry's half-mythical, fantastic heroes of recent times. It will bear no resemblance to Brand, contain no direct polemics and so forth. I have long had the subject in my thoughts; now the entire plan is worked out and written down, and the first act begun. The thing grows as I work at it, and I am certain that you will be satisfied with it."

Two months later (March 8) the poem has "advanced to the middle of the second act." On August 8, he sends to Hegel, from Villa Pisani, Casamicciola, Ischia, the complete manuscript of the first three acts, and writes: "I am curious to hear how you like the poem. I am very hopeful myself. It may interest you to know that Peer Gynt is a real person, who lived in Gudbrandsdal, probably at the end of last, or beginning of this, century; but of his exploits not much more is known than is to be found in Asbjörnsen's Norwegian Fairy Tales, in the section Pictures from the Mountains. Thus I have not had very much to build upon; but so much the more liberty has been left me. It would interest me to know what Clemens Petersen thinks of the work." What Clemens Petersen did think we shall presently learn.

On October 18, Ibsen despatched from Sorrento the remainder of his manuscript, and the book was published on November 14. It has often been pointed out (by myself among others) as a very remarkable fact that two such gigantic creations as Brand and Peer Gynt should have been given to the world in two successive years; but on examination the marvel somewhat dwindles. Peer Gynt did not follow so hot-foot upon Brand as the bare dates of publication would lead us to suppose. Brand was written in the summer of 1865, Peer Gynt (as we have seen) in 1867; so that the poet's mind had lain fallow for a whole year (1866) between the two great efforts. It was a long delay in the publication of Brand that made its successor seem to tread so close upon its heels. As a matter of fact, he spent a longer time over the actual composition of Peer Gynt than over any of his other works, except Emperor and Galilean. It usually took him from six weeks to four months to write a play; but Peer Gynt cost him nine months' labor.

One or two other references to the origin of Peer Gynt may be found in Ibsen's letters. The most important occurs in an autobiographical communication to Peter Hansen, dated Dresden, October 28, 1870: "After Brand came Peer Gynt as though of itself. It was written in Southern Italy, in Ischia and at Sorrentol. So far away from one's readers one becomes reckless. This poem contains much that has its origin in the circumstances of my own youth. My own mother--with the necessary exaggerations --served as the model for Aase. (Likewise for Inga in The Pretenders)" Twelve years later (1882) Ibsen wrote to George Brandes: "My father was a merchant with a large business and wide connections, and he enjoyed dispensing reckless hospitality. In 1836 he failed, and nothing was left to us except a farm near the town. . . .In writing Peer Gynt, I had the circumstances and memories of my own childhood before me when I described the life in the house of 'The rich Jon Gynt'."

Returning to the above-quoted letter to Peter Hanson, we find this further allusion to Peer Gynt and its immediate predecessor and successor in the list of Ibsen's works: "Environment has great influence upon the forms in which imagination creates. May I not, like Christoff in Jakob von Tyboe,[1] point to Brand and Peer Gynt, and say: "See, the wine-cup has done this?" And is there not something in The League of Youth [written in Dresden] that suggests "Knackwurst und Bier"? Not that I would thereby imply any inferiority in the latter play." The transition to prose was no doubt an inevitable step in the evolution of Ibsen's genius; but one wishes he had kept to the "Wine-cup" a little longer.

A masterpiece is not a flawless work, but one which has sufficient vitality to live down its faults, until at last we no longer heed, and almost forget them. Peer Gynt had real faults, not a few; and its great merit, as some of us think--its magnificent, reckless profusion of fantasy--could not but be bewildering to its first critics, who had to pronounce upon it before they had (as Ballested[2] would put it) acclimatised themselves to its atmosphere. Its reception, then, was much more dubious than that of Brand had been. We find even George Brandes writing of it: "What great and noble powers are wasted on this thankless material? Except in the fourth act, which has no connection with what goes before and after, and is witless in its satire, crude in its irony, and in its latter part scarcely comprehensible, there is almost throughout a wealth of poetry and a depth of thought such as we do not find, perhaps, in any of Ibsen's earlier works. . . .It would be unjust to deny that the book contains great beauties, or that it tells us all, and Norwegians in particular, some important truths; but beauties and truths are of far less value than beauty and truth in the singular, and Ibsen's poem is neither beautiful nor true. Contempt for humanity and self-hatred make a bad foundation on which to build a poetic work. What an unlovely and distorting view of life this is! What acrid pleasure can a poet find in thus sullying human nature?"[3] The friendship between Brandes and Ibsen was at this time just beginning and--much to Ibsen's credit--it appears to have suffered no check by reason of this outspoken pronouncement.

On the other hand, he resented deeply a criticism by Clemens Petersen, who seems to have been at this time regarded as the aesthetic lawgiver of Copenhagen. Why he should have done so is not very clear; for Petersen professed to prefer Peer Gynt to Brand, and his criticism on Brand Ibsen had apparently accepted without demur. Most of Petersen's article is couched in a very heavy philosophic idiom; but the following extract, though it refers chiefly to Brand, may convey some idea of his general objection to both poems:--"When a poet, as Ibsen does in Brand, depicts an error, a one-sidedness, which is from first to last presented in an imposing light, it is not sufficient that he should eventually, through a piece of sensational symbolism, let that one-sidedness go to ruin, and it is not sufficient that in the last word of the drama[4] he should utter the name of that with which the one-sidedness should have blended in order to become truth. If he throughout his work shows us this error--in virtue of its strength, if for no other reason--justifying itself as against everything that comes in contact with it, then it is not only in the character depicted that something is lacking, but in the work of art itself. That something is the Ideal, without which the work of art cannot take rank as poetry--the Ideal which here, as so often in art, lies only in the lighting of the picture, but which is nevertheless the saving, the uplifting element. It is to poetry what devotion is to religion. . . .In Peer Gynt, as in Brand, the ideal is lacking. But this must be said rather less strongly of Peer Gynt. There is more fantasy, more real freedom of spirit, less strain and less violence in this poem than in Brand." The critic then speaks of Peer Gynt as being "full of riddles which are insoluble, because there is nothing in them at all." Peer's identification of the Sphinx with the Boyg (Act IV., Sc.12) he characterises as "tankesvindel" --thought-swindling, or, as we might say, juggling with thought. The general upshot of his considerations is that Peer Gynt belongs, with Goldschmidt's Corsaren, to the domain of polemical journalism. It "is not poetry, because in the transmutation of reality into art it falls half-way short of the demands both of art and of reality."

Petersen's review is noteworthy, not for its own sake, but for the effect it produced on Ibsen. His letters to Björnson on the subject are the most vivid and spontaneous he ever wrote. Björnson happened to be in Copenhagen when Petersen's article appeared in Faedrelandet, and Ibsen seems somehow to have blamed him for not preventing its appearance. "All I reproach you with," he says, "is inaction." But Petersen he accuses of lack of "loyalty," of "an intentional crime against truth and justice." "There is a lie involved in Clemens Petersen's article, not in what he says, but in what he refrains from saying. And he intentionally refrains from saying a great deal. . . .Tell me, now, is Peer Gynt himself not a personality, compete and individual? I know that he is. And the mother; is she not?" But the most memorable passage in this memorable letter is the following piece of splendid arrogance: "My book is poetry; and if it is not, then it will be. The conception of poetry in our country, in Norway, shall be made to conform to the book." It certainly seems that any definition of poetry which should be so framed as to exclude Peer Gynt must have something of what Petersen himself called "tankesvindel" about it.

Ibsen's burst of indignation relieved his mind, and three weeks later we find him writing, half apologetically, of the "cargo of nonsense" he had "shipped off" to Björnson, immediately on reading Petersen's review. He even sends a friendly "greeting" to the offending critic. But this is his last (published) letter to Björnson for something like fifteen years. How far the reception of Peer Gynt may have contributed to the breach between them, I do not know. Björnson's own criticism of the poem, as we shall presently see, was very favourable.

Peer Gynt was not, on its appearance, quite so popular as Brand. A second edition was called for in a fortnight; but the third edition did not appear until 1874, by which time the seventh edition of Brand was already on the market. Before the end of the century ten editions of Peer Gynt had appeared in Copenhagen as against fourteen of Brand. The first German translation appeared in 1881, and the present English translation in 1892. A French translation, by Count Prozor, appeared in the Nouvelle Revue in 1896.

After a great deal of discussion as to the stage-arrangement, Peer Gynt, largely abbreviated, was produced, with Edvard Grieg's now famous incidental music, at the Christiania Theatre in February, 1876, Henrik Klausen playing the title-part. It was acted thirty-seven times; but a fire which destroyed some of the scenery put a stop to the performances. In 1892, at the same theatre, the first three acts were revived, with Björn Björnson as Peer, and repeated fifty times. In the repertory of the National Theatre, too (opened in 1899), Peer Gynt has taken a prominent place. It was first given in 1902, and was performed eighty-four times in the subsequent four years. In the version which has established itself on the Norwegian stage, all five acts are given, but the fourth and fifth acts are greatly abbreviated. In the season of 1886 the play was produced at the Dagmar Theatre, Copenhagen. August Lindberg's Swedish Company acted it in Gothenburg in 1892, in Stockholm in 1895, and afterwards toured with it in Norway and Sweden. Count Prozor's translation was acted by "L'Oeuvre" at the Nouveau Théâtre, Paris, in November, 1896, of which remarkable production a lively account may be found in Mr. Bernard Shaw's Dramatic Opinions and Essays, Vol. II, p. 95. At the Deutsches Volkstheater in Vienna, in May 1902, two performances of Peer Gynt were given by the "Akademisch-Litterarische Verein"; and the play has since been produced in Berlin and other German cities. The first production in the English language took place at the Grand Opera House, Chicago, on October 29, 1906, when Mr. Richard Mansfield appeared as Peer Gynt. Mr. Mansfield would seem to have presented portions, at any rate, of all the principle scenes in the play, with the exception of the Saeter-Girl scene and the madhouse scene.

We have seen that the name, Peer Gynt, was suggested to
Ibsen by a folk-tale in Asbjörnsen and Moe's invaluable
collection.   It is one of a group of tales entitled
<u>Reindeer-Hunting in the Rondë Hills</u>,[5] and in the same group occurs
the adventure of Gudbrand Glesnë on the Gendin-edge, which Peer
Gynt works up so unblushingly in Act I., Sc.1. The text of both
these tales will be found in the Appendix, and the reader will
recognise how very slight are the hints which set the poet's
imagination to work.   The encounter with the Saeter-Girls (Act
II., Sc. 3), and the struggle with the Boyg (Act II., Sc. 7), are
foreshadowed in Asbjörnsen, and the concluding remark of Anders
Ulsvolden evidently suggested to Ibsen the idea of incarnating
Fantasy in Peer Gynt, as in Brand he had given us incarnate
Will.   But the Peer Gynt of the drama has really nothing in
common with the Peer Gynt of the story, and the rest of the
characters are not even remotely suggested.   Many scattered
traits and allusions, however, are borrowed from other legends in
the same storehouse of grotesque and marvellous imaginings.   Thus
the story of the devil in a nutshell (Act I., Sc.3) figures in
Asbjörnsen under the title of <u>The Boy and the Devil</u>.[6]   The
appearance of the Green-Clad One with her Ugly Brat, who offers
Peer Gynt a goblet of beer (Act III., Sc. 3), is obviously
suggested by an incident in <u>Berthe Tuppenhaug's Stories</u>.[7]   Old
Berthe, too, supplies the idea of correcting Peer Gynt's eyesight
according to the standard of the hill-trolls (Act II., Sc. 6), as
well as the germ of the fantastic thread-ball episode in the last
Act (sc.6).   The castle, "East of the Sun and West of the Moon"
(Act III., Sc. 4), gives its title to one of Asbjörnsen's
stories,[8] which may be read in English in Mr. Andres Lang's <u>Blue
Fairy Book</u>; and <u>Soria Moria Castle</u> is the title of another
legend.[9]   Herr Passarge (in his <u>Henrik Ibsen</u>, Leipzig, 1883)
goes so far as to trace the idea of Peer Gynt's shrinking from
the casting-ladle, even though hell be the alternative (Act V.,
Sc. 7, etc.), to Asbjörnsen's story of <u>The Smith whom they dared
not let into Hell</u>,[10] but the circumstances are so different, and
Ibsen's idea is such an inseparable part of the ethical scheme of
the drama, that we can scarcely take it to have been suggested by
this (or any other) individual story.[11]   At the same time there
is no doubt that <u>The Folk-Lore of Peer Gynt</u> might form the
subject of a much more extended study than our space or our
knowledge admits of.[12]   The whole atmosphere of the first three
acts and of the fifth is that of the Norwegian Folk and Fairy
Tales.   It must be remembered, too, that in the early 'sixties
Ibsen was commissioned by the Norwegian Government to visit
Romsdal and Söndmöre for the purpose of collection folk-songs and
legends.   To these journeys, no doubt, we are mainly indebted for
the local colour of <u>Brand</u> and <u>Peer Gynt</u>.
   Among the sources of <u>Peer Gynt</u> must also be reckoned an
"apocalyptic comedy," named <u>A Soul after Death</u>, by the Danish

poet and critic J. L. Heiberg, whom Ibsen never ceased to admire, in spite of his harsh criticism of The Vikings. It is especially in the last scenes of the last act that the influence of Heiberg's fantasy is apparent; but traces of the Heiberg manner may also be noted in many other scenes.

In the second volume of Ibsen's Literary Remains, we find over thirty pages of rejected scraps and parings from Peer Gynt; but they contain nothing of very great interest--nothing, certainly, that the poet did wrong to reject. Almost all the fragments, indeed, are actually included in the definitive text, in a polished and perfected form. The only important exception is a whole scene which was apparently to have followed the existing second scene of the Second Act, but has entirely disappeared from the finished play. In it Peer Gynt is playing with the idea of suicide, when Solveig comes upon him. He reproaches her with having driven him mad by refusing to dance with him; and she is, as she was at the wedding feast, half attracted and half frightened by his wild conduct. Then her father and mother, with Aase, come upon the scene, and the father says that Peer may have Solveig, on one condition: namely, that he shall give himself up to justice and undergo the seven years' imprisonment for his crime.[13] "Raise in your heart the Lord's tabernacle," says the old man, "and serve seven years as Jacob served for Rachel." "Seven years is too long," says Aase; "Eternity is longer," replies the old man--and there the fragment ends. There is nothing of much value in the omitted scene. The passage between Peer and Solveig is little more than a repetition of their encounter in the First Act' and the thrilling poetry of Solveig's appearance in Act III., Sc. 3 would have been sadly discounted if this scene had been suffered to stand.

The publication of the fragment known as the "epic Brand" shows us that the incident of the lad who cuts off his finger to escape military service (Act III., Sc. 1) was at first intended to figure in that poem. Brand relates how he saw the youth mutilate himself, and was present next day when the recruiting -commissioners overwhelmed him with scorn, and he fled, an outcast, to his home among the mountains. Here the youth is introduced with unmixed contempt, to typify Norway pleading weakness as a reason for not taking up arms in defence of Denmark. The deeper significance which is given to his case in the Pastor's address (Act V., Sc. 3) was evidently an afterthought.

What are we to say now of the drift, the interpretation of Peer Gynt? The first and most essential thing may be said in Ibsen's own words. On February 24, 1868, he wrote from Rome to

Frederik Hegel: "I learn that the book has created much
excitement in Norway. This does not trouble me in the least; but
both there and in Denmark they have discovered much more satire
in it than was intended by me. Why can they not read the book as
a poem? For as such I wrote it. The satirical passages are
tolerably isolated. But if the Norwegians of the present time
recognise themselves, as it would appear they do, in the
character of Peer Gynt, that is the good people's own affair."
In the last sentence the innocence of intention is, no doubt, that
Ibsen was absolutely sincere in declaring that he wrote it
primarily as a poem, a work of pure imagination, and that as a
work of pure imagination it ought primarily to be read. There is
undeniably an under-current of ethical and satirical meaning in
the play; but no one can properly enjoy or value it who is not
swept along irresistibly by the surface stream of purely poetic
invention and delineation. Peer himself is a character-creation
on the heroic scale, as vital a personality as Falstaff or Don
Quixote. It is here that the poem (as Clemens Petersen vaguely
discerned) has a marked advantage over its predecessor. In spite
of the tremendous energy with which he is depicted, Brand remains
an abstraction or an attitude, rather than a human being. But
Peer Gynt is human in every fibre--too human to be alien to any
one of us. We know him, we understand him, we love him--for who
does not love a genial, imaginative, philosophic rascal? As for
his adventures and vicissitudes, if they do not give us pleasure
in and for themselves, quite apart from any symbolic sub-intention
--just as the adventures of Sindbad, or Gil Blas, or Tom Jones,
or Huckleberry Finn give us pleasure--then assuredly the poem
does not affect us as Ibsen intended that it should. Readers who
approach it for the first time may therefore be counselled to pay
no heed to its ethical or political meanings, and to take it as
it comes, simply as a dramatic romance or phantasmagoria of
purely human humour and pathos. Reading it in this way, they
will naturally find a good deal that seems obscure and arbitrary;
but much of this will be cleared up on a second reading, by the
aid of such side-lights as this Introduction can afford. No
assiduity of study, however, can find in Peer Gynt a clear,
consistent, cut-and-dried allegory, with a place for everything
and everything in its place. It is not an allegory, but (as
aforesaid) a phantasmagory. This is what the early critics did
not realise. They quarrelled with it for the very luxuriance of
its invention, the buoyant irrepressible whimsicality of its
humour, the shimmering iridescence of its style. They stood
before an "undulant and diverse" carnival-pageant, and grumbled
because it would not fit into any recognised form, sanctioned by
their preconceived aesthetic principles.

I am far from maintaining that the reckless, elusive
capriciousness of the poem is an unmixed merit. It would
probably have done no harm if, after the first rapture of compo-

sition had died away, Ibsen had gone over it and pruned it a little here and there. I can by no means endorse the critics' sweeping condemnation of the Fourth Act, which contains some of the most delightful passages in the whole poem; but the first scene of this Act is unquestionably shallow in conception and diffuse in style—a piece of satiric journalism rather than of literature. The concluding scenes of the last Act, too, would certainly have been none the worse for a little compression. The auction scene (Act V., Sc. 4), though it has a sort of fantastic impressiveness, seems to me hopelessly baffling in its relation both to the outward story and to the inner significance of the poem. Here, and perhaps at some half-dozen other points, one may admit that Ibsen appears to have let his fancy run away with him; but the inert, excessive, or utterly enigmatic passages in Peer Gynt are surely few and brief in comparison with the passages in Faust to which the same epithets may be applied. On the other hand, the scenes of poignant and thrilling and haunting poetry are too many to be severally indicated. The First Act, with its inimitable life and movement, Aase's death-scene, and the Pastor's speech in the last Act, are usually cited as the culminating points of the poem; and there can be no doubt that Aase's death-scene, at any rate, is one of the supreme achievements of modern drama.[14] But there are several other scenes that I would place scarcely, if at all, lower than these. In point of weird intensity, there is nothing in the poem more marvellous than the Saeter-Girl scene (Act II., Sc. 3); in point of lyric movement, Peer Gynt's repudiation of Ingird (Act II., Sc.1) is incomparable; and in point of sheer beauty and pathos, Solveig's arrival at the hut (Act III., Sc.3), with the whole of the scene that follows, stands supreme.[15] For my own part, I reckon the shipwreck scenes at the beginning of the Fifth Act among the most impressive, as they are certainly not the least characteristic, in the poem. And, in enumerating its traits of undeniable greatness, one must by no means forget the character of Aase, on which Ibsen himself dwelt with justified complacency. There is not a more lifelike creation in the whole range of drama.

Having now warned the reader against allowing the search for symbolic or satiric meanings to impair his enjoyment of the pure poetry of Peer Gynt, I may proceed to point out some of the implications which do indubitably underlie the surface aspects of the poem. These meanings fall under three heads. First, we have universal-human satire and symbolism, bearing upon human nature in general, irrespective of race or nationality. Next we have satire upon Norwegian human nature in particular, upon the religious and political life of Norway as a nation. Lastly, we find a certain number of local and ephemeral references—what, in the slang of our stage, are called "topical allusions."

In order to provide the reader with a clue to the complex meanings of Peer Gynt, on its higher lines or planes of significance, I cannot do better than quote some paragraphs from the admirable summary of the drama given by Mr. P. H. Wicksteed in his Four Lectures on Henrik Ibsen.[16] Mr. Wicksteed is in such perfect sympathy with Ibsen in the stage of his development marked by Brand and Peer Gynt, that he has understood these poems, in my judgment, at least as well as any other commentator, whether German or Scandinavian. He writes as follows:

"In Brand the hero is an embodied protest against the poverty of spirit and half-heartedness that Ibsen rebelled against in his countrymen. In Peer Gynt the hero is himself the embodiment of that spirit. In Brand the fundamental antithesis, upon which, as its central theme, the drama is constructed, is the contrast between the spirit of compromise on the one hand, and the motto "everything or nothing" on the other. And Peer Gynt is the very incarnation of a compromising dread of decisive committal to any one course. In Brand the problem of self-realisation and the relation of the individual to his surroundings is obscurely struggling for recognition, and in Peer Gynt it becomes the formal theme upon which all the fantastic variations of the drama are built up. In both plays alike the problems of heredity and the influence of early surroundings are more than touched upon; and both alike culminate in the doctrine that the only redeeming power on earth or in heaven is the power of love.

"Peer Gynt, as already stated, stands for the Norwegian people, much as they are sketched in Brand, though with more brightness of colouring. Hence his perpetual "hedging" and determination never so to commit himself that he cannot draw back. Hence his fragmentary life of smatterings. Hence his perpetual brooding over the former grandeur of his family, his idle dreams of the future, and his neglect of every present duty. Hence his deep-rooted selfishness and cynical indifference to all higher motives; and hence, above all, his sordid and superstitious religion; for to him religion is the apotheosis of the art of "hedging."

"But Ibsen's allegories are never stiffly or pedantically worked out. His characters, though typical, are personal. We could read Brand, and could feel the tragedy and learn the lessons of the drama without any knowledge whatever of the circumstances or feelings under which it was written, or the references to the Norwegian character and conduct with which it teems.

"So, too, with Peer Gynt. We may forget the national significance of the sketch, except where special allusions recall it to our minds, and may think only of the universal problems with which the poem deals, and which will retain their awful interest when Ibsen's polemic against his countrymen has sunk into oblivion. The study of Peer Gynt as an occasional poem should be strictly subsidiary and introductory to its study as the tragedy of a lost soul.

"What is it to be one's self? God meant something when he made each one of us. For a man to embody that meaning of God in his words and deeds, and so become in his degree a "word of God made flesh," is to be himself. But thus to be himself he must slay himself. That is to say, he must slay the craving to make himself the centre round which others revolve, and must strive to find his true orbit and swing, self-poised, round the great central light. But what is a poor devil can never puzzle out what on earth God did mean when he made him? Why, then, he must feel it. But how often your "feeling" misses fire! Ay! there you have it. The devil has no stauncher ally than want of perception! [Act V., Sc. 9.]

"But, after all, you may generally find out what God meant you for, if you will face facts. It is easy to find a refuge from facts in lies, in self-deception, and in self-sufficiency. It is easy to take credit to yourself for what circumstances have done for you, and lay upon circumstances what you owe to yourself. It is easy to think you are realising yourself by refusing to become a "pack-horse for the weal and woe of others" [Act IV., Sc. 1], keeping alternatives open and never closing a door behind you or burning your ships, and so always remaining the master of the situation and self-possessed. If you choose to do these easy things you may always "get round" your difficulties [Act II., Sc. 7], but you will never get through them. You will remain master of the situation indeed, but the situation will become poorer and narrower every day. If you never commit yourself, you never express yourself, and your self becomes less and less significant and decisive. Calculating selfishness is the annihilation of self."

So far Mr. Wicksteed. The general significance of the poem, in the terms of that theism which may or may not have been Ibsen's personal creed during the years of its incubation, could scarcely be better expounded.

When we come to subsidiary meanings, we must proceed more carefully, for we have the poet's own word for it that many have been read into the poem whereof he never dreamt. For example, in his first letter to Björnson after reading Clemens Petersen's criticism, he protested against that critic's assumption that the Strange Passenger (Act V., Scs. 1 and 2) was symbolic of "dread." "If my head had been on the block," he said, "and such an explanation would have saved my life, it would never have occurred to me. I never thought of such a thing. I stuck in the scene as a mere caprice." For this element of caprice we must always allow. The whole Fourth Act, the poet told the present writer, was an afterthought, and did not belong to the original scheme of the play.

Here we come upon the question whether Ibsen consciously designed Peer Gynt as a counterblast to Björnson's idyllic peasant-novel, Synnöve Solbakken. This theory, put forward by a judicious French critic, M. Auguste Ehrhard,[17] among others, has always seemed to me very far-fetched; but as Dr. Brandes, in the Introduction to Peer Gynt in the German collected edition, appears to give it his sanction, I quote what he says on the point: "German critics have laid special emphasis on the fact that Ibsen here placed himself in conscious opposition to Björnson's glorification, in his early novels, of the younger generation of Norwegian peasants. Quarrelsomeness and love of fighting were represented in Thorbjörn, the hero of Synnöve Solbakken, as traits of the traditional old-Norse viking spirit; in Arne the poetic proclivities of the people were placed in an engaging light. The vaunted fisticuff-heroism was, in Ibsen's view, nothing but rawness, and the poetic proclivities of Norwegian youth appeared to him, in the last analysis, simply a very prevalent love of lying and gasconading. The Norwegians appear in the caricaturing mirror of this brilliant poem as a people who, in smug contentment, are "to themselves enough," and therefore laud everything that is their own, however insignificant it may be, shrink from all decisive action, and have for their national vice a tendency to fantastication and braggadocio." That Peer Gynt is a counterblast to national romanticism and chauvinism in general there can of course be no doubt; but I see no reason to suppose that Ibsen had Björnson's novels specially in view, or intended anything like a "caricature" of them. It is pretty clear, too, that Björnson himself had no such idea in his mind when he reviewed the poem in the Norsk Folkeblad for November 23, 1867. His long article is almost entirely laudatory, and certainly shows no smallest sign of hostile party-spirit. "Peer Gynt," says Björnson, "is a satire upon Norwegian egoism, narrowness, and self-sufficiency, so executed as to have made me not only again and again laugh till I was sore, but again and again give thanks to the author in my heart--as I here do publicly." Beyond remarking upon the over-exuberance of detail, and criticising the versification, Björnson says little or nothing in dispraise of the poem. On the other hand he says curiously little of its individual beauties. He never mentions Aase, says nothing of her death-scene, or of the Pastor's speech, and picks out as the best thing in the play the thread-ball scene (Act V., Sc.6).

The most obviously satirical passage of the first three acts is the scene in the Dovrë-King's palace (Act II., Sc. 6), with its jibe at Norwegian national vanity:

> The cow gives cakes and the bullock mead
> Ask not if its taste be sour or sweet;
> The main matter is, and you mustn't forget it,
> It's all of it home-brewed.

In the original version of the scene, as it appears in the
Literary Remains, the shafts of satire are even more clearly
driven home than in the finished play. The troll-banquet begins
with a chanting in unison of a parody on the Norwegian national
song, "For Norway, Heroes' Motherland," to the stirring melody of
which Ibsen himself, in the days of his national-romanticism, had
written many a patriotic stanza. Then a "Professor-Troll,"
called upon to pronounce a eulogy on Trolldom, launches forth
into the same speech which he has made year after year on like
occasions--a habit, it is said, of Norwegian Independence Day
(17th May) orators. These too obvious thrusts Ibsen removed on
revision, without thereby in any degree obscuring his satiric
intention. Much more difficult is the interpretation of the
Boyg,[18] that vague, shapeless, ubiquitous, inevitable
invulnerable Thing which Peer encounters in the following scene
(Act II., Sc. 7). Ibsen found it in the folk-tale, and was
attracted, no doubt, by the sheer uncanniness and eerieness of
the idea. Neither can one doubt, however, that in his own mind
he attributed to the monster some symbolic signification. Dr.
Brandes would have us see in it the Spirit of Compromise--the
same evil spirit which is assailed in *Brand*. The Swedish critic,
Vasenius, interprets it as Peer Gynt's own consciousness of his
inability to take a decisive step--to go through an obstacle in
place of skirting round it. Herr Passarge reads in it a symbol
of the mass of mankind, *perpetuum immobile*, opposing its sheer
force of inertia to every forward movement.[19] This would make it
nearly equivalent to "the compact majority " of *An Enemy of the
People*; or, looking at it from a slightly different angle, we
might see in the scene an illustration in action of that
despairing cry of Schiller's Talbot: "Mit der Dummheit kämpfen
Götter selbst vergebens." The truth probably is that the poet
vaguely intended this vague monster to be as elusive in its
symbolism as in its physical constitution. But when, in Act IV.,
Sc. 12, he formally identifies the Boyg with the Sphinx, we may
surely conclude that one of the interpretations present to his
mind was metaphysical. In this aspect, the Boyg would typify the
riddle of existence, with which we grapple in vain, and which we
have to "get round" as best we can.

The Fourth Act contains a good many special allusions, in
addition to the general, and somewhat crude, satire in the
opening scene on the characteristics of different nationalities,
with particular reference to their conduct in the Dano-German
crisis. Peer's dreams of African colonisation (Act IV., Sc. 5),
and of the foundation of a new state to be called Gyntiana, refer
to an attempt made by Ole Bull, between 1852 and 1857, to found,
in the State of Pennsylvania, an ideal commonwealth, which was to
have been christened "Oleana." The attempt and its failure
attracted a good deal of attention in Norway, and were clearly
remembered when *Peer Gynt* was written, some ten years later. But

it is especially in the madhouse scene (Act IV., Sc. 13) that satiric sallies abound. "The Fellah with the royal mummy on his back," says Henrik Jaeger,[20] "is--like Trumpeterstrale--a cut at the Swedes, the mummy being Charles the Twelfth. Like the Fellah, it is implied, the Swedes are extremely proud of their "Hero-king," and yet during the Dano-German war they showed not the smallest sign of having anything in common with him, unless it were that they, like him, "kept still and completely dead." In the delusion of the minister Hussein, who imagines himself a pen, there is a general reference to the futile address- and note -mongering which went on in Norwegian-Swedish officialdom during the Dano-German War, and a more special one to an eminent Swedish statesman [Grev Manderström],[21] who, during the war, had been extremely proud of his official notes, and had imagined that by means of them he might exercise a decisive influence on the course of events."

Most prominent and unmistakable of all the satiric passages, however, is the attack on the language-reformers in the personage of Huhu. In the list of characters, Huhu is set down as a "Malstraever from Zanzibar." Now the Malstraevers are a party which desires to substitute a language compounded from the various local dialects for the Norwegian of the townsfolk and of literature. This they call Danish, and declare to be practically a foreign tongue to the peasants, who form the backbone of the Norwegian nation. Ibsen's satire, it must be said, has had little or no effect on the movement, which has gone on slowly but steadily, and has of late years met with official and legislative recognition. There is a large and increasing literature in the "Mal"; it is taught in schools and it is spoken in the Storthing. Where the movement may end it is hard to say. It must seem to a foreigner, as it seemed to Ibsen, retrograde and obscurantist; but there is doubtless some genuine impulse behind it which the foreigner cannot appreciate.[22]

THE LEAGUE OF YOUTH

After the momentous four years of his first visit to Italy, to which we owe Brand and Peer Gynt, Ibsen left Rome in May, 1868, visited Florence, and then spent the summer at Berchtesgaden in southern Bavaria. There he was busy "mentally wrestling" with the new play which was to take shape as De Unges Forbund (The League of Youth); but he did not begin to put it on paper until, after a short stay at Munich, he settled down in Dresden, in the early autumn. Thence he wrote to his publisher, Hegel, on October 31: "My new work is making rapid progress. . . . The whole outline is finished and written down. The first act is completed, the second will be in the course of a week, and by the end of the year I hope to have the play ready. It will be in prose, and in every way adapted for the stage. The title is The League of Youth; or, The Almighty & Co., a comedy, in five acts." At Hegel's suggestion he omitted the second title, "though," he wrote, "it could have given offence to no one who had read the play."

This was his first play in modern prose, and the medium did not come easy to him. Six or seven years earlier, he wrote the opening scenes of Love's Comedy in prose, but was dissatisfied with the effect, and recast the dialogue in rhymed verse. Having now outgrown his youthful romanticism, and laid down, in Brand and Peer Gynt, the fundamental positions of his criticism of life, he felt that to carry that criticism into detail he must come to close quarters with reality; and to that end he required a suppler instrument than verse. He must cultivate, as he afterwards[1] put it, "the very much more difficult art of writing the genuine, plain language spoken in real life." Probably the mastery of this new art cost him more effort than he anticipated, for, instead of having the play finished by the end of 1868, he did not despatch the manuscript to Copenhagen until March, 1869. It was published on September 30 of that year.

The preliminary sketches for The League of Youth, though they occupy forty pages of the Literary Remains, are fragmentary and of small importance. Ibsen evidently conceived the play from the first very much on the lines which it ultimately followed.

Even the names of the characters in the first draft remain almost unaltered in the finished play, except that Stensgard was originally to have been "Stenborg," Madam Rundholmen "Madam Bagholmen," and Selma "Margrete." The fantastic dialogue between Selma-Margrete, her husband and Stensgard, near the beginning of the second act, is clearly indicated in the draft; but there is no trace of Selma's outburst in the third act. This probably does not mean, however, that the development of her character was an afterthought, but only that he did not happen to make any first study for the scene, or that it has not been preserved. We find several allusions to the sub-title originally contemplated, The Almighty & Co.; indeed it is introduced in quite the orthodox fashion in what may not unfairly be called the "tag." The chief interest of the fragments, in fact, lies in the proof they afford that Ibsen was at this time thoroughly steeped in the current conventions of theatrical manufacture. They also show that he had not yet got over his indignation at what he thought the poltroonery of Norway with reference to the Danish War. He intended to drag in a satiric allusion to it in the second act; but he wisely changed his mind, and used the idea in a poem, entitled "Faith's Foundation."

While the comedy was still in process of conception, Ibsen had written to his publisher: "This new, peaceable work is giving me great pleasure." It thus appears that he considered it less polemical in its character than the poems which had immediately preceded it. If his intentions were pacific, they were entirely frustrated. The play was regarded as a violent and wanton attack on the Norwegian Liberal party, while Stensgard was taken for a personal lampoon on Björnson. Its first performance at the Christiania Theatre (October 18, 1869) passed quietly enough; but at the second and third performances an organised opposition took the field, and disturbances amounting almost to a riot occurred. Public feeling soon calmed down, and the play (the first prose comedy of any importance in Norwegian literature) became one of the most popular pieces in the repertory of the theatre. But it led to an estrangement from Björnson and the Liberal party which was not healed for many a day--not, indeed, until Ghosts had shown the Norwegian public the folly of attempting to make party capital out of the works of a poet who stood far above party.

The estrangement from Björnson had begun some time before the play appeared. A certain misunderstanding had followed the appearance of Peer Gynt,[2] and had been deepened by political differences. Björnson had become an ardent National Liberal, with leanings towards Republicanism; Ibsen was not at all a Republican (he deeply offended Björnson by accepting orders and decorations), and his political sympathies, while not of a partisan nature, were mainly "Scandinavian"--that is to say, directed towards a closer union of the three Scandinavian kingdoms. Distance, and the evil offices of gossiping friends, played their part in begetting dissension. Ibsen's last friendly letter to Björnson (of these years) was written in the last days of 1867; in the first days of 1869, while he was actually busied with The League of Youth, we find him declining to contribute to a Danish magazine for the reason (among others) that Björnson was to be one of its joint editors.

The news of the stormy reception of his comedy reached Ibsen in Egypt, where, as the guest of the Khedive, he was attending the opening of the Suez Canal. He had recorded the incident in a poem, "At Port Said." On his return to Dresden he wrote to Hegel (December 14, 1869): "The reception of The League of Youth pleases me very much; for the disapprobation I was prepared, and it would have been a disappointment to me if there had been none. But what I was not prepared for was that Björnson should feel himself attacked by the play, as rumour says he does. Is this really the case? He must surely see that it is not himself I have had in mind, but his pernicious and "lie-steeped" clique who have served me as models. However, I will write to him to-day or to-morrow, and I hope that the affair, in spite of all differences, will end in a reconciliation." The intended letter does not appear to have been written; nor would it, probably, have produced the desired effect, for Björnson's resentment was very deep. He had already (in November) written a poem to Johan Sverdrup, the leader of the Liberal party, in which he deplored the fact that "the sacred grove of poetry no longer afforded sanctuary against assassination," or as the Norwegian word vigorously expressed it, "sneak-murder." Long afterwards, in 1881, he explained what he meant by this term: "It was not the portrayal of contemporary life and known personages that I called assassination. It was the fact that The League of Youth sought to represent our young Liberal party as a gang of ambitious speculators, whose patriotism was as empty as their phraseology; and particularly that prominent men were first made clearly recognisable, and then had false hearts and shady characters foisted upon them." It is difficult to see, indeed, how Ibsen can have expected Björnson to distinguish very clearly between an attack on his "lie-steeped clique" and a lampoon on himself. Even Stengard's religious phraseology, the confidence with which he claims God as a member of his party, was at that time characteristic of Björnson. The case, in fact, seems to have been very like that of the portraiture of Leigh Hunt in Harold Skimpole. Both Dickens and Ibsen had unconsciously taken more from their respective models than they intended. They imagined, perhaps, that the features which did not belong to the original would conceal the likeness, whereas their actual effect was only to render the portraits libellous.

Eleven years passed before Björnson and Ibsen were reconciled. In 1880 (after the appearance of A Doll's House and

before that of <u>Ghosts</u>) Björnson wrote in an American magazine:
"I think I have a pretty thorough acquaintance with the dramatic
literature of the world, and I have not the slightest hesitation
in saying that Henrik Ibsen possesses more dramatic power than
any other play-writer of our day. The fact that I am not always
partial to the style of his work makes me all the more certain
that I am right in my judgment of him."

   <u>The</u> <u>League</u> <u>of</u> <u>Youth</u> soon became very popular in Norway, and
it had considerable success in Sweden and Denmark. It was acted
with notable excellence at the Royal Theatre in Copenhagen.
Outside of Scandinavia it has never taken any hold of the stage.
At the date of its appearance Ibsen was still quite unknown, even
in Germany; and when he became known, its technique was already
antiquated. It has been acted once or twice both in Germany and
England, and has proved very amusing on the stage; but it is
essentially an experimental, transitional work. The poet is
trying his tools.

   The technical influence of Scribe and his school is apparent
in every scene. Ibsen's determination not to rest content with
the conventions of that school may already be discerned, indeed,
in his disuse of the soliloquy and the aside; but, apart from
these flagrant absurdities, he permits himself to employ almost
all the devices of Scribe. Note, for example, how much of the
action arises from sheer misunderstanding. The whole second act
turns upon the Chamberlain's misunderstanding of the bent of
Stensgard's diatribe in the first act. As the Chamberlain is
deliberately misled by his daughter and Fieldbo, the
misunderstanding is not, perhaps, technically inadmissible. Yet
it has to be maintained by very artificial means. Why, one may
ask, does not Fieldbo, in his long conversation with Stensgard,
in the second act, warn him of the thin ice on which he is
skating? There is no sufficient reason, except that the great
situation at the end of the act would thus be rendered
impossible. It is in the fourth act, however, that the methods
of the vaudevillist are most apparent. It is one string of
blunders of the particular type which the French significantly
call "quiproquos." Some arise through the quite diabolical
genius for malicious wire-pulling developed by old Lundestad; but
most of them are based upon that deliberate and elaborate
vagueness of expression on the part of the characters which is
the favourite artifice of the professor of theatrical
sleight-of-hand. We are not even spared the classic quiproquo of
the proposal by proxy mistaken for a proposal direct--Stensgard's
overtures to Madam Rundholmen on behalf of Bastian being accepted
by her as an offer on his own behalf. We are irresistibly
reminded of Mrs. Bardell's fatal misunderstanding of Mr.
Pickwick's intentions. All this, to be sure, is excellent
farce, but there is no originality in the expedients by which
it is carried on. Equally conventional, and equally redolent of

Scribe, is the conduct of the fifth act. The last drop of effect is wrung out of the quiproquos with an almost mathematical accuracy. We are minded of a game at puss-in-the-four-corners, in which Stensgard tries every corner in turn, only to find himself at last left out in the cold. Then, as the time approaches to ring down the curtain, every one is seized with a fever of amiability, the Chamberlain abandons all his principles and prejudices, even to the point of subscribing for twenty copies of Aslaksen's newspaper, and the whole thing becomes scarcely less unreal than one of the old-comedy endings in which the characters stand in a semicircle while each delivers a couplet of the epilogue. It is difficult to believe that the facile optimism of this conclusion could at any time have satisfied the mind which, only twelve years later, conceived the picture of Oswald Alving shrinking together in his chair and babbling, "Mother--give me the sun."

But, while we realise with what extraordinary rapidity and completeness Ibsen outgrew this phase of his art, we must not overlook the genuine merits of this brilliant comedy. With all its faults, it was an advance on the technique of its day, and was hailed as such by a critic so penetrating as George Brandes. Placing ourselves at the point of view of the time, we may perhaps say that its chief defect is its marked inequality of style. The first act is purely preparatory; the fifth act as we have noted, is a rather perfunctory winding-up. The real play lies in the intervening acts; and each of these belongs to a different order of art. The second act is a piece of high comedy, quite admirable in its kind; the third act, both in tone and substance, verges upon melodrama; while the fourth act is nothing but rattling farce. Even from the Scribe point of view, this jumping from key to key is a fault. Another objection which Scribe would probably have urged is that several of Fieldbo's speeches, and the attitude of the Chamberlain towards him, are, on the face of them, incomprehensible, and are only retrospectively explained. The poetics of that school forbid all reliance on retrospect, perhaps because they do not contemplate the production of any play about which any human being would care to think twice.

The third act, though superficially a rather tame interlude between the vigorous second act and the bustling fourth, is in reality the most characteristic of the five. The second act might be signed Augier, and the fourth Labiche; but in the third the coming Ibsen is manifest. The scene between the Chamberlain and Monsen is, in its disentangling of the past, a preliminary study for much of his later work--a premonition, in fact, of his characteristic method. Here, too, in the character of Selma and her outburst of revolt, we have by far the most original feature of the play. In Selma there is no trace of French influence, spiritual or technical. With admirable perspicacity, Dr. Brandes realised from the outset the significance of this figure. "Selma," he wrote, "is a new creation, and her relation to the family might form the subject of a whole drama. But in the play as it stands she has scarcely room to move." The drama which Brandes here foresaw, Ibsen wrote ten years later in A Doll's House.

With reference to the phrase "De lokale forhold," here lamely represented by "the local situation," Ibsen has a curious remark in a letter to Marcus Grönvold, dated Stockholm, September 3, 1877. His German translator, he says, has rendered the phrase literally "lokale Verhältnisse"--"which is wrong, because no suggestion of comicality or narrow-mindedness is conveyed by this German expression. The rendering ought to be "unsere berechtigten Eigenthümlichkeiten," an expression which conveys the same meaning to Germans as the Norwegian one does to us Scandinavians." This suggestion is, unfortunately, of no help to the English translator, especially when it is remembered in what context Aslaksen uses the phrase "de lokale forhold" in the fifth act of An Enemy of the People.

PILLARS OF SOCIETY

In the eight years that intervened between The League of Youth and Pillars of Society--his second prose play of modern life --Ibsen published a small collection of his poems (1871), and his "World-Historic Drama," Emperor and Galilean (1873). After he had thus dismissed from his mind the figure of Julian the Apostate, which had haunted it ever since his earliest days in Rome, he deliberately abandoned, once for all, what may be called masquerade romanticism--that external stimulus to the imagination which lies in remoteness of time and unfamiliarity of scene and costume. It may be that, for the moment, he also intended to abandon, not merely romanticism, but romance--to deal solely with the literal and commonplace facts of life, studies in the dry light of everyday experience. If that was his purpose, it was very soon to break down; but in Pillars of Society he more nearly achieved it than in any other work.

Many causes contributed to the unusually long pause between Emperor and Galilean and Pillars of Society. The summer of 1874 was occupied with a visit to Norway--the first he had paid since the Hegira of ten years earlier. A good deal of time was devoted to the revision of some of his earlier works, which were republished in Copenhagen; while the increasing vogue of his plays on the stage involved a considerable amount of business correspondence. The Vikings and The Pretenders were acted in these years, not only throughout Scandinavia, but at many of the leading theatres of Germany; and in 1876, after much discussion and negotiation, Peer Gynt was for the first time placed on the stage, in Christiania.

The first mention of Pillars of Society occurs in a letter from Ibsen to his publisher, Hegel, of October 23, 1875 in which he mentions that the first act, "always to me the most difficult part of a play," is ready, and states that it will be "a drama in five acts." Unless this be a mere slip of the pen, it is curious as showing that, even when the first act was finished, Ibsen did not foresee in detail the remainder of the action. In the course of further development an act dropped out of his scheme. On November 25, 1875, he reports to Hegel: "The first act of my new drama is ready--the fair copy written; I am now working at Act Second"; but it was not until the summer of 1877 that the completed manuscript was sent to Copenhagen. The book was published in the early autumn.

We find in the Literary Remains three brief and fragmentary scenarios of this play, two almost complete drafts of the first act, an almost entirely rejected draft of the beginning of the second act, and large fragments of a draft of the fourth act. The "fore-works" of Pillars of Society, as indeed of most of its successors, show that Ibsen was far from being one of the playwrights who have their plays clearly and definitely mapped out before they put pen to paper. Even in the second draft of his first act, he is still fumbling around after his characters and their relations. The germ of the play, I imagine, lay in its title; at any rate, the phrase occurs and is emphasised early in the first draft. The chief "pillars of society" was from the first conceived as one of the energetic manufacturer-merchants, with a score of irons in the fire, who are leading figures in all the minor Norwegian towns; and it was of course evident from the first that this pillar of society must be in some way flawed or hollow. But the precise nature of the flaw seems to have been undetermined even when the first draft of the first act was finished. At any rate, Bernick at that point shows none of the uneasiness which, in the completed play, the return of Johan and Lona naturally causes him; nor is there any preparation in the laying-out of the second act for the great scene between him and Johan in which the true state of matters is revealed. It may be noted that the list of characters includes "Madam Dorf," Dina's mother, the woman with whom Bernick had had the intrigue which he contrived to fasten on Johan Tönnesen. In the completed play she has been dead for years; but in the first draft she is alive, and Dina is in the habit of paying her surreptitious visits. We may assume, I think, that Ibsen contemplated some intervention on her part to clear Johan's character and bring the guilt home to Bernick. With her alive, at any rate, he can scarcely have had the idea of making Bernick try to suppress the scandal by sending Johan his documents to sea in a coffin-ship. This could not occur to him while the best possible witness to the true state of affairs was living at his very doors. So that evidently the matter of the third and fourth acts, the complication of the seaworthy Palm Tree and unseaworthy Indian Girl, and the flight of Olaf on board the latter, was still far from the poet's conception.

A prominent character in both drafts of the first act is Bernick's blind mother, who has quite disappeared from the finished play. Mrs. Bernick, and Johan and Hilmar Tönnesen, are all three children of a blustering old curmudgeon, Mads Tönnesen,

nicknamed "the badger." He was destined to drop out entirely,
his nickname, and some of the traits of his character being
transferred to Morten Kiil in An Enemy of the People. In the
first draft, Bernick is still arguing for the proposed railway,
against the opposition of his business associates; in the
completed play, the whole argument is conducted behind the
scenes, and Bernick has triumphed before he makes his first
appearance. This is a good instance of condensation. Another
instance may be found in the treatment of Johan Tönnesen and Lona
Hessel. In the first draft they are not half-brother and sister,
but only, it would seem, distant cousins; they have been together
in America; and it is by pure chance that they arrive on the same
day. We first hear of Johan in the following passage. Krap,
Bernick's clerk, rushes in and tells of the arrival of a ship in
need of repairs:

    BERNICK. Bravo!. . .What ship is it?
    KRAP. The barque Indian Girl, from New York, with
dye-stuffs from Brazil to Petersburg.
    BERNICK. And the captain?
    KRAP. The captain was swept overboard, and the mate is
lying ill, delirious. But a sailor that was on board as passenger
took the command, and has brought the ship in. . . .
    BERNICK. You have spoken to him, then?
    KRAP. Yes. . . .Here is his card.
    BERNICK. (reads) "John Rawlinson, Esqre., New Orleans."

    In the second draft the name "Rawlinson" is changed to
"Tennyson" which is supposed to be an Anglicised form of
"Tönnesen." Presently Captain Rawlinson and the crew of the
Indian Girl are seen coming up the street, and remarks are made
on their ruffianly appearance:

    MRS. SALVESEN. The captain is almost the worst of them; he
looks just like a robber.
    RECTOR RORLUND. Yes, he's the sort of man that would stick
at nothing.
    BERNICK. They are foreigners, Rector. One mustn't expect
too much of them.

    Then he goes out on the verandah and drops into English:

    BERNICK (bowing and calling out). Good-morning, Master
Rawlinson! This way, if you please, sir! I am Master Bernick!

CAPTAIN RAWLINSON (waves his handkershief and calls). Very well, Karsten; but first, three hurrahs for the old graevling (badger)----

--and the sailors pass on to make a demonstration before the house of Tönnesen, Rawlinson-Tönnesen's father. Meanwhile Lona Hessel has arrived, quite independently, by the Hamburg steamer: in one version, it is this steamer that has towed the Indian Girl into port. We see, then, that Ibsen wrote two complete drafts of the first act before he realised how unnecessary was this intervention of the long arm of coincidence, and made Johan and Lona arrive together and act in concert throughout.

In the earliest draft, there occurs near the end of Act I a farcical scene which would have been very shocking to those critics who are pained by Ibsen's "suburbanism." The reading-party of ladies is on the point of breaking up when:

THE CUSTOM-HOUSE OFFICER'S SERVANT (enters by the garden gate). The master told me to say that the mistress must come home at once; the cook has spoilt the fish-soup.

MRS. RUMMEL. Oh, these servants, these servants! One can't trust them for a moment! Good-bye, good-bye; we shall meet to-morrow. (Exit hastily).

MRS. SALVESEN. Yes, that's what comes of trusting your house to servants.

THE APOTHECARY'S TWO LITTLE GIRLS (at the garden gate). Mamma, mamma, you must come and look after Nicolai; he's fallen into the washing-tub. . . .

MRS. SALVESEN. Oh, these children, these children! Good-bye! I must run as fast as I can. (Rushes out.)

MRS. HOLT. Yes, that's what happens when you have everything standing open. I make it a rule to keep everything under lock and key; and the keys I keep here. (Indicating her pocket.)

THE POSTMAN (comes tearing down the street). Oh, Lord, ma'am, you must make haste home! The steamer will get away without the mail.

MRS. HOLT. The steamer?

THE POSTMAN. Yes; the second bell has rung, and the postmaster can't get on board with the mail until you come home.

MRS. HOLT. What nonsense! Can't he get the mail off without me?

THE POSTMAN. No, for you've locked up his trousers in the wardrobe.

MRS. HOLT. Oh, goodness gracious! These men, these men! They can never do a thing for themselves! (Rushes out with the postman.)

One cannot actually bewail the loss of this scene. I may add that the coffee-parliament of ladies, which disappears after the first act of the completed play, was apparently at first intended to run through the whole action. In the original conception, too, each of the acts was to have passed in a different scene. The process of growth was at the same time a process of condensation.

The theatrical success of Pillars of Society was immediate and striking. First performed in Copenhagen, November 18, 1877, it soon found its way to all the leading stages of Scandinavia. In Berlin, in the early spring of 1878, it was produced at five different theatres within a single fortnight; and it has ever since maintained its hold on the German stage. Before the end of the century it had been acted more than twelve hundred times in Germany and Austria. An adaptation of the play, by the present writer, was produced at the old Gaiety Theatre, London, for a single performance, on the afternoon of December 15, 1880--this being the first time that Ibsen's name had appeared on an English playbill. Again, in 1889, a single performance of it was given at the Opera Comique Theatre; and yet again in May, 1901, the Stage Society gave two performances of it at the Strand Theatre. In the United States it has been acted frequently in German, and Mrs. Fiske has presented it in English, with considerable success. The play did not reach the French stage until 1896, when it was performed by M. Lugné-Poë's organisation, L'Oeuvre. In other countries one hears of a single performance of it, here and there; but, except in Scandinavia and Germany, it has nowhere taken a permanent hold upon the theatre. Nor is the reason far to seek. By the time the English, American, and French public had fully awakened to the existence of Ibsen, he himself had so far outgrown the phase of his development marked by Pillars of Society that the play already seemed commonplace and old-fashioned. It exactly suited the German public of the 'eighties; it was exactly on a level with their theatrical intelligence. But it was above the theatrical intelligence of the English public, and--I had almost said below that of the French public. This is, of course, an exaggeration. What I mean is that there was no possible reason why the countrymen of Augier and Dumas should take any special interest in Pillars of Society. It was not obviously in advance of these masters in technical skill, and the vein of Teutonic sentiment running through it could not greatly appeal to the Parisian public of that period. Thus it is not in the least surprising that, outside of Germany and Scandinavia, Pillars of Society had everywhere to follow in the wake of A Doll's House and Ghosts, and was everywhere found something of an anti-climax.

It is of all Ibsen's works the least characteristic, because, acting on a transitory phase of theory, he has been almost successful in divesting it of poetic charm. There is not even a Selma in it. Of his later plays, only An Enemy of the People is equally prosaic in substance; and it is raised far above the level of the commonplace by the genial humour, the magnificent creative energy, displayed in the character of Stockmann. In Pillars of Society there is nothing that rises above the commonplace. Compared with Stockmann, Bernick seems almost a lay-figure and even Lona Hessel is an intellectual construction--formed of a blend of new theory with old sentiment--rather than an absolute creation, a living and breathing woman, like Nora, or Mrs. Alving, or Rebecca, or Hedda. This is, in brief, the only play of Ibsen's in which plot can be said to preponderate over character. The plot is extraordinarily ingenious and deftly pieced together. Several of the scenes are extremely effective from the theatrical point of view, and in a good many individual touches we may recognise the incomparable master-hand. One of these touches is the scene between Bernick and Rörlund in the third act, in which Bernick's craving for casuistical consolation meets with so painful a rebuff. Only a great dramatist could have devised this scene; but to compare it with a somewhat similar passage in The Pretenders--the scene in the fourth act between King Skule and Jatgeir Skald--is to realise what is meant by the difference between poetry and dramatic prose.

I have called Lona Hessel a composite character because she embodies in a concentrated form the two different strains of feeling that run through the whole play. Beyond the general attack on social pharisaism announced in the very title, we have a clear assertion of the claim of women to moral and economical individuality and independence. Dina, with her insistence on "becoming something for herself" before she will marry Johan, unmistakably foreshadows Nora and Petra. But at the same time the poet is far from having cleared his mind of the old ideal of the infinitely self-sacrificing, dumbly devoted woman whose life has no meaning save in relation to some more or less unworthy male--the Ingeborg-Agnes-Solveig ideal, we may call it. In the original edition of The Pretenders Ingeborg said to Skule: "To love, to sacrifice all, and to be forgotten, that is woman's saga"; and out of that conception arose the very tenderly-touched figure of Martha in this play. If Martha, then, stands for the old ideal--the ideal of the older generation, Lona Hessel hovers between the two. At first sight she seems like an embodiment of the "strong-minded female," the champion of Woman's Rights, and despiser of all feminine graces and foibles. But in the end it appears that her devotion to Bernick has been no less deep and enduring than Martha's devotion to Johan. Her "old friendship does not rust" is a delightful speech; but it points back to the

Ibsen of the past, not forward to the Ibsen of the future. Yet this is not wholly true; for the strain of sentiment which inspired it never became extinct in the poet. He believed to the end in the possibility and the beauty of great, self-forgetful human emotions; and there his philosophy went very much deeper than that of some of his disciples.

In consistency of style, and in architectural symmetry of construction, the play marks a great advance upon The League of Youth. From the end of the first act to the middle of the last, it is a model of skilful plot-development. The exposition, which occupies so much of the first act, is carried out by means of a somewhat cumbrous mechanism. No doubt the "Kaffee-Klatsch" is in great measure justified as a picture of the tattling society of the little town. It does not altogether ignore the principle of economy. But it is curious to note the rapid shrinkage in the poet's expositions. Here we have the necessary information conveyed by a whole party of subsidiary characters. In the next play, A Doll's House, we have still a set exposition, but two characters suffice for it, and one the heroine. In the next play again--that is to say, in Ghosts--the poet has arrived at his own peculiar formula, and the exposition is indistinguishably merged in the action. Still greater is the contrast between the conclusion of Pillars of Society and that of A Doll's House. It would be too much to call Bernick's conversion and promise to turn over a new leaf as conventional as the Chamberlain's right-about-face in The League of Youth. Bernick has passed through a terrible period of mental agony which may well have brought home to him a conviction of sin. Still, the way in which everything suddenly comes right, Olaf is recovered, the Indian Girl is stopped, Aune is reconciled to the use of new machines, and even the weather improves, so as to promise Johan and Dina a prosperous voyage to America--all this is a manifest concession to popular optimism. We are not to conceive, of course, that the poet deliberately compromised with an artistic ideal for the sake of popularity, but rather that he had not yet arrived at the ideal of logical and moral consistency which he was soon afterwards to attain. To use his own metaphor, the ghost of the excellent Eugene Scribe still walked in him. He still instinctively thought of a play as a storm in a tea-cup, which must naturally blow over in the allotted two-hours-and-a-half. Even in his next play--so gradual is the process of evolution--he still makes the external storm, so to speak, blow over at the appointed time. But, instead of the general reconciliation and serenity upon which the curtain falls in The League of Youth and Pillars of Society--instead of the "happy ending" which Helmer so confidently expects--he gives us that famous scene of Nora's revolt and departure, in which he himself may be said to have made his exit from the school of Scribe, banging the door behind him.

The Norwegian title, <u>Samfundets</u> <u>Stötter</u>, means literally
<u>Society's</u> <u>Pillars</u>. In the text, the word "Samfund" has sometimes
been translated "society," sometimes "community." The noun
"stötte," a pillar, has for its correlative the verb, "at
stötte," to support; so that where the English phrase "to support
society" occurs, there is, in the original, a direct allusion to
the title of the play. The leading merchants in Norwegian
seaports often serve as consuls for one or other foreign
Power—whence the title by which Bernick is addressed. Rörlund,
in the original, is called "Adjunkt"—that is to say, he is an
assistant master in a school, subordinate to the head-master or
rector.

A DOLL'S HOUSE

On June 27, 1879, Ibsen wrote from Rome to Marcus Grönvold: "It is now rather hot in Rome, so in about a week we are going to Amalfi, which, being close to the sea, is cooler, and offers opportunity for bathing. I intend to complete there a new dramatic work on which I am now engaged." From Amalfi, on September 20, he wrote to John Paulsen: "A new dramatic work, which I have just completed, has occupied so much of my time during these last months that I have had absolutely none to spare for answering letters." This "new dramatic work" was Et Dukkehjem, which was published in Copenhagen, December 4, 1879. Dr. George Brandes has given some account of the episode in real life which suggested to Ibsen the plot of this play; but the real Nora, it appears, committed forgery, not to save her husband's life, but to redecorate her house. The impulse received from this incident must have been trifling. It is much more to the purpose to remember that the character and situation of Nora had been clearly foreshadowed, ten years earlier, in the figure of Selma in The League of Youth.
Of A Doll's House we find in the Literary Remains a first brief memorandum, a fairly detailed scenario, a complete draft, in quite actable form, and a few detached fragments of dialogue. These documents put out of court a theory of my own[1] that Ibsen originally intended to give the play a "happy ending," and that the relation between Krogstad and Mrs. Linden was devised for that purpose.
Here is the first memorandum:--

NOTES FOR THE[2] TRAGEDY OF TO-DAY

ROME, 19/10/78.
There are two kinds of spiritual laws, two kinds of conscience, one in men and a quite different one in women. They do not understand each other; but the woman is judged in practical life according to the man's law, as if she were not a woman but a man.

The wife in the play finds herself at last entirely at sea
as to what is right and what is wrong; natural feeling on the one
side, and belief in authority on the other, leave her in utter
bewilderment.

A woman cannot be herself in the society of to-day, which is
exclusively a masculine society, with laws written by men, and
with accusers and judges who judge feminine conduct from the
masculine standpoint.

She has committed forgery, and it is her pride; for she did
it for love of her husband, and to save his life. But this
husband, full of everyday rectitude, stands on the basis of the
law and regards the matter with a masculine eye.

Soul-struggles. Oppressed and bewildered by belief in
authority, she loses her faith in her own moral right and ability
to bring up her children. Bitterness. A mother in the society
of to-day, like certain insects, (ought to) go away and die when
she has done her duty towards the continuance of the species.
Love of life, of home, of husband and children and kin. Now and
then a woman-like shaking off of cares. Then a sudden return of
apprehension and dread. She must bear it all alone. The
catastrophe approaches, inexorably, inevitably. Despair,
struggle, and disaster.

In reading Ibsen's statement of the conflict he meant to
portray between the male and female conscience, one cannot but
feel that he somewhat shirked the issue in making Nora's crime a
formal rather than a real one. She had no intention of
defrauding Krogstad; and though it is an interesting point of
casuistry to determine whether, under the stated circumstances,
she had moral right to sign her father's name, opinion on the
point would scarcely be divided along the line of sex. One feels
that, in order to illustrate the "two kinds of conscience," Ibsen
ought to have made his play turn upon some point of conduct (if
such there be) which would sharply divide masculine from feminine
sympathies. The fact that such a point would be extremely hard
to find seems to cast doubt on the ultimate validity of the
thesis. If, for instance, Nora had deliberately stolen the money
from Krogstad, with no intention of repaying it, that would
certainly have revealed a great gulf between her morality and
Helmer's; but would any considerable number of her sex have
sympathised with her? I am not denying a marked difference
between the average man and the average woman in the development
of such characteristics as the sense of justice; but I doubt
whether, when women have their full share in legislation, the
laws relating to forgery will be seriously altered.

A parallel-text edition of the provisional and the final
forms of A Doll's House would be intensely interesting. For the
present, I can note only a few of the most salient differences

between the two versions.

Helmer is at first called "Stenborg";[3] it is not till the scene with Krogstad in the second act that the name Helmer makes its first appearance. Ibsen was constantly changing his characters' names in the course of composition--trying them on, as it were, until he found one that was a perfect fit.

The first scene, down to the entrance of Mrs. Linden, though it contains all that is necessary for the mere development of the plot, runs to only twenty-three speeches, as compared with eighty-one in the completed text. The business of the macaroons is not even indicated; there is none of the charming talk about the Christmas-tree and the children's presents; no request on Nora's part that her present may take the form of money, no indication on Helmer's part that he regards her supposed extravagance as an inheritance from her father. Helmer knows that she toils at copying far into the night in order to earn a few crowns, though of course he has no suspicion as to how she employs the money. Ibsen evidently felt it inconsistent with his character that he should permit this, so in the completed version we learn that Nora, in order to do her copying, locked herself in under the pretext of making decorations for the Christmas-tree, and, when no result appeared, declared that the cat had destroyed her handiwork. The first version, in short, is like a stained glass window seen from without, the second like the same window seen from within.

The long scene between Nora and Mrs. Linden is more fully worked out, though many small touches of character are lacking, such as Nora's remark that some day "when Torvald is not so much in love with me as he is now," she may tell him the great secret of how she saved his life. It is notable throughout that neither Helmer's aestheticism nor the sensual element in his relation to Nora is nearly so much emphasised as in the completed play; while Nora's tendency to small fibbing--that vice of the unfree--is almost an afterthought. In the first appearance of Krogstad, and the indication of his old acquaintance with Mrs. Linden, many small adjustments have been made, all strikingly for the better. The first scene with Dr. Rank,--originally called Dr. Hank--has been almost entirely rewritten. There is in the draft no indication of the doctor's ill-health or of his pessimism; it seems as though he had at first been designed as a mere confidant or raisonneur. This is how he talks:--

HANK. Hallo! what's this? A new carpet? I congratulate you! Now take, for example, a handsome carpet like this; is it a luxury? I say it isn't. Such a carpet is a paying investment; with it underfoot, one has higher, subtler thoughts, and finer feelings, than when one moves over cold, creaking planks in a comfortless room. Especially where there are children in the

house.   The race ennobles itself in a beautiful environment.
    NORA.   Oh, how often I have felt the same, but could never
express it.
    HANK.   No, I dare say not.   It is an observation in
spiritual statistics--a science as yet very little cultivated.

    As to Krogstad, the doctor remarks:--

    If Krogstad's home had been, so to speak, on the sunny side
of life, with all the spiritual windows opening towards the
light. . . .I dare say he might have been a decent enough fellow,
like the rest of us.
    MRS. LINDEN.   You mean that he is not. . . .?
    HANK.   He cannot be.   His marriage was not of the kind to
make it possible.   An unhappy marriage, Mrs. Linden, is like
small-pox: it scars the soul.
    NORA.   And what does a happy marriage do?
    HANK.   It is like a "cure" at the baths; it expels all
peccant humours, and makes all that is good and fine in a man
grow and flourish.

    It is notable that we find in this scene nothing of Nora's
glee on learning that Korgstad is not dependent on her husband;
that fine touch of dramatic irony was an afterthought.   After
Helmer's entrance, the talk is very different in the original
version.   He remarks upon the painful interview he has just had
with Krogstad, whom he is forced to dismiss from the bank; Nora,
in a mild way, pleads for him; and the doctor, in the name of
survival of the fittest,[4] denounces humanitarian sentimentality,
and then goes off to do his best to save a patient who, he
confesses, would be much better dead.   This discussion of the
Krogstad question before Nora has learnt how vital it is to her,
manifestly discounts the effect of the scenes which are to
follow: and Ibsen, on revision did away with it entirely.
    Nora's romp with the children, interrupted by the entrance
of Krogstad, stands very much as in the final version; and in the
scene with Krogstad there is no essential change.   One detail is
worth noting, as an instance of the art of working up an effect.
In the first version, when Krogstad says, "Mrs. Stenborg, you
must see to it that I keep my place in the bank," Nora replies:
"I?   How can you think that I have any such influence with my
husband?"--a natural but not specially effective remark.   But in
the final version she has begun the scene by boasting to Krogstad
of her influence, and telling him that people in a subordinate
position ought to be careful how they offend such influential
persons as herself; so that her subsequent denial that she has any
influence becomes a notable dramatic effect.

The final scene of the act, between Nora and Helmer, is not materially altered in the final version; but the first version contains no hint of the business of decorating the Christmas-tree or of Nora's wheedling Helmer by pretending to need his aid in devising her costume for the fancy dress ball. Indeed, this ball has not yet entered Ibsen's mind. He thinks of it first as a children's party in the flat overhead, to which Helmer's family are invited.

In the opening scene of the second act there are one or two traits that might perhaps have been preserved, such as Nora's prayer: "Oh, God! Oh, God! do something to Torvald's mind to prevent him from enraging that terrible man! Oh, God! Oh, God! I have three little children! Do it for my children's sake." Very natural and touching, too, is her exclamation, "Oh, how glorious it would be if I could only wake up, and come to my senses, and cry, "It was a dream! It was a dream!"" A week, by the way, has passed, instead of a single night, as in the finished play; Nora has been wearing herself out by going to parties every evening. Helmer enters immediately on the nurse's exit; there is no scene with Mrs. Linden in which she remonstrates with Nora for having (as she thinks) borrowed money from Dr. Rank, and so suggests to her the idea of applying to him for aid. In the scene with Helmer, we miss, among many other characteristic traits, his confession that the ultimate reason why he cannot keep Krogstad in the bank is that Krogstad, an old schoolfellow, is so tactless as to tutoyer him. There is a curious little touch in the passage where Helmer draws a contrast between his own strict rectitude and the doubtful character of Nora's father. "I can give you proof of it," he says. "I never cared to mention it before--but the twelve hundred dollars he gave you when you were set on going to Italy he never entered in his books: we have been quite unable to discover where he got them from." When Dr. Rank enters, he speaks to Helmer and Nora together of his failing health; it is an enormous improvement which transfers this passage, in a carefully polished form, to his scene with Nora alone. That scene, in the draft, is almost insignificant. It consists mainly of somewhat melodramatic forecasts of disaster on Nora's part, and the doctor's alarm as to her health. Of the famous silk-stocking scene--that invaluable sidelight on Nora's relation with Helmer there is not a trace. There is no hint of Nora's appeal to Rank for help, nipped in the bud by his declaration of love for her. All these elements we find in a second draft of the scene which has been preserved. In this second draft, Rank says, "Helmer himself might quite well know every thought I have ever had of you; he shall know when I am gone." It might have been better, so far as England is concerned, if Ibsen had retained this speech; it might have prevented much critical misunderstanding of a perfectly harmless and really beautiful episode.

Between the scene with Rank and the scene with Krogstad there intervenes, in the draft, a discussion between Nora and Mrs. Linden, containing this curious passage:--

NORA.   When an unhappy wife is separated from her husband she is not allowed to keep her children?   Is that really so?
MRS. LINDEN.   Yes, I think so.   That's to say, if she is guilty.
NORA.   Oh, guilty, guilty; what does it mean to be guilty? Has a wife no right to love her husband?
MRS. LINDEN.   Yes, precisely, her husband--and him only.
NORA.   Why, of course, who was thinking of anything else? But that law is unjust, Kristina.   You can see clearly that it is the men that have made it.
MRS. LINDEN.   Aha--so you have begun to take up the woman question?
NORA.   No, I don't care a bit about it.

The scene with Krogstad is essentially the same as in the final form, though sharpened, so to speak, at many points.   The question of suicide was originally discussed in a somewhat melodramatic tone:--

NORA.   I have been thinking of nothing else all these days.
KROGSTAD.   Perhaps.   But how to do it?   Poison?   Not so easy to get hold of.   Shooting?   It needs some skill, Mrs. Helmer. Hanging?   Bah--there's something ugly in that. . .
NORA.   Do you hear that rushing sound?
KROGSTAD.   The river?   Yes, of course you have thought of that.   But you haven't pictured the thing to yourself.

And he proceeds to do so for her.   After he has gone, leaving the letter in the box.   Helmer and Rank enter, and Nora implores Helmer to do no work till New Year's Day (the next day) is over. He agrees, but says, "I will just see if any letters have come"; whereupon she rushes to the piano and strikes a few chords.   He stops to listen, and she sits down and plays and sings Anitra's song from Peer Gynt.   When Mrs. Linden presently enters, Nora makes her take her place at the piano, drapes a shawl around her, and dances Anitra's dance.   It must be owned that Ibsen has immensely improved this very strained and arbitrary incident by devising the fancy dress ball and the necessity of rehearsing the tarantella for it; but at the best it remains a piece of theatricalism.

As a study in technique, the re-handling of the last act is immensely interesting. At the beginning, in the earlier form, Nora rushes down from the children's party overhead, and takes a significant farewell of Mrs. Linden, whom she finds awaiting her. Helmer almost forces her to return to the party; and thus the stage is cleared for the scene between Mrs. Linden and Krogstad, which, in the final version, opens the act. Then Nora enters with the two elder children, whom she sends to bed. Helmer immediately follows, and on his heels Dr. Rank, who announces in plain terms that his disease has entered on its last stage, that he is going home to die, and that he will not have Helmer or any one else hanging around his sickroom. In the final version, he says all this to Nora alone in the second act; while in the last act, coming in upon Helmer flushed with wine, and Nora pale and trembling in her masquerade dress, he has a parting scene with them, the significance of which she alone understands. In the earlier version, Rank has several long and heavy speeches in place of the light, swift dialogue of the final form, with its different significance for Helmer and for Nora. There is no trace of the wonderful passage which precedes Rank's exit. To compare the draft with the finished scene is to see a perfect instance of the transmutation of dramatic prose into dramatic poetry.

There is in the draft no indication of Helmer's being warmed with wine, or of the excitement of the senses which gives the final touch of tragedy to Nora's despair. The process of the action is practically the same in both versions; but everywhere in the final form a sharper edge is given to things. One little touch is very significant. In the draft, when Helmer has read the letter with which Krogstad returns the forged bill, he cries, "You are saved, Nora, you are saved!" In the revision, Ibsen cruelly altered this into, "I am saved, Nora, I am saved!" In the final scene, where Nora is telling Helmer how she expected him, when the revelation came, to take all the guilt upon himself, we look in vain, in the first draft, for this passage:--

HELMER. I would gladly work for you night and day, Nora--bear sorrow and want for your sake. But no man sacrifices his honour, even for one he loves.
NORA. Millions of women have done so.

This, then, was an afterthought: was there ever a more brilliant one?

It is with A Doll's House that Ibsen enters upon his kingdom as a world-poet. He had done greater work in the past, and he was to do greater work in the future; but this was the play which was destined to carry his name beyond the limits of Scandinavia, and even of Germany, to the remotest regions of civilisation. Here the Fates were not altogether kind to him. The fact that for many years he was known to thousands of people solely as the author of A Doll's House and it successor, Ghosts, was largely responsible for the extravagant misconceptions of his genius and character which prevailed during the last decade of the nineteenth centry, and are not yet entirely extinct. In these plays he seemed to be delivering a direct assault on marriage, from the standpoint of feminine individualism; wherefore he was taken to be a preacher and pamphleteer rather than a poet. In these plays, and in these only, he made physical disease a considerable factor in the action; whence it was concluded that he had a morbid predilection for "nauseous" subjects. In these plays he laid special and perhaps disproportionate stress on the influence of heredity; whence he was believed to be possessed by a monomania on the point. In these plays, finally, he was trying to act the essentially uncongenial part of the prosaic realist. The effort broke down at many points, and the poet reasserted himself; but these flaws in the prosaic texture were regarded as mere bewildering errors and eccentricities. In short, he was introduced to the world at large through two plays which showed his power, indeed, almost in perfection, but left the higher and subtler qualities of his genius for the most part unrepresented. Hence the grotesquely distorted vision of him which for so long haunted the minds even of intelligent people. Hence, for example, the amazing opinion, given forth as a truism by more than one critic of great ability, that the author of Peer Gynt was devoid of humour.

Within a little more than a fortnight of its publication, A Doll's House was presented by the Royal Theatre, Copenhagen, where Fru Hennings, as Nora, made the great success of her career. The play was soon being acted, as well as read, all over Scandinavia. Nora's startling "declaration of independence" afforded such an inexhaustible theme for heated discussion, that at last it had to be formally barred at social gatherings, just as, in Paris twenty years later, the Dreyfus Case was proclaimed a prohibited topic. The popularity of Pillars of Society in Germany had paved the way for its successor, which spread far and wide over the German stage in the spring of 1880, and has ever since held its place in the repertory of the leading theatres. As his works were at that time wholly unprotected in Germany, Ibsen could not prevent managers from altering the end of the play to suit their taste and fancy. He was thus driven, under protest, to write an alternative ending, in which, at the last moment, the thought of her children restrained Nora from leaving home. He preferred, as he said, "to commit the outrage himself, rather than leave his work to the tender mercies of adaptors."

The patched-up ending soon dropped out of use and out of memory. Ibsen's own account of the matter will be found in his Correspondence, Letter 142.

It took ten years for the play to pass beyond the limits of Scandinavia and Germany. Madame Modjeska, it is true, presented a version of it in Louisville, Kentucky, in 1883, but it attracted no attention. In the following years Messrs. Henry Arthur Jones and Henry Herman produced at the Prince of Wales's Theatre, London, a play entitled Breaking a Butterfly, which was described as being "founded on Ibsen's Norah," but bore only a remote resemblance to the original. In this production Mr. Beerbohm Tree took the part of Dunkley, a melodramatic villain who filled the place of Krogstad. In 1885, again, an adventurous amateur club gave a quaint performance of Miss Lord's translation of the play at a hall in Argyle Street, London. Not until June 7, 1889, was A Doll's House competently, and even brilliantly, presented to the English public, by Mr. Charles Charrington and Miss Janet Achurch, at the Novelty Theatre, London, afterwards re-named the Kingsway Theatre. It was this production that really made Ibsen known to the English-speaking peoples. In other words, it marked his second great stride towards world-wide, as distinct from merely national, renown—if we reckon as the first stride the success of Pillars of Society in Germany. Mr. and Mrs. Charrington took A Doll's House with them on a long Australian tour; Miss Beatrice Cameron (Mrs. Richard Mansfield) was encouraged by the success of the London production to present the play in New York, whence it soon spread to other American cities; while in London itself it was frequently revived and vehemently discussed. The Ibsen controversy, indeed, did not break out in its full virulence until 1891, when Ghosts and Hedda Gabler were produced in London; but from the date of the Novelty production onwards, Ibsen was generally recognised as a potent factor in the intellectual and artistic life of the day.

A French adaptation of Et Dukkehjem was produced in Brussels in March 1889, but attracted little attention. Not until 1894 was the play introduced to the Parisian public, at the Gymnase, with Madame Réjane as Nora. This actress has since played the part frequently, not only in Paris but in London and in America. In Italian the play was first produced in 1889, and soon passed into the repertory of Eleonora Duse, who appeared as Nora in London in 1893. Few heroines in modern drama have been played by so many actresses of the first rank. To those already enumerated must be added Hedwig Niemann-Raabe and Agnes Sorma in Germany, and Minnie Maddern-Fiske and Alla Nazimova in America; and, even so, the list is far from complete. There is probably no country in the world, possessing a theatre on the European model, in which A Doll's House has not been more or less frequently acted.

Undoubtedly the great attraction of the part of Nora to the average actress was the tarantella scene. This was a theatrical effect, of an obvious, unmistakable kind. It might have been--though I am not aware that it ever actually was--made the subject of a picture-poster. But this, as it seems to me, was Ibsen's last concession to the ideal of technique which he had acquired, in the old Bergen days, from his French masters. It was at this point--or, more precisely, a little later, in the middle of the third act--that Ibsen definitely outgrew the theatrical orthodoxy of his earlier years. When the action, in the theatrical sense, was over, he found himself only on the threshold of the essential drama; and in that drama, compressed into the final scene of the play, he proclaimed his true power and his true mission.

How impossible, in his subsequent work, would be such figures as Mrs. Linden, the confidant, and Krogstad, the villain! They are not quite the ordinary confidant and villain, for Ibsen is always Ibsen, and his power of vitalisation is extraordinary. Yet we clearly feel them to belong to a different order of art from that of his later plays. How impossible, too, in the poet's after years, would have been the little tricks of ironic coincidence and picturesque contrast which abound in A Doll's House! The festal atmosphere of the whole play, the Christmas-tree, the tarantella, the masquerade ball, with its distant sounds of music--all the shimmer and tinsel of the background, against which Nora's soul-torture and Rank's despair are thrown into relief, belong to the system of external, artificial antithesis beloved by romantic playwrights from Lope de Vega onward, and carried to its limit by Victor Hugo. The same artificiality is apparent in minor details. "Oh, what a wonderful thing it is to live to be happy!" cries Nora, and instantly "The hall-door bell rings" and Krogstad's shadow falls across the threshold. So, too, for his second entrance, an elaborate effect of contrast is arranged, between Nora's gleeful romp with her children and the sinister figure which stands unannounced in their midst. It would be too much to call these things absolutely unnatural, but the very precision of the coincidence is eloquent of pre-arrangement. At any rate, they belong to an order of effects which in future Ibsen sedulously eschews. The one apparent exception to this rule which I can remember occurs in The Master Builder, where Solness's remark, "Presently the younger generation will come knocking at my door," gives the cue for Hilda's knock and entrance. But here an interesting distinction is to be noted. Throughout The Master Builder the poet subtly indicates the operation of mysterious, unseen agencies--the "helpers and servers" of whom Solness speaks, as well as the Power with which he held converse at the crisis in his life--guiding, or at any rate tampering with, the destinies of the characters. This being so, it is evident that the effect of pre-arrangement produced by Hilda's appearing exactly on the given cue was deliberately aimed at. Like so many other details in the play, it might be a mere coincidence, or it might be a result of inscrutable design--we were purposely left in doubt. But the suggestion of pre-arrangement which helped to create the atmosphere of The Master Builder was wholly out of place in A Doll's House. In the later play it was a subtle stroke of art; in the earlier it was the effect of imperfectly dissembled artifice.

The fact that Ibsen's full originality first reveals itself in the latter half of the third act is proved by the very protests, nay, the actual rebellion, which the last scene called forth. Up to that point he had been doing, approximately, what theatrical orthodoxy demanded of him. But when Nora, having put off her masquerade dress, returned to make up her account with Helmer, and with marriage as Helmer understood it, the poet flew in the face of orthodoxy, and its professors cried out in bewilderment and wrath. But it was just at this point that, in practice, the real grip and thrill of the drama were found to come in. The tarantella scene never, in my experience--and I have seen five or six great actresses in the part--produced an effect in any degree commensurate with the effort involved. But when Nora and Helmer faced each other, one on each side of the table, and set to work to ravel out the skein of their illusions, then one felt oneself face to face with a new thing in drama--an order of experience, at once intellectual and emotional, not hitherto attained in the theatre. This every one felt, I think, who was in any way accessible to that order of experience. For my own part, I shall never forget how surprised I was on first seeing the play, to find this scene, in its naked simplicity, far more exciting and moving than all the artfully-arranged situations of the earlier acts. To the same effect from another point of view, we have the testimony of Fru Hennings, the first actress who ever played the part of Nora. In an interview published soon after Ibsen's death, she spoke of the delight it was to her, in her youth, to embody the Nora of the first and second acts, the "lark," the "squirrel," the irresponsible, butterfly Nora. "When I now play the part," she went on, "the first acts leave me indifferent. Not until the third act am I really interested--but then, intensely." To call the first and second acts positively uninteresting would of course be a gross exaggeration. What one really means is that their workmanship is still a little derivative and immature, and that not until the third act does the poet reveal the full originality and individuality of his genius.

GHOSTS

The winter of 1879-80 Ibsen spent in Munich, and the greater
part of the summer of 1880 at Berchtesgaden. November 1880 saw
him back in Rome, and he passed the summer of 1881 at Sorrento.
There, fourteen years earlier, he had written the last acts of
Peer Cynt: there he now wrote, or at any rate completed,
Gengangere.
   The surviving "foreworks" for this play are very scanty. Of
the dialogue only two or three brief fragments remain.   The
longest is a sketch of the passage in which Oswald shocks Pastor
Manders by his account of artist life in Paris.   We possess,
however, some scattered memoranda relating to the play, some of
them written on the back of an envelope addressed to "Madame
Ibsen, 75 via Capo le Case, Citta" (that is to say, Rome.) They
run as follows:

   The piece will be like an image of life. Faith undermined.
But it does not do to say so.   "The Asylum"--for the sake of
others.   They shall be happy--but this also is only an
appearance--it is all ghosts.
   One main point.   She has been believing and romantic--this
is not wholly obliterated by the stand-point afterwards
attained--"It is all ghosts."
   It brings a Nemesis on the offspring to marry for external
reasons, even if they be religious or moral.
   She, the illegitimate child, may be saved by being married
to--the son--but then-----

   He was in his youth dissipated and worn out; then she, the
religiously awakened, appeared; she saved him; she was rich. He
had wanted to marry a girl who was thought unworthy. He had a
son in his marriage; then he returned to the girl; a daughter----

                    ----

These women of to-day, ill-treated as daughters, as sisters, as wives, not educated according to their gifts, withheld from their vocation, deprived of their heritage, embittered in mind--these it is who furnish the mothers of a new generation. What will be the consequence?

The fundamental note shall be the richly flourishing spiritual life among us in literature, art, etc.; and then, as a contrast, all humanity astray on wrong paths.

The complete human being is no longer a natural product, but a product of art, as corn is, and fruit-trees, and the creole race, and the higher breeds of horses and dogs, the vine, etc.

The fault lies in the fact that all humanity has miscarried. When man demands to live and develop humanly, it is megalomania. All humanity, and most of all the Christians, suffer from megalomania.

Among us we place monuments over the dead, for we recognise duties towards them; we allow people only fit for the hospital [literally, lepers] to marry: but their offspring---? The unborn-----

The fourth and fifth of these six sections seem to have as much bearing on other plays--for instance, An Enemy of the People, and The Lady from the Sea--as on Ghosts. I should take them rather for general memoranda than for notes specially referring to this play.

Gengangere was published in December 1881, after he had returned to Rome. On December 22 he wrote to Ludwig Passarge, one of his German translators, "My new play has now appeared, and has occasioned a terrible uproar in the Scandinavian press; every day I receive letters and newspaper articles decrying or praising it. . . .I consider it utterly impossible that any German theatre should accept the play at present. I hardly believe that they will dare to play it in the Scandinavian countries for some time to come." How rightly he judged we shall see anon.

In the newspapers there was far more obloquy than praise. Two men, however, stood by him from the first: Björnson, from whom he had been practically estranged ever since The League of Youth, and George Brandes. The latter published an article in which he declared (I quote from memory) that the play might or might not be Ibsen's greatest work, but that it was certainly his noblest deed. It was, doubtless, in acknowledgment of this article that Ibsen wrote to Brandes on January 3, 1882:

"Yesterday I had the great pleasure of receiving your brilliantly clear and so warmly appreciative review of Ghosts. . . .All who read your article must, it seems to me, have their eyes opened to what I meant by my new book--assuming, that is, that they have any wish to see. For I cannot get rid of the impression that a very large number of the false interpretations which have appeared in the newspapers are the work of people who know better. In Norway, however, I am willing to believe that the stultification has in most cases been unintentional; and the reason is not far to seek. In that country a great many of the critics are theologians, more or less disguised; and these gentlemen are, as a rule, quite unable to write rationally about creative literature. That enfeeblement of judgment which, at least in the case of the average man, is an inevitable consequence of prolonged occupation with theological studies, betrays itself more especially in the judging of human character, human actions, and human motives. Practical business judgment, on the other hand, does not suffer so much from studies of this order. Therefore the reverend gentlemen are very often excellent members of local boards; but they are unquestionably our worst critics." This passage is interesting as showing clearly the point of view from which Ibsen conceived the character of Manders. In the next paragraph of the same letter he discusses the attitude of "the so-called Liberal press"; but as the paragraph contains the germ of An Enemy of the People, it may most fittingly be quoted in the Introduction to that play.

Three days late (January 6) Ibsen wrote to Schandorph, the Danish novelist: "I was quite prepared for the hubbub. If certain of our Scandinavian reviewers have no talent for anything else, they have an unquestionable talent for thoroughly misunderstanding and misinterpreting those authors whose books they undertake to judge. . . .They endeavour to make me responsible for the opinions which certain of the personages of my drama express. And yet there is not in the whole book a single opinion, a single utterance, which can be laid to the account of the author. I took good care to avoid this. The very method, the order of technique which imposes its form upon the play, forbids the author to appear in the speeches of his characters. My object was to make the reader feel that he was going through a piece of real experience, and nothing could more effectually prevent such an impression than the intrusion of the author's private opinions into the dialogue. Do they imagine at home that I am so inexpert in the theory of drama as not to know this? Of course I know it, and act accordingly. In no other play that I have written is the author so external to the action, so entirely absent from it, as in this last one."

"They say," he continued, "that the book preaches Nihilism. Not at all. It is not concerned to preach anything whatsoever. It merely points to the ferment of Nihilism going on under the surface, at home as elsewhere. A Pastor Manders will always goad one or other Mrs. Alving to revolt. And just because she is a woman, she will, when once she has begun, go to the utmost extremes."

Towards the end of January Ibsen wrote from Rome to Olaf Skavlan: "These last weeks have brought me a wealth of experiences, lessons, and discoveries. I of course foresaw that my new play would call forth a howl from the camp of the stagnationists; and for this I care no more than for the barking of a pack of chained dogs. But the pusillanimity which I have observed among the so-called Liberals has given me cause for reflection. The very day after my play was published, the Dagblad rushed out a hurriedly-written article, evidently designed to purge itself of all suspicion of complicity in my work. This was entirely unnecessary. I myself am responsible for what I write, I, and no one else. I cannot possibly embarrass any party, for to no party do I belong. I stand like a solitary franc-tireur at the outposts, and fight for my own hand. The only man in Norway who has stood up freely, frankly, and courageously for me is Björnson. It is just like him. He has in truth a great, kingly soul, and I shall never forget his action in this matter."

One more quotation completes the history of these stirring January days, as written by Ibsen himself. It occurs in a letter to a Danish journalist, Otto Borchsenius. "It may well be," the poet writes, "that the play is in several respects rather daring. But it seems to me that the time had come for moving some boundary-posts. And this was an undertaking for which a man of the older generation, like myself, was better fitted than the many younger authors who might desire to do something of the kind. I was prepared for a storm; but such storms one must not shrink from encountering. That would be cowardice."

It happened that, just in these days, the present writer had frequent opportunities of conversing with Ibsen, and of bearing from his own lips almost all the view expressed in the above extracts. He was especially emphatic, I remember, in protesting against the notion that the opinions expressed by Mrs. Alving of Oswald were to be attributed to himself. He insisted, on the contrary, that Mrs. Alving's views were merely typical of the moral chaos inevitably produced by reaction from the narrow conventionalism represented by Manders.

With one consent, the leading theatres of the three Scandinavian capitals declined to have anything to do with the play. It was more than eighteen months old before it found its way to the stage at all. In August 1883 it was acted for the first time at Helsingborg, Sweden, by a travelling company under the direction of an eminent Swedish actor, August Lindberg, who himself played Oswald. He took it on tour round the principal cities of Scandinavia, playing it, among the rest, at a minor theatre in Christiania. It happened that the boards of the Christiania Theatre were at the same time occupied by a French farce; and public demonstrations of protest were made against the managerial policy which gave Tête de Linotte the preference over Gengangere. Gradually the prejudice against the play broke down. Already in the autumn of 1883 it was produced at the Royal (Dramatiska) Theatre in Stockholm. When the new National Theatre was opened in Christiania in 1899, Gengangere found an early place in its repertory; and even the Royal Theatre in Copenhagen has since opened its doors to the tragedy.

Not until April 1886 was Gespenster acted in Germany, and then only at a private performance, at the Stadt-theater, Augsburg, the poet himself being present. In the following winter it was acted at the famous Court Theatre at Meiningen, again in the presence of the poet. The first (private) performance in Berlin took place on January 9, 1887, at the Residen Theatre; and when the Freie Bühne, founded on the model of the Paris Théâtre-Libre, began its operations two years later (September 29, 1889), Gespenster was the first play that it produced. The Freie Bühne gave the initial impulse to the whole modern movement which has given Germany a new dramatic literature; and the leaders of the movement, whether authors or critics, were one and all ardent disciples of Ibsen, regarding Gespenster as his typical masterpiece. In Germany, then, the play certainly did, in Ibsen's own words, "move some boundary-posts." The Prussian censorship presently withdrew its veto, and on November 27, 1894, the two leading literary theatres of Berlin, the Deutsches Theater and the Lessing Theater, gave simultaneous performances of the tragedy. Everywhere in Germany and Austria it is now freely performed; but it is naturally one of the least popular of Ibsen's plays.

It was with Les Revenants that Ibsen made his first appearance on the French stage. The play was produced by the Théâtre-Libre (at the Théâtre des Menus-Plaisirs) on May 29, 1890. Here, again, it became the watchword of the new school of authors and critics, and aroused a good deal of opposition among the old school. But the most hostile French criticisms were moderation itself compared with the torrents of abuse which were poured upon Ghosts by the journalists of London when, on March 13, 1891, the Independent Theatre, under the direction of Mr. J. T. Grein, gave a private performance of the play at the Royalty Theatre, Soho. I have elsewhere[1] placed upon record some of the amazing feats of vituperation achieved of the critics, and will not here recall them. It is sufficient to say that if the play had been a tenth part as nauseous as the epithets hurled at it and its author, the Censor's veto would have been amply justified. That veto is still (1911) in force. England enjoys the proud distinction of being the one country in the world where Ghosts may not be publicly acted.

In the United States, the first performance of the play in English took place at the Berkeley Lyceum, New York City, on January 5, 1894. The production was described by Mr. W. D. Howells as "a great theatrical event--the very greatest I have ever known." Other leading men of letters were equally impressed by it. Five years later, a second production took place at the Carnegie Lyceum; and an adventurous manager has even taken the play on tour in the United States. The Italian version of the tragedy, Gli Spettri, has ever since 1892 held a prominent place in the repertory of the great actors Zaccone and Novelli, who have acted it, not only throughout Italy, but in Austria, Germany, Russia, Spain, and South America.

In an interview, published immediately after Ibsen's death, Björnstjerne Björnson, questioned as to what he held to be his brother-poet's greatest work, replied, without a moment's hesitation, Gengangere. This dictum can scarcely, I think, be accepted without some qualification. Even confining our attention to the modern plays, and leaving out of comparison The Pretenders, Brand, and Peer Gynt, we can scarcely call Ghosts Ibsen's richest or most human play, and certainly not his profoundest or most poetical. If some omnipotent Censorship decreed the annihilation of all his works save one, few people, I imagine, would vote that that one should be Ghosts. Even if half a dozen works were to be saved from the wreck, I doubt whether I, for my part, would include Ghosts in the list. It is, in my judgment, a little bare, hard, austere. It is the first work in which Ibsen applies his new technical method--evolved, as I have suggested, during the composition of A Doll's House--and he applies it with something of fanaticism. He is under the sway of a prosaic ideal--confessed in the phrase, "My object was to make the reader feel that he was going through a piece of real experience"--and he is putting some constraint upon the poet within him. The action moves a little stiffly, and all in one rhythm. It lacks variety and suppleness. Moreover, the play affords some slight excuse for the criticism which persists in regarding Ibsen as a preacher rather than as a creator--an author who cares more for ideas and doctrines than for human beings. Though Mrs. Alving, Engstrand and Regina are rounded and breathing characters, it cannot be denied that Manders strikes one as a clerical type rather than an individual, while even Oswald might not quite unfairly be described as simply and solely his father's son, an object-lesson in heredity. We cannot be said to know him, individually and intimately, as we know Helmer or Stockmann, Hialmar Ekdal or Gregers Werle. Then, again, there are one or two curious flaws in the play. The question whether Oswald's "case" is one which actually presents itself in the medical books seems to me of very trifling moment. It is typically true, even if it be not true in detail. The suddenness of the catastrophe may possibly be exaggerated, its premonitions, and even its essential nature, may be misdescribed. On the other hand, I conceive it probable that the poet had documents to found upon, which may be unknown to his critics. I have never taken any pains to satisfy myself upon the point, which seems to me quite immaterial. There is not the slightest doubt that the life-history of a Captain Alving may, and often does, entail upon posterity consequences quite as tragic as those which ensue in Oswald's case, and far more wide-spreading. That being so, the artistic justification of the poet's presentment of the case is certainly not dependent on its absolute scientific accuracy. The flaws above alluded to are of another nature. One of them is the prominence given to the fact that the Asylum is uninsured. No doubt there is some symbolical purport in the circumstance; but I cannot think that it is either sufficiently clear or sufficiently important to justify the emphasis thrown upon it at the end of the second act. Another dubious point is Oswald's argument in the first act as to the expensiveness of marriage as compared with free union. Since the parties to free union, as he describes it, accept all the responsibilities of marriage, and only pretermit the ceremony, the difference of expense, one would suppose, must be neither more nor less than the actual marriage fee. I have never seen this remark of Oswald's adequately explained, either as a matter of economic fact, or as a trait of character. Another blemish, of somewhat greater moment, is the inconceivable facility with which, in the third act, Manders suffers himself to be victimized by Engstrand. All these little things, taken together, detract, as it seems to me, from the artistic completeness of the play, and impair its claim to rank as the poet's masterpiece. Even in prose drama, his greatest and most consummate achievements were yet to come.

Must we, then, wholly dissent from Björnson's judgment? I think not. In a historical, if not in an aesthetic, sense, Ghosts may well rank as Ibsen's greatest work. It was the play which first gave the full measure of his technical and spiritual originality and daring. It has done far more than any other of his plays to "move boundary-posts." It has advanced the frontiers of dramatic art and implanted new ideals, both technical and intellectual, in the minds of a whole generation of playwrights. It ranks with Hernani and La Dame aux Camélias among the epoch-making plays of the nineteenth century, while in point of essential originality it towers above them. We cannot, I think, get nearer to the truth than George Brandes did in the above-quoted phrase from his first notice of the play, describing it as not, perhaps, the poet's greatest work, but certainly his noblest deed. In another essay, Brandes has pointed to it, with equal justice, as marking Ibsen's final breach with his early--one might almost say his hereditary--romanticism. He here becomes, at last, "the most modern of the moderns." "This, I am convinced," says the Danish critic, "is his imperishable glory, and will give lasting life to his works."

AN ENEMY OF THE PEOPLE

From Pillars of Society to John Gabriel Borkman, all Ibsen's plays, with one exception, succeeded each other at intervals of two years. The single exception was An Enemy of the People. The storm of obloquy which greeted Ghosts stirred him to unwonted rapidity of production. Ghosts had appeared in December, 1881; already, in the spring of 1882, Ibsen, then living in Rome, was at work upon its successor; and he finished it at Gossensass, in the Tyrol, in the early autumn. It appeared in Copenhagen at the end of November. Perhaps the rapidity of its composition may account for the fact that we find no sketch or draft of it in the poet's Literary Remains.

John Paulsen[1] relates an anecdote of Ibsen's extreme secretiveness during the process of composition, which may find a place here: "One summer he was travelling by rail with his wife and son. He was engaged upon a new play at the time; but neither Fru Ibsen nor Sigurd had any idea as to what it was about. Of course they were both very curious. It happened that, at a station, Ibsen left the carriage for a few moments. As he did so he dropped a scrap of paper. His wife picked it up, and read on it only the words, "the doctor says. . . ." Nothing more. Fru Ibsen showed it laughingly to Sigurd, and said, "Now we will tease your father a little when he comes back. He will be horrified to find that we know anything of his play." When Ibsen entered the carriage his wife looked at him roguishly, and said, "What doctor is it that figures in your new piece? I am sure he must have many interesting things to say." But if she could have foreseen the effect of her innocent jest, Fru Ibsen would certainly have held her tongue. For Ibsen was speechless with surprise and rage. When at last he recovered his speech, it was to utter a torrent of reproaches. What did this mean? Was he not safe in his own house? Was he surrounded with spies? Had his locks been tampered with, his desk rifled? And so forth, and so forth. His wife, who had listened with a quiet smile to the rising tempest of his wrath, at last handed him the scrap of paper. "We know nothing more than what is written upon this slip which you let fall. Allow me to return it to you." There stood

Ibsen crestfallen. All his suspicions had vanished into thin air. The play on which he was occupied proved to be An Enemy of the People, and the doctor was none other than our old friend Stockmann, the good-hearted and muddleheaded reformer, for whom Jonas Lie partly served as a model."

The indignation which glows in An Enemy of the People was kindled, in the main, by the attitude adopted towards Ghosts by the Norwegian Liberal press and the "compact majority" it represented. But the image on which the play rings the changes was present to the poet's mind before Ghosts was written. On December 19, 1879--a fortnight after the publication of A Doll's House--Ibsen wrote to Professor Dietrichson: "It appears to me doubtful whether better artistic conditions can be attained in Norway before the intellectual soil has been thoroughly turned up and cleansed, and all the swamps drained off." Here we have clearly the germ of An Enemy of the People. The image so took hold of Ibsen that after applying it to social life in this play, he recurred to it in The Wild Duck, in relation to the individual life.

The mood to which we definitely own An Enemy of the People appears very clearly in a letter to George Brandes, dated January 3, 1882, in which Ibsen thanks him for his criticism of Ghosts. "What are we to say," he proceeds, "of the attitude taken up by the so-called Liberal press--by those leaders who speak and write about freedom of action and thought, and at the same time make themselves the slaves of the supposed opinions of their subscribers? I am more and more confirmed in my belief that there is something demoralising in engaging in politics and joining parties. I, at any rate, shall never be able to join a party which has the majority on its side. Björnson says, "The majority is always right"; and as a practical politician he is bound, I suppose, to say so. I, on the contrary, of necessity say, "The minority is always right." Naturally I am not thinking of that minority of stagnationists who are left behind by the great middle party, which with us is called Liberal; I mean that minority which leads the van, and pushes on to points which the majority has not yet reached. I hold that that man is in the right who is most closely in league with the future."

The same letter closes with a passage which foreshadows not only An Enemy of the People, but Rosmersholm: "When I think how slow and heavy and dull the general intelligence is at home, when I notice the low standard by which everything is judged, a deep despondency comes over me, and it often seems to me that I might just as well end my literary activity at once. They really do not need poetry at home; they get along so well with the Parliamentary News and the Lutheran Weekly. And then they have their party papers. I have not the gifts that go to make a good citizen, nor yet the gift of orthodoxy; and what I possess no gift for I keep out of. Liberty is the first and highest condition for me.   At home they do not trouble much about liberty, but only about liberties, a few more or a few less, according to the standpoint of their party.   I feel, too, most painfully affected by the crudity, the plebeian element, in all our public discussion.   The very praiseworthy attempt to make of our people a democratic community has inadvertently gone a good way towards making us a plebeian community.   Distinction of soul seems to be on the decline at home."

So early as March 16, 1882, Ibsen announces to his publisher that he is "fully occupied with preparations for a new play." "This time," he says, "it will be a peaceable production which can be read by Ministers of State and wholesale merchants and their ladies, and from which the theatres will not be obliged to recoil.   Its execution will come very easy to me, and I shall do my best to have it ready pretty early in the autumn."   In this he was successful.   From Gossensass on September 9, he wrote to Hegel: "I have the pleasure of sending you herewith the remainder of the manuscript of my new play.   I have enjoyed writing this piece, and I feel quite lost and lonely now that it is out of hand.   Dr. Stockmann and I got on excellently together; we agree on so many subjects.   But the Doctor is a more muddleheaded person than I am, and he has, moreover, several other characteristics because of which people will stand hearing a good many things from him which they might perhaps not have taken in such very good part had they been said by me."

A letter to Brandes, written six months after the appearance of the play (June 12, 1883), answers some objection which the critic seems to have made--of what nature we can only guess: "As to An Enemy of the People, if we had a chance to discuss it I think we should come to a tolerable agreement.   You are, of course, right in urging that we must all work for the spread of our opinions.   But I maintain that a fighter at the intellectual outposts can never gather a majority around him.   In ten years, perhaps, the majority may occupy the standpoint which Dr. Stockmann held at the public meeting.   But during these ten years the Doctor will not have been standing still; he will still be at least ten years ahead of the majority.   The majority, the mass, the multitude, can never overtake him; he can never have the majority with him.   As for myself, at all events, I am conscious of this incessant progression.   At the point where I stood when I wrote each of my books, there now stands a fairly compact multitude; but I myself am there no longer; I am elsewhere, and, I hope, further ahead."   This is a fine saying, and as just as it is fine, with respect to the series of social plays, down to, and including Rosmersholm.   To the psychological series, which begins with The Lady from the Sea, this law of progression scarcely applies.   The standpoint in each is different; but the movement is not so much one of intellectual advance as of deepening spiritual insight.

   As Ibsen predicted, the Scandinavian theatres seized with
avidity upon An Enemy of the People. Between January and March,
1883, it was produced in Christiania, Bergen, Stockholm, and
Copenhagen. It has always been very popular on the stage, and
was the play chosen to represent Ibsen in the series of festival
performances which inaugurated the National Theatre at
Christiania. The first evening, September 1, 1899, was devoted
to Holberg, the great founder of Norwegian-Danish drama; An Enemy
of the People followed on September 2; and on September 3
Björnson held the stage, with Sigurd Jorsalfar. Oddly enough,
Ein Volksfeind was four years old before it found its way to the
German stage. It was first produced in Berlin, March 5, 1887,
and has since then been very popular throughout Germany. It has
even been presented at the Court Theatres of Berlin and Vienna--a
fact which seems remarkable when we note that in France and Spain
it has been pressed into the service of anarchism as a
revolutionary manifesto. When first produced in Paris in 1895,
and again in 1899, it was made the occasion of anarchist
demonstrations. It was the play chosen for representation in
Paris on Ibsen's seventieth birthday, March 29, 1898. In England
it was first produced by Mr. Beerbohm Tree at the Haymarket
Theatre on the afternoon of June 14, 1893. Mr. (now Sir Herbert)
Tree has repeated his performance of Stockmann a good many times
in London, the provinces, and America. He revived the play at
His Majesty's Theatre in 1905. Mr. Louis Calvert played
Stockmann at the Gentleman's Concert Hall in Manchester, January
27, 1894. I can find no record of the play in America, save
German performances and those given by Mr. Tree; but it seems
incredible that no American actor should have been attracted by
the part of Stockmann. Een Vijand des Volks was produced in
Holland in 1884, before it had even been seen in Germany; and in
Italy Un Nemico del Popolo holds a place in the repertory of the
distinguished actor Ermete Novelli.
   Of all Ibsen's plays, An Enemy of the People is the least
poetical, the least imaginative, the one which makes least appeal
to our sensibilities. Even in The League of Youth there is a
touch of poetic fancy in the character of Selma; while Pillars of
Society is sentimentally conceived throughout, and possess in
Martha a figure of great, though somewhat conventional, pathos.
In this play, on the other hand, there is no appeal either to the
imagination or to the tender emotions. It is a straightforward
satiric comedy, dealing exclusively with the everyday prose of
life. We have only to compare it with its immediate predecessor,
Ghosts, and its immediate successor, The Wild Duck, to feel how
absolutely different is the imaginative effort involved in it.
Realising this, we no longer wonder that the poet should have
thrown it off in half the time he usually required to mature and
execute one of his creations.

Yet An Enemy of the People takes a high place in the second rank of the Ibsen works, in virtue of its buoyant vitality, its great technical excellence, and the geniality of its humour. It seems odd, at first sight, that a distinctly polemical play, which took its rise in a mood of exasperation, should be perhaps the most amiable of all the poet's productions. But the reason is fairly obvious. Ibsen's nature was far too complex, and far too specifically dramatic, to permit of his giving anything like direct expression to a personal mood. The very fact that Dr. Stockmann was to utter much of his own indignation and many of his own ideas forced him to make the worthy Doctor in temperament and manner as unlike himself as possible. Now boisterous geniality, loquacity, irrepressible rashness of utterance, and a total absence of self-criticism and self-irony were the very contradiction of the poet's own characteristics--at any rate, after he had entered upon middle life. He doubtless looked round for models who should be his own antipodes in these respects. John Paulsen, as we have seen, thinks that he took many traits from Jonas Lie; others say[2] that one of his chief models was an old friend named Harald Thaulow, the father of the great painter. Be this as it may, the very effort to disguise himself naturally led him to attribute to his protagonist and mouthpiece a great superficial amiability. I am far from implying that Ibsen's own character was essentially unamiable; it would ill become one whom he always treated with the utmost kindness to say or think anything of the kind. But his amiability was not superficial, effusive, exuberant; it seldom reached that boiling-point which we call geniality; and for that very reason Thomas Stockmann became the most genial of his characters. He may be called Ibsen's Colonel Newcome. We have seen from the letter to Hegel that the poet regarded him with much the same ironic affection which Thackeray must have felt for that other Thomas who, amid many differences, had the same simple-minded, large-hearted, child-like nature.

In technical quality, An Enemy of the People is wholly admirable. We have only to compare it with Pillars of Society, the last play in which Ibsen had painted a broad satiric picture of the life of a Norwegian town, to feel how great an advance he had made in the intervening five years. In naturalness of exposition, suppleness of development, and what may be called general untheatricality of treatment, the later play has every possible advantage over the earlier. In one point only can it be said that Ibsen has allowed a touch of artificiality to creep in. In order to render the peripetia of the third act more striking, he has made Hovstad, Billing, and Aslaksen, in the earlier scenes, unnaturally inapprehensive of the sacrifices implied in Stockmann's scheme of reform. It is scarcely credible that they should be so free and emphatic in their offers of support to the Doctor's agitation, before they have made the

smallest inquiry as to what it is likely to cost the town. They
think, it may be said, that the shareholders of the Baths will
have to bear the whole expense; but surely some misgivings could
not but cross their mind as to whether the shareholders would be
prepared to do so.

THE WILD DUCK

The first mention of The Wild Duck (as yet unnamed) occurs
in a letter from Ibsen to George Brandes, dated Rome, June 12,
1883, some six months after the appearance of An Enemy of the
People. "I am revolving in my mind just now," he says, "the plan
of a new dramatic work in four acts. From time to time a variety
of whimsies gathers in one's mind, and one wants to find an
outlet for them. But as the play will neither deal with the
Supreme Court nor with the Absolute Veto, nor even with the Pure
Flag, it can hardly count upon attracting much attention in
Norway. Let us hope, however, that it may find a hearing
elsewhere." The allusion in this passage is to the great
constitutional struggle of 1880-84, of which some account will
have to be given in the introduction to Rosmersholm. The "Pure
Flag" agitation aimed at, and obtained, the exclusion from the
Norwegian flag of the mark of union with Sweden, and was thus a
preliminary step towards the severance of the two kingdoms. The
word which I have translated "whimsies" is in the original
galskaber, which might be literally rendered "mad fancies" or
"crazy notions." This word, or galskab in the singular, was
Ibsen's favourite term for his conceptions as they grew up in his
mind. I well remember his saying to me, while he was engaged on
The Lady from the Sea, "I hope to have some tomfoolery [galskab]
ready for next year." Sometimes he would vary the expression and
say djoevelskab, or "devilry."
Of this particular "tomfoolery" we hear no more for a full
year. Then, at the end of June, 1884, he writes in almost
identical terms to Brandes and to Theodor Caspari, announcing its
completion in the rough. His letter to Caspari is dated Rome,
June 27. "All last winter," he says, "I have been pondering over
some new whimsies, and have wrestled with them till at last they
took dramatic form in a five-act play which I have just
completed. That is to say, I have completed the rough draft of
it. Now comes the more delicate elaboration, the more energetic
individualisation of the characters and their methods of
expression. In order to find the requisite quiet and solitude
for this work, I am going in a few days to Gossensass, in the

Tyrol." This little glimpse into his workshop is particularly interesting.

It becomes all the more interesting when, on turning to the Literary Remains, we find that the rough draft, which Ibsen took with him to Gossessass, has been preserved, so that we can see, on comparing the two forms, what he meant by "elaboration and individualisation."

The draft of the first act contains 208 speeches, the completed act 302; which practically means that in the process of elaboration the act became half as long again. It is scarcely too much to say that everything that is most characteristic is added in the revision. The idea of making Old Ekdal an ex-officer was an afterthought. In the draft we are told that he was a lawyer, and we gather that he had made himself useful to Werle in some questionable transactions, and was afterwards deserted by him. On the other hand, a small touch of rebellion on Old Ekdal's part against the familiarity with which he is treated by Werle's butler has disappeared from the final form. I venture to think that the chatter of the Chamberlains has not been improved in the revision. Each of them, by the way, figures under his name in the draft, and not under a mere description. Gregers Werle was originally supposed to have been living in Paris, not playing the hermit at "the works." He was apparently conceived as more of a man of the world than he ultimately became. When one of the Chamberlains complains of his digestion, Gregers remarks, "there are remedies for everything, Mr. Flor--else why do you suppose that an all-wise Providence has created mineral waters?"--a speech which another Chamberlain reproves as "Parisian," and which, indeed, would scarcely harmonise with the later conception of his character. The Werle family was originally named "Walle"--the change to Werle suddenly occurs in the middle of the act, at the point where Old Ekdal passes through the room. There is no allusion to the fact of there having been thirteen at table; but the idea had evidently occured to Ibsen before he drafted the second act, in which he made Hialmar say, "There were twelve or fourteen of us." Of the scene between Hialmar and Gregers, so indispensable to the ultimate development, there is only the slightest trace. In the scene between Gregers and Werle, Greger evidently knows that Hialmar is married to his father's ex-mistress, but it is not clear how he has learnt the fact. Old Werle makes no allusion to "people who dive to the bottom the moment they get a couple of slugs in their body," whence it would almost seem that the symbol of the wild duck, which was to give the play its title, had not yet entered the poet's mind.

The draft of the second act is very fragmentary, but we can see that all the leading ideas of the play--except one--are already present to Ibsen's mind. The three remaining acts are pretty fully drafted; nor did the poet seriously depart from the main lines here laid down. What he did was to fill in and enrich the characterisation. Hedvig in particular gains immensely in the revision. In the draft she is comparatively commonplace; much of the delicacy and beauty of the character, which make her fate so heartrending, came to the poet as an afterthought. And it is curious to note how one single invention, apparently trifling in itself, may almost be said to have transformed the character and the play--the invention, I mean, of Werle's weak eyes and Hedvig's threatened blindness. Nowhere in the draft is there any hint of this idea. The most admirably effective strand in the finished fabric was not at first on the poet's loom, but was woven in as an afterthought. It served a multiplicity of purposes: it helped out the plot, it added to the pathos of Hedvig's figure, and it illustrated Hialmar's selfishness in allowing her to strain her eyes over the retouching which he himself ought to have done. One can imagine the artist's joy in achieving so perfect an example of constructive economy. An idea which presents itself in rudimentary form in the draft is that of Hialmar Ekdal's "invention"--here called his "problem." The later development of this wonderful "invention" forms a very good specimen of Ibsen's method. The draft contains no hint of Hialmar's delightful exposition of the part played by the pistol in the tragedy of the House of Ekdal. Everywhere, on a close comparison of the text, we see an intensive imagination lighting up, as it were, what was at first somewhat cold and colourless. In this case, as in many others, Ibsen's final working-over may be compared to a switching-on of the electricity.

From Gossensass he wrote to Hegel on September 2: "Herewith I send you the manuscript of my new play, The Wild Duck, which has occupied me daily for the past four months, and from which I cannot part without a sense of regret. The characters in this play, despite their many frailties, have, in the course of our long daily association, endeared themselves to me. However, I hope they will also find good and kind friends among the great reading public, and not least among the player-folk, to whom they all, without exception, offer problems worth the solving. But the study and presentation of these personages will not be easy. . . .This new play in some ways occupies a place apart among my dramatic productions; its method of development [literally, of advance] is in many respects divergent from that of its predecessors. But for the present I shall say no more on this subject. The critics will no doubt discover the points in question; at all events, they will find a good deal to wrangel about, a good deal to interpret. Moreover, I think The Wild Duck may perhaps lure some of our younger dramatists into new paths, and this I hold to be desirable."

The play was published on November 11, 1884, and was acted at all the leading theatres of Scandinavia in January or February, 1885. Ibsen's estimate of its acting value was fully justified. It everywhere proved itself immensely effective on the stage, and Hialmar, Gina, and Hedvig have made, or greatly enhanced, the reputation of many an actor and actress. Hialmar was one of the chief successes of Emil Poulsen, the leading Danish actor of his day, who placed the second act of The Wild Duck in the programme of his farewell performance. It took more than three years for the play to reach the German stage. It was first acted in Berlin in March, 1888; but thereafter it rapidly spread throughout Germany and Austria, and everywhere took firm hold. It was on several occasions, and in various cities, selected for performance in Ibsen's presence, as representing the best that the local theatre could do. In Paris it was produced at the Théâtre-Libre in 1891, and was pronounced by Francisque Sarcey to be "obscure, incoherent, insupportable," but nevertheless to leave "a profound impression." In London it was first produced by the Independent Theatre Society on May 4, 1894, Mr. W. L. Abingdon playing Hialmar, and Miss Winifred Fraser giving a delightful performance of Hedvig. The late Clement Scott's pronouncement on it was that "to make a fuss about so feeble a production was to insult dramatic literature and to outrage common sense." It was repeated at the Globe Theatre in May, 1897, with Mr. Laurence Irving as Hialmar and Miss Fraser again as Hedvig. In October, 1905, it was revived at the Court Theatre, with Mr. Granville Barker as Hialmar and Miss Dorothy Minto as Hedvig. Of American performances I find no record. It has been acted in Italy and in Greece, I know not with what success. The fact that it has no part for a "leading lady" has rendered it less of an international stock-piece than A Doll's House, Hedda Gabler, or even Rosmersholm.

There can be no doubt that The Wild Duck marks a reaction in the poet's mood, following upon the eager vivacity wherewith, in An Enemy of the People, he had flung his defiance at the "compact Liberal majority," which, as the reception of Ghosts had proved, could not endure to be told the truth. Having said his say and liberated his soul, he now began to ask himself whether human nature was, after all, capable of assimiating the strong meat of truth—whether illusion might not be, for the average man, the only thing that could make life livable. It would be too much to say that the play gives a generally affirmative answer to this question. On the contrary, its last lines express pretty clearly the poet's firm conviction that if life cannot reconcile itself with truth, then life may as well go to the wall. Nevertheless his very devotion to truth forces him to realise and admit that it is an antitoxin which, rashly injected at wrong times or in wrong doses, may produce disastrous results. It ought not to be indiscriminately administered by "quacksalvers."

Gregers Werle is unquestionably a piece of ironic self-portraiture. In his habit of "pestering people, in their poverty, with the claim of the ideal," the poet adumbrates his own conduct from Brand onwards, but especially in Ghosts and An Enemy of the People. Relling, again, is an embodiment of the mood which was dominant during the conception of the play--the mood of pitying contempt for that poor thing human nature, as embodied in Hialmar. An actor who, in playing the part of Relling, made up as Ibsen himself, has been blamed for having committed a fault, not only of taste, but of interpretation, since Gregers (it is maintained) is the true Ibsen. But the fact is that both characters represent the poet. They embody the struggle in his mind between idealism and cynical despondency. There can be no doubt, however, that in some measure he consciously identified himself with Gregers. In a letter to Mr. Gosse, written in 1872, he had employed in his own person the very phrase, den ideale fordring--"the claim of the ideal"--which is Gregers' watchword. The use of this sufficiently obvious phrase, however, does not mean much. Far stronger evidence of identification is afforded by John Paulsen[1] in some anecdotes he relates of Ibsen's habits of "self-help"--evidence which we may all the more safely accept, as Herr Paulsen seems to have been unconscious of its bearing upon the character of Gregers. "Ibsen," he says, "was always bent upon doing things himself, so as not to give trouble to servants. His ideal was "the self-made man."[2] Thus, if a button came off one of his garments he would retire to his own room, lock the door, and after many comical and unnecessary preliminaries proceed to sew on the button himself, with the same care with which he wrote the fair copy of a new play. Such an important task he could not possibly entrust to any one else, not even to his wife. One of his paradoxes was that "a woman never knew how to sew on a button so that it would hold." But if he himself sewed it on, it held to all eternity. Fru Ibsen smiled roguishly and subtly when the creator of Nora came out with such anti-feminist sentiments. Afterwards she told me in confidence, "It is true that Ibsen himself sews on his vagrant buttons; but the fact that they hold so well is my doing, for, without his knowledge, I always 'finish them off,' which he forgets to do. But don't disturb his conviction: it makes him so happy."

"One winter day in Munich," Herr Paulsen continues, "Ibsen asked me with a serious and even anxious countenance, "Tell me one thing, Paulsen--do you black your own boots every morning?" I was taken aback, and doubtless looked quite guilty as I answered, "No." I had a vaguely uncomfortable sense that I had failed in a duty to myself and to society. "But you really ought to do so. It will make you feel a different man. One should never let others do what one can do oneself. If you begin with blacking your boots, you will get on to putting your room in order, laying the fire, etc. In this way you will at last find yourself an emancipated man, independent of Tom, Dick, or Harry." I promised to follow his advice, but have unfortunately not kept my word." It is evident that Ibsen purposely transferred to Gregers this characteristic of his own; and the sentiments with which Gina regards it are probably not unlike those which Fru Ibsen may from time to time have manifested. We could scarcely demand clearer proof that in Gregers the poet was laughing at himself.

To Hedvig, Ibsen gave the name of his only sister, and in many respects she seems to have served as a model for the character. She was the poet's favourite among all his relatives. "You are certainly the best of us," he wrote to her in 1869. Björnstjerne Björnson said, after making her acquaintance, that he now understood what a large element of heredity there was in Ibsen's bent towards mysticism. We may be sure that Hedvig's researches among the books left by the old sea-captain, and her dislike for the frontispiece of Harrison's History of London, are remembered traits from the home-life of the poet's childhood. It does not seem to be known who had the honour of "sitting for" the character of Hialmar. Probably he is composite of many originals. Moreover, he is obviously a younger brother of Peer Gynt. Deprive Peer Gynt of his sense of humour, and clip the wings of his imagination, and you have Hialmar Ekdal.

I confess I do not know quite definitely what Ibsen had in mind when he spoke of The Wild Duck holding "a place apart" among his productions, and exemplifying a technique (for he is evidently thinking of its technical development) "divergent" from that of its predecessors. I should rather say that it marked the continuation and consummation of the technical method which he had been elaborating from Pillars of Society onward. It is the first example of what we may term his retrospective method, in its full complexity. Pillars of Society and A Doll's House may be called semi-retrospective; something like half of the essential action takes place before the eyes of the audience. Ghosts is almost wholly retrospective; as soon as the past has been fully unravelled the action is over, and only the catastrophe remains; but in this case the past to be unravelled is comparatively simple and easy of disentanglement. An Enemy of the People is scarcely retrospective at all; almost the whole of its action falls within the frame of the picture. In The Wild Duck , on the other hand, the unravelling of the past is a task of infinite subtlety and elaborate art. The execution of this task shows a marvellous and hitherto unexampled grasp of mind. Never before, certainly, had the poet displayed such an amazing power of fascinating and absorbing us by the gradual withdrawal of veil after veil from the past; and as every event was also a trait of character, it followed that never before had his dialogue been so saturated, as it were, with character-revelation. The development of the drama reminds one of the practice (in itself a very bad practice) of certain modern stage-managers, who are fond of raising their curtain on a dark scene, and then gradually lighting it up by a series of touches on the electric switchboard. First there comes a glimmer from the right, then a flash from the left; then the background is suffused with light, so that we see objects standing out against it in profile, but cannot as yet discern their details. Then comes a ray from this batten, a gleam from that; here a penetrating shaft of light, there a lambent glow; until at last the footlights are turned on at full, and every nook and cranny of the scene stands revealed in a blaze of luminosity. But Ibsen's switchboard is far more subtly divided than that of even the most modern theatre. At every touch upon it, some single cunningly-placed, ingeniously-dissembled burner kindles, almost unnoticed save by the most watchful eye; so that the full light spreads over the scene as imperceptibly as dawn grows into day.

It seems to me, then, that The Wild Duck is a consummation rather than a new departure. Assuredly it marks the summit of the poet's achievement (in modern prose) up to that date. Its only possible rival is Ghosts; and who does not feel the greater richness, depth, suppleness, and variety of the later play? It gives us, in a word, a larger segment of life.

ROSMERSHOLM

No one who ever saw Henrik Ibsen, in his later years at any rate, could doubt that he was a born aristocrat. It is said that change came over his appearance and manner after the publication of Brand--that he then put off the Bohemian and put on the reserved, correct, punctilious man-of-the-world. When I first saw him in 1881, he had the air of a polished statesman or diplomatist. Distinction was the note of his personality. So early as 1872, he had written to George Brandes, who was then involved in one of his many controversies, "Be dignified! Dignity is the only weapon against such assaults." His actual words, Voer fornem!, mean, literally translated, "Be distinguished!" No democratic movement which implied a levelling-down, could ever command Ibsen's sympathy. He was a leveller-up, or nothing.

This deep-rooted trait in his character found its supreme expression in Rosmersholm.

One of his first remarks (to Brandes, January 3, 1882) after the storm had broken out over Ghosts was: "I feel most painfully affected by the crudity, the plebeian element in all our public discussion. The very praiseworthy attempt to make of our people a democratic community has inadvertently gone a good way towards making us a plebeian community. Distinction of soul seems to be on the decline at home." The same trend of thought makes itself felt again and again in Dr. Stockmann's great speech in the fourth act of An Enemy of the People; but it appears only incidentally in that play, and not at all in The Wild Duck. It was a visit which he paid to Norway in the summer of 1885 that brought the need for "ennoblement" of character into the foreground of his thought, and inspired him with the idea of Rosmersholm. "Since he had last been home," writes Henrik Jaeger, "the great political battle had been fought out, and had left behind it a fanaticism and bitterness of spirit which astounded him. He was struck by the brutality of the prevailing tone; he felt himself painfully affected by the rancorous and vulgar personalities which drowned all rational discussion of the principles at stake; and he observed with sorrow the many enmities to which the contest had given rise. . . .On the whole, he received the impression--as he remarked in conversation--that Norway was inhabited, not by two million human beings, but by two million cats and dogs.   This impression has recorded itself in the picture of party divisions presented in <u>Rosmersholm</u>.   The bitterness of the vanquished is admirably embodied in Rector Kroll; while the victors' craven reluctance to speak out their whole hearts is excellently characterised in the freethinker and opportunist, Mortensgaard."

What was this "great political battle," the echoes of which reverberate through <u>Rosmersholm</u>?   Though a knowledge of its details is in no way essential to the comprehension of the play, the following account[1] of it may not be out of place.

The Norwegian Constitution of 1814 gave the King of Norway and Sweden a suspensive veto on the enactments of the Norwegian Storthing, or Parliament, but provided that a bill passed by three successive triennial Storthings should become law without the Royal assent.   This arrangement worked well enough until about 1870, when the Liberal party became alive to a flaw in the constitution.   The whole legislative and financial power was vested in the Storthing; but the Ministers had no seats in it and acknowledged no responsibility, save to the King.   Thus the overwhelming Liberal majority in the Storthing found itself baulked at every turn by a Conservative ministry, over which it had no effective control.   In 1872, a Bill enacting that Ministers should sit in the Storthing was passed by 80 votes to 29, and was vetoed by the King.   It was passed again and again by successive Storthings, the last time by 93 votes to 20; but now King Oscar came forward with a declaration that <u>on matters affecting the Constitution</u> his veto was not suspensive, but absolute and once more vetoed the Bill.   This measure was met by the Storthing with a resolution (June 9, 1880) that the Act had become law in spite of the veto.   The King ignored the resolution, and, by the advice of his Ministers claimed an absolute veto, not only on constitutional questions, but on measures of supply.   Then the Storthing adopted the last resource provided by the Constitution: it impeached the Ministers before the Supreme Court of the kingdom.   Political rancour ran incredibly high, and there was a great final tussle over the composition of the Supreme Court; but the Liberals were masters of the situation, and carried all before them.   One by one the Ministers were dismissed from office and fined.   The King ostentatiously testified his sympathy with them, and selected a new Ministry from the Extreme Right.   They failed to carry on the government of the country, and matters were at a deadlock.   At last, however, King Oscar gave way.   On June 26, 1884, he sent for Johan Sverdrup, the statesman who for a quarter of a century had guided the counsels of the Liberal party.   Sverdrup consented to form a Ministry, and the battle ended in a Liberal victory along the whole line.

Ten years elapsed between Ibsen's hegira of 1864 and his first brief return to his native land. Before his second visit eleven more years intervened; and during the summer of 1885, which he spent for the most part at Molde, he found the air still quivering with the rancours begotten of the great struggle. In a speech which he addressed to a meeting of workmen at Trondhjem (June 14, 1885) he said that the years of his absence had brought "immense progress in most directions," but that he was disappointed to observe that "the most indispensable individual rights were far less secured than he had hoped and expected to find them under the new order of things." He found neither freedom of thought nor freedom of speech beyond a limit arbitrarily fixed by the dominant majority. "There remains much to be done," he continued, "before we can be said to have attained real liberty. But I fear that our present democracy will not be equal to the task. An element of nobility must be introduced into our national life, into our Parliament, and into our Press. Of course it is not nobility of birth that I am thinking of, nor of money, nor yet of knowledge, nor even of ability and talent: I am thinking of nobility of character, of will, of soul."

When he spoke these words he had been little more than a week in Norway; but it is clear that Rosmersholm was already germinating in his mind.

On his return to Munich he began to think out the play, and on February 14, 1886, he wrote to Carl Snoilsky, the Swedish poet: "I am much taken up with a new play, which I have long had in mind, and for which I made careful studies during my visit to Norway." It may be mentioned that Ibsen had met Snoilsky at Molde during the previous summer, and they had seen a good deal of each other. The manuscript of Rosmersholm was sent to the printers at the end of September, 1886, and a letter to Hegel accompanied it in which Ibsen said: "So far as I can see, the play is not likely to call forth attacks from any quarter; but I hope it will lead to lively discussion. I look for this especially in Sweden." Why in Sweden? Perhaps because, as we shall see presently, the story was partly suggested by a recent episode in Swedish social history. Before proceeding to the question of origins, however, I may quote the only other reference to the play, of any importance, which occurs in Ibsen's letters. The chairman of a debating club in Christiania had addressed to the poet a letter on behalf of the club, which apparently contained some question or suggestion as to the fundamental idea of the play. Ibsen's answer was dated Munich, February 13, 1887. "The call to work," he said, "is certainly distinguishable throughout Rosmersholm. But the play also deals with the struggle with himself which every serious-minded man must face in order to bring his life into harmony with his convictions. For the different spiritual functions do not develop evenly and side by side in any given human being. The acquisitive instinct hastens on from conquest to conquest. The moral consciousness, the conscience, on the other hand is very conservative. It has deep roots in tradition and the past generally. Hence arises the conflict in the individual. But first and foremost, of course, the play is a creative work, dealing with human beings and human destinies."

Dr. George Brandes is our authority for associating Rosmersholm with the social episode above alluded to--an episode which came within Ibsen's ken just while the play was in process of gestation. A swedish nobleman, personally known to Ibsen, and remarkable for that amenity and distinction of manner which he attributes to Rosmer, had been unhappily married to a lady who shared none of his interests, and was intellectually quite unsympathetic to him. Much more sympathetic was a female relative of his wife's. The relation between them attracted attention, and (as in Rosmersholm) was the subject of venomous paragraphs in the local Press. Count Blank left his home and went abroad, was joined by the sympathetic cousin, resigned the high office which he held in his native country, and returned to his wife the fortune she had brought him. Shortly afterwards the Countess dies of consumption, which was, of course, supposed to have been accelerated by her husband's misconduct. The use that Ibsen made of this unhappy story affords a perfect example of the working-up of raw material in the factory of genius. Not one of the traits that constitute the originality and greatness of the play is to be found in the actual circumstances. He remodelled the whole episode; it was plastic as a sculptor's clay in his hands; but doubtless it did give him something to seize upon and re-create. For the character of Rebecca, it is believed (on rather inadequate grounds, it seems to me) that Ibsen borrowed some traits from Charlotte Stieglitz, who committed suicide in 1834, in the vain hope of stimulating the intellectual activity of her husband, a minor poet.[2] For Ulric Brendel, Dr. Brahm relates that Ibsen found a model in an eccentric "dream-genius" known to him in Italy, who created only in his mind, and despised writing. But Brendel is so clearly a piece of the poet's own "devilment" as he used to call it, that it is rather idle to look for his "original." The scene of the play is said to have been suggested to Ibsen by an old family seat near Molde. Be this as it may, Dr. Brandes is certainly mistaken in declaring that there is no such "castle" as Rosmersholm in Norway, and thence arguing that Ibsen had begun to write for a cosmopolitan rather than a Norwegian audience. Rosmersholm is not a "castle" at all; and old houses such as Ibsen describes are far from uncommon.

The Literary Remains enable us to trace Rosmersholm to its completion from a very embryonic form. It was at first to have

been called <u>White Horses</u>.   Here is the earliest memorandum for
it:--

HE, the delicate, distinguished nature, who has gone over to
a liberal (literally, "free-minded") standpoint, and from whom
all his former friends and acquaintances have drawn back.
Widower: has been unhappily married to a melancholic, half-mad
wife, who at last drowned herself.

SHE: his two daughters' governess, emancipated, warm-
blooded, somewhat unscrupulous, but in a refined way.   Is
regarded by the neighbourhood as the evil genius of the house:
is the object of misinterpretation and backbiting.

THE ELDER DAUGHTER: is on the point of breaking down
through loneliness and want of occupation: rich endowment with
no outlet for it.

THE YOUNGER DAUGHTER: observant, budding passions.

THE JOURNALIST: genius, vagabond.

It is evident that the poet has as yet no idea of the
terrible tragedy of Rebecca's relation to Beata; he could
scarcely have described as "somewhat unscrupulous" a woman who,
under the mask of friendship, goaded another to suicide.
Rosmer's two daughters, we see, disappeared from Rosmersholm, to
reappear in <u>The Lady from the Sea</u>, as Boletta and Hilda Wangel.
Ibsen fumbled around a good deal for the names in this
play.   Rosmer appears at first as "Boldt-Romer," and then,
without any warning, he changes into "Rosenhielm." Rebecca is at
first "Miss Badeck" or "Radeck."   Then there was a period during
which she was married to Rosmer.   Through an act and a half she
figures as "Mrs. Rosmer"; and then, in the middle of a draft of
the second act she suddenly comes unmarried again and is called
"Miss Dankert."   While she was Mrs. Rosmer, her Christian name
was "Agatha"; in the "Miss Dankert" stage it was Rebecca; not
until the third act is reached does she become Rebecca West.
Kroll was at first to have been called Hekmann; then he became
"Rector Gylling," a patently inappropriate name, inasmuch as it
suggests the Norwegian word for "chicken."   Ulric Brendel, in one
stage of incubation, adopted Rosmer's cast-off name of
"Rosenhielm"; and somewhat later he became "Seierhielm."

In the earliest draft of the first act that has come down to
us, Rosmer (as Boldt-Romer) speaks to Miss Radeck about his
daughters, saying that he does not like the idea of their skating
on the mill-dam where their mother was drowned, even though they
themselves are ignorant of the fact.   Then Kroll (as Hekmann)
enters, and remonstrates with him for resigning his pastorate;
but the fragment breaks off before Rosmer (now Rosenhielm) has
confessed his "apostasy."   Of a later and more developed draft we

have two acts practically complete. It is in this phase that Rebecca is first "Mrs. Rosmer" and then "Miss Dankert." The two daughters have by this time disappeared; but Rosmer says to Gylling (Kroll), "We do not find it painful to dwell on the thought either of Agneta (Beata) or of little Alfred." This is the only allusion to "little Alfred," and we cannot say with certainty what was in Ibsen's mind when he wrote it. Can he have intended that the dead wife should have had a child, and should have taken the child with her into the mill-race? For the rest, the lines of the completed play seem by this time to be pretty clear in the poet's mind, but its structure is still flaccid and in need of stern compression. It is significant that Rosmer does not, in the first act, confess to Kroll his change of heart. He is on the point of doing so when he is interrupted by the entrance of Rosenhielm (Brendel). The confession being thus deferred till the second act, the first act ends (like the first act of _Pillars of Society_) without any clear announcement of the coming struggle. The student of technique may learn an invaluable lesson in noting the enormous improvement effected by the transference of Rosmer's avowal from the second to the first act. After the draft second act, the further drafts became fragmentary, and are all very much on the lines of the completed play. The one exception may be found in an alternative version of the first Brendel scene, in which Brendel (at this stage called Hetman) expressed his intention of preaching land nationalisation, and is greatly cast down on learning that his theories have been anticipated in a well-known book--an allusion, no doubt, to Henry George's _Progress and Poverty_. Ibsen showed his usual fine instinct in abandoning this idea.

A still more fortunate change was the remodelling of the passage in which we first hear of the White Horse of Rosmersholm. As it originally stood, it afforded an example of the lapses which would now and then occur in Ibsen's sense of humour:--

MRS. ROSMER(Rebecca). What was that you once told me, Madam Helset? You said that, from time immemorial, something strange happened here at Rosmersholm whenever one of the family died.
MADAM HELSET. Yes, it is as true as I stand here. Then the white horse comes.
ROSMER. Oh, that old family legend----
MRS. ROSMER. In it comes at the dead of night. Into the courtyard. Through the closed gate. Neighs loudly. Kicks up its hind legs, gallops once round, and then out again at a tearing gallop?
MADAM HELSET. Yes, that's just how it is. Both my mother and my grandmother have seen it.

Unless we are to suppose that Rebecca is deliberately burlesquing the superstition, the white horse which kicks up its hind legs must be classed with the steamboat in Little Eyolf which has "one red eye and one green." But, unlike the steamboat, the kicking horse did not pursue its mad career into the finished play.

Published on November 23, 1886, Rosmersholm was first acted in Bergen in January, 1887, in Gothenburg in March, in Christiania and Stockholm not till April. Copenhagen did not see it until November, 1887, when it was acted by a Swedish travelling company. Its first production in Germany took place at Augsburg in April, 1887, the poet himself being present. It was produced in Berlin in May, 1887, in Vienna not till May, 1893. There are few of the leading German theatres where it has not been acted, and has not taken a more or less prominent place in the repertory. In Germany indeed (though not elsewhere) it seems to rank among Ibsen's most popular works. In London, Rosmersholm was first acted at the Vaudeville Theatre on February 23, 1891, Mr. F. R. Benson playing Rosmer, and Miss Florence Farr, Rebecca. Four performances of it were given at the Opera Comique in 1893, with Mr. Lewis Waller as Rosmer, and Miss Elizabeth Robins as Rebecca. In 1892, a writer who adopted the pseudonym of "Austin Fryers" produced, at the Globe Theatre, a play called Beata which purported to be a "prologue" to Rosmersholm—the drama which Ibsen (perversely, in Mr. Fryers' judgment) chose to narrate instead of exhibiting it in action. Not until 1893 was Rosmersholm produced in Paris, by the company entitled "L'Oeuvre," under the direction of M. Lugné Poë. This company afterwards acted it in London and in many other cities—among the rest in Christiania. In Italy, Eleonora Duse added the play to her repertory, with scenery designed by Mr. Gordon Craig. In America Rebecca has been acted with great success by Mrs. Fiske.

With Rosmersholm we reach the end of the series of social dramas which began seventeen years earlier with The League of Youth. In all these plays the individual is treated, more or less explicitly, as a social unit, a member of a class, an example of some collective characteristic, or a victim of some collective superstition, injustice, or stupidity. The plays which follow, on the other hand, beginning with The Lady from the Sea, are plays of pure psychology. There are, no doubt, many women like Ellida Wangel or Hedda Gabler; but it is as individuals, not as members of a class, that they interest us; nor is their fate conditioned, like that of Nora or Mrs. Alving, by any social prejudice or pressure. But in Rosmersholm man is still considered as a "political animal." The play, as we have seen, actually took its rise as a protest against a morbid condition of the Norwegian public mind, as observed by the poet at a particular point of time. George Brandes, indeed, has very justly contended that it ought to rank with An Enemy of the People and The Wild Duck as a direct outcome of that momentous incident in Ibsen's career, the fierce attack upon Ghosts. "Rosmer," says Dr. Brandes, "begins where Stockmann left off. He wants to do from the very first what the doctor only wanted to do at the end of An Enemy of the People—to make proud, free, noble beings of his countrymen. At the beginning of the play, Rosmer is believed to be a decided Conservative (which the Norwegians considered Ibsen to be for many years after The League of Youth), and as long as this view is generally held, he is esteemed and admired, while everything that concerns him is interpreted in the most favourable manner. As soon, however, as his complete intellectual emancipation is discovered, and especially when it appears that he himself does not attempt to conceal the change in his views, public opinion turns against him. . . .Ibsen had been almost as much exposed as Rosmer to every sort of attack for some time after the publication of Ghosts, which (from the Conservative point of view) marked his conversion to Radicalism." The analogy between Ibsen's experience and Rosmer's is far too striking not to have been present to the poet's mind.

But, though the play distinctly belongs to the social series, it no less distinctly foreshadows the transition to the psychological series. Rosmer and Rebecca (or I am greatly mistaken) stand out from the social background much more clearly than their predecessors. They seem to grow away from it. At first they are concerned about political duties and social ideals; but, as the action proceeds, all thse considerations drop away from them, or recur but as remembered dreams, and they are alone with their tortured souls. Then we cannot but note the intrusion of pure poetry—imagination scarcely deigning to allege a realistic pretext—in the personage of Ulric Brendel. He is of the same kindred as the Stranger in The Lady from the Sea, and the Rat Wife in Little Eyolf. He marks Ibsen's final rebellion against the prosaic restrictions which from Pillars of Society onwards, he had striven to impose upon his genius.

He was yet to write plays more fascinating than Rosmersholm, but none greater in point of technical mastery. It surpasses The Wild Duck in the simplicity of its material, and in that concentration which renders its effect on the stage, perhaps, a little monotonous, and so detracts from its popularity. In construction it is a very marvel of cunning complexity. It is the consummate example in modern times of the retrospective method of which, in ancient times, the consummate example was the Oedipus Rex. This method has been blamed by many critics; but the first great critic of English drama commended it in the practice of the ancient poets. "They set the audience, as it

were," says Dryden, "at the post where the race is to be
concluded." "In unskilful hands," I have said elsewhere, "the
method might doubtless become very tedious; but when, as in
Rosmersholm, every phase of the retrospect has a definite
reaction upon the drama--the psychological process--actually
passing on the stage, the effect attained is surely one of
peculiar richness and depth. The drama of the past and the drama
of the present are interwoven in such a complex yet clear and
stately harmony as Ibsen himself has not often rivalled."

THE LADY FROM THE SEA

Ibsen's birthplace, Skien, is not on the sea, but at the head of a long and very narrow fjord. At Grimstad, however, and again at Bergen, he had for years lived close to the skerry-bound coast. After he left Bergen, he seldom came in touch with the open sea. The upper part of Christiania Fjord is a mere salt-water lake; and in Germany he never saw the sea, in Italy only on brief visits to Ischia, Sorrento, Amalfi. We find him in 1880,[1] writing to Hegel from Munich: "Of all that I miss down here, I miss the sea most. That is the deprivation to which I can least reconcile myself." Again, in 1885, before the visit which he paid that year to Norway, he writes from Rome to the same correspondent, that he has visions of buying a country-house by the sea, in the neighbourhood of Christiania. "The sight of the sea," he says, "is what I most miss in these regions; and this feeling grows year by year." During the weeks he spent at Molde that year, there can be no doubt that he was gathering, not only the political impressions which he used in Rosmersholm, but the impressions of ocean and fjord, and of the tide of European life flowing past, but not mingling with, the "carp-pond" existence of a small Norwegian town, which he was afterwards to embody in The Lady from the Sea. That invaluable bibliographer, Halvorsen, is almost certainly wrong in suggesting that Veblungsnaes, at the head of the Romsdalfjord, is the scene of the play. The "local situation" is much more like that of Molde itself. There Ibsen must frequently have seen the great English tourist steamer gliding noiselessly to its moorings, before proceeding up the fjord to Veblungsnaes, and then, on the following day, slipping out to sea again.

Two years later, in 1887, Ibsen spent the summer at Frederikshavn and at Saeby in the north of Jutland, not far from Skaw. At Saeby I visited him; and from a letter written at the time I make the following extract: "He said that Fru Ibsen and he had just come from Frederikshavn, which he himself liked very much—he could knock about all day among the shipping, talking to the sailors, and so forth. Besides, he found the neighbourhood of the sea favourable to contemplation and constructive thought.

Here, at Saeby, the sea was not so easily accessible. But Fru Ibsen didn't like Frederikshavn because of the absence of pleasant walks about it; so Saeby was a sort of compromise between him and her." I remember that he enlarged to me at great length on the fascination which the sea exercised over him. He was then, he said, "preparing some tomfoolery for next year." On his return to Munich, he put his ideas into shape, and The Lady from the Sea was published in November, 1888.

Ibsen wrote few letters while the play was in process of preparation, and none of them contains any noteworthy reference to it. On the other hand, we possess a very curious first sketch of the story[2] (dated March 5, 1880), which shows in a most interesting fashion how an idea grew in his mind. Abbreviating freely, I will try to indicate the main points of difference between the sketch and the finished play.

The scene of the action was originally conceived as a much smaller town than it ultimately became, shut in and overshadowed by high, abrupt rocks. (Note that when he wrote the sketch Ibsen had not yet visited Molde). There was to be an hotel and a sanatorium, and a good deal of summer gaiety in the place; but the people were to long, in an impotent, will-less fashion, for release from their imprisonment in the "shadow-life" of this remote corner of the world. Through the short summer, they were always to have the long winter impending over them; and this was to be a type of life: "A bright summer day with the great darkness after it--that is all." This motive, though traces of it remain, is much less emphasised than was at first intended.

The characters were to fall into three groups: inhabitants of the town, summer visitors, and passing tourists. The tourists were simply to "come and go, and enter episodically into the action"; but the other two groups are more or less individualised.

The first group is thus described: "The lawyer married, a second time, to the woman from the open sea outside. Has two young but grown-up daughters by his first marriage. Elegant, distinguished, bitter. His past tarnished by an indiscretion. His career thereby cut short. The disreputable signboard-painter with the artist-dreams, happy in his imaginings. The old, married clerk. Has written a play in his youth, which was only once acted.[3] Is for ever touching it up, and lives in the illusion that it will be published and will make a great success. Takes no steps, however, to bring this about. Nevertheless, accounts himself one of the "literary" class. His wife and children believe blindly in the play. (Perhaps a private tutor, not a clerk.) Tailor Fresvik, the man-midwife of radicalism, who shows his "emancipation" in ludicrous attempts at debauchery--affairs with other men's wives--talks of divorce and so forth."

We see that, in the course of elaboration, not only the profession, but the character of Wangel was entirely altered. It is noteworthy, by the way, that, with Ibsen, lawyers are always more or less unsympathetic characters (Stensgard, Helmer, Krogstad, Brack) while doctors are more or less sympathetic (Fieldbo, Rank, Stockmann, Relling, Wangel, Herdal). We see, too, how he saved up for seventeen years the character of the clerk-dramatist. Found superfluous in The Lady from the Sea, he became the delightful Foldal of John Gabriel Borkman. The radical tailor was destined never to come to life; and the characteristics of the "signboard-painter" were divided between Ballested and Lyngstrand.

In the second group, however—that of the summer visitors—the consumptive sculptor Lyngstrand is already pretty completely sketched. The group was also to have included Lyngstrand's "patron" and his patron's wife—a "stupid, uppish, and tactless woman, who wounds the patient sometimes without meaning it, sometimes on purpose." The patron's wife has entirely disappeared from the completed play, while the patron, though mentioned, has not even a name.

But the oddest fact which this sketch brings to light is that Arnholm and the Stranger were formed by the scission, so to speak, of one character, denominated the "Strange Passenger." Ellida[4] was originally to have been a pastor's daughter. She was to have engaged herself secretly to a "young and unprincipled mate"—a midshipman dismissed the navy. This engagement she broke off, partly at her father's command, partly of her own free will, because she could not forgive what she had learnt of the young sailor's past. Then, after her marriage, she came to feel that in her ignorance and prejudice she had been too hard on him, and to believe that "esentially—in her imagination—it was with him that she had led her married life." This is very like the feeling of Ellida in the play; but her story has become much more strange and romantic. It is not quite clear—the sketch being incomplete—whether the ex-midshipman was to have appeared in person. But there was to have been a "Strange Passenger" (so nicknamed by the other summer visitors) who had been in love with Ellida in the old days, and of whom she was now to make a confidant, very much as she does of Arnholm in the play. His character, however, was to have been quite unlike that of Arnholm; he was to have been "bitter, and given to cutting jests"—somewhat reminiscent, in fact, of the Strange Passenger in Peer Gynt. Ibsen may have meant that the nickname should be given him in allusion to that figure. We see, at any rate, that the Strange Passenger, in his capacity as Ellida's confidant, became Arnholm, who is not in the least strange; while the strangeness was transferred to Ellida's former lover, who, originally conceived as a comparatively commonplace personage, now became distinctly "the Stranger."

Fragments of dialogue are roughly sketched--especially the young sculptor's story of the shipwreck and of the group it has suggested to him. Ellida's fancy that mankind has taken a wrong turning in developing into land-animals instead of water-animals is rather more carefully worked out in the sketch than in the play. It takes the form of a semi-serious biological theory, not attributed to any particular character: "Why should we belong to the dry land? Why not to the air? Why not to the sea? The common longing for wings--the strange dreams that one can fly and that one does fly without feeling the least surprise at the fact--how is all this to be explained?" The suggestion evidently is that these dreams are reminiscences of the bird stage in our development; and then the poet goes on to suggest the same explanation of the intense longing for the sea which he attributes to Ellida: "People who are akin to the sea. Bound to the sea. Dependent on the sea. Must get back to it. A fish-species forms the primoridal link in the evolutionary chain. Do rudiments of it survive in our nature? In the nature of some of us?" He also indicates a fantasy of floating cities to be towed southwards or northwards according to the season. "To learn to control storms and the weather. Some such glorious time will come. And we--we shall not be there to see it." All this over-luxuriant growth of fantasy has been carefully pruned in the completed play.

The main incidents of the first act are sketched out in a form not very different from that which they ultimately assumed--and there the scenario breaks off.

"The Stranger's daemonic power over Ellida was suggested" says John Paulsen, "by Welhaven's strange influence over Camilla Wergeland"; while Dr. Brahm asserts "on credible authority" that the incident of the rings thrown into the sea reproduces an episode of Ibsen's own early life in Bergen. Until the "credible authority" is more clearly specified, we need not pin our faith to the latter assertion; but the former receives some confirmation in a letter which Ibsen addressed on May 3, 1889, to the lady whom Paulsen mentions. This was Camilla Collett, born Wergeland, a sister of the great lyric poet, Henrik Wergeland, and the authoress of a book, From the Camp of the Dumb (1877) which is said to have greatly influenced Ibsen's attitude towards the woman-question, and to have stimulated him to the production of A Doll's House. I do not know the story of her relation to J.S.C. Welhaven, a distinguished poet, and her brother's chief rival; but it is clear from Ibsen's letter that she was in some way present to his mind during the composition of The Lady from the Sea. This is what he wrote: "Allow me to send you a few words of very sincere thanks for your comprehension of The Lady from the Sea. I felt pretty sure in advance that from you more than any one else I could rely upon such comprehension; but it gave me inexpressible pleasure to find my hope confirmed by your letter. Yes, there are points of resemblance--indeed many. And you have seen and felt them--points, I mean, which I could arrive at only by divination. But it is now many years since you, in virtue of your spiritual development, began, in one form or another, to make your presence felt in my work." Camilla Collett died in 1895, at the age of eighty-two.

Nowhere has The Lady from the Sea proved one of Ibsen's most popular works. It was acted in all the Scandinavian capitals, and in several German cities, in February and March, 1889. The poet himself was present at the first performance at the Royal Theatre, Berlin, on March 4, and afterwards (March 14) at a performance at Weimar, where he was called before the curtain after each act, and received a laurel wreath. In a letter to Hoffory, he expressed himself delighted with the actor who played the Stranger at Weimar; "I could not desire, and could scarcely conceive a better embodiment of the part--a long, gaunt figure, with hawk-like features, piercing black eyes, and a fine, deep, veiled voice." The play holds the stage here and there in Germany, but is not very frequently acted.

In London, five performances of Mrs. Marx-Aveling's translation were given, under the direction of Dr. Aveling, at Terry's Theatre in May, 1891--the year of the first performance in England of Ghosts, Rosmersholm, and Hedda Gabler. This wholly inadequate production was followed, eleven years later, by a revival at the Royalty Theatre, by the Stage Society, in which Ellida was played by Miss Janet Achurch, and the Stranger by Mr. Laurence Irving. In Paris, an organisation calling itself "Les Escholiers," produced La Dame de la Mer in 1892. It was afterwards played, both in Paris and on tour, by the Théâtre de l'Oeuvre.

The discovery that The Lady from the Sea was planned so early as 1880 is particularly interesting in view of the fact that, in technical concentration, and even, one is inclined to say, in intellectual power, it falls notably below the level of its immediate predecessors, The Wild Duck and Rosmersholm, and its immediate successors, Hedda Gabler and The Master Builder. It would scarcely be going too far to call it the weakest thing Ibsen produced between A Doll's House and John Gabriel Borkman, both inclusive. I well remember the sense of slackening dramatic fibre with which I read it on its first appearance; the fear that age was beginning to tell upon the poet; and the relief with which I found him, in Hedda Gabler, once more at the very height of his power. Some readers may take exception to this view, and declare that they prefer The Lady from the Sea to several of the plays which I would rank above it. In point of amenity and charm, it doubtless ranks high among Ibsen's works; its poetic merits are great; but the comparative laxity of its technique seems to me quite unmistakable. The main interest--the Ellida-Wangel interest, let us call it--is constantly being

interrupted by two subsidiary interests: the Arnholm-Boletta
interest, and the Boletta-Hilda-Lyngstrand interest. These lines
of interest touch each other, but are not effectually
interwoven. In no other play of Ibsen's, in fact, since
The League of Youth, is there such a marked sub-plot, or, rather,
two sub-plots; and, for my part, judging them by the high Ibsen
standard, I find neither of these sub-plots particularly
interesting. The main action, on the other hand, is not only
interesting but full of psychological truth. Ellida is one of
the most living of Ibsen's women. There are few of his heroines
whom one has not seen and recognised in real life; but Ellida in
particular I happen to have known intimately, though Ibsen never
heard of the lady in question. The character of Wangel, too, is
not only very amiable, but very closely observed. Yet even in
the working out of this main theme, there is, I think, a
technical weakness. We feel that, in the decisive scene of the
last act, Wangel's mere statement that he sets Ellida free is an
insufficient pivot for the revolution which takes place in her
mind. Psychologically, no doubt, it is adequate, but
dramatically it is ineffective. The poet ought, I suggest, to
have devised some more convincing means of bringing home both to
her and to us the fact of her manumission.[5] In default of a
practical proof, a symbolic indication might have served; but
something we want beyond a mere verbal declaration. It may be
taken as a technical principle, I believe, that a change of mind
on which so much depends ought, for purposed of dramatic effect,
to be demonstrated by some outward and visible sign sufficiently
cogent to make the audience fully realise and believe in it.

Another technical weakness, more obvious, though perhaps
less important, is the astounding coincidence by which
Lyngstrand, the one witness to the Stranger's frenzy on reading
of Ellida's faithlessness, is made, by pure change, to encounter
Ellida and to tell her the story. This is, I think the only real
abuse of coincidence in Ibsen's modern plays, from Pillars of
Society onwards.[6] One or two other much slighter
coincidences--such as, in A Doll's House, Mrs. Linden's former
acquaintance with Krogstad--are accounted for by the fact that
Norway is a very small country, in which roughly speaking, every
one of the town-dwelling upper and middle class knows, or has
heard of, every one else.

As I have pointed out in the introduction to Rosmersholm,
The Lady from the Sea is the first play in which Ibsen entirely
abandons social satire and devotes himself to pure psychology.
It is also the first play in which he trenches on the occult. He
was to go much further in this direction in The Master Builder
and Little Eyolf; but already he pursues the plan, which was also
Hawthorne's, of carefully leaving us in doubt as to whether and
how far, any supernormal influence is at work. On the whole,
however, he probably intends us to conclude that the Stranger's
uncanny power over Ellida exists only in her imagination.

HEDDA GABLER

From Munich, on June 29, 1890, Ibsen wrote to the Swedish poet, Count Carl Snoilsky: "Our intention has all along been to spend the summer in the Tyrol again. But circumstances are against our doing so. I am at present engaged upon a new dramatic work, which for several reasons has made very slow progress, and I do not leave Munich until I can take with me the completed first draft. There is little or no prospect of my being able to complete it in July." Ibsen did not leave Munich at all that season. On October 30 he wrote: "At present I am utterly engrossed in a new play. Not one leisure hour have I had for several months." Three weeks later (November 20) he wrote to his French translator, Count Prozor: "My new play is finished; the manuscript went off to Copenhagen the day before yesterday. . . .It produces a curious feeling of emptiness to be thus suddenly separated from a work which has occupied one's time and thoughts for several months, to the exclusion of all else. But it is a good thing, too, to have done with it. The constant intercourse with the fictitious personages was beginning to make me quite nervous." To the same correspondent he wrote on December 4: "The title of the play is Hedda Gabler. My intention in giving it this name was to indicate that Hedda, as a personality, is to be regarded rather as her father's daughter than as her husband's wife. It was not my desire to deal in this play with so-called problems. What I principally wanted to do was to depict human beings, human emotions, and human destinies, upon a groundwork of certain of the social conditions and principles of the present day."

So far we read the history of the play in the official "Correspondence."[1] Some interesting glimpses into the poet's moods during the period between the completion of The Lady from the Sea and the publication of Hedda Gabler are to be found in the series of letters to Fräulein Emilie Bardach, of Vienna, published by Dr. George Brandes.[2] This young lady Ibsen met at Gossensass in the Tyrol in the autumn of 1889. The record of their brief friendship belongs to the history of The Master Builder rather than to that of Hedda Gabler, but the allusions to his work in his letters to her during the winter of 1889 demand some examination.

So early as October 7, 1889, he writes to her: "A new poem begins to dawn in me. I will execute it this winter, and try to transfer to it the bright atmosphere of the summer. But I feel that it will end in sadness--such is my nature." Was this "dawning" poem Hedda Gabler? Or was it rather The Master Builder that was germinating in his mind? Who shall say? The latter hypothesis seems the more probable, for it is hard to believe that at any stage in the incubation of Hedda Gabler he can have conceived it as even beginning in a key of gaiety. A week later, however, he appears to have made up his mind that the time had not come for the poetic utilisation of his recent experiences. He writes on October 15: "Here I sit as usual at my writing-table. Now I would fain work, but am unable to. My fancy, indeed, is very active. But it always wanders away. It wanders where it has no business to wander during working hours. I cannot suppress my summer memories--nor do I wish to. I live through my experiences again and again and yet again. To transmute it all into a poem, I find, in the meantime, impossible." Clearly, then, he felt that his imagination ought to have been engaged on some theme having no relation to his summer experiences--the theme, no doubt, of Hedda Gabler. In his next letter, dated October 29, he writes: "Do not be troubled because I cannot, in the meantime, create (dichten). In reality I am for ever creating, or, at any rate, dreaming of something which, when in the fulness of time it ripens, will reveal itself as a creation (Dichtung)." On November 19 he says: "I am very busily occupied with preparations for my new poem. I sit almost the whole day at my writing-table. Go out only in the evening for a little while." The five following letters contain no allusion to the play; but on September 18, 1890, he wrote: "My wife and son are at present at Riva, on the Lake of Garda, and will probably remain there until the middle of October, or even longer. Thus I am quite alone here, and cannot get away. The new play on which I am at present engaged will probably not be ready until November, though I sit at my writing-table daily, and almost the whole day long."

Here ends the history of Hedda Gabler, so far as the poet's letters carry us. Its hard, clear outlines, and perhaps somewhat bleak atmosphere, seem to have resulted from a sort of reaction against the sentimental "dreamery" begotten of his Gossensass experiences. He sought refuge in the chill materialism of Hedda from the ardent transcendantalism of Hilda, whom he already heard knocking at the door. He was not yet in the mood to deal with her on the plane of poetry.[3]

The Literary Remains contain some interesting jottings in preparation for Hedda Gabler, as well as pretty full drafts of several scenes in the play. The first note runs thus:--

The pale, seemingly cold beauty. Great demands upon life
and upon the joy of life.
He, who has now at last conquered her, is insignificant in
person, but an honorable and gifted, liberal-minded man of
science.

Then come brief scraps of hastily-scribbled dialogue; and
then:

N. B.!

Brack had always thought that Hedda's short engagement to
Tesman would be broken off.
Hedda talks of how she felt herself set aside, step by step,
when her father had fallen out of favour, retired [from the army]
and died leaving no property.--She then felt, and felt bitterly,
as if it had been for his sake that she had been feted.--And she
was already between 25 and 26. On the point of going downhill
unmarried.

She thinks that Tesman in reality feels only a vain
exultation at having won her. His care for her is like that
which one expends upon a fine riding-horse, or a valuable
sporting dog.--She does not, however, feel indignant at this.
She regards it simply as a fact.
Hedda says to Brack that she does not think one can call
Tesman ridiculous. But in reality she does find him so. And
later she finds him pitiful.
TESMAN. Could you not call me by my Christian name?
HEDDA. No, indeed, I can't--unless you had a different name
from the one they have given you.
Tesman takes possession of Lövborg's manuscript, in order
that it may not be lost. It is Hedda who afterwards, as if by a
passing remark, intended to test him, suggests to him the idea of
keeping it.
Then he reads it. A new train of thought is set up within
him. But the situation becomes more tense. Hedda awakens his
jealousy.

*

In the third act there comes one piece of news after another
as to Lövborg's exploits during the night. At last he himself
arrives, in quiet despair. "Where is the manuscript?" "Did I
not leave it behind me here?" He knows that he did not. And, in
any case, what use would the manuscript be to him now! He to
write of "the ethics of the future"! He, who has just got out of

the police cells!

Hedda's despair lies in the idea that there are surely so many possibilities of happiness in the world, but that she cannot discover them. It is the lack of an object in life that tortures her.

When Hedda tempts T. to lead E. L. to ruin, it is to test T.'s character.

It is in Hedda's neighbourbood that the irresistible craving for dissipation always comes over E. L.

Tesman cannot understand that E. L. should be willing to build his future on wrong done to another.

Amid these jottings, too, we find a scrap of dialogue between Hedda and Brack, in which she says: "Remember that I am an old man's child--and more than that, the child of a man who had lived his life. Perhaps that has left its mark on me." Brack replies: "I really believe you have begun to brood over problems"; and she rejoins: "What depths may one not fall to when one has gone and got married?"

From the more detailed drafts it would appear that, in the poet's original conception, Tesman was to be much more of an active intermediary between Hedda and Lövborg than he became in the end. It was Tesman who, at her instigation, was to lure Lövborg to Brack's orgie; and it was apparently Tesman who was actually to make away with or misappropriate Lövborg's manuscript. Both Tesman and Mrs. Elvsted were to have known much more of the former "comradeship" between Lövborg and Hedda than they do in the finished play. There is no hint of any "Mademoiselle Diana" in the draft; when Hedda asks Mrs. Elvsted who the woman is whom Lövborg cannot forget, she replies point-bland, "It is yourself, Hedda." Mrs. Elvsted's luxuriant hair, Hedda's jealousy of it, and threat to "burn it off her head," are afterthoughts; so is the famous conception of Lövborg "with the vine-leaves in his hair." A curious touch, which I am at a loss to explain, occurs in the stage-direction for Hedda's burning of Lövborg's manuscript. It runs thus:--"She goes to the writing-table, takes out the manuscript, seats herself in the arm-chair beside the stove; opens the packet, sorts out the white leaves from the blue, puts the white back in the cover again, and keeps the blue in her lap." Then she opens the stove door and gradually burns the blue leaves, with words very much like those of the final text. What the white leaves can have been I do not know; they must have belonged to some phase in the working-out of the play which has otherwise disappeared.

Hedda Gabler was published in Copenhagen on December 16, 1890. This was the first of Ibsen's plays to be translated from proof-sheets and published in England and America almost simultaneously with its first appearance in Scandinavia. The earliest theatrical performance took place at the Residenz Theater, Munich, on the last day of January 1891, in the presence of the poet, Frau Conrad-Ramlo playing the title-part. The Lessing Theater, Berlin, followed suit on February 10. Not till February 25 was the play seen in Copenhagen, with Fru Hennings as Hedda. On the following night it was given for the first time in Christiania, the Norwegian Hedda being Fröken Constance Bruun. It was this production which the poet saw when he visited the Christiania Theater for the first time after his return to Norway, August 28, 1891. It would take pages to give even the baldest list of the productions and revivals of Hedda Gabler in Scandinavia and Germany, where it has always ranked among Ibsen's most popular works. ⌐ The admirable production of the play by Miss Elizabeth Robins and Miss Marion Lea, at the Vaudeville Theatre, London, April 20, 1891, may rank as the second great step towards the popularisation of Ibsen in England,⌐ the first being the Charrington-Achurch production of A Doll's House in 1889. Miss Robins afterwards repeated her fine performance of Hedda many times, in London, in the English provinces, and in New York. The character has also been acted in London by Eleonora Duse, and by Mrs. Patrick Campbell. In America Hedda has been acted with great success by Mrs. Fiske and by Madame Nazimova; in Australia, by Miss Nance O'Neill. The first French Hedda Gabler was Mlle. Marthe Brandes, who played the part at the Vaudeville Theatre, Paris, on December 17, 1891, the performance being introduced by a lecture by M. Jules Lemaître. In Holland, in Italy, in Russia, the play has been acted times without number. In short (as might easily have been foretold) it has rivalled A Doll's House in world-wide popularity.

It has been suggested,[4] I think without sufficient ground, that Ibsen deliberately conceived Hedda Gabler as an "international" play, and that the scene is really the "west end" of any great European city. To me it seems quite clear that Ibsen had Christiania in mind, and the Christiania of a somewhat earlier period than the 'nineties. The electric cars, telephones, and other conspicuous factors in the life of a modern capital are notably absent from the play. There is no electric light in Secretary Falk's villa. It is still the habit for ladies to return on foot from evening parties, with gallant swains escorting them. This "suburbanism" which so distressed the London critics of 1891, was characteristic of the Christiania Ibsen himself had known in the 'sixties--the Christiania of Love's Comedy--rather than of the greatly extended and modernised city of the end of the century. Moreover, Lövborg's allusions to the fjord, and the suggested picture of Sheriff Elvsted, his family and his avocations, are all distinctly Norwegian. The truth seems to be very simple--the environment and the subsidiary personages are all thoroughly national, but Hedda herself is an "international" type, a product of civilisation by no means peculiar to Norway.

We cannot point to any individual model or models who "sat to" Ibsen for the character of Hedda.[5] The late Grant Allen declared that Hedda was "nothing more nor less than the girl we take down to dinner in London nineteen times out of twenty"; in which case Ibsen must have suffered from a superfluity of models, rather than from any difficulty in finding one. But the fact is that in this, as in all other instances, the word "model" must be taken in a very different sense from that in which it is commonly used in painting. Ibsen undoubtedly used models for this trait and that, but never for a whole figure. If his characters can be called portraits at all, they are composite portraits. Even when it seems pretty clear that the initial impulse towards the creation of a particular character came from some individual, the original figure is entirely transmuted in the process of harmonisation with the dramatic scheme. We need not, therefore, look for a definite prototype of Hedda; but Dr. Brandes shows that two of that lady's exploits were probably suggested by the anecdotic history of the day.

Ibsen had no doubt heard how the wife of a well-known Norwegian composer, in a fit of raging jealousy excited by her husband's prolonged absence from home, burnt the manuscript of a symphony which he had just finished. The circumstances under which Hedda burns Lövborg's manuscript are, of course, entirely different and infinitely more dramatic; but here we have merely another instance of the dramatisation or "poetisation" of the raw material of life. Again, a still more painful incident probably came to his knowledge about the same time. A beautiful and very intellectual woman was married to a well-known man who had been addicted to drink, but had entirely conquered the vice. One day a mad whim seized her to put his self-mastery and her power over him to the test. As it happened to be his birthday, she rolled into his study a small keg of brandy, and then withdrew. She returned some time afterwards to find that he had broached the keg, and lay insensible on the floor. In this anecdote we cannot but recognise the germ, not only of Hedda's temptation of Lövborg, but of a large part of her character.

"Thus," says Dr. Brandes, "out of small and scattered traits of reality Ibsen fashioned his close-knit and profoundly thought-out works of art."

For the character of Eilert Lövborg, again, Ibsen seems unquestionably to have borrowed several traits from a definite original. A young Danish man of letters, whom Dr. Brandes calls Holm, was an enthusiastic admirer of Ibsen, and came to be on very friendly terms with him. One day Ibsen was astonished to receive, in Munich, a parcel addressed from Berlin by this young man, containing, without word of explanation, a packet of his (Ibsen's) letters, and a photograph which he had presented to Holm. Ibsen brooded and brooded over the incident, and at last came to the conclusion that the young man had intended to return her letters and photograph to a young lady to whom he was known to be attached, and had in a fit of aberration mixed up the two objects of his worship. Some time after, Holm appeared at Ibsen's rooms. He talked quite rationally, but professed to have no knowledge whatever of the letter-incident, though he admitted the truth of Ibsen's conjecture that the "belle dame sans merci" had demanded the return of her letters and portrait. Ibsen was determined to get at the root of the mystery; and a little inquiry into his young friend's habits revealed the fact that he broke his fast on a bottle of port wine, consumed a bottle of Rhine wine at lunch, of Burgundy at dinner, and finished off the evening with one or two more bottles of port. Then he heard, too, how, in the course of a night's carouse, Holm had lost the manuscript of a book; and in these traits he saw the outline of the figure of Eilert Lövborg.

Some time elapsed, and again Ibsen received a postal packet from Holm. This one contained his will, in which Ibsen figured as his residuary legatee. But many other legatees were mentioned in the instrument--all of them ladies, such as Fräulein Alma Rothbart, of Bremen, and Fräulein Elise Kraushaar, of Berlin. The bequests to these meritorious spinsters were so generous that their sum considerably exceeded the amount of the testator's property. Ibsen gently but firmly declined the proffered inheritance; but Holm's will no doubt suggested to him the figure of that red-haired "Mademoiselle Diana," who is heard of but not seen in Hedda Gabler, and enabled him to add some further traits to the portraiture of Lovborg. When the play appeared, Holm recognised himself with glee in the character of the bibulous man of letters, and thereafter adopted "Eilert Lövborg" as his pseudonym. I do not, therefore, see why Dr. Brandes should suppress his real name; but I willingly imitate him in erring on the side of discretion. The poor fellow died several years ago.

Some critics have been greatly troubled as to the precise meaning of Hedda's fantastic vision of Lövborg "with vine-leaves in his hair." Surely this is a very obvious image or symbol of the beautiful, the ideal, aspect of bacchic elation and revelry. Antique art, or I am much mistaken, shows us many figures of Dionysus himself and his followers with vine-leaves entwined in their hair. To Ibsen's mind, at any rate, the image had long been familiar. In Peer Gynt (Act iv. sc. 8), when Peer, having carried off Anitra, finds himself in a particularly festive mood, he cries: "Were there vine-leaves around, I would garland my brow." Again, in Emperor and Galilean (Pt. ii. Act 1) where Julian, in the procession of Dionysus, impersonates the god himself, it is directed that he shall wear a wreath of vine-leaves. Professor Dietrichson relates that among the young artists whose society Ibsen frequented during his first years in Rome, it was customary, at their little festivals, for the revellers to deck themselves in this fashion. But the image is so obvious that there is no need to trace it to any personal experience. The attempt to place Hedda's vine-leaves among Ibsen's obscurities is an example of the firm resolution not to understand which animated the criticism of the 'nineties.

Dr. Brandes has dealt very severely with the character of Eilert Lövborg, alleging that we cannot believe in the genius attributed to him. But where is he described as a genius? The poet represents him as a very able student of sociology; but that is a quite different thing from attributing to him such genius as must necessarily shine forth in every word he utters. Dr. Brandes, indeed, declines to believe even in his ability as a sociologist, on the ground that it is idle to write about the social development of the future. "To our prosaic minds," he says, "it may seem as if the most sensible utterance on the subject is that of the fool of the play: "The future! Good heavens, we know nothing of the future."" The best retort to this criticism is that which Eilert himself makes: "There's a thing or two to be said about it all the same." The intelligent forecasting of the future (as Mr. H. G. Wells has shown) is not only clearly distinguishable from fantastic Utopianism, but is indispensable to any large statesmanship or enlightened social activity. With very real and very great respect for Dr. Brandes, I cannot think that he has been fortunate in his treatment of Lövborg's character. It has been represented as an absurdity that he should think of reading abstracts from his new book to a man like Tesman, whom he despises. But though Tesman is a ninny, he is, as Hedda says, a "specialist"—he is a competent, plodding student of his subject. Lövborg may quite naturally wish to see how his new method, or his excursion into a new field, strikes the average scholar of the Tesman type. He is, in fact, "trying it on the dog"—neither an unreasonable nor an unusual proceeding. There is a certain improbability in the way in which Lövborg is represented as carrying his manuscript around, and especially in Mrs. Elvsted's production of his rough draft from her pocket; but these are mechanical trifles, on which only a niggling criticism would dream of laying stress.

Of all Ibsen's works, Hedda Gabler is the most detached, the most objective—a character-study pure and simple. It is impossible—or so it seems to me—to extract any sort of general idea from it. One cannot even call it a satire, unless one is prepared to apply that term to the record of a "case" in a work on criminology. Reverting to Dumas's dictum that a play should contain "a painting, a judgment, an ideal," we may say that Hedda Gabler fulfils only the first of these requirements. The poet does not even pass judgment on his heroine: he simply paints her full-length portrait with scientific impassivity. But what a portrait! How searching in insight, how brilliant in colouring, how rich in detail! Grant Allen's remark, above quoted, was, of course, a whimsical exaggeration: the Hedda type is not so common as all that, else the world would quickly come to an end. But particular traits and tendencies of the Hedda type are very common in modern life, and not only among women. Hyperaesthesia lies at the root of her tragedy. With a keenly critical, relentlessly solvent intelligence, she combines a morbid shrinking from all the gross and prosaic detail of the sensual life. She has nothing to take her out of herself--not a single intellectual interest or moral enthusiasm. She cherishes, in a languid way, a petty social ambition; and even that she finds obstructed and baffled. At the same time she learns that another woman has had the courage to love and venture all, where she, in her cowardice, only hankered and refrained. Her malign egoism rises up uncontrolled, and calls to its aid her quick and subtle intellect. She ruins the other woman's happiness, but in doing so incurs a danger from which her sense of personal dignity revolts. Life has no such charm for her that she cares to purchase it at the cost of squalid humiliation and self-contempt. The good and the bad in her alike impel her to have done with it all; and a pistol-shot ends what is surely one of the most poignant character-tragedies in literature.[6] Ibsen's brain never worked at higher pressure than in the conception and adjustment of those "crowded hours" in which Hedda, tangled in the web of Will and Circumstance, struggles on till she is too weary to struggle any more.

It may not be superfluous to note that the "a" in "Gabler" should be sounded long and full, like the "a" in "garden"-- not like the "a" in "gable" or in "gabble."

THE MASTER BUILDER

With The Master Builder--or Master Builder Solness, as the title runs in the original--we enter upon the final stage in Ibsen's career. "You are essentially right," the poet wrote to Count Prozor in March, 1900, "when you say that the series which closes with the Epilogue (When We Dead Awaken) began with Master Builder Solness."

"Ibsen," says Dr. Brahm, "wrote in Christiania all the four works which he thus seems to bracket together-- Solness, Eyolf, Borkman, and When We Dead Awaken. He returned to Norway in July, 1891, for a stay of indefinite length; but the restless wanderer over Europe was destined to leave his home no more. . . .He had not returned, however, to throw himself, as of old, into the battle of the passing day. Polemics are entirely absent from the poetry of his old age. He leaves the State and Society at peace. He who had departed as the creator of Falk [in Love's Comedy] now, on his return, gazes, not satirically, but rather in a lyric mood, into the secret places of human nature and the wonders of his own soul."

Dr. Brahm, however, seems to be mistaken in thinking that Ibsen returned to Norway with no definite intention of settling down. Dr. Julius Elias (an excellent authority) reports that shortly before Ibsen left Munich in 1891, he remarked one day, "I must get back to the North!" "Is that a sudden impulse?" asked Elias. "Oh no," was the reply; "I want to be a good head of a household and have my affairs in order. To that end I must consolidate my property, lay it down in good securities, and get it under control--and that one can best do where one has rights of citizenship." Some critics will no doubt be shocked to find the poet whom they have written down an "anarchist" confessing such bourgeois motives.

After his return to Norway, Ibsen's correspondence became very scant, and we have no letters dating from the period when he was at work on The Master Builder. On the other hand, we possess a curious lyrical prelude to the play, which he put on paper on March 16, 1892. It is said to have been his habit, before setting to work on a play, to "crystallise in a poem the mood

which then possessed him"; but the following is the only one of
these keynote poems which has been published. I give it in the
original language, with a literal translation:

DE SAD DER, DE TO--

De sad der, de to, i saa lunt et hus
ved höst og i vinterdage,
Saa braendte huset. Alt ligger i grus.
De to faar i asken rage.

For nede i den er et smykke gemt,--
et smykke, som aldrig kan braende.
Og leder de trofast, haender det nemt
at det findes af ham eller hende.

Men finder de end, de brandlidte to,
det dyre, ildfaste smykke,--
aldrig hun finder sin braendte tro,
han aldrig sin braendte lykke.

THEY SAT THERE, THE TWO--

They sat there, the two, in so cosy a house, through autumn
and winter days. Then the house burned down. Everything lies in
ruins. The two must grope among the ashes.
     For among them is hidden a jewel--a jewel that never can
burn. And if they search faithfully, it may easily happen that
he or she may find it.
     But even should they find it, the burnt-out two--find this
precious unburnable jewel--never will she find her burnt faith,
he never his burnt happiness.

This is the latest piece of Ibsen's verse that has been given to
the world; but one of his earliest poems--first printed in
1858--was also, in some sort, a prelude to The Master Builder.
Of this a literal translation may suffice. It is called

BUILDING-PLANS

     I remember as clearly as if it had been to-day the evening
when, in the paper, I saw my first poem in print. There I sat in
my den, and, with long-drawn puffs, I smoked and I dreamed in
blissful self-complacency.
     "I will build a cloud-castle. It shall shine all over the
North. It shall have two wings: one little and one great. The

great wing shall shelter a deathless poet; the little wing shall
serve as a young girl's bower."

The plan seemed to me nobly harmonious; but as time went on
it fell into confusion. When the master grew reasonable, the
castle turned utterly crazy; the great wing became too little,
the little wing fell to ruin.

Thus we see that, thirty-five years before the date of The Master
Builder, Ibsen's imagination was preoccupied with the symbol of a
master building a castle in the air, and a young girl in one of
its towers.

There has been some competition among the poet's young lady
friends for the honour of having served as his model for Hilda.
Several, no doubt, are entitled to some share in it. One is not
surprised to learn that among the papers he left behind were
sheaves upon sheaves of letters from women. "All these ladies,"
says Dr. Julius Elias, "demanded something of him--some cure for
their agonies of soul, or for the incomprehension from which they
suffered; some solution of the riddle of their nature. Almost
every one of them regarded herself as a problem to which Ibsen
could not but have the time and the interest to apply himself.
They all thought they had a claim on the creator of Nora. . . .Of
this chapter of his experience, Fru Ibsen spoke with ironic
humour. "Ibsen (I have often said to him), Ibsen, keep these
swarms of over-strained womenfolk at arm's length." "Oh no
(he would reply), let them alone. I want to observe them more
closely." His observations would take a longer or shorter time
as the case might be, and would always contribute to some work of
art."

The principal model for Hilda was doubtless Fräulein Emilie
Bardach, of Vienna, whom he met at Gossensass in the autumn of
1889. He was then sixty-one years of age; she is said to have
been seventeen. As the lady herself handed his letters to Dr.
Brandes for publication, there can be no indiscretion in speaking
of them freely. Some passages from them I have quoted in the
introduction to Hedda Gabler--passages which show that at first
the poet deliberately put aside his Gossensass impressions for
use when he should stand at a greater distance from them, and
meanwhile devoted himself to work in a totally different key. On
October 15, 1889, he writes, in his second letter to Fräulein
Bardach: "I cannot repress my summer memories, nor do I want
to. I live through my experiences again and again, and yet
again. To transmute it all into a poem I find, in the meantime,
impossible. In the meantime? Shall I succeed in doing so some
time in the future? And do I really wish to succeed? In the
meantime, at any rate, I do not. . . .And yet it must come in
time." The letters number twelve in all and are couched in a
tone of sentimental regret for the brief, bright summer days of

their acquaintanceship. The keynote is struck in the inscription
on the back of a photograph which he gave her before they
parted: <u>An die Maisonne eines Septemberlebens--</u> in <u>Tiroli</u>,[1]
27/9/89. In her album he had written the words:

> Hohes, schmerzliches Glück--
> um das Unerreichbare zu ringen![2]

in which we may, if we like, see a foreshadowing of the Solness
frame of mind. In the fifth letter of the series he refers to
her as "an enigmatic Princess"; in the sixth he twice calls her
"my dear Princess"; but this is the only point at which the
letters definitely and unmistakably point forward to <u>The Master
Builder</u>. In the ninth letter (February 6, 1890) he says: "I
feel it a matter of conscience to end, or at any rate, to
restrict, our correspondence." The tenth letter, six months
later, is one of kindly condolence on the death of the young
lady's father. In the eleventh (very short) note, dated December
30, 1890, he acknowledges some small gift, but says: "Please,
for the present, do not write to me again. . . .I will soon send
you my new play [Hedda Gabler]. Receive it in friendship, but in
silence!" This injunction she apparently obeyed. When <u>The
Master Builder</u> appeared, it would seem that Ibsen did not even
send her a copy of the play; and we gather that he was rather
annoyed when she sent him a photograph signed "Princess of
Orangia." On his seventieth birthday, however, she telegraphed
her congratulations, to which he returned a very cordial reply.
And here their relations ended.

That she was right, however, in regarding herself as his
principal model for Hilda appears from an anecdote related by Dr.
Elias.[3] It is not an altogether pleasing anecdote, but Dr. Elias
is an unexceptionable witness, and it can by no means be omitted
from an examination into the origins of <u>The Master Builder</u>.
Ibsen had come to Berlin in February, 1891, for the first
performance of <u>Hedda Gabler</u>. Such experiences were always a trial
to him, and he felt greatly relieved when they were over.
Packing, too, he detested; and Elias having helped him through
this terrible ordeal, the two sat down to lunch together, while
awaiting the train. An expansive mood descended upon Ibsen, and
chuckling over his champagne glass, he said: "Do you know, my
next play is already hovering before me--of course in vague
outline. But of one thing I have got firm hold. An experience:
a woman's figure. Very interesting, very interesting indeed.
Again a spice of devilry in it." Then he related how he had
met in the Tyrol a Viennese girl of very remarkable character.
She had at once made him her confidant. The gist of her
confessions was that she did not care a bit about one day
marrying a well brought-up young man--most likely she would never
marry. What tempted and charmed and delighted her was to lure

other women's husbands away from them. She was a little
daemonic wrecker; she often appeared to him like a little bird of
prey, that would fain have made him, too, her booty. He had
studied her very, very closely. For the rest, she had had no
great success with him. "She did not get hold of me, but I got
hold of her--for my play. Then I fancy" (here he chuckled again)
"she consoled herself with some one else." Love seemed to mean
for her only a sort of morbid imagination. This, however, was
only one side of her nature. His little model had had a great
deal of heart and of womanly understanding; and every woman,
thanks to the spontaneous power she could gain over him, might,
if she wished it, guide some man towards the good. "Thus Ibsen
spoke," says Elias, "calmly and coolly, gazing as it were into
the far distance, like an artist taking an objective view of some
experience--like Rubek speaking of his soul-thefts. He had
stolen a soul, and put it to a double employment. Thea Elvsted
and Hilda Wangel are intimately related--are, indeed, only
different expressions of the same nature." If Ibsen actually
declared Thea and Hilda to be drawn from one model, we must of
course take his word for it; but the relationship is hard to
discern.

There can be no reasonable doubt, then, that the Gossensass
episode gave the primary impulse to The Master Builder. But it
seems pretty well established, too, that another lady, whom he
met in Christiania after his return in 1891, also contributed
largely to the character of Hilda. This may have been the reason
why he resented Fräulein Bardach's appropriating to herself the
title of "Princess of Orangia."

The preliminary studies for The Master Builder, published in
the Literary Remains, are scanty and of slight interest. They
are little more, indeed, than fragments of the finished play,
nowhere indicating any considerable change of plan. Perhaps the
most interesting trait in them occurs where Solness is giving
Hilda an account of his progress in his profession. His work is
in demand, he says, far and wide; "and now, of late years, they
are beginning to take an interest in me abroad." No doubt this
touch was deleted because it pointed too clearly to the identity
of Solness and his creator.

The play was published in the middle of December, 1892. It
was acted both in Germany and England before it was seen in the
Scandinavian capitals. Its first performance took place at the
Lessing Theatre, Berlin, January 19, 1893, with Emmanuel Reicher
as Solness and Frl. Reisenhofer as Hilda. In London it was first
performed at the Trafalgar Square Theatre (now the Duke of
York's) on February 20, 1893, under the direction of Mr. Herbert
Waring and Miss Elizabeth Robins, who played Solness and Hilda.
This was one of the most brilliant and successful of English
Ibsen productions. Miss Robins was almost an ideal Hilda, and
Mr. Waring's Solness was exceedingly able. Some thirty

performances were given in all, and the play was reproduced at
the Opera Comique later in the season, with Mr. Lewis Waller in
Solness.   In the spring of 1911, Hilda and Solness were acted at
the Little Theatre by Miss Lillah McCarthy and Mr. Norman
McKinnell, respectively.   In Christiania and Copenhagen the play
was produced on the same evening, March 8, 1893; the Copenhagen
Solness and Hilda were Emil Poulsen and Fru Hennings.   A Swedish
production, by Lindberg, soon followed, both in Stockholm and
Gothenburg.   In Paris Solness le constructeur was not seen until
April 3, 1894, when it was produced by "L'Oeuvre" with M.
Lugné-Poë as Solness.   This company, sometimes with Mme. Suzanne
Desprès and sometimes with Mme. Berthe Bady as Hilda, in 1894 and
1895 presented the play in London, Brussels, Amsterdam, Milan,
and other cities.   In October, 1894, they visited Christiania,
where Ibsen was present at one of their performances, and is
reported by Herman Bang to have been so enraptured with it that
he exclaimed, "This is the resurrection of my play!"   On this
occasion Mme. Bady was the Hilda.   The first performance of the
play in America took place at the Carnegie Lyceum, New York, on
January 16, 1900, with Mr. William H. Pascoe as Solness and Miss
Florence Kahn as Hilda.   The performance was repeated in the
course of the same month, both at Washington and Boston.   Mme.
Nazimova has since found in Hilda one of her most notable parts.

    In England, and probably elsewhere as well, The Master
Builder produced a curious double effect.   It alienated many of
the poet's staunchest admirers, and it powerfully attracted many
people who had hitherto been hostile to him.   Looking back, it is
easy to see why this should have been so; for here was certainly
a new thing in drama, which could not but set up many novel
reactions.   A greater contrast could scarcely be imagined than
that between the hard, cold, precise outlines of Hedda Gabler and
the vague mysterious atmosphere of The Master Builder, in which,
though the dialogue is sternly restrained within the limits of
prose, the art of drama seems for ever on the point of floating
away to blend with the art of music.   Substantially, the play is
one long dialogue between Solness and Hilda; and it would be
quite possible to analyse this dialogue in terms of music, noting
(for example) the announcement first of this theme and then of
that, the resumption and reinforcement of a theme which seemed to
have been dropped, the contrapuntal interweaving of two or more
motives, a scherzo here, a fugal passage there.   Leaving this
exercise to some one more skilled in music (or less unskilled)
than myself, I may note that in The Master Builder Ibsen resumes
his favourite retrospective method, from which in Hedda Gabler he
had in great measure departed.   But the retrospect with which we
are here concerned is purely psychological.   The external events
involved in it are few and simple in comparison with the external
events which are successively unveiled in the retrospective
passages of The Wild Duck or Rosmersholm.   The matter of the play

is the soul-history of Halvard Solness, recounted to an impassioned listener--so impassioned, indeed, that the soul-changes it begets in her form an absorbing and thrilling drama. The gradations, retardations, accelerations of Solness's self-revealment are managed with the subtlest art, so as to keep the interest of the spectator ever on the stretch. The technical method was not new; it was simply that which Ibsen had been perfecting from <u>Pillars of Society</u> onward; but it was applied to a subject of a nature not only new to him, but new to literature.

That the play is full of symbolism it would be futile to deny; and the symbolism is mainly autobiographic. The churches which Solness sets out by building doubtless represent Ibsen's early romantic plays, the "homes for human beings" his social dramas; while the houses with high towers, merging into "castles in the air," stand for those spiritual dramas, with a wide outlook over the metaphysical environment of humanity, on which he was henceforth to be engaged. Perhaps it is not altogether fanciful to read a personal reference into Solness's refusal to call himself an architect, on the ground that his training has not been systematic--that he is a self-taught man. Ibsen too was in all essentials self-taught; his philosophy was entirely unsystematic; and, like Solness, he was no student of books. There may be an introspective note also in that dread of the younger generation to which Solness confesses. It is certain that the old Master-Builder was not lavish of his certificates of competence to young aspirants, though there is nothing to show that his reticence ever depressed or quenched any rising genius.

On the whole, then, it cannot be doubted that several symbolic motives are inwoven into the iridescent fabric of the play. But is is a great mistake to regard it as essentially and inseparably a piece of symbolism. Essentially it is the history of a sickly conscience, worked out in terms of pure psychology. Or rather, it is a study of a sickly and a robust conscience side by side. "The conscience is very conservative," Ibsen has somewhere said; and here Solness's conservatism is contrasted with Hilda's radicalism--or rather would-be radicalism, for we are led to suspect, towards the close, that the radical too is a conservative in spite of herself. The fact that Solness cannot climb as high as he builds implies, I take it, that he cannot act as freely as he thinks, or as Hilda would goad him into thinking. At such an altitude his conscience would turn dizzy, and life would become impossible to him. But here I am straying back to the interpretation of symbols. My present purpose is to insist that there is nothing in the play which has no meaning on the natural-psychological plane, and absolutely requires a symbolic interpretation to make it comprehensible. The symbols are harmonic undertones; the psychological melody is clear and consistent without any reference to them.[4] It is true that, in order to accept the action on what we may call the realistic level, we must suppose Solness to possess and to exercise, sometimes in spite of himself, and sometimes unconsciously, a considerable measure of hypnotic power. But the time is surely past when we could reckon hypnotism among "super-natural" phenomena. Whether the particular forms of hypnotic influence attributed to Solness do actually exist is a question we need not determine. The poet does not demand our absolute credence, as though he were giving evidence in the witness-box. What he requires is our imaginative acceptance of certain incidents which he purposely leaves hovering on the border between the natural and the preternatural, the explained and the unexplained. In this play, as in The Lady from the Sea and Little Eyolf, he shows a delicacy of art in his dalliance with the occult which irresistibly recalls the exquisite genius of Nathaniel Hawthorne.[5]

The critics who insist on finding nothing but symbolism in the play have fastened on Mrs. Solness's "nine lovely dolls," and provided the most amazing interpretations for them. A letter which I contributed in 1893 to the Westminster Gazette records an incident which throws a curious light on the subject, and may be worth preserving. "At a recent first night," I wrote, "I happened to be seated just behind a well-known critic. He turned round to me and said, "I want you to tell me what is your theory of those "nine lovely dolls." Of course one can see that they are entirely symbolical." "I am not so sure of that," I replied, remembering a Norwegian cousin of my own who treasured a favourite doll until she was nearer thirty than twenty. "They of course symbolise the unsatisfied passion of motherhood in Mrs. Solness's heart, but I have very little doubt that Ibsen makes use of this "symbol" because he has observed a similar case, or cases, in real life." "What!" cried the critic. "He has seen a grown-up, a middle-aged, woman continuing to "live with" her dolls!" I was about to say that it did not seem to me so very improbable, when a lady who was seated next me, a total stranger to both of us, leant forward and said, "Excuse my interrupting you, but it may perhaps interest you to know that I have three dolls to which I am deeply attached!" I will not be so rude as to conjecture this lady's age, but we may be sure that a very young woman would not have had the courage to make such an avowal. Does it not seem that Ibsen knows a thing or two about human nature--English as well as Norwegian--which we dramatic critics, though bound by our calling to be subtle psychologists, have not yet fathomed?" In the course of the correspondence which followed, one very apposite anecdote was quoted from an American paper, the Argonaut: "An old Virginia lady said to a friend, on finding a treasured old teacup cracked by a careless maid, "I know of nothing to compare with the affliction of losing a handsome piece of old china." "Surely," said the friend, "it is not so bad as losing one's children." "Yes, it is," replied the old lady, "for when your children die, you do have the consolations of religion, you know.""

It would be a paradox to call The Master Builder Ibsen's greatest work, but one of his three or four greatest it assuredly is. Of all his writings, it is probably the most original, the most individual, the most unlike any other drama by any other writer. The form of Brand and Peer Gynt was doubtless suggested by other dramatic poems--notably by Faust. In The Wild Duck, in Rosmersholm, in Hedda Gabler, even in Little Eyolf and John Gabriel Borkman, there remain faint traces of the French leaven which was so strong in the earlier plays. But The Master Builder had no model and has no parallel. It shows no slightest vestige of outside influence. It is Ibsen, and nothing but Ibsen.

LITTLE EYOLF

Little Eyolf was written in Christiania during 1894, and published in Copenhagen on December 11 in that year. By this time Ibsen's correspondence has become so scanty as to afford us no clue to what may be called the biographical antecedents of the play. Even of anecdotic history very little attaches to it. For only one of the characters has a definite model been suggested. Ibsen himself told his French translator, Count Prozor, that the original of the Rat-Wife was "a little old woman who came to kill rats at the school where he was educated. She carried a little dog in a bag, and it was said that children had been drowned through following her." This means that Ibsen did not himself adapt to his uses the legend so familiar to us in Browning's Pied Piper of Hamelin, but found it ready adapted by the popular imagination of his native place, Skien. "This idea," Ibsen continued to Count Prozor, "was just what I wanted for bringing about the disappearance of Little Eyolf, in whom the infatuation[1] and the feebleness of his father are reproduced, but concentrated, exaggerated, as one often sees them in the son of such a father." Dr. Elias tells us that a well-known lady-artist, who in middle life suggested to Ibsen the figure of Lona Hessel, was in later years the model for the Rat-Wife. There is no inconsistency between these two accounts of the matter. The idea was doubtless suggested by his recollection of the rat-catcher of Skien, while traits of manner and physiognomy might be borrowed from the lady in question.

The Literary Remains contain a first draft of Little Eyolf, with several gaps in it, and yet fairly complete. It shows once more how after having invented a play, the poet set about re-inventing it, and how the re-invention was apt to determine its poetic value. In this case he had extraordinary difficulty with the characters' names, which he changed about incessantly. His first list of characters ran thus:

Harold Borgheim.
Johanna, his wife.
Rita, his sister.

Alfred, his son, eleven years old.
Eivind Almer, road-engineer.
Miss Varg, Johanna's aunt.

Miss Varg is the character who ultimately became the grimly-fascinating Rat-Wife. After he ceased to be "Borgheim" Allmers became "Skioldheim." Eyolf, after beginning as "Alfred" was for some time "Eivind." Rita was "Andrea" all through the second act. Not till the third act was reached had the names been finally allotted. It seems that the poet's first idea was simply to study a rather commonplace wife's jealousy of a rather commonplace child. The lameness of Eyolf was an afterthought; there is no trace of it in the draft. And as Eyolf is not lame, the terrible cry of "the crutch is floating" must also have been an afterthought, as well as the almost intolerable scene of recrimination between Allmers and Rita as to the accident which caused his lameness. In fact, nearly everything that gives the play its depth, its horror, and its elevation came as an afterthought. There is a slight--a very slight--hint of the "evil eye" motive, but the idea is in no way developed. Instead of the exquisite beauty of Rita's resolve to try to "make her peace with the great open eyes," and to fill the blank within her with "something that is a little like love," we have a page of almost common sentimentalizing over Eyolf's continued existence in their hearts. And instead of Alfred's wonderful tale of his meeting with Death in the mountains, we find a poem which he reads to Rita!--the verses Ibsen had written as a first hint for The Master Builder. In no case, perhaps, did Ibsen's revision work such a transfiguration as in this play.

The verse quoted on pp. 52 and 53 is the last line of a very well-known poem by Johan Sebastian Welhaven, entitled Republikanerne, written in 1839. An unknown guest in a Paris restaurant has been challenged by a noisy party of young Frenchmen to join them in drinking a health to Poland. He refuses; they denounce him as a craven and a slave; he bares his breast and shows the scars of wounds received in fighting for the country whose lost cause has become a subject for conventional enthusiasm and windy rhetoric.

"De saae paa hverandre. Han vandred sin vei.
De havde champagne, men rörte den ei.

"They looked at each other. He sent on his way. There stood their champagne, but they did not touch it." The champagne incident leads me to wonder whether the relation between Rita and Allmers may not have been partly suggested to Ibsen by the relation between Charlotte Stieglitz and her weakling of a husband. Their story must have been known to him through George Brandes's Young Germany, if not more directly. "From time to time," says Dr. Brandes, "there came over her what she calls her champagne-mood; she grieves that this is no longer the case with him."[2] Did the germ of the incident lie in these words?

The first performance of the play in Norway took place at the Christiania Theatre on January 15, 1895, Fru Wettergren playing Rita and Fru Dybwad, Asta. In Copenhagen (March 13, 1895) Fru Oda Nielsen and Fru Hennings played Rita and Asta respectively, while Emil Poulsen played Allmers. The first German Rita (Deutsches Theater, Berlin, January 12, 1895) was Frau Agnes Sorma, with Reicher as Allmers. Six weeks later Frl. Sandrock played Rita at the Burg-theater, Vienna. In May, 1895, the play was acted by M. Lugné-Poë's company in Paris. The first performance in English took place at the Avenue Theatre, London, on the afternoon of November 23, 1896, with Miss Janet Achurch as Rita, Miss Elizabeth Robins as Asta, and Mrs. Patrick Campbell as the Rat-Wife. Miss Achurch's Rita made a profound impression. Mrs. Patrick Campbell afterwards played the part in a short series of evening performances. In the spring of 1895 the play was acted in Chicago by a company of Scandinavian amateurs, presumably in Norwegian, but it was not acted in English in America until Madame Nazimova added it to her repertory in the season of 1907-1908.

As the external history of Little Eyolf is so short, I am tempted to depart from my usual practice, and say a few words as to its matter and meaning.

George Brandes, writing of this play, has rightly observed that "a kind of dualism has always been perceptible in Ibsen; he pleads the cause of Nature, and he castigates Nature with mystic morality; only sometimes Nature is allowed the first voice, sometimes morality. In The Master Builder and in Ghosts the lover of Nature in Ibsen was predominant; here, as in Brand and The Wild Duck, the castigator is in the ascendant." So clearly is this the case in Little Eyolf that Ibsen seems almost to fall into line with Mr. Thomas Hardy. To say nothing of analogies of detail between Little Eyolf and Jude the Obscure, there is this radical analogy, that they are both utterances of a profound pessimism, both indictments of Nature.

But while Mr. Hardy's pessimism is plaintive and passive, Ibsen's is stoical and almost bracing. It is true that in this play he is no longer the mere "indignation-pessimist" whom Dr. Brandes quite justly recognised in his earlier works. His analysis has gone deeper into the heart of things, and he has put off the satirist and the iconoclast. But there is in his thought an incompressible energy of revolt. A pessimist in contemplation, he remains a meliorist in action. He is not, like Mr. Hardy, content to let the flag droop half-mast high; his protagonist still runs it up to the mast-head, and looks forward steadily to the "heavy day of work" before him. But although the note of the conclusion is resolute, almost, serene, the play

remains none the less an indictment of Nature, or at least of
that egoism of passion which is one of her most potent
subtleties. In this view, Allmers becomes a type of what we may
roughly call the "free moral agent"; Eyolf, a type of humanity
conceived as passive and suffering, thrust will-less into
existence, with boundless aspirations and cruelly limited powers;
Rita, a type of the egoistic instinct which is "a consuming
fire"; and Asta, a type of the beneficent love which is possible
only so long as it is exempt from "the law of change." Allmers,
then, is self-conscious egoism, egoism which can now and then
break its chains, look in its own visage, realise and shrink from
itself; while Rita, until she has passed through the awful crisis
which forms the matter of the play, is unconscious, reckless, and
ruthless egoism, exigent and jealous, "holding to its rights,"
and incapable even of rising into the secondary stage of maternal
love. The offspring and the victim of these egoisms is Eyolf,
"little wounded warrior," who longs to scale the heights and dive
into the depths, but must remain for ever chained to the crutch
of human infirmity. For years Allmers has been a restless and
half-reluctant slave to Rita's imperious temperament. He has
dreamed and theorised about "responsibility," and has kept Eyolf
poring over his books, in the hope that, despite his misfortune,
he may one day minister to parental vanity. Finally he breaks
away from Rita, for the first time "in all these ten years," goes
up "into the infinite solitudes," looks Death in the face, and
returns shrinking from passion, yearning towards selfless love,
and filled with a profound and remorseful pity for the lot of
poor maimed humanity. He will "help Eyolf to bring his desires
into harmony with what lies attainable before him." He will
"create a conscious happiness in his mind." And here the drama
opens.

Before the Rat-Wife enters, let me pause for a moment to
point out that here again Ibsen adopts that characteristic method
which, in writing of The Lady from the Sea and The Master
Builder, I have compared to the method of Hawthorne. The story
he tells is not really, or rather not inevitably, supernatural.
Everything is explicable within the limits of nature; but
supernatural agency is also vaguely suggested, and the reader's
imagination is stimulated, without any absolute violence to his
sense of reality. On the plane of everyday life, then, the
Rat-Wife is a crazy and uncanny old woman, fabled by the peasants
to be a werewolf in her leisure moments, who goes about the
country killing vermin. Coming across an impressionable child,
she tells him a preposterous tale, adapted from the old "Pied
Piper" legends, of her method of fascinating her victims. The
child, whose imagination has long dwelt on this personage, is in
fact hypnotised by her, follows her down to the sea, and,
watching her row away, turns dizzy, falls in, and is drowned.
There is nothing impossible, nothing even improbable, in this.

At the same time, there cannot be the least doubt, I think, that
in the poet's mind the Rat-Wife is the symbol of Death, of the
"still, soft darkness" that is at once so fearful and so
fascinating to humanity. This is clear not only in the text of
her single scene, but in the fact that Allmers, in the last act,
treats her and his "fellow-traveller" of that night among the
mountains, not precisely as identical, but as interchangeable,
ideas. To tell the truth, I have even my own suspicions as to
who is meant by "her sweetheart," whom she "lured" long ago, and
who is now "down where all the rats are." This theory I shall
keep to myself; it may be purely fantastic, and is at best
inessential. What is certain is that death carried off little
Eyolf, and that, of all he was, only the crutch is left, mute
witness to his hapless lot.

He is gone; there was so little to bind him to life that he
made not even a moment's struggle against the allurement of the
"long, sweet sleep." Then, for the first time, the depth of the
egoism which had created and conditioned his little life bursts
upon his parents' horror-stricken gaze. Like accomplices in
crime, they turn upon and accuse each other--"sorrow makes them
wicked and hateful." Allmers, as the one whose eyes were already
half opened, is the first to carry the war into the enemy's
country; but Rita is not slow to retort, and presently they both
have to admit that their recriminations are only a vain attempt
to drown the voice of self-reproach. In a sort of fierce frenzy
they tear away veil after veil from their souls, until they
realise that Eyolf never existed at all, so to speak, for his own
sake, but only for the sake of their passions and vanities.
"Isn't it curious," says Rita, summing up the matter, "that we
should grieve like this over a little stranger boy?"

In blind self-absorption they have played with life and
death, and now "the great open eyes" of the stranger boy will be
for ever upon them. Allmers would fain take refuge in a love
untainted by the egoism, and unexposed to the revulsions, of
passion. But not only is Asta's pity for Rita too strong to let
her countenance this desertion: she has discovered that her
relation to Allmers is not "exempt from the law of change," and
she "takes flight from him--and from herself." Meanwhile it
appears that the agony which Allmers and Rita have endured in
probing their wounds has been, as Halvard Solness would say,
"salutary self-torture." The consuming fire of passion is now
quenched, but "it has left an empty place within them," and they
feel a common need "to fill it up with something that is a little
like love." They come to remember that there are other children
in the world on whom reckless instinct has thrust the gift of
life--neglected children, stunted and maimed in mind if not in
body. And now that her egoism is seared to the quick, the
mother-instinct asserts itself in Rita. She will take these
children to her--these children to whom her hand and her heart

have hitherto been closed. They shall be outwardly in Eyolf's place, and perhaps in time they may fill the place in her heart that should have been Eyolf's. Thus she will try to "make her peace with the great open eyes." For now, at last, she has divined the secret of the unwritten book on "human responsibility," and has realised that motherhood means--atonement.

So I read this terrible and beautiful work of art. This, I think, is a meaning inherent in it--not perhaps the meaning, and still less all the meanings. Indeed, its peculiar fascination for me, among all Ibsen's works, lies in the fact that it seems to touch life at so many different points. But I must not be understood as implying that Ibsen constructed the play with any such definitely allegoric design as is here set forth. I do not believe that this creator of men and women ever started from an abstract conception. He did not first compose his philosophic tune and then set his puppets dancing to it. The germ in his mind was dramatic, not ethical; it was only as the drama developed that its meanings dawned upon him; and he left them implicit and fragmentary, like the symbolism of life itself, seldom formulated, never worked out with schematic precision. He simply took a cutting from the tree of life, and, planting it in the rich soil of his imagination, let it ramify and burgeon as it would.

Even if one did not know the date of Little Eyolf, one could confidently assign it to the latest period of Ibsen's career, on noting a certain difference of scale between its foundations and its superstructure. In his earlier plays, down to and including Hedda Gabler, we feel his invention at work to the very last moment, often with more intensity in the last act than in the first; in his later plays he seems to be in haste to pass as early as possible from invention to pure analysis. In this play, after the death of Eyolf (surely one of the most inspired "situations" in all drama) there is practically no external action whatsoever. Nothing happens save in the souls of the characters; there is no further invention, but rather what one may perhaps call inquisition. This does not prevent the second act from being quite the most poignant, or the third act from being one of the most moving, that Ibsen ever wrote. Far from wishing to depreciate the play, I rate it more highly, perhaps, than most critics--among the very greatest of Ibsen's achievements. I merely note as a characteristic of the poet's latest manner this disparity of scale between the work foreshadowed, so to speak, and the work completed. We shall find it still more evident in the case of John Gabriel Borkman.

JOHN GABRIEL BORKMAN

The anecdotic history of John Gabriel Borkman is even scantier than that of Little Eyolf. It is true that two mentions of it occur in Ibsen's letters, but they throw no light whatever upon its spiritual antecedents. Writing to George Brandes from Christiania, on April 24, 1896, Ibsen says: "In your last letter you make the suggestion that I should visit London. If I knew enough English, I might perhaps go. But as I unfortunately do not, I must give up the idea altogether. Besides, I am engaged in preparing for a big new work, and I do not wish to put off the writing of it longer than necessary. It might so easily happen that a roof-tile fell on my head before I had "found time to make the last verse." And what then?" On October 3 of the same year, writing to the same correspondent, he again alludes to his work as "a new long play, which must be completed as soon as possible." It was, as a matter of fact, completed with very little delay, for it appeared in Copenhagen on December 15, 1896.

The irresponsible gossip of the time made out that Björnson discerned in the play some personal allusions to himself; but this Björnson emphatically denied. I am not aware that any attempt has been made to identify the originals of the various characters. It need scarcely be pointed out that in the sisters Gunhild and Ella we have the pair of women, one strong and masterful, the other tender and devoted, who run through so many of Ibsen's plays, from The Feast at Solhoug onwards—nay, even from Catiline. In my Introduction to The Lady from the Sea it is pointed out that Ibsen had the character of Foldal clearly in his mind when, in March, 1880, he made the first draft of that play. The character there appears as: "The old married clerk. Has written a play in his youth which was only once acted. Is for ever touching it up, and lives in the illusion that it will be published and will make a great success. Takes no steps, however, to bring this about. Nevertheless accounts himself one of the "literary" class. His wife and children believe blindly in the play." By the time Foldal actually came to life, the faith of his wife and children had sadly dwindled away.

We find in the Literary Remains only brief and unimportant fragments of the preliminary studies for this play. They tell us nothing more notable than that Borkman at first bore the incurably prosaic name of Jens, and that he was originally conceived as occupying his leisure by playing Beethoven on the violin, to a pianoforte accompaniment provided by Frida Foldal. There was scarcely a theatre in Scandinavia or Finland at which John Gabriel Borkman was not acted in the course of January 1897. Helsingfors led the way with performances both at the Swedish and at the Finnish Theatres on January 10. Christiania and Stockholm followed on January 25, Copenhagen on January 31; and meanwhile the piece had been presented at many provincial theatres as well. In Christiania, Borkman, Gunhild, and Ella were played by Garmann, Fru Gundersen, and Fröken Reimers respectively; in Copenhagen, by Emil Poulsen, Fru Eckhardt, and Fru Hennings. In the course of 1897 it spread all over Germany, beginning with Frankfort on Main, where oddly enough, it was somewhat maltreated by the Censorship. In London, an organisation calling itself the New Century Theatre presented John Gabriel Borkman at the Strand Theatre on the afternoon of May 3, 1897, with Mr. W. H. Vernon as Borkman, Miss Genevieve Ward as Gunhild, Miss Elizabeth Robins as Ella Rentheim, Mr. Martin Harvey as Erhart, Mr. James Welch as Foldal, and Mrs. Beerbohm Tree as Mrs. Wilton. The first performance in America was given by the Criterion Independent Theatre of New York on November 18, 1897, Mr. E. J. Henley playing Borkman, Mr. John Blair Erhart, Miss Maude Banks Gunhild, and Miss Ann Warrington Ella. For some reason, which I can only conjecture to be the weakness of the third act, the play seems nowhere to have taken a very firm hold on the stage.

Dr. Brahm has drawn attention to the great similarity between the theme of John Gabriel Borkman and that of Pillars of Society. "In both," he says, "we have a business man of great ability who is guilty of a crime; in both this man is placed between two sisters; and in both he renounces a marriage of inclination for the sake of a marriage that shall further his business interests." The likeness is undeniable; and yet how utterly unlike are the two plays! and how immeasurably superior the later one! It may seem on a superficial view, that in John Gabriel Borkman Ibsen had returned to prose and the common earth after his excursion into poetry and the possibly supernatural, if I may so call it, in The Master Builder and Little Eyolf. But this is a very superficial view indeed. We have only to compare the whole invention of John Gabriel Borkman with the invention of Pillars of Society, to realise the difference between the poetry and the prose of drama. The quality of imagination which conceived the story of the House of Bernick is utterly unlike that which conceived the tragedy of the House of Borkman. The difference is not greater between (say) The Merchant of Venice and King Lear.

The technical feat which Ibsen here achieves of carrying through without a single break the whole action of a four-act play has been much commented on and admired. The imaginary time of the drama is actually shorter than the real time of representation, since the poet does not even leave intervals for the changing of the scenes. This feat, however, is more curious than important. Nothing particular is gained by such a literal observance of the unity of time. For the rest, we feel definitely in John Gabriel Borkman what we already felt vaguely in Little Eyolf--that the poet's technical staying-power is beginning to fail him. We feel that the initial design was larger and more detailed than the finished work. If the last acts of The Wild Duck and Hedda Gabler be compared with the last acts of Little Eyolf and Borkman, it will be seen that in the earlier plays his constructive faculty is working at its highest tension up to the very end, while in the later plays it relaxes towards the close, to make room for pure imagination and lyric beauty. The actual drama is over long before the curtain falls on either play, and in the one case we have Rita and Allmers, in the other Ella and Borkman, looking back over their shattered lives and playing chorus to their own tragedy. For my part, I set the highest value on these choral odes, these mournful antiphones, in which the poet definitely triumphs over the mere playwright. They seem to be noble and beautiful in themselves, and as truly artistic, if not as theatrical, as any abrupter catastrophe could be. But I am not quite sure that they are exactly the conclusions the poet originally projected, and still less am I satisfied that they are reached by precisely the paths which he at first designed to pursue.

The traces of a change of scheme in John Gabriel Borkman seem to me almost unmistakable. The first two acts laid the foundation for a larger and more complex superstructure than is ultimately erected. Ibsen seems to have designed that Hinkel, the man who "betrayed" Borkman in the past, should play some efficient part in the alienation of Erhart from his family and home. Otherwise, why this insistence on a "party" at the Hinkels', which is apparently to serve as a sort of "send-off" for Erhart and Mrs. Wilton? It appears in the third act that the "party" was imaginary. "Erhart and I were the whole party," says Mrs. Wilton, "and little Frida, of course." We might, then, suppose it to have been a mere blind to enable Erhart to escape from home; but, in the first place, as Erhart does not live at home, there is no need for any such pretext, in the second place, it appears that the trio do actually go to the Hinkels' house (since Mrs. Borkman's servant finds them there), and do actually make it their starting-point. Erhart comes and goes with the utmost freedom in Mrs. Wilton's own house; what possible reason can they have for not setting out from there? No reason is shown or hinted. We cannot even imagine that the Hinkels have been instrumental in bringing Erhart and Mrs. Wilton together; it is expressly stated that Erhart made her acquaintance and saw a great deal of her in town, before she moved out into the country. The whole conception of the party at the Hinkels' is, as it stands, mysterious and a little cumbersome. We are forced to conclude, I think, that something more was at one time intended to come of it, and that, when the poet abandoned the idea, he did not think it worth while to remove the scaffolding. To this change of plan, too, we may possibly trace what I take to be the one serious flaw in the play--the comparative weakness of the second half of the third act. The scene of Erhart's rebellion against the claims of mother, aunt, and father strikes one as the symmetrical working out of a problem rather than a passage of living drama.

All this means, of course, that there is a certain looseness of fibre in <u>John Gabriel Borkman</u> which we do not find in the best of Ibsen's earlier works. But in point of intellectual power and poetic beauty it yields to none of its predecessors. The conception of the three leading figures is one of the great things of literature; the second act, with the exquisite humour of the Foldal scene, and the dramatic intensity of the encounter between Borkman and Ella, is perhaps the finest single act Ibsen ever wrote, in prose at all events; and the last scene is a thing of rare and exalted beauty. One could wish that the poet's last words to us had been those haunting lives with which Gunhild and Ella join hands over Borkman's body:

> We twin sisters--over him we both have loved.
> We two shadows--over the dead man.[1]

Among many verbal difficulties which this play presents, the greatest, perhaps, has been to find an equivalent for the work "opreisning," which occurs again and again in the first and second acts. No one English word that I could discover would fit in all the different contexts; so I have had to employ three: "redemption," "restoration," and in one place "rehabilitation." The reader may bear in mind that these three terms represent one idea in the original.

Borkman in Act II. uses a very odd expression--"overshurkens moral," which I have rendered "the morals of the higher rascality." I cannot but suspect (though for this I have no authority) that in the word "overshurk," which might be represented in German by "Ueberschurke," Borkman is parodying the expression "Uebermensch," of which so much has been heard of late. When I once suggested this to Ibsen, he neither affirmed nor denied it. I understood him to say, however, that in speaking of "overskurken" he had a particular man in view. Somewhat pusillanimously, perhaps, I pursued my inquiries no further.

WHEN WE DEAD AWAKEN

From *Pillars of Society* to *John Gabriel Borkman*, Ibsen's plays had followed each other at regular intervals of two years, save when his indignation over the abuse heaped upon *Ghosts* reduced to a single year the interval between that play and *An Enemy of the People*. *John Gabriel Borkman* having appeared in 1896, its successor was expected in 1898; but Christmas came and brought no rumour of a new play. In a man now over seventy, this breach of a long-established habit seemed ominous. The new National Theatre in Christiania was opened in September of the following year; and when I then met Ibsen (for the last time) he told me that he was actually at work on a new play, which he thought of calling a "Dramatic Epilogue." He wrote *When We Dead Awaken*," says Dr. Elias, "with such labour and such passionate agitation, so spasmodically and so ferverishly, that those around him were almost alarmed. He must get on with it, he must get on! He seemed to hear the beating of dark pinions over his head. He seemed to feel the grim Visitant, who had accompanied Alfred Allmers on the mountain paths, already standing behind him with uplifted hand. His relatives are firmly convinced that he knew quite clearly that this would be his last play, that he was to write no more. And soon the blow fell."

The *Literary Remains* contain some preliminary jottings for *When We Dead Awaken*, and a rejected draft of the final scene. From the jottings it appears that the play was to have been called *The Resurrection Day*, and that Ibsen originally thought of introducing at least two characters whom he ultimately suppressed—the Physician at the Baths, "a youngish, intelligent man," and "the Tattling Lady from the capital" who "is considered immensely amusing by the patients," and is "malicious out of thoughtlessness." At the end of a rough scenario of the first act there occurs the following curious reflection: "In this country it is only the mountains which have any resonance [literally "give an echo"] not the people." In the draft of the last scene, Rubek, Irene, Ulfheim and Maia are all assembled outside Ulfheim's hut. The fragment begins thus:

MAIA (interrupting). Is it not strange that we four should meet here in the middle of the wild mountains?
RUBEK. You with an eagle-shooter, and I with--(to Irene)--with what shall I say?
IRENE. With a shot eagle.
MAIA. Shot?
IRENE. Winged, madam.

Ulfheim unlocks the hut, and produces from it champagne and glasses, which he fills.

ULFHEIM (to Maia). What shall we drink to, honoured lady?
MAIA. Let us drink to freedom!
    (She empties her glass at one draught.)
RUBEK. Yes, let us drink to freedom. (He drinks.)
IRENE. And to the courage which dares to use it.
    (She takes a sip from her glass and pours the rest on
    the ground.)

After Ulfheim and Maia have departed, Rubek and Irene have a last conversation which ends thus:--

IRENE. The craving for life is dead in me. Now I have arisen, and I see that life lies on a corpse. The whole of life lies on its bier--(The clouds droop slowly down in the form of a clammy mist). See how the shroud is drooping over us, too! But I will not die over again, Arnold!--Save me! Save me, if you can and if you will!
RUBEK. Above the mists I see the mountain peak. It stands there glittering in the sunrise. We must climb to it--through the night mists, up into the light of morning.
            (The mists droop closer and closer over the scene.
             RUBEK and IRENE descend into the mist-veil and are
             gradually lost to sight.)
            (The SISTER OF MERCY'S head, spying, comes in sight in
             a rift in the mist.)
            (High up above the sea of the mist, the peak shines in
             the morning sun.)

And that is the end.

When We Dead Awaken was published very shortly before Christmas 1899. Ibsen had still a year of comparative health before him. We find him, in March 1900, writing to Count Prozor: "I cannot say yet whether or not I shall write another drama; but if I continue to retain the vigour of body and mind which I at present enjoy, I do not imagine that I shall be able to keep permanently away from the old battlefields. However, if I were to make my appearance again, it would be with new weapons and in new armour." Was he hinting at the desire, which he had long ago confessed to Professor Herford, that his last work should be a drama in verse? Whatever his dream, it was not to be realised. His last letter (defending his attitude of philosophic impartiality with regard to the South African war) is dated December 9, 1900. With the dawn of the new century, the curtain descended upon the mind of the great dramatic poet of the age which had passed away.

When We Dead Awaken was acted during 1900 at most of the leading theatres in Scandinavia and Germany. In some German cities (notably in Frankfort on Main) it even attained a considerable number of representations. I cannot learn, however, that it has anywhere held the stage. It was produced in London, by the Stage Society, at the Imperial Theatre, on January 25 and 26, 1903. Mr. G. S. Titheradge played Rubek, Miss Henrietta Watson Irene, Miss Mabel Hackney Maia, and Mr. Laurence Irving Ulfheim. In New York it was acted at the Knickerbocker Theatre, the part of Irene being taken by Miss Florence Kahn, and that of Rubek by Mr. Frederick Lewis.

In the above-mentioned letter to Count Prozor, Ibsen confirmed that critic's conjecture that "the series which ends with the Epilogue really began with The Master Builder." As the last confession, so to speak, of a great artist, the Epilogue will always be read with interest. It contains, moreover, many flashes of the old genius, many strokes of the old incommunicable magic. One may say with perfect sincerity that there is more fascination in the dregs of Ibsen's mind than in the "first sprightly running" of more commonplace talents. But to his sane admirers the interest of the play must always be melancholy, because it is purely pathological. To deny this is, in my opinion, to cast a slur over all the poet's previous work, and in great measure to justify the criticisms of his most violent detractors. For When We Dead Awaken is very like the sort of play that haunted the "anti-Ibsenite" imagination in the year 1893 or thereabouts. It is a piece of self-caricature, a series of echoes from all the earlier plays, an exaggeration of manner to the pitch of mannerism. Moreover, in his treatment of his symbolic motives, Ibsen did exactly what he had hitherto, with perfect justice, plumed himself upon never doing: he sacrificed the surface reality to the underlying meaning. Take, for instance, the history of Rubek's statue and its development into a group. In actual sculpture this development is a grostesque impossibility. In conceiving it we are deserting the domain of reality, and plunging into some fourth dimension where the properties of matter are other than those we know. This is an abandonment of the fundamental principle which Ibsen over and over again emphatically expressed--namely, that any symbolism his work might be found to contain was entirely incidental, and subordinate to the truth and consistency of his picture of life.

Even when he dallied with the supernatural, as in <u>The Master Builder</u> and <u>Little Eyolf</u>, he was always careful, as I have tried to show, not to overstep decisively the boundaries of the natural. Here, on the other hand, without any suggestion of the supernatural, we are confronted with the wholly impossible, the inconceivable. How remote is this alike from his principles of art and from the consistent, unvarying practice of his better years! So great is the chasm between <u>John Gabriel Borkman</u> and <u>When We Dead Awaken</u> that one could almost suppose his mental breakdown to have preceded instead of followed the writing of the latter play. Certainly it is one of the premonitions of the coming end. It is Ibsen's <u>Count Robert of Paris</u>. To pretend to rank it with his masterpieces is to show a very imperfect sense of the nature of their mastery.

NOTES

FOOTNOTES

PART ONE

IBSEN AND ENGLISH CRITICISM

1.   Robert Elsmere is a novel of 1888, widely read at the time, written by Mrs. Humphrey [Mary Augusta] Ward (1851-1920).

2.   Source unidentified; curiosity remains.

3.   Rachel [born Élisa Felix] (1820-58) was a great tragic actress of the French stage, best known for her Phèdre.   She performed in London in the 1840's.

4.   Aimée Desclée (1836-74), also a French actress, was famous for her emotional power in serious roles.

5.   This phrase is used by Dr. Stockmann in Ibsen's An Enemy of the People.

6.   S. T. Coleridge said this of the Shakespearean actor Edmund Kean (1787/90-1833), who played the evil roles with passionate intensity.

7.   Boanerges--or "sons of thunder"--is the titled Christ bestowed on the brothers James and John, sons of Zebedee (Mark 3:17), probably because of their violent tempers.

8.   Archer saw A Doll's House in Christiania (Oslo) in 1883.

9.   [Archer's footnote]   It so happens that two or three formal generalizations of Ibsen's have recently been going the round of the press; but they are taken from letters or speeches, not from his plays.

10. Mr. Podsnap is a smug, narrowminded, and chauvinistic bourgeois in Charles Dickens' Our Mutual Friend.

11. "to make an ape blush."

12. During the early period of the Ibsen controversy (1880-1895) Archer continually expressed doubts about the acceptance of serious drama in the English theatres, while of course fighting for such acceptance relentlessly.

GHOSTS AND GIBBERINGS

1. August Friedrich Ferdinand von Kotzebue (1761-1819) was a German dramatist who wrote quite popular and sentimental melodramas.

2. Lord Campbell's Act of 1857 was for the suppression of obscene publications.

3. The office of Lord Chamberlain acted as censor for the stage. Ghosts was banned until 1914. The censor, E. F. S. Pigott, stated in 1892 in his report to the Select Committee on Censorship that he did not censor any other Ibsen plays submitted to him because "all Ibsen's characters were morally deranged," so the plays were "too absurd altogether to be injurious to public morals."

4. The Schimpf-Lexicon of Wagner, a collection of attacks on his music, was compiled by Wilhelm Tappert and published in Leipzig in 1877. Its full title" A Dictionary of Impoliteness, Containing Rude, Sneering, Malicious, Slanderous Expressions Which Were Used by Enemies and Mockers against Meister Richard Wagner, His Works, and His Followers.

5. Billingsgate was a London market area along the river, famous for smelly fish and abusive language.

6. Hamlet (I, i, 116).

7. Truth, by the American playwright Bronson Howard (1842-1908), ran for 27 performances in 1890 at the Criterion Theatre.

8. Clement Scott (1841-1904), who wrote for the Daily Telegraph, was London's most popular and widely-read theatre critic. Both conservative and sentimental, he was truly revolted by Ibsen's drama.

THE QUINTESSENCE OF IBSENISM:
AN OPEN LETTER TO GEORGE BERNARD SHAW

1.   A. B. Walkley (1855-1926) was a theatre critic, usually in the pro-Ibsen camp.

2.   "Walden Pond" was the name Archer borrowed for his country home.

3.   Archer was the first of several people to accuse Shaw of depending too much on German philosophy, including the works of Arthur Schopenhauer (1788-1860), whose major book, The World as Will and Idea (1818), was published in England in 1883.

4.   Shaw's novel about boxing, Cashel Byron's Profession, was published in 1886.

5.   Shaw had not yet read Brand because it was not translated until after he wrote Quintessence. He had depended upon Archer's private readings to him.

6.   The Rev. Philip H. Wicksteed, a classical scholar and translator of Dante, was one of the early supports of Ibsen in England. He lectured on Ibsen in 1888 at the Chelsea Town Hall (after being denied space at the University of London). Two of these lectures were subsequently published in The Contemporary Review (1889 & 1891). Then in 1892 he published a book, Four Lectures on Henrik Ibsen (Sonnenschein). Like Archer, he argued for Ibsen the poet over Ibsen the social philosopher.

7.   Jeremy Bentham (1748-1832), the English philosopher, was the founder of Utilitarianism, which argued for a social ethic based upon the idea of the greatest happiness for the greatest number of people.

8.   Augustine Birrell (1850-1933) wrote prolifically on literary topics, and especially on literary figures of the nineteenth century, including Thomas Babington Macaulay (1800-1859), the historian and essayist.

9.   "I do not see the necessity." Shaw quotes Voltaire to this effect, from the "Discours preliminaire" to his play, Alzire. But originally it was Comte d'Argental, censor of the press to Louis XV, who made this statement when a political writer excused his own political squibs by saying, "I must live."

10.   John Dryden (1631-1700), Don Sabastian (II, i).

11.   Archer is, of course, teasing Shaw by way of The Wild Duck.

THE MAUSOLEUM OF IBSEN

1.   The actress Florence Farr [Mrs. Edward Emery] (1860-1917) played Rebecca West in Rosmersholm, which Archer co-directed.

2.   [Archer's footnote]   Reprinted in part in Mr. G. Bernard Shaw's Quintessence of Ibsenism.

3.   Together Elizabeth Robins (1862-1952) and Marion Lea [later Mrs. Langdon E. Mitchell] (1864-1944), both American actresses, produced and acted in Hedda Gabler.   Archer co-directed.

4.   The production of Hedda Gabler opened April 20 and ran for five weeks.

5.   The [slaying] hammer for heretics.

6.   Jacob Thomas Grein (1862-1927), a "Dutchman," founded the Independent Theatre Society, which produced Ghosts in 1891.

7.   The parody by James M. Barrie (1860-1937), who later became famous for such plays as Peter Pan and The Admirable Crichton, was first performed May 30, 1891.   It was supposedly the "fifth act" of Hedda Gabler, and included Ibsen as a character who commits suicide because he is depressed by the misery of his characters.

8.   Herbert Waring (1857-1932), a popular and versatile actor with a long career, was Torvald in the 1889 production of A Doll's House and Solness in 1893 production of The Master Builder.   Much later he was Major Crespin in Archer's successful melodrama, The Green Goddess (1921).

9.   [Archer's footnote]   He is just as much of a socialist as Mr. Herbert Spencer is--that is to say, the very reverse of a socialist.   But these nice distinctions are beyond the critical intellect.

10.   [Archer's footnote]   This of course includes sales in America and the colonies; but as a matter of fact the great bulk of these editions has been sold in the United Kingdom.

11.   [Archer's footnote]   Mr. Scott, as aforesaid, has sold

over 31,000 volumes, and we may quite safely assume a sale of 9,000 for the six single plays issued by other publishers.

12.   [Archer's footnote]   The deplorable perversions of _Faust_, and the crude melodramas made out of one or two of Hugo's plays, must certainly be reckoned as adaptations, not translations.

13.   [Archer's footnote]   "That Mr. Ibsen's fantastic balderdash has been supported during the present week by playgoers who have paid to see it, I decline to believe."   So says the indefatigable "Rapier" of the _Sporting and Dramatic News_ (March 4).   It was "supported," and liberally supported, by the paying public.   Does "Rapier" think it a quite legitimate trick of the fence to make injurious inuendoes on matters of which he knows nothing?   Another paragraphist, pursuing the same maganimous tactics, states that to his certain knowledge the receipts have at their highest never risen to a sum to which, as a matter of fact, they have at their lowest never fallen.   Such are the methods of anti-Ibsenism.

14.   This production, produced by Dr. Edward Aveling and Eleanor Marx-Aveling, (and translated by Marx-Aveling), ran for five performances, May 11-15, 1891.   Miss Rose Meller played Ellida Wangel and Oscar Adye played Dr. Wangel.

15.   [Archer's footnote]   Performances at the Crystal Palace are included in this calculation.

16.   [Archer's footnote]   The first, and very successful, production of _A Doll's House_ took place at the Novelty Theatre, a house utterly unknown to the majority of playgoers, and hidden away in a by-street on the very confines of theatrical civilization.   The Vaudeville, where _Hedda Gabler_ was produced, has been, and is, a popular theatre, but scarcely with the class of playgoers to whom Ibsen most directly appeals.   The Trafalgar Square Theatre, where _The Master Builder_ was produced, is one of the pleasantest and best-appointed houses in London, but has the disadvantage of being quite new.   It takes the public a long time to discover the existence of a new theatre.

17.   During a two-week period, May 29 - June 10, 1893, Elizabeth Robins successfully, even triumphantly, played four leading roles in Ibsen: Hedda Gabler, Rebecca West in _Rosmersholm_, Hilde Wangel in _The Master Builder_, and Agnes in _Brand_, Act IV.   Archer was involved in these productions as translator and co-director.

THE REAL IBSEN

1.   Archer translated Brandes' study of Ibsen and Björnstjerne Björnson in 1899 (Heinemann).

2.   This phrase, "cup and saucer drama," was used to describe the drama of T. W. Robertson (1829-71), whose plays called for realistic set design and props, down to the cups and saucers.   The "epigrammatic" quality of his dialogue is not notable.

3.   Alexandre Dumas fils (1824-95) was one of the French masters of the "well-made play," although he modified the Scribean model so that it could be a "thesis play" that expressed his social views.   In his Preface to Un Pere prodigue (1868), for example, he discussed his dramatic technique.   Francisque Sarcey (1832-1901), the influential French theatre critic, was famous for his maxims on how to write drama.

4.   Giacomo Leopardi (1798-1837), an Italian poet, published his views on life in Operette morali (1824).   His bitter pessimism is also expressed in his Idylls.

5.   The Gay Lord Quex (1899) by Arthur Wing Pinero (1855-1934) is a sexual comedy of seduction, pitting an immoral aristocrat against a "vulgar" woman from the lower classes. Various ideas of honor are toyed with by Pinero.

6.   A fictitious person, Mrs. Grundy (here augmented by a husband) was a popular name for anyone who held narrowminded ideas on social convention and behavior.   The source of her identity is a play by Tom Morton, Speed the Plough (1798), in which the characters worry about the opinion of a busybody neighbor: "What will Mrs. Grundy say?"

7.   Mrs. Hardcastle is a character in Oliver Goldsmith's She Stoops to Conquer; Mrs. Micawber is in Charles Dickens' David Copperfield.

8.   Sir Willoughby Patterne is the main character in George Meredith's autobiographical novel, The Egoist (1879);   Numa Roumestan is the title character in a novel of 1879 by Alphonse Daudet (1840-97).

9.   W. L. Courtney, theater critic and professor, published The Idea of Tragedy in Ancient and Modern Drama in 1900.   Archer reviewed it that year on June 15 in the Daily Chronicle.

10.   [Archer's footnote]   Writing for American readers, I
ought to explain that South Hampstead is a middle-class suburb of
London, while Carlton House Terrace, overlooking St. James' Park,
is largely inhabited by Ambassadors and Cabinet Ministers.   So to
illustrate Ibsen's "parochialism," Mr. Courtney employs an image
which can mean nothing to people who do not happen to be familiar
with the topography of London.   The paragraph certainly does
illustrate parochialism--but is it Ibsen's?

11.   F.   Anstey [Thomas Anstey Guthrie] published his
parody, Mr. Punch's Pocket Ibsen, in Punch first, then in book
form in 1893.   It includes satires of A Doll's House, Hedda
Gabler, Rosmersholm, The Wild Duck, and The Master Builder.

12.   The Belle of New York, a musical comedy by Hugh Morton
(libretto) and Gustave Kerker (music), ran for 693 performances
in London, from April 12, 1898 to Dec. 30, 1899.   The Second Mrs.
Tanqueray, by A. W. Pinero, ran for 223 performances, from May
27, 1893 to July 28, 1893 and then again from Nov. 11, 1893 to
April 21, 1894.

13.   John Dryden, Absalom and Achitophel, 1. 545.   Actually,
Archer has it slightly wrong.   It reads: A man so various, that
he seemed to be/ Not one, but all mankind's epitome:/ Stiff in
opinions, always in the wrong;/ Was everything by starts, and
nothing long."

IBSEN'S APPRENTICESHIP

1.   Eugène Scribe (1791-1861), a prolific French playwright
who produce, alone and in collaboration, over 400 plays, was the
originator of what came to be called the pièce bien faite (or
well-made play).   Elaborately plotted by formula, these
clock-work plays are long on intrigue and short on idea and
characterization.   Possibly the best known in English are The
Glass of Water and Adrienne Lecourvreur.   Several famous operas,
such as Verdi's Un Ballo in Maschera and Donizetti's Elisir
d'Amore, are based on Scribe's librettos.   Dramatists in Scribe's
"school" included Émile Augier (1820-89), Victorien Sardou
(1831-1908), and Alexandre Dumas fils (1824-95).

2.   Now Oslo.

3.   Ludwig Holberg (1684-1754), a Norwegian by birth, lived
most of his life in Copenhagen, where he was a professor of
philosophy at the University.   He became director of the Danish
theater in 1721, and proceeded to write what did not exist until

then: a Danish drama of vernacular comedy. He wrote 33 plays, many still popular today in Scandinavia and Germany. The best known in English is Jeppe of the Mountains (Jeppe paa Bjerget). He was Ibsen's favorite writer.

4. Björnstjerne Björnson (1832-1910) and Ibsen were the two major dramatists of Norway. In 1903 Björnson received the Novel Prize. His early plays were historical, his middle plays were realistic social dramas, and his late ones were spiritual. Probably Beyond Human Power (Over AEvne I) is the best known in English.

5. T. Blanc, Nörges forste nationale scene (Christiania, 1884).

6. Lorentz Dietrichson (1834-1917), whom Ibsen first met in Rome in 1864, was librarian of the Scandinavian Association of Rome, and later professor in Christiania.

7. Le Gendre de M. Poirier (1854) was written by Émile Augier (1820-89) and Jules Sandeau (1811-83).

HENRIK IBSEN: PHILOSOPHER OR POET?

1. [Archer's footnote] Svanhild in Love's Comedy is the nearest approach we can find in this period to a rebellious, intellectually independent woman who stops short of crime; but she is so far from taking the modern view of woman as a self-sufficing entity that she actually accepts as her destiny a marriage of convenience.

2. A letter to Sophus Schandorph, 6 Jan. 1882.

3. Jean Martin Charcot (1825-93), a French neurologist, did research in the nature of hysteria, among other things, at his famous clinic in Paris, La Salpetriere. Freud studied under him.

4. The occasion was a speech by Ibsen to the Norwegian League for Women's Rights, Christiania, May 26, 1898. It is printed in Evert Sprinchorn's edition of the letters and speeches.

5. Gregers Werle, of course, in The Wild Duck.

IBSEN IN HIS LETTERS

1. Björnstjerne Björnson (1832-1910), Norwegian dramatist, was generally more popular, if not more respected,
than Ibsen during the second half of the nineteenth century.
Unlike Ibsen, he stayed home and took part in the social, moral,
and artistic life of Norway. There are certain similarities,
however, between their writing: both wrote history plays in the
beginning of their careers, realistic social drama in the middle,
and more spiritual plays at the end. For this reason alone there
was both rivalry and respect between the two men.

2. Georg Brandes (1842-1927), one of the major literary
critics of the nineteenth century, best known today for his
six-volume study, Main Currents in Nineteenth Century Literature,
became a good friend of Ibsen's. Brandes' arguments for realism
had definite influence on Ibsen's decision to write realistic
social drama rather than poetic drama.

3. Romeo and Juliet (V, i).

4. Adam Gottlob Oehlenschlaeger (1779-1850) was a Danish
poet and dramatist who wrote plays based upon the national
sagas.

5. Edmund Gosse (1849-1928) was an English critic who
wrote the first essays in England on Ibsen. He translated a few
of the plays, including two with Archer, and in 1907 he published
a biography of Ibsen.

6. Count Moritz Prozor (b. 1849), a Lithuanian who worked
for the Russian diplomacy, translated several of Ibsen's plays
into French.

7. As Michael Meyer notes in his biography, Ibsen's
judgment on the English artwork displayed at the Exhibition was
less than reliable. Archer, who also saw the English works,
called them "glaringly inferior."

8. This is, of course, Wordsworth's famous dictum from the
Preface to the Lyrical Ballads.

9. Sir Willoughby Patterne is the main character in
Meredith's novel, The Egoist (1879). Meredith's confession was
to Robert Louis Stevenson.

10. Actually, as Bernard Dukore pointed out to me, Shaw used
this word, "impossibilist," seven years earlier in Act III of
Captain Brassbound's Conversion, as the holograph facsimile
reveals.

11. George Wyndham (1863-1913) was a Tory politician and a literary critic.

12. Lorentz Dietrichson (1834-1917) was the librarian of the Scandinavian Association in Rome, 1862-1865. Ibsen replaced him in this position, thus attaining a free house and modest income. Dietrichson became a professor at the University of Christiania. He and Ibsen were good friends, until a quarrel in 1885.

13. Marcus Grönvold, a Norwegian painter, wrote about Ibsen in his Fra Ulrikken til Alperne (Oslo, 1925).

14. Clemens Petersen (b. 1834), the leading Danish critic at the time, had some good things to say about Brand, but he dismissed Peer Gynt as polemical journalism, not worthy to be called poetry. Ibsen went into a rage, as Archer records above.

15. Although Archer passes over this quotation without comment, surely he means us to see that this description fits Ibsen more than Björnson.

IBSEN AS I KNEW HIM

1. This letter and the others in this essay were written by Archer to his brother. Many of them can be found in Charles Archer's biography of Archer.

2. Edmund Gosse (1849-1928), the English literary critic, had written a review essay ("Peer Gynt," Spectator, 20 July 1872), in which he translated some of the lines and praised Ibsen as a poet.

3. [Archer's footnote] Many years later he told Professor Herford that he would like to write his last play in verse, "if only one could tell which play was to be last."

4. [Archer's footnote] Carl Ploug, the Danish poet and journalist, had fallen into this ridiculous misunderstanding of an incident in Ghosts.

5. Other reports, however, do not support Archer's skepticism.

6. [Archer's footnote] A Danish theologian who is commonly said to have been the original of Ibsen's Brand. See the Revue de Paris, July 1901.

7.   The Morgenbladet was a Christiania newspaper.

8.   Friedrich Spielhagen (1829-1911) wrote social-political novels that attacked aristocrats and bourgeois materialists.

9.   Paul Heyse (1830-1914) wrote plays, novels, and stories that were self-consciously stylistic.   He disapproved of naturalism and subscribed to his own particular idea of aestheticism.   In 1910 he won the Nobel Prize.

10.   The S. P. Q. R. or Senatus Populusque Romanus was the public authority of Rome.

11.   [Archer's footnote]   There must have been some mistake about this.   When I was last in Rome (1904) the house was very slightly altered.   It had become a hotel--the Hotel Suez, if I remember rightly.

12.   The Aftenposten was a Christiania newspaper.

13.   Other parts of this letter can be found in Charles Archer, William Archer: Life, Work, and Friendships (London: George Allen & Unwin, 1931).

14.   Charles Charrington (-1926) and Janet Achurch (1864-1916) played Dr. Rank and Nora in the production, which Archer co-directed with Charrington.

15.   Ibsen's son.

16.   See J. L. Wisenthal, Shaw and Ibsen (Toronto, 1979), for a detailed clarification of this whole episode, which grew out of a reporter's misrepresentation of Shaw's Fabian lecture on Ibsen.

17.   H. L. Braekstad, a Norwegian who lived in London and worked in publishing, was a close acquaintance of both Archer and Ibsen.

18.   Paul Schlenther was active with Otto Brahm and others in the revival of theatre in Germany during the 1880's and 1890's.

IBSEN'S CRAFTSMANSHIP

1.   Ibsen's Apprenticeship," Jan. 1904.

2.   [Archer's footnote]   I do not here inquire into the question of Scribe's originality, or his relation to his immediate predecessors, from Beaumarchais onwards.   Probably he was not a great innovator, even in technique, but is rather to be regarded as the representative figure in a general movement which would have taken no very different course even if he had never existed.   The human mind will never rest content until it has exhausted the possibilities of any given instrument; and the Scribe style of play was one of the possibilities, and at first sight one of the most fascinating, of the highly complex instrument that we call the modern theatre.   It was an inevitable phase of development, the philosophy of which has yet to be thoroughly studied.

3.   Francisque Sarcey (1827-99) was a very influential theater critic in late nineteenth-century France.   His most famous maxim stated that a play calls for certain scenes that must be treated-- scènes à faire.   They must dramatize--not merely narrate--an action that the play has been leading up to. Horace, in his Ars Poetica, had similar things to say about what must be properly treated in art.   Archer's phrase for this was "obligatory scene."

4.   Which, in fact, Archer did the following year in "Ibsen's Imperialism," the following essay in this collection.

5.   Les Pates de Mouche by Victorien Sardou (1831-1908) is a textbook example of the well-made play.

IBSEN'S IMPERIALISM

1.   Frederik Hegel, the Copenhagen publisher, brought out all of Ibsen's plays from Brand in 1865 to When We Dead Awaken in 1899.

2.   Edmund Gosse published three essays on Ibsen in 1872: "Ibsen's New Poems," "Peer Gynt," and "The Pretenders."   These essays formed part of his analysis of Ibsen in his book Studies in the Literature of Northern Europe (1879).

3.   This reference to Nietzsche need not be taken as a sign of Archer's readings in or respect for German philosophy.   No doubt he had a passing knowledge of the popular ideas of Nietzsche and Schopenhauer, in some part, but he was not sympathetic to those ideas.   Thus, we should note that although he talks here about "World-Will" and the dialectical organization of Ibsen's play, the only Hegel he mentions is the publisher.

4. "I will not venture to say with as much assurance as M. Naville that anthropomorphism is entirely foreign to him." Gaston Boissier, La fin du paganisme (Paris, 1891); Adrien Naville, Julien l'apostat et sa philosophie du polythéisme (Paris, 1877).

5. George Meredith, The Egoist (1879).

6. Houndsditch was a lower-class area of London.

7. [Archer's footnote] Between fifteen and twenty are enumerated by Allard (Julien l'Apostat), a writer who gravely reproduces all the stereotyped figments of the hagiographers.

8. The Sign of the Cross, a "Christian drama," by Wilson Barrett, had a successful run of 438 performances in London (Lyric Theatre), from 4 Jan. 1896 to 30 Jan. 1897. Archer's review, which attacked the play, is in Theatrical World of 1896 (London: W. Scott, 1897), pp. 9-11. This melodramatic play about Nero and the Christians was also a great success financially in America, and it made a fortune for Barrett, who was an actor-manager in London.

9. Those whom God wishes to destroy He first deprives of their senses.

10. Delusions of grandeur.

THE TRUE GREATNESS OF IBSEN

1. James Thomson (1834–82), English poet and essayist, published The City of Dreadful Night in installments in 1874 in the National Reformer, then in book form in 1880. He sometimes signed his work B. V. or Bysshe Vanolis, a pseudonym for his two favorite poets, Shelley and Novalis.

2. The summer of 1872.

3. Archer quoted this passage, and others in this essay, in Norwegian because Edda, where he published the lecture, is a Norwegian journal. For convenience I have put these passages back into English, using the translations from his edition of the plays.

4. Houndsditch was a miserable area of London.

5.   This is from C. H. Herford's translation, 1894, which Archer placed in his edition of the plays.   Much is missing here, so Archer's point may seem less than convincing.

6.   John Newton (1725-1807) was an English clergyman and hymn writer.

7.   Mr. Gröndahl, the Norwegian Minster, to England, was present at Archer's lecture and supported the study of Scandinavian languages and literature at University College, London.

PART TWO

All footnotes for these essays on the individual plays are by Archer, unless otherwise noted.

THE PRETENDERS

1.   The original title Kongsemnerne might be more literally translated "The Scions of Royalty." It is rendered by Brandes in German "Königsmaterie," or "the stuff from which kings are made."

2.   This remark does not apply, of course, to the satiric "parabasis" uttered by the Bishop's ghost in the fifth act. That is a totally different matter.

3.   In America it was acted in April, 1907, by the Yale University Dramatic Association, but has not as yet (1911) found its way to the professional stage.

4.   The followers of Haakon's grandfather, King Sverre.

5.   On page 323 will be found a reference to Brandes's Ibsen and Björnson; but I may as well give here the substance of the passage. In the original form of the play, three speeches of Ingeborg's in her scene with Skule, ran as follows: "It is man's right to forget," "It is woman's happiness to remember," and "To have to sacrifice all and be forgotten, that is woman's saga." It was only on Brandes's remonstrance that Ibsen substituted the present form of these speeches, in which they became, not the generalised expression of an ideal, but merely utterances of Ingeborg's individual character.

PEER GYNT

1.   One of Holberg's most famous comedies.

2.   See The Lady from the Sea.

3.　　Brandes:　Ibsen and Björnson, p. 35.　London, Heinemann, 1899. Except in regard to the Fourth Act, Dr. Brandes has, in the introduction to Peer Gynt in the German collected edition, recanted his early condemnation of the poem.

4.　The last words are "deus caritatis."

5.　Norske Huldre-Eventyr og Folkesagn, Christiania, 1848, p. 47. See also Copenhagen edition, 1896, p. 163.

6.　Norske Folke-og Huldre-Eventyr, Copenhagen, 1896, p. 48.

7.　Ibid., p. 129.

8.　Ibid., p. 259.

9.　Not included in the Copenhagen edition.　See edition, Christiania, 1866, p. 115.　See also Sir George Webbe Dasent's Popular Tales from the Norse, Edinburgh, 1859; new ed. 1903, p. 396.　More or less representative selections from the storehouse of Asbjörnsen and Moe may also be found in Tales from the Fjeld, by G. W. Dasent, London, 1874, and in Round the Yule Log, by H. L. Braekstad, London, 1881.

10.　Copenhagen ed. 1896, p. 148.

11.　In this story, however, he probably found the suggestion of the "cross-roads" which figure so largely in the Fifth Act.　In Asbjörnsen, they are explicitly stated to be the point where the ways to Heaven and Hell diverge.

12.　Further gleanings of legendary lore concerning Peer Gynt may be found in the Norwegian periodical Syn og Segn, 1903, pp. 119-130.　The writer, Per Aasmundstad, is of opinion that Peer Gynt's real name was Peer Haagaa (the owner of Haagaa farm) and that Gynt was either a name given him by the huldra-folk, or else a local nickname for humourists of his kind.　According to this authority, he probably lived as far back as the seventeenth century.　Per Aasmundstad's article is written in the local dialect, with such ruthless phonetic accuracy that I read it with difficulty; but he does not seem to have discovered anything that has a definite bearing on Ibsen's work.　From the wording of Ibsen's letters to Hegel, however (p. viii), it would seem that he had some knowledge of the Gynt legend over and above what was to be found in Asbjörnsen.　(For access to Syn og Segn, and for other obliging assistance, I am indebted to Herr Halvdan Koht, the author of the excellent biographical introduction to Ibsen's Letters.)

13. It is perhaps worth noting that his idea of expiating crime by undergoing the legal punishment reappears in A Doll's House, where Helmer says that Krogstad could have retrieved his character had he taken that manly course.

14. It is pretty clear that the poet designed Aase's death as a deliberate contrast to the death of Brand's mother.

15. In all these remarks I have in mind, of course, the scenes in their original form. The reader will easily understand the loss which they inevitably suffer in being deprived of the crowning grace of richly-elaborated rhyme.

16. London: Sonnenschein, 1892.

17. Henrik Ibsen et le Théâtre Contemporain. Paris, 1892.

18. Deeming it unnecessary to trouble our readers with niceties of pronunciation, we have represented the "Boig" of the original by the more easily pronounceable "Boyg." The root-idea seems to be that of bending, of sinuousness; compare Norwegian boië, German biegen, to bend. In Aasmundstad's version of the Peer Gynt legends (see footnote 12) when the Boyg names itself, Peer answers, "Antel du ae rak hell bogjë, saa fae du sleppe mé fram"--"Whether you are straight or crooked, you must let me pass." The German translator, both in the folk-tale and in the drama, renders "Böigen" by "der Krumme." So far as we are aware, the name occurs in no other folk-tale save that of Peer Gynt. It is not generic, but denotes an individual troll-monster.

19. Dr. A. von Hanstein (Ibsen als Idealist, Leipzig, 1897, p. 67) states that Ibsen himself endorsed this interpretation; but I do not know on what evidence his statement is founded.

20. Henrik Ibsen, 1828-1888. Et Literoert Livsbillede, Copenhagen, 1888. English Translation, London, Heinemann, 1890.

21. A writer in the Danish Dagblad for December 15, 1863, said of Manderström: "Many people have imagined they saw in him a new Oxenstjerna, a Northern Cavour. It remains to be seen whether he is a real statesman or only an adroit pen."

22. [Editor's Note: Because of space limitations, I have removed the last part of Archer's essay on Peer Gynt. This final section is exclusively concerned with decisions of translation, yet of interest to anyone considering the poem's verse forms.]

THE LEAGUE OF YOUTH

1. Letter to Lucie Wolf, May 1883. <u>Correspondence</u>, Letter 171.

2. See <u>Correspondence</u>, Letters 44 and 45.

A DOLL'S HOUSE

1. Stated in the <u>Fortnightly</u> <u>Review</u>, July 1906, and repeated in the first edition of this Introduction.

2. The definite article does not, I think, imply that Ibsen ever intended this to be the title of the play, but merely that the notes refer to "the" tragedy of contemporary life which he has had for some time in his mind.

3. This name seems to have haunted Ibsen. It was also the original name of Stensgaard in <u>The</u> <u>League</u> <u>of</u> <u>Youth</u>.

4. It is noteworthy that Darwin's two great books were translated into Danish very shortly before Ibsen began to work at <u>A</u> <u>Doll's</u> <u>House</u>.

GHOSTS

1. See "The Mausoleum of Ibsen." <u>Fortnightly</u> <u>Review</u>, August 1893. See also Mr. Bernard Shaw's <u>Quintessence</u> <u>of</u> <u>Ibsenism</u>, p. 89, and my introduction to <u>Ghosts</u> in the single-volume edition.

AN ENEMY OF THE PEOPLE

1. <u>Samliv</u> <u>med</u> <u>Ibsen</u>, p. 173.

2. See article by Julius Elias in <u>Die</u> <u>neue</u> <u>Rundschau</u>, December, 1906, p. 1461.

THE WILD DUCK

1. <u>Samliv</u> <u>med</u> <u>Ibsen</u>, p. 33.

2.   Herr Paulsen uses the English words; but it will appear from the sequel that Ibsen's ideal was not so much the self-made as the self-mended man.

ROSMERSHOLM

1.   Condensed from an article in the Fortnightly Review, September, 1885.

2.   See note (in the Norwegian and German editions) to Ibsen's Letters, No. 146.   As to Charlotte Stieglitz, see Brandes' Main Currents in Nineteenth Century Literature, vol. vi., p. 296.

THE LADY FROM THE SEA

1.   The date is July 16.   On March 5 of the same year he had (as we shall see later) written down the first outline of what was afterwards to become The Lady from the Sea.

2.   Published in Die neue Rundschau, December, 1906.   The Literary Remains contain, besides this sketch, a first draft of the play, somewhat fragmentary, yet covering nearly the whole ground, and showing that it underwent no essential remodelling in the course of revision.

3.   I met in Rome, in 1881-82, when Ibsen was living there, a minor official of the Vatican Library, then a middle-aged man, who had written eighteen or twenty tragedies, all of which I saw in exquisite manuscript.   One of them, Coriolano, had been acted once, on the day, I think, before the Italian troops entered Rome in 1870.   Is it possible that Ibsen, too, had come across this rival dramatist?

4.   The name originally assigned her was "Thora."   Readers who know anything of Norway will probably realise how absolutely right was the substitution of "Ellida."   It is a master-stroke in the art of nomenclature.   Boletta was originally called Thea, and afterwards Annette.   Hilda first appears under the name of Frida.   Arnholm is at first Hesler, and afterwards Arenholdt.

5.   In the draft, Wangel says at the decisive moment: "It would be easy for me to prevent you from going away with this strange man.   I do nothing to prevent you.   You are now a free woman, at full liberty to go where you will."

6. It is suggested that the coincidence is to be regarded as part of the "occult" atmosphere of the play. But I doubt whether this was in the poet's mind; and, in any case, the defence does not seem a very good one.

HEDDA GABLER

1. Letters 214, 216, 217, 219.

2. In the Ibsen volume of Die Literatur (Berlin).

3. Dr. Julius Elias (Neue deutsche Rundschau, December 1906, p. 1462) makes the curious assertion that the character of Thea Elvsted was in part borrowed from this "Gossensasser Hildetypus." It is hard to see how even Ibsen's ingenuity could distil from the same flower two such different essences as Thea and Hilda.

4. See article by Herman Bang in Neue deutsche Rundschau, December 1906, p. 1495.

5. Dr. Brahm (Neue deutsche Rundschau, December 1906, p. 1422) says that after the first performance of Hedda Gabler in Berlin Ibsen confided to him that the character had been suggested by a German lady whom he met in Munich, and who did not shoot, but poisoned herself. Nothing more seems to be known of this lady. See, too, an article by Julius Elias in the same magazine, p. 1460.

6. Hedda's case cannot but recall that stoic maxim of A. E. Housman's:

> If your hand or foot offend you,
>   Cut it off, lad and be whole;
> But play the man, stand up and end you,
>   When your sickness is your soul.
>
>   -- A Shropshire Lad, XLV

THE MASTER BUILDER

1. "To the May-sun of a September life--in Tyrol."

2.   "High, painful happiness--to struggle for the unattainable!"

3. <u>Neue</u> <u>deutsche</u> <u>Rundschau</u>, December, 1906, p. 1462.

4.   This conception I have worked out at much greater length in an essay, entitled <u>The</u> <u>Melody</u> <u>of</u> <u>the</u> <u>Master</u> <u>Builder</u>, appended to the shilling edition of the play, published in 1893 (London, Heinemann). I there retell the story, transplanting it to England and making the hero a journalist instead of an architect, in order to show that (if we grant the reality of certain commonly-accepted phenomena of hypnotism) there is nothing incredible or even extravagantly improbable about it. The argument is far too long to be included here, but the reader who is interested in the subject may find it worth referring to.

5.   For an instance of the technical methods by which he suggested the supernormal element in the atmosphere of the play, see Introduction to <u>A</u> <u>Doll's</u> <u>House</u>.

LITTLE EYOLF

1.   The French word used by Count Prozor is "infatuation." I can think of no other rendering for it; but I do not quite know what it means as applied to Allmers and Eyolf.

2.   <u>Main</u> <u>Currents</u> <u>of</u> <u>Nineteenth</u> <u>Century</u> <u>Literature</u>, vol. vi. p. 299.

JOHN GABRIEL BORKMAN

1. In the first draft this passage runs thus:

ELLA RENTHEIM: The cold has killed him.
MRS. BORKMAN: Ah, Ella, the cold had killed him long ago.
ELLA RENTHEIM: Us too.
MRS. BORKMAN: You are right there.
ELLA RENTHEIM: We are three dead people--we three here.
MRS. BORKMAN: We are. So perhaps we two can join hands, Ella.
ELLA RENTHEIM: (<u>Quietly</u>.) Over the third. Yes.

How the poet has transfigured the passage in re-writing it!

INDEX

Topics:

About the Editor

THOMAS POSTLEWAIT is Assistant Professor, Department of Drama and Theatre Arts, at the University of Georgia in Athens. He received his Ph.D. from the University of Minnesota. Professor Postlewait is the author of *Victorian Science and Victorian Values: Literary Perspectives* (1980), with James Paradis. He has also published articles in *Twentieth Century Literature* and *Comparative Drama*.

Recent Titles in
Contributions in Drama and Theatre Studies
Series Editor: Joseph Donohue

American Popular Entertainment: Papers and Proceedings of the Conference
on the History of American Popular Entertainment
Myron Matlaw, editor

George Frederick Cooke: Machiavel of the Stage
Don B. Wilmeth

Greek Theatre Practice
J. Michael Walton

Gordon Craig's Moscow *Hamlet*: A Reconstruction
Laurence Senelick

Theatrical Touring and Founding in North America
L. W. Conolly, editor

Bernhardt and the Theatre of Her Time
Eric Salmon, editor

Revolution in the Theatre: French Romantic Theories of Drama
Barry V. Daniels

Serf Actor: The Life and Career of Mikhail Shchepkin
Laurence Senelick

Musical Theatre in America: Papers and Proceedings
of the Conference on the Musical Theatre in America
Glenn Loney, editor
The American Society for Theatre Research, The Sonneck Society,
and the Theatre Library Association, joint sponsors

Garrick Claims the Stage: Acting as Social Emblem in Eighteenth-Century England
Leigh Woods

A Whirlwind in Dublin: *The Plough and the Stars* Riots
Robert G. Lowery, editor

German Actors of the Eighteenth and Nineteenth Centuries:
Idealism, Romanticism, and Realism
Simon Williams